Entrepreneurship and Small Firms

Entrepreneurship and Small Firms
David Deakins and Mark Freel
ISBN-13 978-0-07-713645-1
ISBN-10 0-07-7136454

Published by McGraw-Hill Education
Shoppenhangers Road
Maidenhead
Berkshire
SL6 2QL
Telephone: 44 (0) 1628 502 500
Fax: 44 (0) 1628 770 224
Website: www.mcgraw-hill.co.uk

British Library Cataloguing in Publication Data
A catalogue record for this book is available from the British Library

Library of Congress Cataloguing in Publication Data
The Library of Congress data for this book has been applied for from the Library of Congress

Acquisitions Editor: Leiah Batchelor
Development Editor: Jennifer Yendell
Production Editor: Alison Davis
Marketing Manager: Alexis Thomas

Text Design by HL Studios
Cover design by Adam Renvoize
Printed in Spain by Grafo Industrias Gráficas

ISBN-13 978-0-07-713645-1
ISBN-10 0-07-7136454

Entrepreneurship and Small Firms
Sixth edition

David Deakins and Mark Freel

McGraw-Hill
Higher Education

London   Boston   Burr Ridge, IL   Dubuque, IA   Madison, WI   New York   San Francisco
St. Louis   Bangkok   Bogotá   Caracas   Kuala Lumpur   Lisbon   Madrid   Mexico City
Milan   Montreal   New Delhi   Santiago   Seoul   Singapore   Sydney   Taipei   Toronto

Brief table of contents

Detailed table of contents

Preface

At the time of writing, the effects of the 'financial crisis', that followed the collapse of Lehman Brothers in September 2008, linger on. Having shrunk by some 0.6 per cent in the final quarter of 2010, the UK economy is likely to record modest growth of around 1 per cent in 2011, with a similar gloomy forecast for 2012. The UK, of course, is not alone in its travails. The IMF's *World Economic Outlook*, published in September 2011, 'paints a sobering picture about the likelihood of a double-dip recession[1] in France, the United Kingdom, and the United States' (p. 55). Meanwhile, sovereign debt crises across the Eurozone have had profound effects on member countries, with the EU's 'bailout' of Greece alone running into the hundreds of billion euros.

All of this suggests troubling times for entrepreneurs and would-be entrepreneurs. As Chapter 2 discusses, many forms of entrepreneurial activity are pro-cyclical. That is, they tend to follow the fortunes of the economy as a whole. Businesses whose low entry-barriers make them easy to start in good times, such as restaurants or small retail stores, are also those most likely to fail in a recession as potential customers tighten their belts. In this sense, the High Street is an excellent barometer for the economy as a whole. Of course, we know that periods of high unemployment tend to be followed by periods of high self-employment as unemployment lowers the opportunity costs of entrepreneurship. But what makes the current recession different from its counterparts in the '70s, '80s and '90s is who is being made redundant. Unlike in previous recessions, the rise in unemployment this time is being driven, in large part, by public-sector cuts – putting people out of work who may be less able or less inclined to pursue entrepreneurial careers. Confounding these difficulties are the slow recovery and the shortage of reasonably priced debt finance.

Certainly, not all forms of entrepreneurship are pro-cyclical. Some, such as discount stores or similarly inspired ventures, may be counter-cyclical as uncertainty and changing spending patterns create opportunities for entrepreneurs. Others, with large entry and exit costs, may appear more or less independent of the cycle. What is clear is that many believe that stimulating entrepreneurship is an important component of any economic recovery and development plan. This belief is clearly manifest in government commitments to supporting 'enterprise'. Recent examples include the UK's fledgling New Enterprise Allowance, which provides the unemployed (Jobseeker's Allowance claimants who have been claiming for 26 weeks) access to a volunteer business-mentor, a 'soft' start-up loan and a small 'wage' as they start their own businesses. Of course, Margaret Thatcher's first Conservative government introduced a similar scheme to address unemployment concerns in the early 1980s. Despite assisting some individuals who became involved in high-profile successes (e.g. Alan McGee of Creation Records and the founders of *Viz* magazine) this earlier scheme was subject to considerable contemporary and subsequent criticism. Concerns include the limited employment creation potential of assisted firms, the high failure-rates, and the extent to which subsidizing new entrants to compete against existing firms is good policy.

Regardless, these sorts of activities and the difficult economic climate make it still more important that we strive for greater understanding of entrepreneurship and small firms. Economic and financial contexts change, but entrepreneurs will still seek and exploit opportunities, small firms will still be at the forefront of innovation and our future prosperity will depend upon their increasing importance in our economy.

STRUCTURE OF THE BOOK

This sixth edition of *Entrepreneurship and Small Firms* continues our policy with this text of using the new editions as an opportunity to revise all the chapters and to introduce new material, reflecting current issues,

---

[1] A double-dip recession refers to a period of recession followed by a short-lived recovery followed by another recession.

research and academic debate on entrepreneurship and small firms. For example, in this edition, the reader will find a new chapter on 'Corporate entrepreneurship', reflecting a growing belief in an increasing entrepreneurial imperative for large corporations and other large organisations. We have also taken the opportunity to revise completely some of the chapters; those that have undergone a complete rewriting with new material include: Chapter 4 on 'Diversity in entrepreneurship' with new material from Dr Laura Galloway; Chapter 8 on 'Venture finance', which has been given a more international focus and incorporates data from key developing economies; Chapter 9 on 'Innovation and entrepreneurship', which has been rewritten to include new material on open innovation; and Chapter 12 on 'Issues in business start-up' has been revised to include new material on support agencies. Readers familiar with previous editions of the text will also note significant 'updating' in all the chapters. These efforts reflect our commitment to present students and teachers with current thinking, underpinned by the most up-to-date data. Many of the chapters also incorporate new case material, with further new material in the Online Learning Centre.

But perhaps the biggest change in this edition is the structuring of the text around four 'parts'. These parts group together chapters with similar themes or intents and help signpost the reader through the text. The opening part, for instance, is concerned with setting the scene. In it, Chapter 1 introduces the reader to longstanding theoretical debates on the nature of entrepreneurship and newer material on entrepreneurial learning; while Chapter 2 explores the role of small firms, as vehicles for entrepreneurship, in a range of different economic settings. Part 2 focuses on various 'domains' of entrepreneurship. As the text consistently stresses, entrepreneurship is a heterogeneous phenomenon and understanding it involves better understanding the multiplicity of contexts in which it occurs. To this end, Part 2 includes chapters on 'Family businesses' (Chapter 3), 'Diversity in entrepreneurship' (Chapter 4), 'Social entrepreneurship' (Chapter 5) and 'Corporate entrepreneurship' (Chapter 6). Part 3 places the focus more firmly on the development of smaller businesses and on the strategic issues that concern owner-managers. This part is not a 'how-to' manual. Rather it elaborates the processes and challenges that many firms will face as they attempt to access finance (Chapter 7), deal with venture capitalists (Chapter 8), push to innovate or grow (Chapters 9 and 10) or venture into new markets outside their home country (Chapter 11). Finally, part 4 concerns itself with 'making it happen'. In Chapter 12, we recount many of the key issues in business start-up, elaborating upon the different stages involved in launching a new venture and the various resource challenges prospective entrepreneurs may face. The text closes with Chapter 13, which provides important material on constructing business plans and, more importantly, on the planning process.

To complement this restructuring of the text, we have been fortunate in sourcing a series of 'integrative' case studies that serve as section openers. These cases have been drawn from the *European Entrepreneurship Case Study Resource Centre* (www.eecsrc.eu). In this we are grateful for the help and guidance provided by Tom Cooney and to the authors of the cases used. The versions which appear in the text are abridged and full versions are contained in the Online Learning Centre (OLC) that accompanies the text. The EECSRC is funded by the European Commission and is an excellent and timely (and free!) resource for anyone involved in entrepreneurship education. It provides exposure for those writing case studies and a bank of edited cases for those trying to enthuse students about entrepreneurship.

Despite these structural changes, the overall style has been retained. Many of the successful features introduced in the third edition, such as 'Entrepreneurship in action' boxes, case studies and suggested assignments, remain and we hope that the text continues to be readable. As in the fifth edition, we have sought to bolster the Online Learning Centre, which contains much new and some old material. In part, this is about space constraints in the main text and was driven by reviewer comments on earlier editions. It is also about providing our readers and adopters with valuable additional material. To get the most benefit from this edition, students should consult this online resource material. We have, of course, retained and revised the tutors' online resource material, which contains lecture slides and additional material not available to students.

This sixth edition has also retained the learning and pedagogical features that were introduced with previous editions. Learning outcomes are given at the start of each chapter; boxed examples, titled 'Entrepreneurship in action', are provided where appropriate throughout the text, and review questions are also incorporated to review the material and to allow the reader to reflect upon the material and develop alternative concepts. Suggested assignments are given for each chapter; some of these incorporate or draw upon the additional material available in the student online material. Finally, the reader should find that the references have been completely updated, reflecting recent developments in academic debate and changes in the policy agenda, and also that the recommended reading sections have been updated and are included at the end of each chapter.

USING THE TEXT

This text is aimed at undergraduate and postgraduate students of entrepreneurship, enterprise, small firms and business venturing. Comments on using the text are provided here for students and lecturers.

Students will find that the text has been designed to be read in digestible sections. Chapters are broken up with highlights such as the 'Entrepreneurship in action' features and with review questions at the end of the chapter. These questions do not treat each of these sections in isolation; rather they try to encourage the student to consider some of the implications raised in the chapter's content and material and attempt to get them to think further and perhaps link the material to that in other chapters of the text. Hints are given to enable them to do this. Suggested answers to the review questions are provided in the student's online resources material. These are not meant to be prescriptive, but provide an indication of the ways to think about the questions set, which may be in a discussion form.

The text is designed to cover entrepreneurial and small-firm theory, concepts, evidence, policy and practice. It is designed to link these areas together. For example, discussion of entrepreneurial concepts is followed by practical mini-case examples or discussion of theoretical issues in small-firm development; discussion of the growth of small firms is followed by a discussion of evidence; discussion of business creation is followed by discussion of some of the policy implications and policy measures, as well as practical examples. You are encouraged to link these distinct elements together through the review questions and suggested assignments. For example, you may be asked to relate entrepreneurial concepts to a practical case study.

The detailed case studies, most of which are in the online student resources for this edition, are all real entrepreneurial cases. In some of them, names have been changed to preserve anonymity. They are designed to take you to a decision point in the case study, to put you in the place of the entrepreneur. This may form part of a class group discussion in which you discuss the different paths the entrepreneur(s) may take and give a recommended course of action. It is important to realize that there is ambiguity in entrepreneurial decision-making. An ability to recognize different options can be as important as the actual decision made. A number of options can be equally valid courses of action; in other words, there is not necessarily one right answer. However, there are, for some of the detailed case studies, further sections provided in the online student learning material and further information in the online tutors' material (some of this information is available for registered tutors only).

While much of the material in this text is designed to enable you to understand entrepreneurship and small-firm and enterprise development, to apply concepts, to understand case studies and to understand new policy developments, Chapter 13 also provides a guide to preparing *for* entrepreneurship through the coverage of research, design and writing of business plans. Of course, other chapters of the book also provide an opportunity to develop skills and to prepare for entrepreneurship through the discussion of case material and practical examples, but Chapter 13 focuses specifically on sources of information, research methods and the planning process. Throughout the text, we combine a focus on *understanding* with *doing*; a combination of enterprise skills should be developed if you use the review questions, material, case studies and assignments in the book throughout your course. These enterprise skills include problem solving, creative thinking, research and information gathering, presentation and strategic planning. The value of developing these enterprise skills is that they are *transferable*, whatever career is undertaken. Increasingly employers are seeking graduates with transferable enterprise skills, who can think entrepreneurially, be creative and innovative and communicate new ideas. This is part of the reason for the increased emphasis governments are placing on enterprise education initiatives. We believe that this book will help you to develop those skills and apply them in different problem-solving situations, whether you decide to follow an entrepreneurial career or not. More important, research indicates that most entrepreneurial students do not wish to enter entrepreneurship when they graduate; rather they intend to enter entrepreneurship or self-employment after a period of employment, but having undertaken study of entrepreneurship and small firms they are better prepared for such a change of career.

Lecturers will able to use this text for undergraduate and postgraduate courses in entrepreneurship and small firms. As discussed above, it combines concepts and theory with practical entrepreneurial case studies and examples, although the more detailed in-depth cases have now been placed in the student online resources to create additional room in this edition for the discussion of concepts and content on additional topics, such as the new chapter on 'Corporate entrepreneurship' (Chapter 6). It also has policy-related sections, where these are relevant, so that the material is placed in the context of recent developments in entrepreneurship and economic development. As indicated above, additional case material and suggested answers to the review questions are available to students through the student online resources.

For this sixth edition, we have retained the tutor online material, but revised for this edition. This provides additional course lecture slides and material for teaching purposes, which can be used in teaching alongside this text. The online resource for tutors also contains further information on using the case material in the text. Apart from these additional features, lecturers familiar with previous editions should find that we have rewritten the text to take account of new developments, new research and new policy initiatives in field.

Other users should find that they are able to use this text for a variety of purposes; for example, for training courses for new entrepreneurs, for an understanding of new developments in entrepreneurship and for an appreciation of concepts applied to practical examples. We hope that this new text will continue to appeal and be of use to a large and varied audience, including potential entrepreneurs, trainers, policy-makers and other users with an interest in entrepreneurship and small firms.

CHAPTER CONTENT

The first two chapters are foundation chapters, covering entrepreneurship (Chapter 1) and small firms (Chapter 2); they provide the underlying theory and concepts for much of the material presented in the text. Chapter 1 provides a foundation for many of the concepts on entrepreneurship. It examines the three approaches to entrepreneurship: from economic writers, from a psychological perspective and from the socio-behavioural view. Alternative paradigms are also considered. Although the emphasis of the chapter is on different conceptual approaches, underlying evidence to support these approaches is considered with a critical review that emphasizes the importance of entrepreneurial learning and entrepreneurship as a process. Chapter 2 builds upon this foundation by covering the importance of small firms and entrepreneurial activity for European economies, with comparisons of importance in different European countries, including those of eastern Europe. Measures of entrepreneurial activity are considered with a critical examination of the relationship between entrepreneurial activity and economic performance.

Chapter 3, on family businesses, examines the nature of relationships in family businesses, which are now an important part of modern entrepreneurial economies. The chapter also examines specific issues in this area, notably succession planning, with a discussion of general principles applied to specific case studies. Chapter 4 provides an assessment of the importance of diversity of entrepreneurship. The chapter covers the issues of women's enterprise and ethnic-minority entrepreneurship and examines some of the factors that affect the participation of women and ethnic minorities in entrepreneurial activity. Diversity is a theme running through much of the material of the text and, therefore, this chapter provides a further important step in understanding the nature and importance of entrepreneurship and small firms.

Chapter 5 addresses the growing phenomenon of social entrepreneurship and the increasingly important 'third sector' of the economy which includes social, voluntary and charitable organizations. The chapter reviews their importance and factors in their success and development. New case material on social entrepreneurs has been specially written for this chapter. Chapter 6 is a wholly new chapter on corporate entrepreneurship (CE). This chapter recognises entrepreneurial behaviour as not solely the domain of new start-ups, but of new ventures and development initiatives within large corporations or public-sector organisations. The chapter explores how CE activity relates to classical forms of entrepreneurship and outlines recent work which attempts to quantify certain forms of CE.

The next two chapters, 7 and 8, discuss the nature of the financial environment for entrepreneurs and small firms, primarily focusing on the UK, although with important international comparisons. As with previous editions, the first of these chapters focuses mainly on debt finance – that is, the banks – and the latter on equity finance – that is, formal and informal venture finance. Both chapters make reference to the global financial crisis of autumn 2008; its impact on the commercial banks and on equity providers; on their policies and lending or investing practices.

Chapters 9, 10 and 11 discuss the nature of rapidly changing environments and concepts in entrepreneurship and small firms concerned with innovation, growth and internationalisation. Chapter 9 discusses the relationship between innovation and entrepreneurship, building on and developing many of the concepts that were introduced in Chapter 1. The chapter develops additional concepts in innovation and examines the advantages and disadvantages of small firms in the innovation process. The nature and process of entrepreneurial growth firms is discussed in Chapter 10, with discussion of both theory and evidence on growth firms and new material on barriers to growth. Chapter 11 examines processes of internationalization in small firms, again with discussion of theory and evidence. Chapters 10 and 11 draw out some of the similarities to be found in models of the processes of growth and internationalisation which, of course, are not mutually exclusive.

The last two chapters focus on business start-up and creation. Chapter 12 discusses issues in business start-up, including creativity, opportunity recognition and business development. This chapter provides the basis for the more practical approach of Chapter 13, which focuses on the planning process for business start-up, including the design, writing and implementation of business plans. The material in the final two chapters, especially in Chapter 12, has been revised and updated for the sixth edition.

David Deakins and Mark Freel
October 2011

Guided tour

Learning Outcomes

Each chapter opens with a set of learning outcomes, summarising what knowledge, skills or understanding readers should acquire from each chapter.

Examples

Each chapter has example boxes that highlight major topics to aid the understanding of the concepts and theories discussed.

Entrepreneurship in Action

Throughout the book these boxes provide practical examples demonstrating the application of concepts, followed by discussion questions to encourage you to analyse and discuss real-life issues.

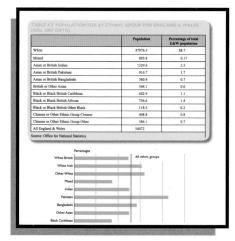

Figures and Tables

Each chapter provides a number of figures and tables to help you visualize the information, and to illustrate and summarize important concepts

Chapter Conclusion

This briefly reviews and reinforces the main topics you will have covered in each chapter to ensure you have acquired a solid understanding of the key topics. Use it in conjunction with the learning objectives as a quick reference to check you have understood the ideas explored in the chapter.

CONCLUSIONS

In this chapter we have explored the meaning of social entrepreneu economic development. Social entrepreneurship has a long and somewh gins in the nineteenth century through to the present day when it ha academic and policy circles. Social entrepreneurship can be defined change that necessitates the enrolment of others into the cause. As such social value as well as economic value, but also an awareness of oppor problems, accountability to a greater good, and an element of risk-takin

It has been estimated that over one million people in the UK are inv and that there are over 50,000 British social enterprises.[36] However, sector, social enterprises and social entrepreneurship, two points need to whole has largely kept pace with both the public and private sectors ove Second, the distribution of the third sector is highly uneven across Brit and south-west England having higher proportions of social enterprise

Consequently, there may be limitations to the role that social entrep nomic development.[10] Despite this caveat, we can argue that social impact on the development of communities through the encouragen defined social capital as the reciprocal relationships in a social netwo and access to information.[44] It also highlighted how it is important to c capital in order to understand the impact of social entrepreneurship. F

REVIEW QUESTIONS

1 Contrast the Schumpeterian view of the entrepreneur with th
2 List the key contributions to our understanding of entreprene
   • Knight
   • Casson
   • Kirzner
   • Schumpeter
3 Why is the environment important to our understanding of di entrepreneurship?
4 How does Schumpeter help to explain the dotcom bubble of of failing dotcom entrepreneurs?

Hint: see also Chapter 9.

5 Suggest key personality characteristics associated with succe
6 Suggest additional key personality characteristics that may be (for example, consider perseverance required to overcome ini
7 Which of the personality characteristics you have listed in yc acquired through learning?
8 Critically review the entrepreneurial personality approach w

Review Questions

These questions encourage you to review and apply the knowledge you have acquired from each chapter. They are pitched at different levels.

SUGGESTED ASSIGNMENTS

These questions refer to the Aquamotive case study, which is available centre.

As a basis for discussion

1 With hindsight, was the strategy to use MBS to gain time and finance experience, correct?

2 What are the difficulties faced by entrepreneurs in the innovation pr Aquamotive?

3 How can these be overcome?

4 What are the risks for a potential investor in Aquamotive?

As a role play

Students are allocated roles through a briefing sheet that asks them to a

• Two students play the roles of Alex and Marion.

• One student plays the role of a business angel who has £100,000 engineering opportunity.

• Students who take on the roles of Marion and Alex must sell thei then has to justify his/her decision as to whether or not to inve

Suggested Assignments

These end-of-chapter features provide tasks or discussions to reinforce the subjects covered and to help enable you to gain the most benefit from each chapter.

DAVID LYSAGHT[1]

by Thomas Cooney
Dublin Institute of Technology

INTRODUCTION

David Lysaght understood from the moment that his business idea was c would be a challenging prospect and that the possibility of failing would of 2010, the economic recession that Ireland was suffering had taken its to wondered if he should abandon his plans to establish a not-for-profit bi walking and mountain-trekking to raise funds for charitable organisations become extremely competitive in Ireland because: (1) there was substant the public and private sectors to give to charities; (2) there had been a shar because the wealth of high-worth individuals had been badly hit by the re large increase in the number of not-for-profit organisations seeking to sec additional challenge that few other entrepreneurs have to face: he has cere erally characterized by an inability fully to control one's motor functions co-ordination. While David had a very positive attitude to life, he wonder a good business choice for someone with his condition. He also thought al people frequently changed their behaviour when they met him and saw meeting with his business mentor in seven days' time, and David decided the positive and negative aspects to his personal and business situation in j analysis would help him determine the next step in the development of hi

Case Studies

These up-to-date examples give you the opportunity to apply what you have learnt through real-life scenarios.

REFERENCES

1 **Small Business Service (2004)** *A Government Action Plan for Small Businesses: The Evidence Base*, SBS/DTI, London.

2 **ONS** (2007) *Population Estimates*, Office for National Statistics, London.

3 **Ram, M. and Jones, T.** (2007) 'Ethnic minority businesses in the UK: A review of research and policy developments', report for the ESRC, paper presented to an ESRC/CRE/DTI/EMDA seminar, February, London.

4 **Langowitz, N. and Minniti, M.** (2007) 'The entrepreneurial propensity of women', *Entrepreneurship, Theory and Practice*, vol. 31, no. 3, pp. 341–364.

5 **Carter, S. and Shaw, E.** (2006) *Women's Business Ownership: Recent Research and Policy Developments*, Report to the Small Business Service, available at www.berr.gov.uk/files/

accounts of the role of women in founding and establishing family businesses', *International Small Business Journal*, vol. 24, no. 3, pp. 253–271.

9 **Verheul, I., van Stel, A. and Thurik, R.** (2006) 'Explaining female and male entrepreneurship at the country level', *Entrepreneurship and Regional Development*, vol. 18, pp. 151–183.

10 **Sarri, K. and Trihopoulou, A.** (2005) 'Female entrepreneurs' personal characteristics and motivations: a review of the Greek situation', *Women in Management Review*, vol. 20, no. 1, pp. 24–36.

11 **Morris, M.H., Nola, M.N., Craig, W.E. and Coombes, S.M.** (2006) 'The dilemma of growth: understanding venture sizehoices of women entrepreneurs',*Journal of Small Business Management*, vol. 44, no. 2, pp. 221–244.

References and Recommended Reading

Each chapter ends with a list of suggested further reading, listing international research and sources – journals, papers and books – in entrepreneurship. Use this list as a starting-point for your reading for assignments or class preparation.

Technology to enhance learning and teaching

Online Learning Centre (OLC)

STUDENTS – HELPING YOU TO CONNECT, LEARN AND SUCCEED

We understand that studying for your module is not just about reading this textbook. It's also about researching online, revising key terms, preparing for assignments, and passing the exam. The website above provides you with a number of **FREE** resources to help you succeed on your module, including:

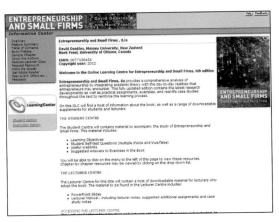

- *Multiple choice questions* to prepare you for tests and exams
- *Glossary* of key terms to revise core concepts
- *Web links* to online sources of information to help you prepare for class

LECTURER SUPPORT – HELPING YOU TO HELP YOUR STUDENTS

The Online Learning Centre also offers lecturers adopting this book a range of resources designed to offer:

- **Faster course preparation** – time-saving support for your module
- **High-calibre content to support your students** – resources written by your academic peers, who understand your need for rigorous and reliable content
- **Flexibility** – edit, adapt or repurpose; test in EZ Test or your department's Course Management System. The choice is yours.

The materials created specifically for lecturers adopting this textbook include:

- *Lecturer's Manual to support your module preparation*
- *PowerPoint presentations to use in lecture presentations*
- *Image library of artwork from the textbook*
- *Suggested answers to exercises in the textbook*
- *Case notes with guide answers to case questions, written to help support your students in understanding and analysing the cases in the textbook*

To request your password to access these resources, contact your McGraw-Hill representative or visit **www.mcgraw-hill.co.uk/textbooks/deakins**

Let us help make our **content** your **solution**

At McGraw-Hill Education our aim is to help lecturers to find the most suitable content for their needs delivered to their students in the most appropriate way. Our **custom publishing solutions** offer the ideal combination of content delivered in the way which best suits lecturer and students.

Our custom publishing programme offers lecturers the opportunity to select just the chapters or sections of material they wish to deliver to their students from a database called CREATE™ at

www.mcgrawhillcreate.co.uk

CREATE™ contains over two million pages of content from:

- textbooks
- professional books
- case books – Harvard Articles, Insead, Ivey, Darden, Thunderbird and BusinessWeek
- Taking Sides – debate materials

Across the following imprints:

- McGraw-Hill Education
- Open University Press
- Harvard Business Publishing
- US and European material

There is also the option to include additional material authored by lecturers in the custom product – this does not necessarily have to be in English.

We will take care of everything from start to finish in the process of developing and delivering a custom product to ensure that lecturers and students receive exactly the material needed in the most suitable way.

With a custom publishing solution, students enjoy the best selection of material deemed to be the most suitable for learning everything they need for their courses – something of real value to support their learning. Teachers are able to use exactly the material they want, in the way they want, to support their teaching on the course.

Please contact your local McGraw-Hill representative with any questions or alternatively contact Warren Eels **e: warren_eels@mcgraw-hill.com.**

Make the grade

Acknowledgements

Our thanks go to the following reviewers for their comments at various stages in the text's development.

Publisher's acknowledgements

Trevor Andrews, Portsmouth University
Jock Anderson, Queen Margaret University
Justin O'Brien, Royal Holloway, University of London
Haya Al-Dajani, University of East Anglia
Emmanuil Noikokyris, University of Essex
Alan Benson, University of Exeter
Sheena Bell, University of Glasgow
Allan Discua Cruz, Lancaster University
Dermot Breslin, University of Sheffield
Rasmus Rahm, Stockholm School of Entrepreneurship
Spinder Dhaliwal, University of Surrey

We would also like to thank the following people for their contributions to the case and chapter content.

Spinder Dhaliwal, University of Surrey
Kean Birch, University of Toronto
Laura Galloway, Herriot Watt University
Geoff Whittam, University of West Sussex

About the authors

PROFESSOR DAVID DEAKINS

David Deakins holds a Chair in Small Business in the School of Management, Massey University and is Director of the New Zealand Centre for SME Research (NZSMERC), a research centre in the College of Business. He joined the Centre in September 2009 after spending 15 years at the former University of Paisley in Scotland, where his research interests covered many aspects of small firm innovation, growth and development, but focused on access to finance and ethnic minority entrepreneurship. While at Paisley he set up the Paisley Enterprise Research Centre and completed projects for the Scottish Government on women's enterprise, minority ethnic enterprise and SMEs' access to bank finance. At NZSMERC he has led projects for the New Zealand Government's Inland Revenue Department and Ministry of Economic Development.

DR MARK FREEL

Mark Freel is Professor of Innovation and Entrepreneurship and the Mark R. Bruneau Fellow for Global Business and Entrepreneurship at the Tefler School of Management, University of Ottawa, Canada.

PART ONE
INTRODUCING ENTREPRENEURSHIP AND SMALL FIRMS

In this first part of the text we examine the domain of entrepreneurship and small firms. The foundation of core concepts in entrepreneurship and the importance of the role of small firms in modern economies is explained and explored in Chapters 1 and 2. These two chapters provide an understanding of the importance of the role of entrepreneurs and small firms in economic development.

Entrepreneurship is an emerging discipline, and like any academic discipline, there are different theories, concepts and controversies that are presented and examined in Chapter 1. Theory and real-world evidence are presented on what makes an entrepreneur, whether they are different and whether they need special qualities. The concepts introduced and discussed in Chapter 1, such as entrepreneurial opportunity recognition and exploitation, are an important foundation that will underpin discussions and theories used in later chapters.

Chapter 2 reviews evidence on the importance of entrepreneurial activity, small firms and their importance in economic development. Some of the challenges of comparing different definitions of small firms are examined. This chapter will set the context, provide evidence and review developments in measurement of small firms for the discussion that occurs in Part 2 on the Domains of Entrepreneurship and in Part 3 on Strategy and the Small Firm.

VIROBUSTER

by Paula Englis, Marianne ven der Steen, Rainer Harms and Rickie A Moore
University of Twente

INTRODUCTION

Herbert Silderhuis drove slowly from Enschede city centre on his way to his office, deeply lost in thought. It was early March 2009 and although the work week was nearly over, he was thinking about the local newspaper article that he had read that morning – 'Immediate Closure of Hospitals in Enschede and Hengelo due to Deadly Virus'. The story was the talk of the town during the lunch hour with people wondering how this could happen to their local hospital. Herbert was a scientist and a serial entrepreneur and so he was intrigued by the question: how could people avoid this type of disaster happening again in the future? Over three decades he had launched five companies, all of whom specialized in a different aspect of health hygiene and had been successful in the hospital sector. Throughout this period, he had also been conducting research on treating viruses and had several of his protocols adopted in the preparation of flu medicines. Indeed, he had just launched Virobuster to promote a range of clean-air technologies and protocols.

Herbert was getting ever deeper in thought on the questions raised by the possible closure of the hospitals because for him it was a potential opportunity. He had seen the problem coming and like all of his other products, he had started Virobuster knowing that hospitals would eventually become interested in his products. The closure of the hospitals in Enschede and Hengelo would be devastating to the communities, and if this was happening in Enschede and Hengelo, then it was surely happening elsewhere also in Europe, and indeed around the world. He wondered whether Virobuster could offer a solution for Enschede and Hengelo. And could Virobuster offer a solution to the rest of Europe? What should he do? How should he proceed? Herbert realised that if Virobuster went after the Enschede and Henglo opportunity, he would be venturing into a new situation as the company would have to deal with not one but two nearby public hospitals simultaneously. He wondered if he would be able to leverage his reputation and experience in air sterilization in the health and food sectors to break into this new market. He also realised that if he succeeded with Enschede and Henglo he would be in a stronger position to set his sights on the rest of Europe. Herbert considered his options because he could either expand through his own sales team on a country-by-country basis or alternatively he could license out the technology to other suppliers which would allow him to enter many markets across Europe simultaneously. There were positives and negatives to whichever option he might finally select.

COMPANY HISTORY

Like many people with an entrepreneurial spirit, Herbert began the company when he saw an issue and wanted to be the solution. Beginning in 2002, Herbert had begun to work on air-sterilization processes due to the ever-increasing levels of death and sickness acquired while people attended Dutch hospitals. But these problems were not limited to the Dutch context as a report in 2005 by the Center for Diseases Control (CDC) reflected:

> over two million hospital patients in the USA had been infected by bacteria or viruses unrelated to the primary reason for their visit. Of these, 90,000 had died because of such infections. Dying from such infections in hospital was ranked fourth in the USA as a cause of death.

Due to these alarming statistics, Virobuster stepped in to find a cure for this problem and through its operations Herbert thought that the company could make an impact in Holland, as well as in other European countries with the same problems. Airborne diseases such as MRSA, SARS and others were costing hospitals internationally millions of euros on an annual basis, but more importantly, the death rate from these diseases inside hospitals was alarming. Virobuster aimed to make devices that would not only prevent the spread of these airborne diseases but would actually eliminate them completely.

Herbert had always viewed the company as a 'born global firm' (i.e. a venture that pursues opportunities across national borders by combining resources and selling outputs around the world from inception) and in less than eight years Virobuster had become a major player in the industry. With a solid line of products all designed to attack air sterilization, Virobuster had exploded onto the scene as a leader, pioneer and a model for the industry. While Herbert had started the company because he saw an opportunity to improve hospital conditions, he had turned the company into a successful, profitable, but most importantly life-saving, global business. Continuing to grow and implement a global strategy had helped Virobuster to maintain its leadership status in the industry, to be successful with their clients, and really to focus on research and development to continually improve upon their products. Herbert believed that the better equipped that Virobuster was as a firm to build a powerful and successful global brand image and products, the more they would be able to differentiate themselves from their competition.

CONCLUSION

Since his early entrepreneurial beginnings, Herbert had created products that had eliminated diseases in the air and been successful in reversing the negative trends that the European hospitals had been experiencing. He and the board had just named Alain le Loux as the CEO of Virobuster as he wanted to pursue the non-commercial side of Virobuster's activities. Personally, Herbert was obsessed with finding opportunities to perfect the air quality and make the world a safer place to live. He was also very concerned about the problem in Enschede and Hengelo. Could Virobuster offer a solution for Enschede and Hengelo? Who did they know in the Ministry of Health, and in the Regional Council and the city governments of Enschede and Hengelo? From previous experience, he knew that selling to hospitals was not a walk in the park. Could Virobuster offer a solution to the rest of Europe – if so, what should they do? He stopped at the kiosk and grabbed a copy of the local newspaper. As he entered his office, he asked his secretary to scan the article on the hospital situation. Then he walked over to Alain's office, showed him the article and said, 'I think we need to talk'!

1 THE ENTREPRENEUR: CONCEPTS AND EVIDENCE

LEARNING OUTCOMES

At the end of this chapter you should be able to:

- Describe the main theories and concepts of the entrepreneur.
- Compare and contrast different theories on the role of the entrepreneur.
- Describe the process of entrepreneurship and discuss influences on that process.
- Describe some of the problems and limitations of research into the personality of the entrepreneur.
- Discuss the social and environmental factors that influence the extent of entrepreneurial activity.
- Describe the role of entrepreneurial capital in the process of entrepreneurship.
- Compare the characteristics of two start-up entrepreneurs from a case study.

INTRODUCTION

- What makes an entrepreneur or small-business owner?
- Is an entrepreneur different from other individuals or can anyone be an entrepreneur given sufficient resources?
- Can anyone set up in business or do you need to have special skills and characteristics?

These are questions that have occupied researchers and theorists for some time; indeed theories on what makes an entrepreneur date from the early Industrial Revolution. We will attempt to answer some of these questions later when we examine factors that can encourage successful new business creation and entrepreneurial success. We will also introduce the first part of an entrepreneurial case study on Skype, which provides an opportunity to examine the characteristics of two start-up entrepreneurs: Niklas Zennström and Janus Friis.

However, it is useful to review the contribution of the major theorists on entrepreneurship first. It is only when these have been examined that we can understand the characteristics, traits and factors that researchers have sought to find in the modern entrepreneur. Later we question much of this research effort into the characteristics of the entrepreneur; it may, for example, be better to concentrate on the management skills and competencies that are required of business owners.

This chapter is concerned with three approaches to entrepreneurship, which are illustrated in Figure 1.1. The three approaches shown in Figure 1.1 are associated with the following sources:

- The contributions of economic writers and theorists on the role of the entrepreneur in economic development and the application of economic theory
- The psychological trait approach on personality characteristics of the entrepreneur
- A social-behavioural approach, which stresses the influence of the social and cultural environment as well as personality characteristics

Each approach is considered in this chapter and it can be claimed that all three approaches have something to contribute to our understanding of the entrepreneurship process. However, it will be seen that the value of psychological traits and social approaches is more controversial. Indeed, there is some dispute over whether 'entrepreneurial' traits or characteristics can be identified at all.

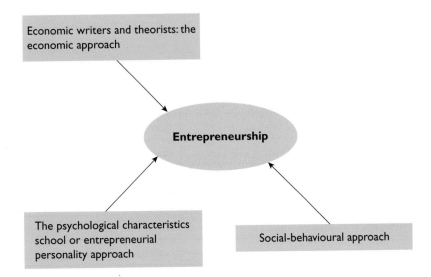

FIGURE 1.1

Approaches to entrepreneurship

There are many writers who have contributed to theories about the entrepreneur, but there is insufficient space in this text to consider more than the major contributors. For a detailed analysis of other theorists and contributors, the student is advised to consult the recommended reading at the end of this chapter.

THE ENTREPRENEUR

If we examine conventional economic theory, the term 'entrepreneur' is noticeable only by its absence. In mainstream or neoclassical economic theory, the entrepreneur can be viewed as someone who co-ordinates different factors of production, but the important distinction is that this role is viewed as a non-important one. The entrepreneur becomes merged with the capitalist employer, the owner-manager, who has the wealth to enable production to take place, but otherwise does not contain any special attributes. The entrepreneur, if recognized at all, is a pure risk-taker, the reward being the ability to appropriate profits. It is a remarkable fact that the main body of conventional economic theory has developed without a place for the entrepreneur, yet there is no shortage of writers who have contributed to the development of views on the role and concept of the entrepreneur.

The idea that the entrepreneur has a significant role in economic development has been developed by writers outside mainstream economic thinking. Their contributions now have an important place, but it is only relatively recently that the importance of these contributions has been recognized. As attention has become more focused on the importance of the small and medium-sized enterprise (SME) sector for economic development and job creation, so greater attention has also been directed at theories of entrepreneurship. We examine the most important of these theories which are accepted today; they are summarized in Table 1.1 by their key insights.

The term 'entrepreneur' is French in origin and a literal meaning might translate as 'one who takes between'. There are some important French writers who contributed views on the role of the entrepreneur, the most important being Cantillon and Say.

- Cantillon was the first to recognize the crucial role of the entrepreneur in economic development, which was founded on individual property rights. Of the three classes in society recognized by Cantillon,

TABLE 1.1 KEY CONTRIBUTIONS OF ECONOMIC WRITERS ON THE ROLE OF THE ENTREPRENEUR

Writer	Key role of entrepreneur	Additional insights
Say	Organizer of factors of production	Catalyst for economic change
Cantillon	Organizer of factors of production	Catalyst for economic change
Kirzner	Ability to spot opportunity	Entrepreneur's key ability is 'creative' alertness
Schumpeter	Innovator	Entrepreneur as 'hero' figure
Knight	Risk taker	Profit is reward for risk-taking
Casson	Organizer of resources	Key influence of the environment
Shackle	Creativity	Uncertainty creates opportunities for profit
Hayek	Visionary	Opportunity recognition via knowledge

entrepreneurs were the important class and were the central economic actors. The other two classes were landowners and workers.

- Say also made the entrepreneur the pivot of the economy and a catalyst for economic change and development. The entrepreneur provided a commercial stage in three stages of production. In this way, the entrepreneur could be seen as close to the traditional mainstream and as someone willing to take the risk of bringing different factors of production together.

Both Cantillon and Say belonged to a French school of thought known as the 'physiocrats', so called because of the physical nature of the agrarian economy that dominated their thinking. It could be because of this view that developments in the concept of the entrepreneur were not seen as being relevant to the nineteenth-century industrial economy. It was much later before more modern concepts of the entrepreneur were developed. Some of these views have been developed within the 'Austrian School' of thought; however, this is such a wide-ranging term that there is not one particular view associated with this school for the entrepreneur. What is different is that the entrepreneur is seen as being crucial to economic development and a catalyst for dynamic change. We turn now to these Austrian School writers who underpin much of the current theories of the entrepreneur.

KIRZNER

For Kirzner, the entrepreneur is someone who is *alert* to profitable opportunities for exchange. Recognizing the possibilities for exchange enables the entrepreneur to benefit by acting as a 'middleman' who facilitates the exchange. The Kirznerian entrepreneur is alert to opportunities for trade. He or she is able to identify suppliers and customers and act as the intermediary. Note that there is no necessity to own resources and that profit arises out of the intermediary function.

These possibilities for profitable exchange exist because of imperfect knowledge. The entrepreneur has some additional knowledge, which is not possessed by others, and this permits the entrepreneur to take advantage of profitable opportunities. The information is costless – it arises when someone notices an opportunity which may have been available all the time. It can often seem obvious after the service or product has been provided, but it still takes someone with additional knowledge to recognize and exploit the opportunity.

The role of information in the marketplace is important for the Kirznerian entrepreneur. Market exchange itself is an entrepreneurial process, but people can profit from exchange because of information gaps in the market. In this view, the entrepreneur may be seen as little more than a market trader taking advantage of opportunities to trade; yet for Kirzner the entrepreneur is someone who is still creative. The possession of additional knowledge provides opportunities for creative discoveries. However, in contrast to the Schumpeterian view below, anyone could potentially possess the additional knowledge and be alert to opportunities for exchange and trade.

The Kirznerian view can be compared to the entrepreneurs who founded Skype in our entrepreneurial case study which is introduced in this chapter.

SCHUMPETER

By contrast, Schumpeter's entrepreneur is a special person. Although Schumpeter is a writer classified in the Austrian School, his views on the entrepreneurial function are quite different from those of Kirzner.

The Schumpeterian entrepreneur is an *innovator*. The entrepreneur brings about change through the introduction of new technological processes or products. For Kirzner, anyone has the potential to be an entrepreneur and he or she operates within set production constraints. For Schumpeter, only certain extraordinary people have the ability to be entrepreneurs and they bring about extraordinary events. The Schumpeterian entrepreneur changes technological possibilities, alters convention through innovative activity and, hence, moves production constraints. He or she develops new technology, whereas the Kirznerian entrepreneur operates on opportunities that arise out of new technology.

Although the entrepreneur is again an important catalyst for economic change, the entrepreneur is essentially temporary for Schumpeter. Schumpeter predicted the demise of the function of the entrepreneur, that

THE INTERNET BOOM AND THE RELEVANCE OF SCHUMPETER

The dotcom 'boom and bust' situation bears comparison to Schumpeter's cycles of 'creative destruction'. At the turn of the twenty-first century, explosive growth in the use of the Internet created opportunities for many dotcom enterprises and e-entrepreneurs, among the most famous in the UK being lastminute. com, established by Martha Lane-Fox and Brent Hoberman. The case study on Skype provides another example of a very successful Internet-based start-up. The Internet technology had made new ways of trading possible and there was a rush of money from institutions and small shareholders into such new e-entrepreneurial firms at vastly inflated share prices. At the height of the boom, lastminute.com shares were issued at a price of £3.20 and briefly reached £3.80. After the dotcom bubble burst after March 2000, the shares in such companies collapsed and many ceased trading, although lastminute.com is now one of the more successful dotcom companies, having established a trading base across Europe. Schumpeter predicted that such new technology waves (or swarms) would occur from time to time in the economy, but that the life of many such new entrepreneurs would be short-lived; in order to create change it was necessary to have creative destruction – brought by new technology – but out of this, new opportunities would be available and have since been exploited by some very successful Internet companies. Such dotcom entrepreneurs could be seen to be innovative – they were pioneering new ways of trading, using new technology and, in some cases, revolutionized ways of trading and doing business (such as the low-cost airlines' ticketing policies and booking through the Internet).

For a full discussion of the implications of e-commerce see the additional material on e-business in the students' online learning centre.

technological advance and change would be carried out by teams of workers and scientists operating in large organizations. This is because, for Schumpeter, large monopolistic firms have distinct advantages over small firms in the technological process.

The concept that large firms are more successful than small firms in new technology-based industries is more correctly attributable to Galbraith. However, this concept has come to be associated with Schumpeter, even though he was more concerned with the advantages of monopolistic market structure than firm size. The small-firm entrepreneur faces considerable disadvantages in research and development (R&D); for example, R&D is expensive, it has long development times, it is viewed as high risk by funders, and teams of researchers are able to benefit by feeding off one another's ideas. If the entrepreneur is an innovator, then this argument suggests that they will find it difficult to establish a new small firm. Technological change is carried out by large firms. The entrepreneur may still exist in large firms and is sometimes termed an 'intrapreneur', an individual, who may have control of resources and teams, and is capable of risk-taking, innovation and initiating change in large firms (see Chapter 6 on Corporate Entrepreneurship).

The concept that the entrepreneur is someone who is different, someone who is an innovator, is important. Some writers have carried this forward to distinguish entrepreneurs (business owners who wish to develop and expand their businesses) from other small-business owners who have no ambition to expand their business or who wish to remain just self-employed. The essential distinguishing feature for such writers is that the entrepreneur is a Schumpeterian innovator, although here the term 'innovator' would be more loosely defined to include a person who wishes to manage change or initiate change in some way. For example, Curran and Stanworth[1] state that:

> **Entrepreneurship, rigorously defined, refers to the creation of a new economic entity centred on a novel product or service or, at the very least, one which differs significantly from products or services offered elsewhere in the market.**
>
> (p. 12)

KNIGHT

The commonly held view of the entrepreneur as a calculated risk-taker comes close to the view of Knight. For Knight, the entrepreneur is an individual who is prepared to undertake risk and the reward – profit – is the return for bearing uncertainty, which is an uninsurable risk.

The opportunity for profit arises out of uncertainty surrounding change. If change is perfectly predictable then no opportunity for profit exists. The entrepreneur is someone who is prepared to undertake risk in an uncertain world.

Knight made an important distinction between risk and uncertainty. Risk exists when we have uncertain outcomes, but those outcomes can be predicted with a certain degree of probability. For example, the outcome that your car will be stolen or not stolen is uncertain, but the risk that your car will be stolen can be calculated with some degree of probability and this risk can be insured against. True uncertainty arises when the probability of outcomes cannot be calculated. Thus, anyone can set up in business, but that person cannot insure against business failure because that particular outcome cannot be predicted with any degree of probability. The entrepreneur then is someone who is willing to accept the remaining risk that cannot be transferred through insurance. Issues such as the extent to which the entrepreneur assesses, accepts and transfers risk have still to be properly explored.

This distinction helps to distinguish a small-firm manager from the entrepreneur/owner. One of the characteristics of entrepreneurs (following Knight) could be considered to be the responsibility for one's own actions. If a manager assumes this, then he or she is performing some entrepreneurial functions. We can also use this distinction as a criticism of some research into entrepreneurship which concentrates solely on personality traits and ignores management skills.

However, for a discussion of the extent of the different meanings of entrepreneurship in the literature see Galloway and Wilson.[2] An exception is also provided by Shailer.[3] For example, Shailer considers that:

> [The] entrepreneur is now a widely used term, with considerable contemporary diversity in meaning associated with the intended interests of its users. ... Owner-managers do not necessarily fit any of the current popular definitions of 'entrepreneur'.
>
> (p. 34)

Shailer prefers to adopt the view of entrepreneurship as a process and refers to a stage of the firm when it is in owner-management. Again we have the important concept of management of the firm, the willingness to accept risks and responsibilities. If the firm grows, it is possible to transfer this entrepreneurial function, but still retain part-ownership through the issue of shares. The manager, as opposed to the owner, now takes on the function of the entrepreneur. The fact that behaviour of the previous owner-entrepreneur is likely to alter has been established (theoretically) by writers such as Jensen and Meckling[4] by applying agency theory. Interestingly there are cases of very successful entrepreneurs that have not been comfortable with the loss of control when a firm is floated by the issuing of shares as a plc. For example, see the Entrepreneurship in Action case of easyJet and Stelios Haji-Ioannou, discussed in Chapter 12.

The concept of the importance of small-business management skills is also discussed by Ray.[5] He considers that the search for the prototype (entrepreneur) has been ill-conceived and considers that: 'There is no empirical evidence or conceptual base to say much, if anything, about entrepreneurs and risk taking' (p. 347). Ray considers that we should concentrate on the development of skills and how managers acquire them.

The concept of entrepreneurship as a process has also been highlighted by Stevenson and Jarillo[6] who suggest that: 'entrepreneurship is a process by which individuals . . . pursue opportunities without regard to the resources they control' (p. 23). Stevenson and Jarillo usefully denote the approach of economic writers to entrepreneurship as being concerned with what happens when entrepreneurs act, or with the results and consequences of entrepreneurship, whereas they view the psychological characteristics approach as being concerned with how entrepreneurs act, or with the study of entrepreneurial management.[6]

We could say, then, that the Knightian entrepreneur is anyone who is prepared to undertake the risk of setting up their own business. However, equally it could be any risk-taker (and this is a source of criticism). The entrepreneur is someone who has the confidence and is venturesome enough to make judgements about the uncertain future and reward for this is profit.

SHACKLE

Shackle's entrepreneur is someone who is creative and imaginative. Whereas Kirzner's entrepreneur *perceives* opportunities, Shackle's *imagines* opportunities. Everyone potentially has this creative ability, which is exercised in making choices.

The role of uncertainty and imperfect information is crucial for the view of the role of the entrepreneur by Shackle. Uncertainty gives rise to opportunities for certain individuals to imagine opportunities for profit. Shackle's entrepreneur is creative and original. The act of imagination is important for identifying the potential of opportunities. This potential is compared to resources available, which can lead to the decision to produce, hence the act of entrepreneurship. Shackle's creative entrepreneur indicates that *creativity* is an important element in the entrepreneurship process. However, how this creative process occurs, and the factors which might influence it, remain areas that are only just beginning to be explored. A host of factors will influence an individual's ability to be creative, including personal background, education and attitudes; but it is likely that such influences will combine to affect the extent to which that individual is *prepared* to recognize and exploit opportunities. It is only recently that pre-entrepreneurial experiences (including education, employment and learning) are beginning to be recognized as important influences on nascent (pre-start) entrepreneurs.[7]

The study of important factors influencing pre-start – or the process of nascent – entrepreneurship has received attention, given its potential importance for modern economies,[7] with much research effort now undertaken by the Global Entrepreneurship Monitor programme.[8]

HAYEK

Hayek's view is in the Austrian tradition, that information asymmetries create differences in *knowledge* held by individuals, or differences in kinds of knowledge, which provide the basis for exploitation of the discovery of entrepreneurial opportunities, although this can be a speculative process, subject to dynamic competition with elements of surprise from unexpected outcomes.[9] Hayek was concerned with economic planning, seeking to highlight the decentralisation of decision-making with the importance of individual decision-making such as that of business people, which he might have seen as managers and today we see as entrepreneurs.

CASSON

Casson attempts to synthesize some of these entrepreneurial attributes and concepts that have been discussed with the major writers. Casson recognizes that the entrepreneur will have different skills from others. These skills enable the entrepreneur to make judgements, to co-ordinate scarce resources. The entrepreneur makes judgemental decisions that involve the reallocation or organization of resources.

Casson emphasizes that entrepreneurs require command over resources if he or she is to back their judgements and that this is likely to imply that they will have personal wealth. Lack of financial capital would thus be a barrier to successful entrepreneurship.

Casson's view is closer to that of Knight than other writers. The entrepreneur operates within a set of technological conditions; by making difficult judgemental decisions they are able to enjoy the reward of profit (for bearing uninsurable risk). This enables the entrepreneur to co-ordinate demand and supply under uncertainty.

In Figure 1.2 the demand curve represents the return to each entrepreneur as their numbers increase and is part of a map of such curves. The supply curve of entrepreneurs depends on access to resources and thus depends on the local economy and environment. Casson's analysis attempts to explain why in some economies entrepreneurs can flourish, yet in others there are low participation rates for people who own their own businesses. For example, in the UK, the South East has higher participation rates of people in small business ownership than the Midlands, which in turn has higher participation rates than Scotland. The low participation rates in Scotland have been partly attributed, for example, to relatively low home-ownership, which limits the amount of equity that a nascent entrepreneur might have to invest in a start-up firm.[10] Thus Casson's point about the access to resources would appear to be an important one. The clear implication, when we examine

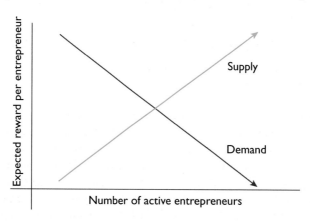

FIGURE 1.2

Casson's demand and supply of entrepreneurs

such participation rates, is that the environment can be a more powerful influence than any predilection amongst the local population for entrepreneurship.

Casson's insight is to view change as an accompaniment to entrepreneurship. The pace of change provides opportunities and the entrepreneur chooses which one to back. Entrepreneurs can vie with each other as their numbers increase, the supply of entrepreneurs depending on their access to resources. The supply curve shown in Figure 1.2 will thus depend on the propensity of any given set of circumstances and the extent to which potential entrepreneurs have access to resources. This will depend on factors such as social mobility and institutional factors such as the ability to access capital. An equilibrium position will result from the interaction of these factors, as shown in Figure 1.2.

A number of other economic writers and theorists have considered the development of the role of the entrepreneur. These include, for example, Thünen who could be seen as a forerunner of Knight. Thünen recognized the function of the entrepreneur as a risk-taker, involving risks that cannot be transferred through insurance. For Thünen, however, the entrepreneur was also concerned with innovation and problem-solving.

It would be untrue to say that the neoclassical school of economists added little to the concept of the entrepreneur. For example, Marshall recognized a distinction between the capitalist and the entrepreneur through his 'undertaker' who was alert to opportunities, but also innovative in devising new methods of production.

SECTION SUMMARY AND REVIEW

A consensus has emerged that, in conditions of uncertainty and change, the entrepreneur is a key actor in the economy. The different views on the role of the entrepreneur are summarized in Table 1.1, but two major lines of thinking have developed: the Knightian approach which highlights the risk-bearing and uncertainty-reducing role of entrepreneurs; and the Schumpeterian approach in which the entrepreneur is an innovator.

Other perspectives highlight the knowledge and insight of the entrepreneur to new possibilities. This co-ordinating role has been developed and emphasized by Casson, but in addition it is clear that there are other factors that influence participation in entrepreneurship, such as access to resources and facilities in the local environment. The entrepreneurial act of business creation is part of a process that will be affected by many historical factors as well as the opportunities arising from economic change, such as the example of the Internet. As the pace of economic change increases, so opportunities increase; yet our understanding of the complete entrepreneurship process, and why participation rates (of different groups in society) are far from equitable, remains limited.

THE ENTREPRENEURIAL PERSONALITY

The second approach to entrepreneurship is to identify certain personality characteristics or 'traits' in individuals that appear to be possessed by successful entrepreneurs. The characteristics literature has been concerned with testing and applying some perceived characteristics in individuals. From this approach, it is possible to argue that the supply of potential entrepreneurs is limited to a finite number of people that have innate abilities, that have a set of characteristics that marks them out as special, and have particular insights not possessed by others. This has led to some controversy and, in terms of policy, it has significant implications. Obviously, if entrepreneurial characteristics are inherent then there is little to be gained from direct interventions to encourage new entrepreneurs to start new businesses, although interventions into improving the infrastructure or environment may still have an effect.

We examine some of these personality 'traits', although we do not accept the hypothesis that there is a fixed limit to the supply of potential entrepreneurs. For example, many of the characteristics which are often said to be special to successful entrepreneurs are the same abilities and skills that could be applied to most successful managers and it is therefore difficult to separate out specific characteristics of entrepreneurs.

Some of this research stems from the original work carried out by McClelland,[11] who identified the historical role model influence of prominent leaders on subsequent generations. Such influence induced a high need for achievement on the population of the subsequent generations. McClellend, however, is also associated with identifying the following key competencies of successful entrepreneurs.

PROPOSED KEY COMPETENCIES OF SUCCESSFUL ENTREPRENEURS

- Proactivity: initiative and assertiveness
- Achievement orientation: ability to see and act on opportunities
- Commitment to others

Much has been made of the need for achievement trait, as though this was the one characteristic that set potential entrepreneurs apart from others. An implicit assumption with this approach is that the individual bears responsibility for his or her lack of entrepreneurial activity and this proposition could be used by policy-makers to divert interventions away from regions that have low rates of participation in small-firm ownership.

Considering the work of writers on the entrepreneurship personality, we can identify certain key characteristics which have been identified in the literature as being important abilities of any entrepreneur (see the accompanying box).

THE ENTREPRENEURIAL PERSONALITY – KEY CHARACTERISTICS

- McClelland's need for achievement
- Calculated risk-taker
- High internal locus of control
- Creativity
- Innovative
- Need for autonomy
- Ambiguity tolerance
- Vision
- Self-efficacy

Some writers subscribe to the view of McClelland – that the key characteristic is achievement motivation, or a high need for achievement, which can be described as a desire to excel, to achieve a goal in relation to a set of standards. High achievers are those that accept responsibility for decisions and for achieving solutions to problems, but standards will be set carefully so that they can be achieved. Satisfaction is gained from finding the solution to a problem rather than with monetary reward. Yet, partly because such a characteristic is difficult to measure, the evidence on the importance of this personality characteristic has proved to be contradictory. A high need for achievement can also be an important characteristic for success for people in many occupations, not just entrepreneurs.

Another characteristic that has been advocated is the internal locus of control. Individuals with a high internal locus of control like to be in charge of their environment and of their own destiny. Again, as with the need for achievement trait, it has not been possible to reconcile conflicting evidence with entrepreneurs with this approach to one or two important personality traits. For a critique of the characteristics literature see Chell et al.[12] In a review of this approach, Delmar[13] comments that 'the [research] results have been poor and it has been difficult to discern any specific traits to entrepreneurial behaviour' (p. 145).

A further example is provided by Meredith et al.[14] who give five core traits:

- Self-confidence
- Risk-taking activity
- Flexibility
- Need for achievement
- Strong desire to be independent

A high degree of self-confidence or perceived self-confidence, called self-efficacy, has been advocated by some writers as an important concept in entrepreneurship. High self-efficacy in entrepreneurship translates into self-belief in one's capabilities to mobilize resources, motivate others and produce change (business start-up). Although there is some evidence that perceived self-efficacy is related to business performance,[14] researchers have been concerned with whether successful entrepreneurs display psychological traits which separate them out as individuals from others. However, such an approach can be criticized in a number of ways.

CRITICISMS OF THE PERSONALITY CHARACTERISTICS APPROACH

- It is inappropriate to search for a significant single trait.
- It ignores environmental factors that may be more important than personality.
- It comprises an essentially static analysis approach to the dynamic process of entrepreneurship.
- It ignores the role of learning, preparation and serendipity in the process of entrepreneurship (these factors are discussed later in this chapter).

A more negative characteristic, that of the deviant (non-conformist) personality, is associated with Kets de Vries.[15] The deviant personality is associated with the third approach to the entrepreneur, that of the social-behavioural school. A deviant character is associated with individuals who do not easily fit in with their existing employment – for instance someone who is out of place in a large firm. The non-conformist behaviour precipitates a desire to start their own business, rather than operate within the regulations of a large organization.

However, this would seem to rule out the possibility of the dynamic employee wishing to create change in the large firm, the intrapreneur.

Writers such as Timmons[16] have attempted to summarize the personality characteristics of successful entrepreneurs and to categorize characteristics that can be acquired and those that are more innate. While Timmons does admit that many of these characteristics can be acquired, through learning or from experience, Timmons also considers that there are some attributes which cannot be acquired, which are innate, and perhaps mark out 'born entrepreneurs' from 'made entrepreneurs'.

Timmons considers that both need for achievement and locus of control can be acquired along with other leadership abilities and competencies such as the ability to take responsibility for actions/decisions. Many of these characteristics are management skills. Entrepreneurs obviously need to be ambitious, but need to be satisfied that they have achieved personal goals and ambitions.

We can assume that profit or monetary reward is not the only driving force behind entrepreneurs. There is also the need to build and achieve personally set goals, hence implying that entrepreneurs have a high need for achievement in order to establish a growing business or 'entrepreneurial' firm (this is discussed in more detail in Chapter 10). Similarly, the internal locus of control has been identified as an important characteristic of potential entrepreneurs. Timmons considers that these characteristics can be acquired; many of these abilities can be taught or, at the very least, scenarios can be provided which stimulate the acquisition of these skills and abilities.

In practice, many of the entrepreneurial characteristics are those associated with any successful manager or indeed with any successful individual. It is therefore difficult to justify a separate set of characteristics for a successful career in entrepreneurship.

Timmons also gives additional attributes which are more innate. These are listed as:

- High energy coupled with emotional stability
- Creative and innovative ability
- Conceptual ability
- Vision combined with a capacity to inspire

Although it may be claimed that this set of characteristics is more innate in terms of identifying people who are potential entrepreneurs, it is difficult to justify that these abilities mark people out for entrepreneurship. Also it does not mean that they cannot be acquired. By the use of planning scenarios and problem-solving it is still possible to demonstrate how opportunities can be exploited, how resources can be acquired and how creative solutions can be developed.

Some institutions and writers have attempted to develop tests of potential entrepreneurial ability or enterprise. Caird, for example, has developed a measure of enterprising traits (or entrepreneurial abilities) called the General Enterprise Tendency (GET).[17] It consists of a scale of different questions within the following categories:

- 12 that measure need for achievement
- 12 that assess internal locus of control
- 12 to determine creative tendency
- 12 to gauge calculated risk-taking
- 6 to measure need for autonomy

Entrepreneurial or enterprise tendency tests, however, suffer from the same limitations as the characteristics approach. Not surprisingly, these tests have been found to be inconsistent in their application or selection. However, more recent work, carried out by Johnson and Suet Fan Ma,[18] with an expanded scaled test with nine dimensions, appears to claim more promising results as an enterprise tendency test.

Problems arise whenever attempts are made to measure these characteristics. For example:

- Characteristics are not stable and change over time.
- They can describe actions that require subjective judgements that do not lend themselves to objective measurement. For example, how do we define being innovative? It can simply be the ability to deal with change and the ability to cope with new processes and solutions. How do we measure the calculated risk-taker? In many respects there are unsatisfactory definitions of actions associated with these concepts which makes their measurement difficult to justify.
- Concentrating on personality characteristics means that we are in danger of ignoring environmental and cultural influences, which can be just as, if not more, important than any set of personality traits.
- Placing too much importance on an inherent set of personality characteristics reduces the role of education and training. Learning is a very valuable process that allows potential entrepreneurs to acquire skills, to develop methods of business planning. While we would agree that many people are not suited to entrepreneurship, there is still much that can be learned and acquired by potential entrepreneurs and this process is not yet fully understood.

There is a danger that these approaches can influence and dominate approaches to small-firm ownership and entrepreneurship so that important influences on entrepreneurship, such as quality of the infrastructure provided in the environment, are ignored. There are a number of problems with these approaches and they include ignoring issues such as gender, age, social class and education, all of which can have a bearing on the propensity of an individual to enter entrepreneurship.

SOCIO-BEHAVIOURAL APPROACHES

Socio-behavioural approaches recognize the importance of some of these factors, but especially the environment and the influence of culture on individuals. It can be argued that a society's culture is a more powerful influence on the extent to which individuals can successfully pursue entrepreneurship. An example is provided by a nation's tolerance of failure.

DEALING WITH FAILURE

Timmons considers that dealing with failure can be an important attribute of entrepreneurs. However, the ability to tolerate failure depends on the culture. In the USA failure is viewed as a learning experience and that people can benefit from it, can learn from their experience and can go on to form successful companies as a result. In other countries, including Britain, the culture is less tolerant of failure and, too often, highly talented individuals have not been able to recover from it. According to a report, in the European Union (EU) as many as 40 per cent of people would not start a business due to fear of failure, whereas the equivalent in the USA is 26 per cent.[19] The culture and environment are crucial to tolerance of failure. There is little doubt that Britain has lost many potentially successful entrepreneurs because, having failed once, they have not been allowed to recover from that failure, perhaps from an inability to raise capital following bankruptcy. Failure is a very valuable learning experience, as many entrepreneurs have admitted. In Britain, in the past, new entrepreneurs have not been allowed a further opportunity so that they can benefit from their experience, apply lessons learned and build a successful business. Recent changes in the UK bankruptcy laws, easing the severe restrictions on the actions of individuals in bankruptcy, have been made, in part, to allow individuals at least an opportunity to learn from previous failure and to restart.

THE INFLUENCE OF THE ENVIRONMENT: DIFFERENT ENTREPRENEURSHIP PARTICIPATION RATES

We turn now to consider some of the empirical evidence on the factors that influence entrepreneurship. An example can be taken from the UK, where there are low participation rates in entrepreneurship by women and by African-Caribbeans (see Chapter 4). As Ram[20] has pointed out, the Asian community has high rates of participation in small-business ownership and entrepreneurship, yet this has had more to do with negative factors of barriers to employment elsewhere than any predisposition for entrepreneurship.

The ideas and concepts surrounding the entrepreneur, which have been outlined in previous sections, are used as a basis by researchers for detecting traits in successful small-business owners and entrepreneurs. As in any scientific method, theory can be used for developing hypotheses about the behaviour of successful entrepreneurs. These hypotheses are then tested against the observed characteristics of entrepreneurs and small-business owners in the real world. However, there are a number of problems with this approach, among which is the assumption that additional factors affecting participation rates will be constant.

ENTREPRENEURIAL PARTICIPATION RATES VARY

- Different participation rates in different regions
- Different participation rates by gender
- Different participation rates by ethnic minority groups
- Active inter-firm networks vary by region

First, some regions are more favoured than others for establishing successful small businesses and entrepreneurs, and hence their economic development is more successful. The question of whether this is due to characteristics in the population, or due to certain aspects of the environment and infrastructure that enable potential entrepreneurs to more easily exploit their skills and opportunities, remains, at this stage, an open one.

Research undertaken for Scottish Enterprise[10] after concern at low participation rates in entrepreneurship, showed that a complex series of factors contributed to low participation rates. For example, the historical dependence on a limited number of large employers, coupled with inward investment (North Sea oil) had produced a 'dependency culture' – that is, people were used to depending on large firms for employment. Thus, the thought of going into business on their own account did not come easily to them. Other factors were found to be important as well, such as difficulties in accessing finance. Scottish Enterprise introduced a Business Birth Rate Strategy in 1993[21] with a raft of measures designed to improve access to environmental factors affecting entrepreneurship; after seven years a comprehensive review of the strategy[22] concluded that although the environment had been improved, little difference had been made to the business birth rate. This example shows that participation rates can vary in different geographical areas, but explanations of such spatial variations involve complex reasons and appear to be very difficult to change through public policy measures.

Second, concern has been addressed at the existence of latent entrepreneurial talent. For example, why are there relatively few female high-growth entrepreneurs? In Scotland, a compilation and promotion of over 400 high-growth entrepreneurs (conducted by Scottish Enterprise[23] in an attempt to provide more role models that might influence possible or potential nascent entrepreneurs) contained only 16 per cent who were female entrepreneurs. Why is the participation rate of Black Africans and Black Caribbeans, in the UK, in entrepreneurship low? Again these remain open questions which appear to have no simple solution but, rather, are caused by a complex combination of social and economic reasons.

Limited research has been conducted specifically on these groups in the UK, although a UK study involving the author[24] with Black Africans and Black Caribbeans and the other main ethnic-minority entrepreneurs in the UK has provided more information on motivation, aspirations and issues facing these groups (for a more detailed discussion on ethnic-minority entrepreneurship, see Chapter 4).

Third, attention has focused on the role of networks in successful entrepreneurial development. For example, some research suggests that inter-firm networks contribute to successful entrepreneurship.

Official statistics indicate that a high proportion of new firms fail within three years of start-up. For example, in the UK, 30 per cent of new firms appear to cease trading by the third year and 50 per cent by the fifth year.[25] Official statistics need to be treated with caution and are likely to overstate the true failure rate. For example, a successful start-up firm may cease to exist when taken over by another firm; some business-owners leave and re-enter self-employment, dependent on labour market conditions. However, it is accepted that there are only a small proportion of new firms that grow to employ 50 or more workers. One of the factors that might affect such limited numbers of high-growth firms is the potential loss of control faced by the entrepreneur as the firm grows. New small firms and entrepreneurs that are successful are predominantly located in the South East in the UK, which suggests that the environment and infrastructure are at least as important as the characteristics of the entrepreneur. It is also likely that the development of inter-firm networks is more advanced in the South East than in other regions of the UK.

The inter-organizational networks that link firms after they are established have been found to be important to the ongoing success of firms.[26] Efficient networks that foster good communications between firms contribute to entrepreneurial behaviour and success.[27]

THE ROLE OF SOCIAL CAPITAL

A concept that may help to explain differing participation rates in entrepreneurship is that of the value and role of social capital, which may vary between regions and different groups in society. Conceptually, social capital refers to the ability of decision-makers, such as entrepreneurs, to draw on resources from their social networks[28; 29] or the ability to use resources from social exchange.[30] In a government review of the literature on social capital, it was defined as: 'social capital consists of the networks, norms, relationships, values and informal sanctions that shape the quantity and co-operative quality of a society's social interactions'.[31]

Such social networks, relationships and values may be based on a number of different, but complementary (and possibly competing) networks, including family, community and organizational business networks such as local business clubs and business forums. Social capital, then, is an 'umbrella term'[32] covering a potential multitude of relationships between entrepreneurs, their families, their friends and their community. The importance of the role of social capital may be indicated by the attention given by a number of commentators to its role in ethnic-minority businesses, which it is argued will have strong social capital due to strong ties with family and their local ethnic communities, partly because of cultural factors that lead to high value being placed on (extended) family and community ties and because, as a minority immigrant group within a host society, exclusion tends to increase the strength of community bonding.

Sirmon and Hitt[33] recognize and discuss the role of social capital in entrepreneurial family firms in relation to the roles of forms of capital which they label as human, financial and 'survivability'. Their discussion sees social capital as an important resource in the resource-based view (RBV) of the firm, where entrepreneurial and competitive advantage are derived from advantages obtained through resources; therefore, social capital assists in gaining important resources which can give a competitive advantage. They argue that:

> Social capital can affect a number of important firm activities such as interunit and interfirm resource exchange, the creation of intellectual capital, interfirm learning, supplier interactions, product innovation and entrepreneurship ... (and) ... as such social capital is a highly important resource.
>
> (p. 342)

The nature of social capital, i.e. whether it bonds or bridges or performs additional roles, has also been the focus of discussion by some writers; for example, bonding social capital, that strengthens ties, and bridging social capital, that strengthens relationships and networks across different groups (such as different class forms and ethnic groups). Anderson and Jack take this further by discussing the role of social capital as either 'glue' or 'lubricant', taking up the concept that social capital can have different roles.[34] They eventually conclude that such 'expressions' of social capital are part of the process of social capital. 'In fact both dimensions are merely *expressions* of social capital, while social capital itself is a process' (their emphasis).

The Shapero model[35] has also suggested that strong social capital through networks can be a factor in determining entrepreneurial entry. It is argued that social capital has an important influence with nascent entrepreneurs for determining the entrepreneurial entry decision. For example, Davidsson and Honig take up the concept of the bonding role of social capital and claim that strong bonding and strong social ties are important factors that explain start-up entrepreneurial decision-making.[32]

> Bonding social capital based on strong ties, such as having parents who owned businesses or close friends who owned businesses, was a good predictor in differentiating those engaged in nascent entrepreneurship from the control population, as was active encouragement from family and friends.
>
> (p. 304)

The nature of successful networks depends on the level of trust, which itself will depend on the nature of the business environment (e.g. rural v. urban), on culture and on regulations. It is arguable that weak ties, for example, with other business-owners as peers, may be more important than strong ties, for example, family bonds and can certainly be more beneficial.[36] Writers on women's enterprise have argued that women entrepreneurs will bring a different set of networks that do not easily match to the institutionalized existing business networks, which are of course male dominated.[37] It is arguable that policymakers need to understand these different social ties and social networks of male and female entrepreneurs.[37]

It is likely that the role of social capital in the entrepreneurial process is complex and variable. Research undertaken by the author with ethnic-minority businesses in Scotland found the role of social capital to be complex and diverse, with both advantages and restrictions on the start-up and development of such businesses. Strong social capital provided benefits in accessing resources (for example, finance and advice), but it could also be more restrictive where the advice could limit entrepreneurial development.[38]

THE ABILITY TO LEARN

As discussed in previous sections, a fertile area that deserves further work is the understanding of factors affecting the ability of entrepreneurs to learn. Although there have been recent advances in understanding, for example, following work by Cope and Watts and Rae,[39; 40] there is still a need to improve our knowledge on how entrepreneurs learn, yet it is accepted that there is a learning experience from merely establishing a new enterprise. The learning process that is involved in business and enterprise development is still imperfectly understood, yet programmes have been designed and interventions are made in business development. The problem with these interventions (at least in the past) is that they were often task orientated.

They were built around particular tasks and skills in terms of business planning; for example, on bookkeeping or financial skills or on liquidity or controlling for debt. As such, they concentrated on specific tasks of running a business. A failing of such interventions is that they do little to alter the approach of the entrepreneur to solving business problems and reflective learning. However, in recent years in the UK, there has been evidence of the introduction of more mentoring-style assistance. Overall, though, it is not surprising that Storey and West-head,[41] from a survey of the literature, found that there was little evidence of a link between formal training and improved performance of small firms, indicating that formal personal-management development and training of the entrepreneur appears, paradoxically, to have no impact on improved performance. Gibb,[42] however, proposes that development of the entrepreneur is affected by the extent of interaction with 'stakeholders' in the small-firm environment (for example, customers, bankers, creditors and supply chain relationships), thus implying that intervening to improve learning from interaction and experience should improve entrepreneurial ability and performance. According to Gibb:

> Learning better from experience implies bringing knowledge, skills, values and attitudes together to interact upon the learning process; it therefore fundamentally demands an action-learning approach.
>
> (p. 16)

Gibb's 'stakeholder' model of entrepreneurial learning is illustrated in Figure 1.3. It sees the small business as a learning organization and places importance on the small-firm relationships with the external environment.

The relationships in Figure 1.3 illustrate three sources of entrepreneurial learning:

- Practice-based: this source includes learning from incidental forms of management development and, therefore, from day-to-day activities. However, it may also include informal learning arising from processes and practice within the business
- Proximal: this source refers to untapped and latent *potential* from existing development activities to solve managerial problems, as there will be within any firm latent potential development from problem-solving using previous experience and that of trusted advisers, peers and mentors[43]
- Distal learning: refers to learning that is external to the firm and may be both informal through membership of peer groups and formal through structured and arranged programmes

It is the untapped potential from proximal and some distal sources that many of the policy interventions have failed to capture and caused Gibb to call for more action-learning based approaches.[42]

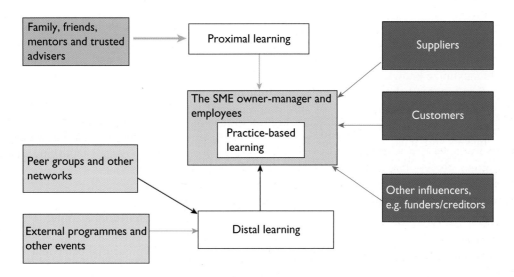

FIGURE 1.3

Sources of learning and SMEs as learning organizations

(Following Gibb (1997) *The Small Business as a Learning Organisation.*)

The 'stakeholder model' can be contrasted with an alternative approach based on an evolutionary theory of learning and entrepreneurial behaviour. Drawing on evolutionary theories, Costello,[44] for example, has shown that, with technology-based small firms, entrepreneurs learn to adapt behaviour into 'routines' that enable knowledge to be acquired and it is the routine (a set of rules) that enables learning to evolve. This, however, also implies that such learning becomes 'path dependent'[45] taking a critical event to change a routine.

Entrepreneurship involves a learning process, an ability to cope with problems and to learn from those problems. An ability to recognize why problems occur, to be able to deal with them and, more importantly, understand why they occur, will ensure that the entrepreneur will be able not only to deal with those problems, but also to learn from the experience and ensure that processes are put in place within the firm to ensure that either the problem does not occur again or that the firm can manage similar issues. If much learning is practice-based, then the entrepreneur needs to know how to reflect and absorb any lessons, so that the small business achieves features of a learning company.[46]

Case studies of the features of learning organizations have been developed in some detail,[47] yet little equivalent research has been undertaken within small firms, partly because of the lack of appropriate ethnographic and case-study approaches that are capable of revealing the complex, and often subtle, mix of factors that will affect entrepreneurial learning. At the same time, we need developments of theories and concepts that are appropriate to entrepreneurship. Learning organization concepts are derived from large organizations; more promising are developments in evolutionary approaches to learning and the entrepreneur. In part, these stem from a Schumpeterian dynamics analysis of the forces of change and attempt to explain how the entrepreneur can adapt, change and thus learn from dealing with uncertainty.[48] The interaction between learning and the entrepreneurship process has been highlighted by Levinthal[49] who stresses the adaptive role of entrepreneurs as they adjust to their environment, to their learning experience and, as a result, change behaviour. The nature of learning may follow a trial and error and discovery activity; entrepreneurial behaviour becomes adapted in an evolutionary way to the discovery of information from trial and error. It is suggested that such evolutionary theories may be able to model the nature of entrepreneurial behaviour and development, although there is a need for further work in this area.

The ability of the entrepreneur, or entrepreneurial team, to learn is crucial to their behaviour and ability to succeed. To be successful, entrepreneurs must be able to learn from decisions, from mistakes, from experience and from their networks. It is a process that is characterized by significant and critical *learning events*. To be able to maximize knowledge as a result of experiencing these learning events will determine how successful their firm eventually becomes. There seems little doubt that there are methods of enhancing the learning activity, such as the careful choice of an entrepreneurial team with complementary skills. We have suggested, however, that at present there is a need for further theoretical development, which will help to guide policymakers and, thus, interventions. Entrepreneurial behaviour is a dynamic response to a constantly changing environment. Large-firm organizational theory does not capture the dynamic of learning in such an environment.

The author's view is that these dichotomous approaches to entrepreneurial learning (as represented by Gibb and Costello) have something to offer in understanding the nature of entrepreneurial learning. The author has suggested that entrepreneurial learning occurs as a result of a combination of the processes involved in these two approaches.[50] The important contribution of these theories is that entrepreneurial behaviour is a dynamic process, where the entrepreneur learns to adjust decision-making, and consequently we cannot view the ability of the entrepreneur as something that is static; rather it is continually evolving.

The previous academic work directly on entrepreneurial learning can be classified into three categories: from the application of theories of adult learning, from the application of environmental and social explanations, and from applications of organizational behaviour and (hence) organizational learning theories.

Application of Theories of Adult Learning

Much of the conceptual literature in this area draws upon and modifies theories of adult learning. Partly this is because entrepreneurial learning is assumed to be experiential in nature. Politis[51] considers that there is a need to consider how experience (gained) is transformed into knowledge. Cope[52] considers that entrepreneurs adapt and develop new behaviour over a period of time so that there is a need to consider adult learning theories that allow for the cumulative nature of learning and the importance of dynamic and cyclical explanations.[53]

It is arguable that dynamic, rather than static, and longitudinal, rather than cross-sectional or survey, approaches are necessary to increase our understanding of entrepreneurial learning. In Rae's study[54] he focused upon the life stories of interviewed entrepreneurs to understand how individual respondents learned to develop entrepreneurial behaviour. He has suggested that such 'learned entrepreneurial behaviour' could be identified through the dynamic nature of 'learning episodes', involving discrete extended periods of time in which entrepreneurs drew upon learning and reflection from experiences that have formulated their approaches and behaviour. Other writers have identified dynamic 'critical events' as the catalyst for learning and changes in entrepreneurial behaviour.[55] Cope and Watts[56] have applied critical incident methodology to a longitudinal case study approach and claim that, although very diverse in nature, critical events provide the basis for the development of 'higher-level' learning, where the concept of deep learning is the outcome of the experience of the identified critical events leading to changed entrepreneurial behaviour. However, they also conclude that, because of the complex and diverse nature of entrepreneurial learning:[56] 'In terms of theory building we are a long way from the development of sufficiently broad-based frameworks to illustrate this diversity' (p. 118).

Environmental and Social Explanations

Environmental and social explanations of the nature of entrepreneurial learning identify behavioural factors affecting both the firm and the entrepreneur. These approaches treat entrepreneurial learning as a product of the social environment within which the entrepreneur operates. These are not necessarily separate from conceptual writers mentioned in the first category and elements of such approaches have been used by Rae[54] and Cope.[52]

Organizational Learning Theory Applications

Organizational learning (OL) theories stem from explanations of collective learning within large organizations.[57] However, more recently Zhang et al.[58] have used an OL approach to explain learning processes on innovation within manufacturing SMEs and claim that: '[Our] findings confirm early studies on the importance of organisation-wide (intra-organisation) learning in innovative firms' (p. 312). They also claim that the application of OL theories in SMEs helps to explain those that were 'innovative' compared to those that were 'stable'. An earlier study by Wyer et al.[59] has also argued that OL theories can provide insights into 'collective learning' within small firms.

Despite the recent increase in the number of papers in the academic literature, the previous research evidence directly on entrepreneurial learning is limited and recent papers have been conceptual, aiming to provide a framework for further research or to set a research agenda.[51; 53; 50] Given some of the features of the nature of entrepreneurial learning, which have been discussed in the academic literature, it is not surprising that the investigations that have involved direct research evidence have been based upon largely qualitative approaches and with the main focus on entrepreneurial case studies. For example, Cope[60] reported findings from six case studies and Rae[54] reported narrative life stories from 12 interviews. However, more recent research has employed programmes of interviews or surveys: for example Thorpe et al.[61] report the findings of 44 email 'postcard' responses and Zhang et al.[58] discuss the analysis of 26 interviews.

In summary, the recent developments in contributions to our understanding of entrepreneurial learning from these different approaches have been very welcome advances and have demonstrated the importance of complex factors which are discontinuous and experiential in nature within the entrepreneurial process. It is worth bearing in mind the conceptual concepts of entrepreneurial learning with the following case study on Skype Part 1.

ENTREPRENEURSHIP IN ACTION

The following case material is extracted from a case study written by Professor Hans Bent Martinsen at Aarhus Business School, Denmark and we are grateful for the permission to use it.

Source: Martinsen (2006) *Why were Janus Friis and Niklas Zennström successful with Kazaa and Skype?*, Aarhus Business School, Denmark.

SKYPE PART 1
Early Developments

Three important technological trends occurred in the 1990s:

- The growth of digital recordings via CDs and move away from analogue recordings
- The growth of home PC use
- The growth and availability of the Internet allowing the possibility of sharing digital files with other users

During the 1990s the music industry had seen the introduction of digital CDs, and with the advent and take-up of home PCs copying CDs and retaining quality of sound became viable. The Internet brought the possibility of sharing and exchanging files.

In 1999 Napster was created by American student Shawn Fanning. This was a software program that made MP3 files available for all other Napster users via the Internet. In this way Napster turned thousands of computers into one huge server. However, the Recording Industry Association of America (RIAA) took Napster to court and Napster was forced to close its server in August 2000.

But Napster had shown the way and soon there were a whole swarm of peer-to-peer file servers on the Internet. The result was that companies could try to get court injunctions, but because servers could be anywhere in the world, the growth of downloading digital recordings via the Internet continued unabated.

THE PARTNERSHIP IS FORMED

Tele2 is a Swedish telecom company operating in 23 European countries. In 1993, Tele2 launched fixed telephony as a virtual operator and across several European countries by 1998.

In 1997 Niklas Zennström, a 32-year-old MSc Computer Science graduate was working for Tele2 and was tasked with building an ISP for Tele2 in Denmark. Janus Friis was 22 years old, had left school without formal qualifications and was working at an Internet service provider (ISP) in Denmark, called Cybercity. During 1997, Janus Friis was hired by Niklas Zennström to work on the establishment of the Tele2 ISP and by 1998 they had forged a working partnership with Friis providing the creative ideas and Zennström the business and strategic leadership. They worked on setting up ISP centres in other nations in Europe, including Luxembourg and Amsterdam. The nature of the partnership has been illustrated by the following extract:

> In October 2004, Søren Krogsgaard from Beringske Nyhedsmagasin described Janus Friis as the visionary generator of ideas, while Niklas Zennström seemed to be the organiser bringing ideas into being. (Politiken, 14 August 2005)

Krogsgaard goes on to say:

> The differences are clear to everyone. Friis is ten years younger than his Swedish counterpart. He wears T-shirts and a rucksack, while Zennström seems to prefer a pin-striped suit and an attaché case—Friis wants to develop ideas that generate popular movements, Zennström speaks about ideas that will be big business.

THE CLEVER BIT: SOLVING THE PROBLEM OF MASS DISTRIBUTION ON THE INTERNET

The development of the ISP business across Europe had led to some issues regarding capacity and bandwidth. This effectively determined the extent of traffic that could be handled by an ISP, obviously in turn limiting capacity for business and income generation from subscribers. Peer-to-peer (P2P) distributed computing offered an alternative. This technology uses the Internet but avoids central servers by using each other's PC for storage while online: the Internet is purely the connection. This cleverly solves the problem of mass distribution on the Internet; it avoids situations where systems can crash because thousands of subscribers try to download files simultaneously. The P2P principle works well with very popular files, which use the principle to create greater accessibility. It side-steps neatly the need for server provision and is impossible to control by the major recording companies and the movie industry.

FROM ESTONIA WITH LOVE: KAZAA

These developments coincided with the dotcom boom (see earlier comment in this chapter), when venture capital money was chasing new start-up ideas. By now Friis and Zennström had experience of Internet business development, saw the potential for P2P and decided to launch their own joint venture, but without any clear idea of exactly which service they would provide. They based themselves in Amsterdam at Zennström's apartment with Friis in the guest room and the office in the kitchen. Zennström told Politiken that at the time:

> We knew we'd come up with something, or, at least, we hoped we would.

Neither Zennström nor Friis were programmers, but they could see the potential for P2P on the Internet especially as the legal cases against Napster in the USA had shown that an alternative solution needed to be found.

Kazaa uses a P2P principle developed by Estonian software engineers working in a garage. Three Estonian programmers were led by Jaan Tallinn who had meet Zennström and Friis while working for Tele2. Zennström commented:

> These are the best software developers I have ever seen in my life—and—they are very skilful at problem-solving.

The software developers came up with a program called Kazaa, which outsourced its server needs to its users; it became a self-organizing network with supernodes which were represented by people's PCs with fast broadband connections.

After four months of development, Zennström and Friis launched their new start-up company which they called FastTrack with the Kazaa file-sharing service. Zennström founded the company with his savings, there was no borrowing and no venture capital and zero expenditure on marketing and advertising. Friis:

> We uploaded the programs to a web server and entered links on http://download.com and other shareware sites. Then we just sat down and waited for something to happen.

◀

DISCUSSION QUESTIONS

1 What are the features and characteristics of the partnership between Niklas Zennström and Janus Friis that would form the foundation of an entrepreneurial partnership?

2 Are Zennström and Friis examples of Schumpeterian or Kirznerian entrepreneurs? What are the features of the case that support your answer?

3 What role did serendipity play in this case and how important do you think it was?

4 Will Zennström and Friis be able to make money out of the FastTrack company?

5 What do you expect them to do next?

6 Why will the experience and entrepreneurial learning with FastTrack be important for the future decision-making of Niklas Zennström and Janus Friis?

CONCLUSIONS

We can see that attempts to develop tests on entrepreneurial characteristics owe something to the development of theories of entrepreneurship. Shackle's creator and Schumpeter's innovator are included in the measures of creative tendency. There is Knight's calculated risk-taker. The role of co-ordinator of Casson and Kirzner is included by the need to have an internal locus of control and autonomy. These theories have been the guidelines for tests of entrepreneurial ability. Concern with the entrepreneurial personality has diverted attention away from the learning and development process in entrepreneurship and enterprise development, away from the recognition that the individual entrepreneur *acquires* skills and abilities, which are learned from the very process of entrepreneurship. Recent research with entrepreneurial learning has revealed important findings on the discontinuous nature of entrepreneurial development in the entrepreneurial process; these have been welcome developments. At least in theory, support for entrepreneurship should benefit by being better informed to enable individuals to acquire management skills that enable them to learn from their experience, and from their solution of problems.

There is little doubt, however, that the social and economic environment can be just as important as personal management skills for successful entrepreneurship. It affects the ability of the entrepreneur to acquire resources, including social capital. This has important implications for policy and the support of SMEs. Some of these issues will reoccur when we examine entrepreneurial and small business support later in this book. If the environment is not conducive then entrepreneurial talent will lie dormant. The importance of identifying entrepreneurial characteristics lies in encouraging potential entrepreneurs to start their own businesses. Schemes that give blanket coverage run the risk of persuading people to enter business who are not suited to the task of controlling and running their own business (however good the business idea may be) and will eventually fail. There is evidence that policy has become more focused on start-ups and increasing the level of entrepreneurial activity;[19] but it is also important to ensure that policies encourage high-quality sustainable businesses.

There are some myths associated with entrepreneurship (see the text by Read et al.[62]), one of which is that you need to be a special individual with special resources, experience and with a special vision or foresight. While some personal qualities are important, we will see from the examination of the cases in this text that entrepreneurs are drawn from a diverse range of backgrounds and experience, and have a wide range of different abilities, making prescriptive comments about the qualities of entrepreneurs difficult to make with any consistency. Hence we will focus on entrepreneurship as a process.

REVIEW QUESTIONS

1 Contrast the Schumpeterian view of the entrepreneur with that of Kirzner. Give examples.
2 List the key contributions to our understanding of entrepreneurial abilities by each of the following:
   • Knight
   • Casson
   • Kirzner
   • Schumpeter
3 Why is the environment important to our understanding of differing participation rates in entrepreneurship?
4 How does Schumpeter help to explain the dotcom bubble of 1999–2000 and the subsequent fall-out of failing dotcom entrepreneurs?

Hint: see also Chapter 9.

5 Suggest key personality characteristics associated with successful entrepreneurs.
6 Suggest additional key personality characteristics that may be required to be a successful entrepreneur (for example, consider perseverance required to overcome initial rejection of a new idea by funders).
7 Which of the personality characteristics you have listed in your answer to question 5 could be acquired through learning?
8 Critically review the entrepreneurial personality approach with a series of bullet points.
9 Using case material in this chapter, why are alertness to opportunity recognition and ability to learn key attributes of the entrepreneur?
10 Review the three approaches to entrepreneurship discussed in this chapter; why do they each have something to contribute to our understanding of entrepreneurship?
11 Why is it important to treat entrepreneurship as a process?

SUGGESTED ASSIGNMENTS

1 Students undertake a small research study by interviewing small-firm owner-managers about their concepts of management and entrepreneurship. For example, do they consider themselves as entrepreneurs? Small groups of students can each interview one small-firm owner and discuss results in class.

2 Students debate the skills of entrepreneurs. Students are each given one of two briefs indicating which case they have to argue from:
   • Entrepreneurs are special and have to be born.
   • Entrepreneurship skills can be acquired and the environment that fosters entrepreneurship is important.

3 Consider the case study on Skype Part 1 and compare the founders Niklas Zennström and Janus Friis to another well-known entrepreneur in your country. What similarities and differences are apparent?

REFERENCES

1   **Curran, J. and Stanworth, J.** (1989) 'Education and training for enterprise: some problems of classification, evaluation, policy and research', *International Small Business Journal*, vol. 7, no. 2, pp. 11–22.

2   **Galloway, L. and Wilson, L.** (2003) 'The use and abuse of the entrepreneur', Management School Working Paper, Heriot-Watt University, Edinburgh.

3   **Shailer, G.** (1994) 'Capitalists and entrepreneurs in owner-managed firms', *International Small Business Journal*, vol. 12, no. 3, pp. 33–41.

4   **Jensen, M.C. and Meckling, W.H.** (1976) 'Theory of the firm: managerial behaviour, agency costs and ownership structure', *Journal of Financial Economics*, vol. 3, no. 2, pp. 305–60.

5   **Ray, D.** (1993) 'Understanding the entrepreneur: entrepreneurial attributes, experience and skills', *Entrepreneurship and Regional Development*, vol. 5, no. 4, pp. 345–57.

6   **Stevenson, H.H. and Jarillo, J.C.** (1990) 'A paradigm of entrepreneurship: entrepreneurial management', *Strategic Management Journal*, vol. 11, special issue, pp. 17–27.

7   **Reynolds, P.D. and White, S.B.** (1997) *The Entrepreneurial Process: Economic Growth, Men, Women and Minorities*, Quorum, Westport, CT.

8   **Global Entrepreneurship Monitor** Research Network and Programme (GEM) http://www.gemconsortium.org.

9   **Hayek, F.A**. (1945) 'The use of knowledge in society', *The American Economic Review*, vol. 35, no. 4, pp. 519–30.

10   **Scottish Enterprise** (1993) *Scotland's Business Birth Rate: A National Enquiry*, Scottish Enterprise, Glasgow.

11   **McClelland, D.C.** (1961) *The Achieving Society*, Van Nostrand, New York.

12   **Chell, E., Haworth, J. and Brearley, S.** (1991) *The Entrepreneurial Personality, Concepts, Cases and Categories*, Routledge, London.

13   **Delmar, F.** (2000) 'The psychology of the entrepreneur', in S. Carter and D. Jones-Evans (eds), *Enterprise and Small Business: Principles, Practice and Policy*, FT/Prentice Hall, London, pp. 132–54.

14   **Meredith, G.G., Nelson, R.E. and Neck, P.A.** (1982) *The Practice of Entrepreneurship*, International Labour Office, Geneva.

15   **Kets de Vries, M.** (1977) 'The entrepreneurial personality: a person at the crossroads', *Journal of Management Studies*, vol. 14, no. 1, pp. 34–57.

16   **Timmons, J.A.** (1994) *New Venture Creation: Entrepreneurship for the 21st Century*, 4th edn, Irwin, Chicago, IL.

17   **Cromie, S. and O'Donoghue, J.** (1992) 'Assessing entrepreneurial inclinations', *International Small Business Journal*, vol. 10, no. 2, pp. 66–71.

18   **Johnson, D. and Suet Fan Ma, R.** (1995) 'Research note: a method for selecting and training entrants on new business start-up programmes', *International Small Business Journal*, vol. 13, no. 3, pp. 80–4.

19   **Small Business Service** (2004) *A Government Action Plan for Small Business; The Evidence Base*, SBS, DTI, London.

20   **Ram, M.** (1993) *Managing to Survive: Working Lives in Small Firms*, Blackwell, Oxford.

21   **Scottish Enterprise** (1993) *A National Strategy for Scotland*, Scottish Enterprise, Glasgow.

22   **Fraser of Allander Institute** (2001) *Promoting Business Start-ups: A New Strategic Formula, Stage 1 Final Report*, Scottish Enterprise, Glasgow.

23   **Scottish Enterprise** (1997) *Local Heroes*, Scottish Enterprise, Glasgow.

24   **Ram, M., Smallbone, D. and Deakins, D.** (2002) *Ethnic Minority Businesses in the UK: Access to Finance and Business Support*, British Bankers' Association, London.

25   **DTI** (1997) *Small Firms in Britain Report 1996*, DTI, London.

26   **Butler, J.E. and Hansen, G.S.** (1991) 'Network evolution, entrepreneurial success and regional development', *Entrepreneurship and Regional Development*, vol. 3, no. 1, pp. 1–16.

27   **Greve, A. and Salaff, J.W.** (2003) 'Social networks and entrepreneurship', *Entrepreneurship Theory and Practice*, vol. 28, no. 1, pp. 1–22.

28   **Lin, N., Ensel, W. and Vaughan, J.** (1981) 'Social resources and strength of ties: structural factors in occupational status attainment', *American Sociological Review*, vol. 46, no. 4, pp. 393–405.

29   **Portes, A.** (1998) 'Social capital', *Annual Review of Sociology*, vol. 23, pp. 1–24.

30   **Emerson, R.** (1972) 'Exchange theory', in J. Berger, M. Zelditch and B. Anderson (eds), *Sociological Theories in Progress*, Houghton Mifflin, Boston, MA.

31 **Cabinet Office** (2002) *Social Capital: A Discussion Paper*, Performance and Innovation Unit, Cabinet Office, London.

32 **Davidsson, P. and Honig, B.** (2003) 'The role of social and human capital among nascent entrepreneurs', *Journal of Business Venturing*, vol. 18, no. 3, pp. 301–31.

33 **Sirmon, D.G. and Hitt, M.A.** (2003) 'Managing resources: linking unique resources, management and wealth creation in family firms', *Entrepreneurship, Theory and Practice*, vol. 27, no. 4, pp. 339–58.

34 **Anderson, A.R. and Jack, S.H.** (2002) 'The articulation of social capital in entrepreneurial networks: a glue or a lubricant', *Entrepreneurship and Regional Development*, vol. 14, no. 2, pp. 193–210.

35 **Shapero, A. and Sokol, L.** (1982) 'The social dimensions of entrepreneurship', in C.A. Kent, D.L. Sexton and K.H. Vesper (eds), *Encyclopedia of Entrepreneurship*, Prentice Hall, Englewood Cliffs, NJ, pp. 72–90.

36 **Granovetter, M.** (1973) 'The strength of weak ties', *American Journal of Sociology*, vol. 78, pp. 1360–80.

37 **Wilson, L., Whittam, G. and Deakins, D.** (2004) 'Women's enterprise: a critical examination of national policies to support women's enterprise', *Environment and Planning C; Government and Policy*, vol. 20, no. 5, pp. 799–815.

38 **Deakins, D., Ishaq, M., Smallbone, D., Whittam, G. and Wyper, J.** (2007) 'The role of social capital and ethnic minority businesses in Scotland', *International Small Business Journal*, vol. 25, no. 3, pp. 307–26.

39 **Cope, J. and Watts, G.** (2000) 'Learning by doing: an exploration of experience, critical incidents and reflection in entrepreneurial learning', *International Journal of Entrepreneurial Behaviour and Research*, vol. 6, no. 3, pp. 104–24.

40 **Rae, D.** (2003) '*Entrepreneurial identity and capability: the role of learning*', PhD thesis, Nottingham Trent University, Nottingham.

41 **Storey, D.J. and Westhead, P.** (1996) 'Management training and small firm performance: why is the link so weak?', *International Small Business Journal*, vol. 14, no. 4, pp. 13–24.

42 **Gibb, A.** (1997) 'Small firms' training and competitiveness. Building upon the small business as a learning organisation', *International Small Business Journal*, vol. 15, no. 3, pp. 13–29.

43 **Vygotsky, L.S.** (1978). *Mind and Society: The Development of Higher Psychological Processes*, Harvard University Press, Cambridge, MA.

44 **Costello, N.** (1996) 'Learning and routines in high-tech SMEs: analysing rich case study material', *Journal of Economic Issues*, vol. 30, no. 2, pp. 591–97.

45 **Freel, M.** (1998) 'Evolution, innovation and learning: evidence from case studies', *Entrepreneurship and Regional Development*, vol. 10, no. 2, pp. 137–49.

46 **Pedler, M., Burgoyne, J. and Boydell, T.** (1991) *The Learning Company: A Strategy for Sustainable Development*, McGraw-Hill, Maidenhead.

47 **Kline, P. and Saunders, B.** (1993) *Ten Steps to a Learning Organisation*, Great Ocean, Arlington, VA.

48 **Nelson, R. and Winter, S.** (1982) *An Evolutionary Theory of Economic Change*, Harvard University Press, Boston, MA.

49 **Levinthal, D.** (1996) 'Learning and Schumpeterian dynamics', in G. Dosi and F. Malerba (eds), *Organisation and Strategy in the Evolution of Enterprise*, Macmillan, London.

50 **Deakins, D.** (1999) 'Editorial: "Entrepreneurial learning"', *International Journal of Entrepreneurial Behaviour and Research*, vol. 5, no. 3.

51 **Politis, D.** (2005) 'The process of entrepreneurial learning: a conceptual framework', *Entrepreneurship Theory and Practice*, vol. 29, no. 4, pp. 399–424.

52 **Cope, J.** (2005) 'Toward a dynamic learning perspective of entrepreneurship', *Entrepreneurship Theory and Practice*, vol. 29, no. 4, pp. 373–98.

53 **Corbett, A.C.** (2005) 'Experiential learning within the process of opportunity identification and exploitation', *Entrepreneurship Theory and Practice*, vol. 29, no. 4, pp. 473–92.

54 **Rae, D. and Carswell, M.** (2001) 'Towards a conceptual understanding of entrepreneurial learning', *Journal of Small Business and Enterprise Development*, vol. 8, no. 2, pp. 150–58.

55 **Deakins, D. and Freel, M.** (1998) 'Entrepreneurial learning and the growth process in SMEs', *The Learning Organisation*, vol. 5, no. 3, pp. 144–55.

56 **Cope, J. and Watts, G.** (2000) 'Learning by doing: an exploration of experience, critical incidents and reflection in entrepreneurial learning', *International Journal of Entrepreneurial Behaviour and Research*, vol. 6, no. 3, pp. 104–24.

57 **Easterby-Smith, M., Thorpe, R. and Lowe, A.** (2002) *Management Research: An Introduction*, 2nd edn, Sage, London.

58 **Zhang, M., Macpherson, A. and Jones, O.** (2006) 'Conceptualising

the learning process in SMEs: improving innovation through external orientation', *International Small Business Journal*, vol. 24, no. 3, pp. 299–323.

59 **Wyer, P., Mason, J. and Theo-dorakopoulos, N.** (2000) 'Small business development and the "learning organisation"', *International Journal of Entrepreneurial Behaviour and Research*, vol. 6, no. 4, pp. 239–59.

60 **Cope, J.** (2003) 'Entrepreneurial learning and critical reflection: discontinuous events as triggers for higher level learning', *Management Learning*, vol. 34, no. 4, pp. 429–50.

61 **Thorpe, R., Gold, J., Holt, R. and Clarke, J.** (2006) 'Immatu-rity: the constraining of entrepre-neurship', *International Small Business Journal*, vol. 24, no. 3, pp. 232–52.

62 **Read, S., Sarasvathy, S., Dow, N., Wiltbank, R. and Ohlsson, A.-V.** (2011) *Effectual Entrepre-neurship*, Routledge, Oxford.

RECOMMENDED READING

Read, S., Sarasvathy, S., Dow, N., Wiltbank, R. and Ohlsson, A.-V. (2011) *Effectual Entrepreneurship*, Routledge, Oxford.

Global Entrepreneurship Monitor (2011) *Executive Report*, Kauffman Center for Entrepreneurial Leadership, Babson College, Boston, MA.

Handy, C. (1999) *The New Alchemists*, Hutchinson, London.

Reynolds, P.D. and White, S.B. (1997) *The Entrepreneurial Process: Economic Growth, Men, Women and Minorities*, Quorum, Westport, CT.

2 ENTREPRENEURIAL ACTIVITY, THE ECONOMY AND THE IMPORTANCE OF SMALL FIRMS

LEARNING OUTCOMES

At the end of this chapter you should be able to:

- Discuss different approaches to the definitions of small firms.
- Describe the importance of small firms in European economies.
- Describe the importance of small firms for job creation.
- Discuss the association between entrepreneurial activity and economic growth.
- Discuss international comparisons on the importance of small firms.
- Describe the factors that account for the increased importance of small firms in modern economies.
- Discuss differences in the importance of small firms in European transition economies.

INTRODUCTION

This chapter focuses on the importance of small firms in the UK and in other economies, particularly European economies. It includes a section on European transition economies for comparative purposes. The reader should also refer to Chapter 11, which covers additional material on international entrepreneurship and also considers entrepreneurship in transition economies. This chapter, however, focuses on data on the importance of small firms.

Texts of this type inevitably beg the question 'Why study entrepreneurship and small firms?' The simple answer is that they 'matter'. Indeed, there is an established consensus, at least within policy circles, that they matter a great deal. For instance, in a recent speech to an international policy forum, Jean-Philippe Cotis (OECD Chief Economist) noted that:

> Entrepreneurship is a hot topic these days. It features frequently in discussions among policy makers, academic researchers, and even in more mundane talk shows. There is a large consensus that entrepreneurship is good and should be encouraged. There is also growing scientific evidence that entrepreneurial activities matter for employment, productivity and, ultimately economic growth.[1]

In 2005 the European Commission relaunched the 'Lisbon Strategy', placing small firms at the heart of the agenda. The 'Strategy for Growth and Jobs' (as the Lisbon strategy is now called) promised that particular attention will be paid to the concerns and needs of small firms, and asserts that the 'Think Small First principle' will apply across all EU activities. Certainly, SME policies are now more integrated into the revised strategy, giving them greater visibility.[2] This appears to add substance to the earlier Green Paper on Entrepreneurship in Europe,[3] which noted that 'Europe . . . needs more new and thriving firms', with a clear implication that the bulk of these firms would be small. Within individual member states and further afield, the policy focus on small firms is clearer still. In the UK, for instance, the Department for Business, Innovation and Skills (formerly the Department for Business, Enterprise and Regulatory Reform)[4] has set itself the key target of helping to 'build an enterprise society in which small firms of all kinds thrive and achieve their potential' (p. 49). In a similar vein, the OECD's recent flagship publication *SMEs, Entrepreneurship and Innovation*[5] opens with the insistence that 'an important shift has occurred from the "managed" to the "entrepreneurial" economy, associated with a fall in the importance of economies of scale in production, management, finance and R&D' and that 'SMEs and new business ventures are important players in this environment' (p. 23). SMEs and entrepreneurship are now widely recognised as a key source of dynamism, innovation and flexibility in advanced countries, as well as in emerging and developing economies. They have been shown to be responsible for most net job creation in OECD countries and make significant contributions to innovation, productivity and economic growth.

Undoubtedly, small firms matter and it is encouraging that policymakers recognise this. But why do they matter? And why do they matter, or appear to matter, more now than, say, 30 or 40 years ago? Answering these supplementary questions is central to understanding why we study entrepreneurship and small firms, and why our attitudes towards the sector have changed in relatively recent times.

DEFINITIONS AND MEASUREMENT

Before attempting to answer these questions, it is important to clarify what we mean by 'small firms'. Intuitively most people will have a sense of what constitutes 'smallness' in any given context. However, it is this issue of context that leads to general ambiguity. For instance, a car manufacturer that employs 700 people (independent British specialist sports-car manufacturer Aston Martin is one example – http://www.astonmartin.com) is likely to be considered very small. Yet, in contrast, and with fewer staff, Manchester United is among the largest football clubs in the world and was, until recently, a public limited company. Clearly, the precise answer to the question 'What is a small firm?', should be 'it depends'. And it depends upon a number of factors. Among the most obvious of these are the industry sector and market in which a given firm operates. Taking our car manufacturer Aston Martin, for example, it is clearly very small when compared to familiar industry names such as Ford or General Motors. However, in the market for specialist sports cars it is actually relatively large when compared with its key competitors, such as Caterham and Morgan.

Moreover, in addition to industry and market considerations, time also matters when discussing firm size – at least to the extent that size is measured by the number of employees. For instance, European labour productivity (measured as GDP per hours worked) has more than doubled since 1970.[6] Simplistically, one might reasonably suggest that the same amount may be produced today with less than half the number of employees required 35 years ago. Accordingly, our conception of small, medium and large must also be altered. Or, indeed, it may be that in some instances (e.g. industries that experience persistently high productivity growth) measures of firm size that rely on staffing levels are simply less appropriate.

As a result of these difficulties in defining or classifying small firms, it is likely that no single objective or statistical measure will suit the purpose. Nonetheless, in light of its attempt properly to address the issues, a popular point of departure is provided by the UK Committee of Inquiry on Small Firms,[7] chaired by Sir John Bolton (hereafter termed the Bolton Committee). The Bolton Committee distinguished both 'statistical' and 'economic' definitions (see Table 2.1). In terms of its statistical definition, the committee recognized that size is relative to sector. Moreover, it recognized that it may be appropriate to define size by the number of employees in some sectors but more appropriate to use turnover or assets in others. Clearly the sectors identified by the Bolton Committee are not exhaustive and are a function of both the time and the place in which the definitions were devised. Certainly, they are not comprehensive, nor have they been 'updated'. However, it is the principle of, and reasons for, employing multiple measures that are the important legacy.

More interesting than the statistical, quantitative measures offered by the Bolton Committee are the 'economic', qualitative measures. Indeed, these have enjoyed a certain durability, at least within UK policy circles. And have had considerable influence over a generation of policy-oriented academics in the UK and elsewhere. Undoubtedly, there is a comfortable, if a little superficial, underpinning logic and firms that satisfy these criteria will, in all likelihood, be small. However, notwithstanding their enduring popularity, the Bolton

TABLE 2.1 BOLTON'S DEFINITIONS OF SMALL FIRMS

The 'statistical' definitions	
Manufacturing	200 employees or less
Construction, mining and quarrying	25 employees or less
Retail and miscellaneous services	Turnover of £50,000 or less
Motor trades	Turnover of £100,000 or less
Wholesale trades	Turnover of £200,000 or less
Road transport	5 vehicles or less
Catering	All; excluding multiple and brewery managed houses
The 'economic' definitions	
Small firms are those which:	
1 Have a relatively small share of their marketplace	
2 Are managed by owners or part-owners in a personalised way, and not through the medium of a formalised management structure	
3 Are independent, in the sense of not being part of a large enterprise	

Committee's 'economic' definitions have not been above criticism. Storey[8] for instance, notes that 'the Bolton criterion that a small business is "managed by its owners or part-owners and not through the medium of a formal management structure" is almost certainly incompatible with its "statistical" definition of small manufacturing firms which could have up to 200 employees' (p. 10). Indeed, there is evidence that managerial appointments are made when firm size reaches between 10 and 20 employees.[9] As such, it seems unlikely that a firm that employs over 100 staff will not have evolved some degree of managerial formality that involves substantial delegation of decision-making.

Storey[8] also questions the Bolton Committee's emphasis on the small firm's inability to influence its environment, and the implication that small firms are inevitably price-takers. Here he draws the distinction between the economic concept of perfect competition, which he believes influenced the Committee, and the reality of small-firm competition as largely monopolistic, with many firms occupying market 'niches'. In this way, they 'provide a highly specialised service or product, possibly in a geographically isolated area, and often do not perceive themselves to have clear competitors' (p. 10).

In spite of these legitimate criticisms, the value of the Bolton Committee definition lies in its willingness to address the complexities involved in accurately defining small firms, and its engagement with the issue of context. Nonetheless, these strengths may also be the source of the definition's principal weakness – that is, an awareness of the specificities of context necessarily retards general and consistent application in practice: a sensible prerequisite for government schemes aimed at assisting small firms, in which it is necessary to have simple, unambiguous qualifying criteria to ensure that administration is not overly complex or costly.

As a result of problems in the practical application of Bolton's 'economic' definitions, and despite the difficulties in objectively defining small firms, the most commonly used measure of 'smallness' relates to employment levels. To this end, small firms are considered by the OECD[5] to be 'non-subsidiary independent firms which employ fewer than a given number of employees' (p. 7). Though the threshold number varies across countries (the USA, for example, includes firms with fewer than 500 employees, while the Netherlands collects data on firms with fewer than 100 employees), perhaps the most commonly adopted definition is provided by the European Commission (EC). With the intention of overcoming the identified problems of earlier statistical and economic definitions, the EC coined the phrase 'small and medium-sized enterprises' (SMEs).

The SME sector itself was disaggregated into three subsets (see accompanying box).

EC DEFINITIONS OF SMALL FIRMS

- Micro enterprises – those of between 0 and 9 employees.
- Small enterprises – those of between 10 and 99 employees (11–50 as of February 1996).
- Medium enterprises – those of between 100 and 499 employees (51–250 as of February 1996).

Financial criteria are also used in the EC definition. For instance, from 2005, micro-firms were those employing fewer than 10 people whose annual turnover and/or balance sheet did not exceed € 2 million. Small firms were those employing fewer than 50 people whose annual turnover and/or balance sheet did not exceed € 10 million. Finally, medium-sized firms were those employing fewer than 250 people whose annual turnover and/or balance sheet did not exceed € 50 and € 43 million respectively. Nevertheless, it is employment size bands that are most commonly cited and that, to all intents and purposes, are used as the standard working definition. These definitions hold for all industries (except agriculture, hunting, forestry and fishing) and, having been explicitly adopted by most member states, form the basis for both domestic and EU policy development in the area. Accordingly, they are the definitions used in this text.

It is important to note, however, that none of the principal criticisms of the earlier definitions has been answered. The EC definition still treats the small-firm sector as an homogeneous whole and will still be liable to significant misclassification errors. Essentially, it is a measure of convenience.

SMALL FIRMS IN THE ECONOMY

Turning now to why small firms matter, perhaps the simplest way of illustrating this is to point to their prevalence and the contribution they make to common measures of economic well-being, such as employment and income. To this end, Tables 2.2–2.4 detail the distribution of private sector enterprises, and of private sector employment and value added, by firm-size class for EU countries.

Addressing Table 2.2, in the first instance, it seems clear that most firms are small firms. In all of the economies, SMEs represent in excess of 99 per cent of private enterprises. Moreover, the vast majority of these firms are micro-enterprises. While there is some variation in terms of the distributions across size bands (e.g. in economies where large-scale manufacturing, such as automobiles in Slovakia or computer hardware and packaged software in Ireland, continues to be important, micro firms are proportionately fewer), the picture is reasonably consistent across EU economies. Simply put, one might argue that we should be interested in small firms because most firms are small. Indeed, and building upon a similar trend throughout the 1990s, recent evidence points to the particular expansion of the micro and small firms sectors (Figure 2.1) – so strengthening this observation.

However, merely remarking that SMEs dominate EU economies may, in itself, be insufficient to explain the current level of interest focused upon them. Rather, policymakers and academics are inevitably more

TABLE 2.2 DISTRIBUTION OF (NON-FINANCIAL) ENTERPRISES BY SIZE CLASS: 2008

	Micro	Small	Medium	SME	LSE
Austria	87.52	10.52	1.62	99.66	0.34
Belgium	92.15	6.69	0.97	99.80	0.20
Bulgaria	89.32	8.69	1.71	99.73	0.27
Cyprus	92.00	6.86	0.99	99.86	0.14
Czech Republic	95.11	3.92	0.80	99.83	0.17
Denmark	86.83	10.97	1.87	99.67	0.33
Estonia	83.09	13.89	2.66	99.64	0.36
Finland	92.82	5.80	1.10	99.72	0.28
France	92.33	6.48	0.98	99.79	0.21
Germany	83.11	14.07	2.34	99.52	0.48
Greece	96.49	3.03	0.42	99.95	0.05
Hungary	94.36	4.71	0.77	99.85	0.15
Ireland	82.76	14.05	2.70	99.52	0.48
Italy	94.61	4.80	0.51	99.92	0.08
Latvia	83.08	13.98	2.60	99.67	0.33
Lithuania	88.37	9.33	2.03	99.73	0.27
Luxembourg	86.74	10.73	2.11	99.58	0.42
Malta	95.73	3.54	0.61	99.89	0.11
Netherlands	90.04	8.30	1.41	99.75	0.25
Poland	95.99	2.84	0.97	99.80	0.20
Portugal	94.58	4.68	0.65	99.91	0.09
Romania	88.12	9.39	2.08	99.59	0.41
Slovakia	76.07	19.05	3.92	99.05	0.95
Slovenia	92.82	5.66	1.26	99.73	0.27
Spain	92.23	6.83	0.82	99.88	0.12
Sweden	94.22	4.77	0.84	99.83	0.17
UK	87.46	10.49	1.68	99.63	0.37
Norway	91.76	7.05	0.98	99.79	0.21

Source: Annual Report on EU SMEs 2009, EIM/European Commission.

interested in smaller firms' contribution to employment and income – as more direct indicators of their role in the economy. To that end, the data in Table 2.3 indicate the distribution of employment, by firm-size band, for the EU economies. Once again, it is clear that small firms 'matter'. SMEs account for in excess of 50 per cent of non-financial employment in all of the economies and, for instance, as much as 87 per cent in Greece.

TABLE 2.3 DISTRIBUTION OF EMPLOYMENT BY SIZE CLASS: 2008 (NON-FINANCIAL BUSINESS ECONOMY)

	Micro	**Small**	**Medium**	**SME**	**LSE**
Austria	25	23	19	67	33
Belgium	30	22	16	67	33
Bulgaria	28	23	23	74	26
Cyprus	39	25	20	84	16
Czech Republic	29	19	20	68	32
Denmark	20	25	21	66	34
Estonia	24	28	26	79	21
Finland	23	19	18	60	40
France	25	21	16	62	38
Germany	19	22	19	60	40
Greece	58	17	12	87	13
Hungary	35	19	16	71	29
Ireland	21	25	23	69	31
Italy	47	22	12	81	19
Latvia	22	28	26	76	24
Lithuania	23	25	26	75	25
Luxembourg	19	24	24	67	33
Malta	40	18	18	77	23
Netherlands	29	21	17	67	33
Poland	39	12	19	69	31
Portugal	42	23	16	81	19
Romania	21	20	23	64	36
Slovakia	15	18	23	55	45
Slovenia	28	18	21	67	33
Spain	38	26	15	78	22
Sweden	25	21	18	64	36
UK	22	18	15	55	45
Norway	27	25	18	70	30

Source: Annual Report on EU SMEs 2009, EIM/European Commission.

Indeed, there is considerably more between-country variation in the small-firm contribution to employment than the data in Table 2.2 might have indicated. Moreover, some of this variation may be systematic. Certainly, in western Europe there is tentative evidence of a north-south divide. That is, small firms appear to be more important providers of jobs in the southern European economies of Greece, Italy, Spain and Portugal than they do in the northern European economies of, for example, the UK, Germany, Finland or Sweden. Alas, identifying

TABLE 2.4 DISTRIBUTION OF VALUE ADDED BY SIZE CLASS: 2008 (NON-
FINANCIAL BUSINESS ECONOMY) AND THE SME/LARGE FIRM
PRODUCTIVITY RATIO

	Micro	Small	Medium	SME	LSE	SME/LSE productivity
Austria	19	20	21	60	40	0.720227
Belgium	19	20	19	58	42	0.676066
Bulgaria	14	19	21	54	46	0.413183
Cyprus	31	26	22	79	21	0.744811
Czech Republic	19	16	20	55	45	0.580061
Denmark	28	21	19	68	32	1.088469
Estonia	21	25	30	76	24	0.876189
Finland	19	16	18	54	46	0.783227
France	21	19	16	55	45	0.765144
Germany	16	18	19	53	47	0.729748
Greece	35	20	17	73	27	0.394406
Hungary	18	16	18	52	48	0.438946
Ireland	15	14	23	52	48	0.491521
Italy	33	23	16	72	28	0.597720
Latvia	19	27	29	74	26	0.892008
Lithuania	12	23	29	64	36	0.605925
Luxembourg	24	20	20	64	36	0.882882
Malta	28	19	17	64	36	0.532105
Netherlands	20	21	21	62	38	0.802679
Poland	18	12	22	52	48	0.483326
Portugal	24	22	21	67	33	0.467911
Romania	12	14	16	42	58	0.418003
Slovakia	13	15	18	46	54	0.697423
Slovenia	20	19	21	60	40	0.730986
Spain	27	24	17	68	32	0.595584
Sweden	20	18	18	56	44	0.718617
UK	18	16	17	51	49	0.845634
Norway	30	16	19	65	35	0.794876

Source: Annual Report on EU SMEs 2009, EIM/European Commission.

why this might be the case is not likely to be a simple matter, though one is tempted to suggest that enduring craft traditions, sectoral variations (such as the relative importance of textiles and clothing) and culture will feature in any account. The pattern in eastern European economies is more mixed, ranging from 55 per cent in Slovakias to 79 per cent in Estonia – reflecting, in large part, differences in the sectoral make-up of these economies. Beyond Europe, SMEs consistently account for over 50 per cent of employment in other OECD economies

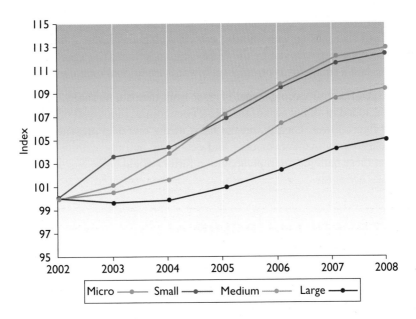

FIGURE 2.1

Development of number of enterprises, non-financial business economy, by size-class, EU-27, 2002–2008

SOURCE: Annual Report on EU SMEs 2009.

(though not shown, SMEs provide 65 per cent and 51 per cent of private-sector employment in Canada and the USA[a]) – including a remarkable 69.1 per cent in Japan.

The tentative western European north-south divide also appears in the data relating to value added (Table 2.4). Here, there is further evidence of the relatively more or less significant economic role of SMEs in some southern and northern European economies (compare, for example, Greece and the UK). In addition, consideration of the ratio of contributions to labour productivity (essentially looking at the value-added created per person employed – the final column in Table 2.4) suggests some interesting inter-country differences. For instance, while there may be relatively more SMEs in southern European economies, and they may make more contribution to employment and to value added, they also record much lower labour productivity than their larger within-country peers – as low as 40 per cent in Greece – than do northern European SMEs. Of course, it may well be that variations in labour productivity merely represent underlying sectoral variations. Certainly, it does not inevitably suggest poorer economic performance on the part of those countries where the SME share in value added is low. Interestingly, for those who would counsel expansion and support of the small-business sector as some form of economic panacea, Ireland's growth during the 1990s was driven by successful inward direct investment by American and European multinationals and by strong export performance.[10] Indeed, much of the apparent relative poor performance of Irish small manufacturers may simply reflect widespread transfer pricing on the part of large, foreign-owned, multinationals. Similarly, the Finnish economy is dominated by a large public sector, with state-owned enterprises and a few large, and successful, private-sector firms. For instance, past evidence suggests that Nokia and its first-tier suppliers were responsible for over a third of Finland's GDP growth during the late 1990s.[11]

---

[a] These countries are not included in the tables because directly comparable data are unavailable.

Regardless, with one remarkable exception (Denmark), labour productivity across Europe appears to be positively correlated with firm size – as is, importantly, *growth* in labour productivity.[12] Larger firms are more productive and the gap is widening – driven by the increasing importance of export markets, faster technological change in large firms and a small-firms orientation towards traditional manufacturing sectors and services.

Irrespective of these specific observations, what is clear from the data in Table 2.4 is that SMEs account for over 50 per cent of value added in all but two of the EU-27 economies (and in all of the EU-15). Only in Romania and Slovakia is the figure lower. Clearly, on the basis of the raw data presented in Tables 2.2–2.4, small firms matter a great deal to employment, income and economic activity within Europe. Moreover, there is substantial evidence that these patterns are representative further afield.[5; 13]

LINKING ENTREPRENEURSHIP AND ECONOMIC GROWTH

Perhaps more important than the immediate contribution small firms make to employment and income is the widely held belief that there exists a positive link between entrepreneurship and economic growth. And, while entrepreneurship is not the exclusive province of small firms, the two are often conflated in policy and academic discussions. To this end, small firms are thought to act as agents of change and are the sources of considerable innovative activity.[14] A vibrant small-firm sector stimulates industry evolution and generates a disproportionate share of new jobs. Accordingly, as Wennekers and Thurik[15] observe, 'Many economists and politicians now have an *intuition* that there is a positive impact of entrepreneurship on the growth of GDP and employment' (p. 29, emphasis added). Unfortunately, this 'intuition' has yet to be unequivocally supported by empirical evidence.

Among the foremost proponents of the positive entrepreneurship–economic growth link is the ambitious, and highly influential, annual Global Entrepreneurship Monitor (GEM). The GEM project undertakes surveys of the adult population in a sample of countries[b] to establish a Total Entrepreneurial Activity (TEA) index for each country. The TEA[16] is a measure of 'the proportion of individuals in the working age population who are actively trying to start their own business, including self-employment, or running their own business that is less than 3½ years old' (p. 9). In the early GEM reports, starting in 1999,[17] 'the evidence was compelling' (p. 3). Until recently, the GEM consortium was in no doubt that there was a strong positive (and linear) correlation between entrepreneurial activity in a country and economic growth. On the evidence they presented, this thesis was hard to resist. For instance, Figure 2.2, using data from GEM 2004,[18] plots one-year lagged growth in GDP against TEA for the 40 countries studied.[c] While not perfect, there does seem to be evidence of the anticipated positive relationship. Moreover, this apparent relationship between TEA and GDP growth is statistically significant, with a strong correlation coefficient ($R = 0.45$). The policy conclusion that seemed to flow from this may best be expressed as 'more entrepreneurship leads to higher economic growth'.

Certainly, in the face of the evidence presented by successive GEM reports, and notwithstanding some methodological concerns, one is happy to accept the existence of some form of positive relationship between entrepreneurship and economic growth.

However, it is not clear that the relationship is as simple as is intimated or, more importantly, that the arrow of causation is as described. While there is a comfortable logic in arguing that entrepreneurship 'causes' economic growth, it is equally plausible to argue the reverse. That is, as the economy grows and more money flows

---

[b] The TEA is presented for 59 countries in the 2010 report.

[c] Each point represents a country and year, though only the extremes of the distribution are labelled.

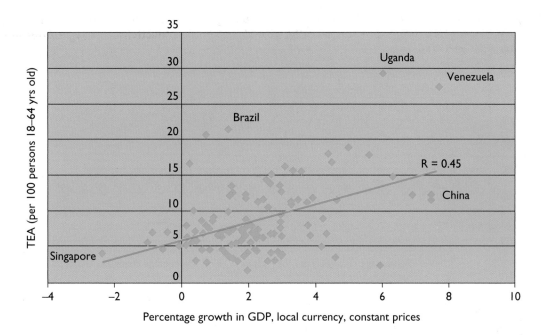

FIGURE 2.2

TEA rates and national economic growth: one year lag (pooled data)

NOTE: Each data point represents the TEA and lagged growth rates for individual countries, covering years for which GEM data are available. Accordingly, some countries are represented by only one data point and others by up to four. Limited labels given are for illustration purposes.

SOURCE: GEM (2004).

around the system, opportunities for entrepreneurship are created. Indeed, casual observation would seem to support this. Think of the average High Street during either recessions or booms. The opening and closure of shops and restaurants is palpable evidence of economic good and bad times. In these sectors (and in others such as construction or business services) the barriers to both entry and exit are relatively low and businesses tend to be particularly sensitive to changes in the business cycle. Economists term such industries 'pro-cyclical' – they experience greater activity when the economy grows. Importantly, they are likely to include much of the entrepreneurship captured by GEM's population surveys.

Figure 2.3 explores this idea empirically. Using data from the UK (because of its ready availability), the chart plots changes in the stock of value-added tax (VAT) registered firms and GDP growth for the period 1980–2004 (with no lags). The stock of VAT-registered firms is certainly different from the TEA used by GEM. However, they both crudely measure the same sort of thing and VAT data have the benefit of greater objectivity.[d] A cursory glance at the figure seems to suggest that entrepreneurial activity (i.e. changes in the stock of VAT-registered firms) follows, rather than precedes changes in GDP growth rates. That is, entrepreneurial activity is a consequence, rather than a cause, of economic growth. Or, aggregate entrepreneurial activity is pro-cyclical.

More formally, if one conducts a simple bivariate regression using the VAT data (and lagging GDP growth by one year, in line with GEM practice), one is able to generate similar results to the GEM project. That is, there appears to be a statistically significant positive relationship between net business start-ups and GDP growth

---

[d] Though there are a great many other weaknesses (see Storey,[8] pp. 84–85).

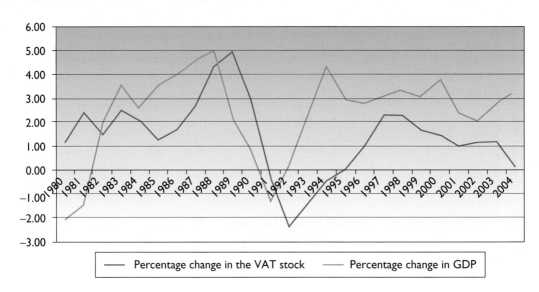

FIGURE 2.3

GDP growth and changes in the stock of VAT-registered firms (UK, 1980–2004)

SOURCE: http://stats.bis.gov.uk/ed/vat/index.htm. Crown copyright material is reproduced with the permission of the Controller of HMSO and the Queen's Printer for Scotland.

(p = 0.027 and R = 0.466). However, working in the opposite direction (i.e. lagging the VAT stock by two years as suggested by the data in Figure 2.3) increases both the explanatory power and the degree of statistical significance (p = 0.015 and R = 0.524).

Unsurprisingly, one can make the statistics tell both stories. However, on the basis of this very crude analysis, there does appear to be a stronger case for arguing that entrepreneurship is 'consequence', rather than 'cause' of growth. Nevertheless, the purpose of this exercise is not to suggest that entrepreneurship is an unimportant factor in generating economic growth. This would be both counter-intuitive and foolish. Rather, it is merely to note that the evidence remains patchy and the complexities of the relationship warrant considerably more attention, before 'more small firms' or 'more self-employment' is enshrined as some sort of economic development panacea.

To this end, two recent lines of academic enquiry warrant brief elaboration here. First, work by David Audretsch and Roy Thurik,[19] building on earlier work,[20] and ongoing work at the Dutch-based EIM, has suggested a U-shaped relationship between a country's stage of development (proxied by per capita GDP) and the level of entrepreneurial activity. This argument is intuitively appealing. For instance, GEM 2010 recorded the highest TEA rates for the developing economies of Vanuatu, Bolivia, Ghana and Zambia, respectively. In contrast Italy, Japan, Belgium and Denmark featured among the lowest TEA rates recorded. Figure 2.4 (reproduced from GEM 2010) records the position of various countries along the curve. According to the most recent GEM reports, this pattern reflects changing labour-market opportunities and their implications for entrepreneurship. For example, the initial downward-sloping curve for developing countries may reflect the growth in waged employment opportunities and a consequent fall in levels of *necessity* entrepreneurship as economies grow. At the other end of the curve, as countries become very rich, more individuals have the financial wherewithal to go into business for themselves, often in search of independence, in an economic environment that allows opportunity exploitation. Thus, the rising curve reflects the growth in *opportunity* entrepreneurship. In the middle, the low levels of entrepreneurship in the developed economies of western Europe, for instance, are likely to reflect both inflexible labour markets and extensive welfare systems. That is, abundant wage opportunities and job security dull incentives for opportunity entrepreneurship, while the welfare safety net does likewise for

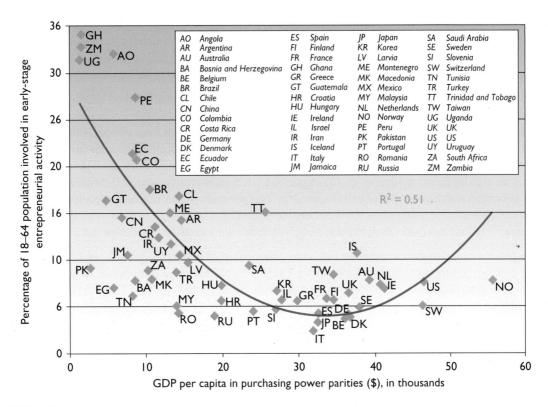

FIGURE 2.4

The relationship between income per capita and entrepreneurship rate

SOURCE: GEM (2010).

necessity entrepreneurship. In this view, falls in the prevalence of early-stage entrepreneurship may actually be a positive indicator in developing economies:

> It could signal greater sustainability, especially if this is accompanied by economic growth and political stability. As such, it represents a natural evolution in development, as an economy relies increasingly on established organisations with scale.
>
> (p. 26)[16]

However, in the developed economies, the positive link between entrepreneurship and economic growth is likely to remain.

The idea of varying entrepreneurial imperatives was a key component of Audretsch and Thurik's[19] earlier work. Crucially, they suggest the concept of an 'optimal industry structure', such that a country may have 'either too few or two many SMEs' (p. 19), given its level of economic development. In other words, there may be an equilibrium level of entrepreneurship, which varies with levels of economic development. If one accepts this contention, then there are clearly implications for deviations from this equilibrium. For instance, deviations above or below the equilibrium could mean either loss of economy of scale efficiencies, or underdeveloped or unexploited opportunities, respectively. Accordingly, the policy conclusion is conditional: if the level of entrepreneurship is too high, expanding business ownership would reduce economic growth; if the level is too low, then increasing the number of entrepreneurial firms would be rewarded by[19] 'growth dividends and reduced unemployment' (p. 29). Regardless of this contingency, Audretsch and Thurik[19] do suggest that, for OECD economies at least, 'those countries that have experienced an increase in entrepreneurial activity have also enjoyed higher rates of growth and greater reductions in unemployment' (p. 26). However, for the less developed economies outside the OECD, the standard small-firm prescription may be less appropriate.

Beyond this, Wennekers and Thurik[15] point to the importance of 'competition and selection amidst variety' (p. 51), with the clear allusion that policy should seek to keep both entry and exit barriers low as a means of finding the equilibrium number of firms. Indeed, it has long been recognised that high rates of both firm entry and exit are important factors influencing the dynamics of economic development.[21; 22] Economists term this phenomenon 'turbulence' and, as Audretsch et al.[23] note, 'high rates of innovation, growth and entry are characteristics of young industries with high levels of turbulence' (p. 10). Again, the UK figures clearly suggest that higher rates of entry are generally associated with higher rates of exit (Figure 2.5). This perspective sees economic development as an evolutionary process, wherein entry facilitates the necessary variety, and market competition provides the 'rules' for selection, enabling[15] individuals (and firms) to learn from both their own and others' successes and failures' (p. 51).

Yet, despite their determined attempt to link entrepreneurship to economic growth, and the generally confirmatory conclusions they reach, Wennekers and Thurik[15] note that 'the importance of institutions for the development of entrepreneurship is paramount and deserves further study' (p. 51). This then leads to the second thesis worthy of elaboration.

This 'institutional' view regards relative levels of entrepreneurship as consequences of economic development rather than causes. Arguing from an Austrian perspective,[24] it is suggested that since 'entrepreneurship is an omnipresent aspect of human action such that all individuals are entrepreneurs . . . entrepreneurship cannot

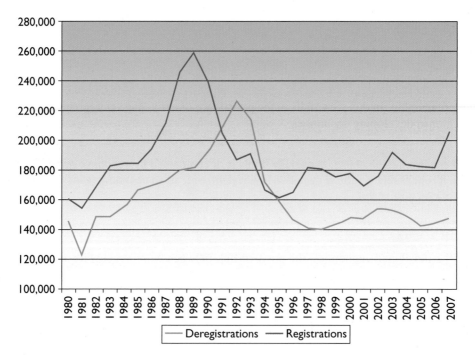

FIGURE 2.5

VAT registrations and deregistrations (UK, 1980–2007)

SOURCE: http://stats.bis.gov.uk/ed/vat/index.htm. Crown copyright material is reproduced with the permission of the Controller of HMSO and the Queen's Printer for Scotland.

be the cause of economic development. Instead we must look at the rules of the game and determine the behaviours which those incentives encourage and discourage' (p. 23). In this way, entrepreneurship is a consequence of a country's economic development, and of the adoption and development of institutions that 'encourage the entrepreneurial aspect of human action'. Development is caused by the adoption of certain institutions, which in turn concentrates and promotes entrepreneurship and enterprising behaviour, which in turn spurs economic growth. Appropriate institutions may range from cultural attitudes to work and to risk, the structure of educational provision and skills training, the make-up of capital marks, and many more besides. However, Boettke and Coyne[24] believe that the 'two most important "core" institutions for encouraging entrepreneurship are well-defined property rights and the rule of law' (p. 17), with all others flowing from these. This is not an entirely new idea; 250 years ago, Adam Smith (1755) commented that:

> Little else is requisite to carry a state to the highest degree of opulence from the lowest barbarism, but peace, easy taxes, and a tolerable administration of justice; all the rest being brought about by the natural course of things.

This may well overstate the case, but it serves as a useful reminder to policymakers that, in encouraging entrepreneurship and economic development, the institutional infrastructure cannot be neglected. The most recent GEM report explicitly recognizes this,[16] noting that a shift from *necessity* entrepreneurship to *opportunity* entrepreneurship is conditioned upon the development of appropriate economic and financial institutions:

> To the extent these institutions are able to accommodate and support opportunity-seeking entrepreneurship activity, innovative entrepreneurial firms may emerge as significant drivers of economic growth and wealth creation.
>
> (p. 14)

Recognising the facilitating role played by 'institutions' is important; however, a great deal of work remains to be done to determine which institutional arrangements are causative and which are simply noise. Moreover, and notwithstanding these ongoing developments, the general view[25] remains that entrepreneurship is 'at the heart of national advantage' (p. 125). The role of the entrepreneur, most often through the medium of the small firm, in carrying through innovations and in enhancing competitive rivalry is thought to be central to economic growth. Less is known about quite how the mechanisms linking entrepreneurship and economic growth operate. Yet, most commentators appear to agree that some form of positive link exists, and the consensus has been sufficient to drive policy.

THE CHANGING ROLE OF SMALL FIRMS

Having discussed the contribution of small firms to the economy and to economic growth, it is worth considering why they feature more prominently in policy deliberations now than they did 30 years ago. To that end, it is commonplace, at least within the Anglo-Saxon economies of the UK and North America, to point to one or two landmark events. Unquestionably, the first of these was the publication, in 1979, of David Birch's *The Job Generation Process*.[26]

Birch's work undermined the established belief that large corporations were the principal drivers of growth in the economy.[27] Using Dun & Bradstreet data relating to over 5.6 million firms, Birch's research suggested that small firms (i.e. those with fewer than 100 employees) created over 80 per cent of net new jobs in the US economy between 1969 and 1976. Rather pithily, Birch[28] concluded that 'whatever else they are doing, large firms are no longer the major providers of new jobs for Americans' (p. 8). Such bold claims have inevitably drawn scrutiny and the work has since been subject to considerable criticism (principally relating to methodology). For example, Storey[29] suggests that, since jobs in small firms tend to have less permanency, if one concentrates solely on job generation and not 'job disappearance', one is likely to overstate the contribution of small firms to this measure of economic activity. However, notwithstanding the legitimacy of much of the critique, *The Job Generation Process* was, and continues to be, highly influential. The common acceptance of small business as the primary source of net new jobs has led to government commitment, in most industrialised countries, to a wide variety of programmes designed to foster small firms and entrepreneurship. In this sense, the influence of Birch's work has been truly global.

More or less coincidental to the publication of *The Job Generation Process*, both the UK and the USA witnessed the election of political administrations with markedly different economic philosophies to those they succeeded. Both the first Thatcher government in the UK (1979) and the Reagan administration in the USA (1981) were committed to: reducing the role of government; reducing the marginal tax rates on income from both labour and capital; reducing regulation; and reducing inflation by controlling the growth of the money supply. Under these regimes, reliance upon social services and the welfare state was to be discouraged and a premium was placed upon personal enterprise.

In the UK, this philosophy was caricatured in Norman Tebbit's infamous 'get on your bike and look for work' speech at the Conservative Party conference in 1981. However, irrespective of the merits of the economic thesis and its political manifestation, there is little doubt that, since the respective elections, a great deal of emphasis has been placed, by government spokespersons on both sides of the Atlantic, on the virtues of an expanding small-business sector.[30] Accordingly, there has been a natural temptation to view these events not only as landmarks in our attitudes towards small firms, but also as landmarks in the expansion of the small-firm sector itself. Proponents of this latter argument would undoubtedly point to such factors as: the market-making opportunities afforded by privatisation and deregulation policies; the role of lower levels of income tax as an incentive to self-employment; falling real unemployment benefit rates as a means of lowering the opportunity cost to entrepreneurship; government fostering of an 'enterprise culture' and the myriad associated policy initiatives; and greater labour market flexibility (see Storey[8] for a fuller discussion). However, notwithstanding the validity or otherwise of such an argument, it is unlikely that theories based upon local factors alone will be able to explain the more generalised shift towards smaller firm size experienced by every developed western economy (though with variations in timing and extent).[31]

In (the former Federal Republic of) Germany, for instance, Fritsch[32] noted a steadily increasing concentration of employment in large firms from 1907–1970, and a reversal of this trend thereafter. Similar patterns have been observed for countries as diverse as Italy,[33] the Netherlands[34] and the USA. Data for UK manufacturing[30] illustrate this general trend well (Figure 2.6). While the nadir for small firms comes a little earlier in the UK (mid-1960s rather than 1970s), the broad pattern is consistent with that observed elsewhere. In short, the small-firm sector's role in the economy was at its least significant during the height of Fordist mass production, preceding the oil crisis of the early 1970s, a time that allowed prominent economists, such as the late J.K. Galbraith,[35] to confidently predict that large firms would prevail in economic life, due to higher efficiency (through scale economies) and superior technology. However, by the 1980s it had become clear that the importance of Fordist mass production was on the decline and a new thesis of 'flexible specialisation'[36] was developed to explain the relative success of small firms in certain industries and locales.

There are a number of related explanations given for this widespread shift in firm-size distribution. However, the clearest starting point is probably to note the general shift from manufacturing to services witnessed throughout the industrialised West. In the UK, for instance, the manufacturing sector's contribution to GDP fell from 31 per cent in 1972 to 19 per cent in 2000. Similarly, employees in employment in UK manufacturing fell from 8 million to fewer than 4 million over the same period. By contrast, over the last three decades of the twentieth century, services contribution to UK GDP rose from 59 to 72 per cent and employment from less than 14 million to over 20 million.

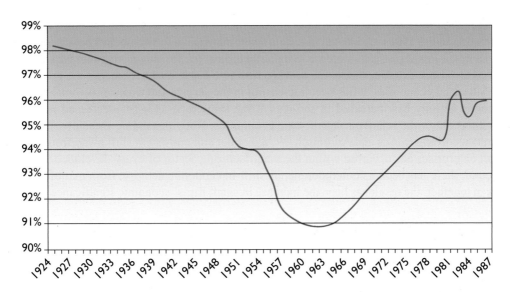

FIGURE 2.6

Proportion of UK manufacturing establishments employing fewer than 200 (1924–87)

SOURCE: Extrapolated from Hughes (1993).

For the former Federal Republic of Germany (FRG), Fritsch[32] noted that 'the main reason for the increasing share of small firm employment in the FRG is simply the change in the sectoral composition of employment during this period' (p. 44). Service firms tend, in the main, to be smaller than manufacturing firms. In the jargon of economics, they have a smaller minimum efficient scale. Accordingly, one would expect a shift from manufacturing to services to be accompanied by an apparent increasing role for small firms.

Perhaps the most obvious reason for the contraction of the manufacturing sectors of industrialised economies relates[37] to 'deagglomeration or specialisation: the selling off or disinvestment of non-core business in order to free up scarce resources (particularly management time) to defend and nurture core business activities' (p. 21) in the face of low unit labour cost competition from the developing world. As John Travolta's President in the film *Primary Colors* tells a US shipyard, 'muscle jobs are going to go where muscle is cheap, and that's not here' (thought to be an indirect quote from former US President Bill Clinton).

However, the rise of small firms is not simply a result of the contraction of incumbent firms. Rather, two parallel processes appear to be in play. In addition to the decline in average size of existing firms, there is substantial evidence of a significant net inflow of new small firms.[33; 31] To explain this second phenomenon, Carlsson[37] points to 'the emergence of new computer-based technology which improves the productivity of small and medium-scaled production relative to standardised mass production techniques which dominated for the previous 150 years' (p. 21). The implementation of such flexible technologies has served to diminish the importance of scale economies over the last three decades and may account, in part, for changes in firm size distributions. According to Dosi:[38]

As an historical example, I suggest that we are currently observing, at least in the industrial countries, a process of change in the size distribution of plants and firms that is significantly influenced by the new flexibility–scale trade-offs associated with electronic production technologies . . . in mass production industries the higher flexibility of the new forms of automation is likely to allow the efficient survival of relatively smaller firms [as compared to the past].

(pp. 1155–56)

However, this final argument warrants a couple of qualifications. First, as Hughes[30] notes for the UK, 'new business formation in the 1980s . . . has led to a significant increase in the number of businesses in the service sector, but to a much less significant increase in manufacturing' (p. 35), suggesting that where there has been entry, there has also been exit. Second, while average firm size has been decreasing in the manufacturing sectors of most industrial economies, it has been increasing in the service and finance sectors.[31] The concentration of economic activity has increased in services at the same time as it has decreased in manufacturing, begging questions about the relative roles of scale economies. Notwithstanding these provisos, some things are clear. First, according to Acs and Audretsch,[31] 'a distinct and consistent shift away from large firms and towards small enterprises has occurred within the manufacturing sector of every developed western country' (p. 227). Second, there has been a contemporaneous shift in economic activity, from manufacturing towards services. Taken together, the result has been the increase in small firms' economic significance that is so evident in the data.

Importantly, this is not to suggest that such structural change was inevitable, at least to the extent witnessed, and that local factors have had no influence. Rather, policy action is likely to have facilitated and, perhaps, quickened the necessary restructuring, which may have taken longer in its absence. However, the evidence seems to suggest that the transformation in the fortunes of the small business sector was, and is, a continuation of long-run trends that predated the flurry of focused policy activity associated with the 1980s and 1990s.

ENTREPRENEURSHIP IN EMERGING ECONOMIES

Unsurprisingly, much of the preceding discussion has concentrated on data and trends in western industrialised economies. This is an inevitable consequence of both the majority readership and, more importantly, data availability. In particular, the discussion of long-term trends in entrepreneurship (above) is exclusively concerned with OECD economies. Indeed, a large part of the material that this section draws upon is to be found in a single edited text published in 1993.[39] Perhaps this may seem a little dated. Yet, for the OECD economies considered, the period of principal interest runs from around 1970–1990 and the text is admirably fit for purpose. Importantly, the text was also explicitly concerned with illuminating an 'East–West perspective', and includes chapters on (the former) Czechoslovakia, East Germany and Poland. The timing of the text is intriguingly coincidental. Most of the datasets used terminate in the late 1980s, immediately preceding the fall of the Berlin Wall (November 1989) and the disintegration of the former Soviet Union (December 1991). Up to this point, the picture painted of small firms in eastern Europe stood in stark contrast to its western equivalent. As Acs and Audretsch[31] noted:

> There are two striking consistencies emerging from the country studies of Eastern Europe. First, the role of small firms throughout the Eastern European countries is remarkably small, especially when compared to that in Western nations . . . Second, while the developed Western economies all experienced a shift in economic activity in manufacturing away from large firms and towards small enterprises, the trend was exactly the opposite in Eastern Europe.
>
> (p. 228)

Undoubtedly, these trends reflected deliberate policies to centralise and concentrate economic assets under state planning. However, it is what has happened since that is of interest here. Following the collapse of the Warsaw Pact in 1991, many former Soviet republics and other eastern European nations began a process of transition from socialism to market capitalism. While much of the contemporaneous debate revolved around the importance of privatising existing firms, private-sector entrepreneurship (and, in particular, the creation of new firms) became central to the creation of wealth and economic development.[40] The greater flexibility in prices, wages and production decisions, which followed initial reforms, created profit opportunities for entrepreneurs. According to McMillan and Woodruff,[40] 'Entrepreneurs responded by starting enterprises at a rapid – though varying – rate in each of the transition economies' (p. 154). Over a period of around ten years, private-sector enterprise rose from illegality to contributing 60–80 per cent of GDP in the transition economies of central Europe and the newly independent Baltic states.[41] Unfortunately, until recently, detailed comparative data were not widely or easily available for most transition economies. Now, as recent members of the EU, data from Bulgaria, the Czech Republic, Estonia, Hungary, Latvia, Lithuania, Poland, Romania, Slovakia and Slovenia is more readily available. Accordingly, Tables 2.2–2.4 recorded the distributions of enterprises, employment and value-added for these economies. Looking at this snapshot data, there is no obvious East-West pattern. Neighbours, such as Slovakia (with its large-scale manufacturing FDI) and the Czech Republic (which, with over 80 SMEs per 1000 inhabitants, has more than double the EU average) seem as different from each other as any other pair. There is, perhaps, some tentative evidence that SMEs in former Eastern Bloc countries are less productive than their same-country peers: for instance, in the newest EU countries, Bulgaria and Romania, SME productivity is less than 42 per cent of large firm productivity. This, in turn, may reflect some of our earlier discussion on economic development and the prevalence of necessity versus opportunity entrepreneurship – or 'booty' capitalism versus more productive forms of entrepreneurship. One suspects more longitudinal data would illuminate more.

Certainly, we know that the process of transition has not been uniform across transition economies. For instance, there is some evidence that it has stalled in Russia, while EU membership may mark out notable 'success stories'.[41] It is tempting to argue that transition progress is somehow a function of either an earlier start or closer proximity to western Europe, and simple consideration of the 'better' performers would seem to support this view. Yet, perhaps a more compelling rationalisation reflects upon the institutional arguments touched upon previously.[24]

In a recent study of a sample of European transition economies, Ovaska and Sobel[41] examined the policies and institutions most highly correlated with transition success – where success is equated with entrepreneurial activity and economic growth. These authors conclude that high rates of entrepreneurial activity were associated with credit availability, contract enforcement, low government corruption, high foreign direct investment, sound monetary policy and 'policies (such as low regulations and taxation) that are consistent with giving citizens a high degree of economic freedom' (p. 2). Of these, credit availability and lower levels of government corruption tended to be most important in encouraging new firm formation. Interestingly, however, these authors also suggest that policies that foster new firm formation do not, inevitably, also promote the higher rates of technological innovation thought central to economic growth:

> To be successful, these countries not only need to institute policies consistent with fostering the creation of new businesses but also have to have in place policies conducive with fostering new high-tech innovation. One of the most important of these factors is the presence of economic freedom – low taxes, low regulation, and secure property rights.
>
> (pp. 3–4)

This seems to comfortably echo Adam Smith's 'peace, easy taxes, and a tolerable administration of justice'. That is, while, at the micro level, these imperatives may be manifest in a variety of managerial challenges, at the macro level creating the appropriate institutions may be the primary task. McMillan and Woodruff[40] provide a remarkable illustration of the importance of such institutions in providing incentives to entrepreneurship.

Drawing upon data from a survey of start-up manufacturing firms in Russia, Poland, Slovakia, Ukraine and Romania,[42] these authors record that:

> Managers were asked . . . whether they would invest $100 today if they expected to receive $200 in two years (an implied annual rate of return of 40 percent). The responses to this question give an indication of both the opportunity cost and the security of property. A striking 99 percent of the Russian managers said they would not, compared with 22 percent of the Polish managers.
>
> (p. 155)

Recent work suggests that, in the absence of effective market-based institutions to protect property rights and ensure fair competition, entrepreneurs in transition economies may be more likely to direct their efforts towards necessity entrepreneurship.[43] This focuses Scase's earlier argument:

> . . . in Eastern Europe it is necessary to make a conceptual distinction between entrepreneurial activity on the one hand and small-scale business proprietorship on the other. It is the latter that is expanding rapidly as increasing numbers of individuals strive to protect themselves from the uncertainties of the newly-emerging market economies . . . proprietorship offers possibilities for generating cash flows that can be consumed for raising personal living standards rather than for business expansion.
>
> (p. 14)

For Scase, this is Max Weber's 'booty capitalism', a term which refers to trading activities haphazardly pursued for the purposes of personal advantage, rather than longer-term capital accumulation. Moreover, it implies investments in exchange and consumption, rather than production (where, at least some of, the rewards are reinvested rather than consumed). The data presented in Figures 2.2–2.4 are unlikely to capture this phenomenon. However, as noted, it may be in this context that the relatively low small-firm productivity figures may best be understood.

Of course, emerging economies are not solely located in eastern and central Europe. Rather, one may think of them, more generally, as 'economies that are increasingly moving to market orientation and seeking to rapidly advance economically'[44] (p.1). Alas, the research on entrepreneurship in emerging economies has been disproportionately concerned with countries of the former Soviet Union and its satellites'[44] – though China, in particular, has been an increasing focus of academic study. On the face of it, China's transition has been quite different from the former Soviet-Bloc countries. While the transition from central planning to a more mixed-market economy has been similar, China's path has been more gradual. Economic reforms followed the 'open door' policy of 1978, which intended to open world markets to Chinese goods, and to open China to world markets and foreign investment.[45] These economic reforms re-legitimised private enterprise, allowing individuals to own the means of production and exploit their labour to earn a living in a privately trading economy. Some argue that private entrepreneurship in China has gone through stages: of strict prohibition, tolerance, accommodation and encouragement.[46] Currently, encouragement and accommodation are to the fore. For instance, in 2001, President Jiang Zemin suggested that the Chinese Communist Party should actively recruit private entrepreneurs since they represent advanced productive forces.[46] The 'crossing the river by feeling the stones' reform mentality, proposed by Deng Xiaoping, meant that market reforms have been gradualist, with partial reforms introduced as localized experiments and allowed to spread gradually.[45]

Within China, it is estimated that SMEs are now responsible for approximately 75 per cent of the workforce in cities and towns[47] and 75 per cent of new jobs.[48] In Beijing, the focus of this study, there were approximately

965,773 SMEs registered in the city in 2006, representing 82.92 per cent of all firms (*China Private Enterprises Year Book 2004-2006*, p. 217). More than in all of Belgium and the Netherlands combined.

Certainly, one intuitively feels that general comments on the importance of regulatory and normative institutions (and the implications, in their absence, for necessity *versus* opportunity entrepreneurship) are likely to apply to the emerging economies of Africa, Asia and South America, as well as to their eastern European counterparts. However, there is a pressing need for more research to better understand the similarities and differences in challenges faced by this wider set of emerging economies. Not least as projections indicate that the BRIC economies (Brazil, Russia, India and China) will be larger than the G6 economies (USA, UK, Japan, Germany, France and Italy) by 2050.[49]

CONCLUSIONS

In this chapter we have tried to provide some answers to the question 'Why study entrepreneurship and small firms?' To this end, we began by pointing to the simple statistics illustrating the extent to which small firms dominate the business stock, and the contributions they make to both employment and income. In every European economy, over 99 per cent of all firms are small firms. Moreover, in most of these economies small firms account for over 60 per cent of total employment and over 50 per cent of value added. Clearly, on this basis small firms 'matter'.

However, the chapter was also concerned with the more dynamic contribution small firms may make to economic well-being. With this in mind, we outlined the widely held belief that entrepreneurship (most often embodied in small firms) positively impacts upon economic growth. Casual reading of the literature and attention to policy announcements would leave one in little doubt that, as expressed by Wennekers and Thurik[15] 'Entrepreneurship matters [and] In modern open economies it is more important for economic growth than it has ever been' (p. 51). Unfortunately, while one may share this intuition, the evidence to date is far from unequivocal. Nonetheless, this general view has already had considerable influence on policy.

In addition, the chapter tried to understand why small firms appear to matter more now than they have in the recent past or, at least, why our interest in them has grown. Here, the influence of David Birch's work and the coincidence of changing political circumstance in the UK and USA are acknowledged. However, the trends in the growth of the small-firm sector appear to predate these landmark events. Moreover, the changes have not been limited to the Anglo-Saxon economies of the UK and North America. Rather, they have occurred in every developed western economy, though with some variations in timing and extent. Such a widespread phenomenon calls for more general explanations and the chapter suggests two: first, a structural shift from manufacturing towards services; and, second, the development of new flexible manufacturing technologies, which, in some sectors, have diminished the importance of scale economies. Numerous other factors are likely to have contributed to the pace of change; however, the power of these two alone is quite compelling.

Finally, the chapter commented briefly on the development of, and challenges to, entrepreneurship in emerging economies. Here the development of suitable supporting institutions seems crucial if economies are to direct activities away from short-term necessity entrepreneurship to accumulative, sustainable, opportunity entrepreneurship. Unfortunately, to date, we know too little about entrepreneurship in economies beyond Europe and North America.

REVIEW QUESTIONS

1 What factors account for the increased policy attention given to entrepreneurial activity and the small firm sector?
2 What are the accepted definitions of:
   - micro firms
   - small firms
   - medium-sized firms?
3 Account for the growth in entrepreneurial activity in the last 20 years. Discuss, in your view, whether this constitutes an entrepreneurial revolution.
4 Should policymakers focus merely on encouraging more entrepreneurial activity and new firm start-ups?
5 Why should an emphasis of policy on quality start-ups (rather than blanket support) be worthwhile?
6 Should under-represented groups (e.g. women) be targeted by policymakers?
7 What factors might account for small-firm volatility or stability?
8 Why is new entrepreneurial activity important to the health of a nation's economy?
9 Why are different views held on the volatility or otherwise of small-firm formation and failure rates?
10 Why is it important to establish consistent definitions of small firms?
11 What is the EU definition of a small firm?

SUGGESTED ASSIGNMENTS

1 Students are allocated to small working groups and are required to present and contrast the growth in the numbers of small firms in the UK compared to large firms. Student groups are required to discuss their definition adopted of a small firm and account for the differences shown.

2 Students are allocated to groups to discuss factors that have contributed to the growth in the numbers of small firms. Their task is to suggest why small-business ownership has become an attractive alternative career for many people compared to large-firm employment in the modern labour market.

3 Students select one economy in western Europe, one economy from eastern Europe and compare and contrast the importance of small firms. What factors will account for the differences?

REFERENCES

1 **Cotis, J.-P.** (2007) 'Entrepreneurship as the engine of growth: evidence and policy challenges', GEM forum, London, 10 January (available at http://www.oecd.org/dataoecd/4/51/38031895.pdf) (accessed at 28 October 2011).

2 **European Commission** (2005) 'Working together for growth and jobs – A new start for the Lisbon strategy', Brussels, http://eur-lex.europa.eu/LexUriServ/LexUriServ.do?uri=COM:2005:0024:FIN:en:PDF (accessed at 28 October 2011).

3 **European Commission** (2003) *Entrepreneurship in Europe*, Green Paper, Brussels, http://eur-lex.europa.eu/LexUriServ/site/en/com/2003/com2003_0027en01.pdf (accessed at 28 October 2011).

4 **Small Business Service** (2002) *Small Business and Government – The Way Forward*, HMSO, London, http://www2.accaglobal.com/pdfs/smallbusiness/sb_gov_thewayforward.pdf (accessed at 28 October 2011).

5 **OECD** (2010) *SMEs, Entrepreneurship and Innovation*, OECD, Paris.

6 **Cotis, J.-P.** (2004) *Alternatives for Stable Economic Growth: Increasing Productivity, Greater Competitiveness and Entrepreneurial Innovation*, paper presented at the Economist Conference, Madrid, 29 June.

7 **Bolton, J.** (1971) *Report of the Committee of Inquiry on Small Firms*, Cmnd 4811, HMSO, London.

8 **Storey, D.** (1994) *Understanding the Small Firm Sector*, Routledge, London.

9 **Atkinson, J. and Meagre, N.** (1994) 'Running to a stand still: the small business in the labour market', in Atkinson, J. and Storey, D. (eds), *Employment, the Small Firm and the Labour Market*, Routledge, London.

10 **Stevenson, L. and Lundström, A.** (2001) *Patterns and Trends in Entrepreneurship/SME Policy and Practice in Ten Economies*, vol. 3 of the 'Entrepreneurship Policy for the Future' series, Swedish Foundation for Small Business Research.

11 **Reynolds, P., Hay, M. and Camp, S.** (1999) *Global Entrepreneurship Monitor, 1999 Executive Report*, Babson College, Kauffman Foundation and London Business School, http://www.gemconsortium.org/download/1319813179527/GEM%20Global%201999%20report.pdf (accessed at 28 October 2011).

12 **DGEI/EIM** (2009) *European SMEs Under Pressure: The Annual Report in EU SMEs 2009*, Zoetermeer, The Netherlands.

13 **OECD** (2000) *Small and Medium Enterprise Outlook*, 2000 edn, OECD, Paris.

14 **Acs, Z. and Audretsch, D.** (1990) *Innovation and Small Firms*, MIT Press, Cambridge, MA.

15 **Wennekers, S. and Thurik, R.** (1999) 'Linking entrepreneurship and economic growth', *Small Business Economics*, vol. 13, pp. 27–55.

16 **GEM** (2010) *Global Entrepreneurship Monitor, 2010 Global Report*, Babson College, Universidad del Desarollo and London Business School, http://www.gemconsortium.org/download/1319813179527/GEM%20Global%201999%20report.pdf (accessed at 28 October 2011).

17 **GEM** (1999) *Global Entrepreneurship Monitor, 1999 Executive Report*, Babson College, Kauffman Foundation and London Business School www.gemconsortium.org (accessed at 28 October 2011).

18 **GEM** (2004) *Global Entrepreneurship Monitor, 2004 Executive Report*, Babson College, Kauffman Foundation and London Business School www.gemconsortium.org (accessed at 28 October 2011).

19 **Audretsch, D. and Thurik, R.** (2001) 'Linking entrepreneurship to growth', STI Working Papers 2001/2, OECD, Paris.

20 **Acs, Z., Audretsch, D. and Evans, D.** (1994) *The Determinants of Variations in Self-employment Rates Across Countries and Over Time*, Cambridge, MA (unpublished manuscript).

21 **Audretsch, D.** (1995) 'Innovation, growth and survival', *International Journal of Industrial Organisation*, vol. 13, pp. 441–57.

22 **Geroski, P.A.** (1995) 'What do we know about entry?', *International Journal of Industrial Organisation*, vol. 13, pp. 421–40.

23 **Audretsch, D., Houweling, P. and Thurik, R.** (1997) *New-Firm Survival: Industry Versus Firm Effects*, DP 97-063, Tinbergen Institute, Rotterdam.

24 **Boettke, P. and Coyne, C.** (2002) 'Entrepreneurship and development: cause or consequence?', Global Prosperity Initiative WP 6, George Mason University.

25 **Porter, M.** (1990) *The Competitive Advantage of Nations*, The Free Press, New York.

26 **Birch, D.** (1979) *The Job Generation Process*, MIT Programme on Neighborhood and Regional Change, Cambridge, MA.

27 **Kirchhoff, B.A. and Greene, P.G.** (1995) 'Response to renewed attacks on the small business job creation hypothesis', in *Frontiers of Entrepreneurship Research*, Babson College, Boston, MA.

28 **Birch, D.** (1981) 'Who creates jobs?', *The Public Interest*, vol. 65, Fall, pp. 3–14.

29 **Storey, D.** (1990) 'Firm performance and size', in Acs, Z. and Audretsch, D. (eds), *The Economics of Small Firms: A European Challenge*, Kluwer, Dordrecht.

30 **Hughes, A.** (1993) 'Industrial concentration and small firms in the United Kingdom: The 1980s in historical perspective', in Acs, Z. and Audretsch, D. (eds), *Small Firms and Entrepreneurship: An East–West Perspective*, Cambridge University Press, Cambridge, pp. 15–37.

31 **Acs, Z. and Audretsch, D.** (1993) 'Conclusion', in Acs, Z. and Audretsch, D. (eds), *Small Firms and Entrepreneurship: An East–West Perspective*, Cambridge University Press, Cambridge, pp. 227–32.

32 **Fritsch, M.** (1993) 'The role of small firms in West Germany', in Acs, Z. and Audretsch, D. (eds), *Small Firms and Entrepreneurship: An East–West Perspective*, Cambridge University Press, Cambridge, pp. 38–54.

33 **Invernizzi, B. and Revelli, R.** (1993) 'Small firms and the Italian economy: structural changes and evidence of turbulence', in Acs, Z. and Audretsch, D. (eds), *Small Firms and Entrepreneurship: An East–West Perspective*, Cambridge University Press, Cambridge, pp. 123–54.

34 **Thurik, R.** (1993) 'Recent development in the firmsize distribution and economies of scale in Dutch manufacturing', in Acs, Z. and Audretsch, D. (eds), *Small Firms and Entrepreneurship: An East–West Perspective*, Cambridge University Press, Cambridge, pp. 78–109.

35 **Galbraith, J.K.** (1967) *The New Industrial State*, Houghton Mifflin, Boston, MA.

36 **Piore, M. and Sabel, C.** (1984) *Second Industrial Divide: Possibilities for Prosperity*, Basic Books, New York.

37 **Carlsson, B.** (1989) 'The evolution of manufacturing technology and its impact on industrial structure: an international study', *Small Business Economics*, vol. 1, pp. 21–38.

38 **Dosi, G.** (1988) 'Sources, procedures and microeconomic effects of innovation', *Journal of Economic Literature*, vol. 26, pp. 1120–71.

39 **Acs, Z. and Audretsch, D.** (eds) (1993) *Small Firms and Entrepreneurship: An East–West Perspective*, Cambridge University Press, Cambridge.

40 **McMillan, J. and Woodruff, C.** (2002) 'The central role of entrepreneurs in transition economies', *Journal of Economic Perspectives*, vol. 16, pp. 153–70.

41 **Ovaska, T. and Sobel, R.** (2004) 'Entrepreneurship in Post-socialist Economies*', WP 04-06, Economics Department, University of West Virginia.

42 **Johnson, S., McMillan, J. and Woodruff, C.** (2002) 'Property rights and finance', *American Economic Review*, vol. 92, pp. 1335–56.

43 **Manolova, T., Rangamohan, E. and Bojidar, G.** (2008) 'Institutional environments for entrepreneurship: evidence from emerging economies in Eastern Europe', *Entrepreneurship Theory and Practice*, vol. 32, no. 1, pp. 203–18.

44 **Bruton, G., Ahlstrom, D. and Krzysztof, O.** (2008) 'Entrepreneurship in emerging economies: where we are now and where should the research go in the future', *Entrepreneurship Theory and Practice*, vol. 32, no. 1, pp. 1–14.

45 **Anderson, A.R., Li, J.-H., Harrison R.T. and Robson P.J.A.** (2003) 'The increasing role of small business in the Chinese economy', *Journal of Small Business Management*, 41(3), 310–16.

46 **Peng, Y.** (2004) 'Kinship networks and entrepreneurs in China's transitional economy', *American Journal of Sociology*, vol. 109, no. 5, pp. 10545–74.

47 **Hussain, J., Millman, C. and Matlay, H.** (2006) 'SMEs financing in the UK and in China: a comparative perspective', *Journal of Small Business and Enterprise Development*, vol. 13(4), 584–99.

48 **Zou, P.** (2006) 'SMEs absorb 75 percent of the work force', *Dazhong Daily*, 17 November, http://news.sina.com.cn/c/2006-11-17/073110525012s.shtml. (in Chinese) (accessed at 28 October 2011).

49 **Wilson, D. and Purushothaman, R.** (2003) *Dreaming with BRICS: The Path to 2050*, Goldman Sachs Global Economics Paper No. 99, available online: http://www.worldbpoforum.com/files/casestudy/2case.pdf (accessed at 28 October 2011).

RECOMMENDED READING

GEM (2010) *Global Entrepreneurship Monitor, 2010 Global Report*, Babson College, Universidad del Desarollo and London Business School (http://www. gemconsortium.org) (accessed at 28 October 2011).

DGEI/EIM (2009) *European SMEs Under Pressure: The Annual Report in EU SMEs 2009*, Zoetermeer, The Netherlands.

Bruton, G., Ahlstrom, D. and Krzysztof, O. (2008) 'Entrepreneurship in emerging economies: where we are now and where should the research go in the future', *Entrepreneurship Theory and Practice*, vol. 32, no. 1, pp. 1-14.

PART TWO
THE DOMAINS OF ENTREPRENEURSHIP

Part 2 contains four chapters that develop concepts introduced in Part 1 in different domains of entrepreneurship. The role of the entrepreneur is examined within different organisations and in different domains.

Many firms are family businesses and Chapter 3 examines the role of the entrepreneur in family businesses and develops theory relevant to this domain, yet placed against *'Entrepreneurship in Action'* case examples of entrepreneurial family firms. The role of women and ethnic minorities as entrepreneurs is examined in Chapter 4. Challenges that face such 'minority' entrepreneurs are discussed and compared and we build further issues around the concepts of entrepreneurial opportunity and recognition set against the challenges. Entrepreneurial diversity provides the theme for discussion of opportunities and challenges. *'Entrepreneurship in Action'* cases provide examples of such diversity to provide the context for consideration of different issues that determine firm development.

Chapters 5 and 6 continue the theme of diversity in entrepreneurial domains by examining the role of social and corporate entrepreneurs and how our earlier entrepreneurial concepts need to be modified in the light of different organisational contexts. Entrepreneurial opportunity and recognition are still important concepts, but they need to be re-examined in the light of these different contexts. *'Entrepreneurship in Action'* cases provide further examples of how entrepreneurs operate in different environments and in different organisations.

DAVID LYSAGHT[1]

by Thomas Cooney
Dublin Institute of Technology

INTRODUCTION

David Lysaght understood from the moment that his business idea was conceived that starting a business would be a challenging prospect and that the possibility of failing would be high. During the late summer of 2010, the economic recession that Ireland was suffering had taken its toll on many businesses, and David wondered if he should abandon his plans to establish a not-for-profit business that would organise hill-walking and mountain-trekking to raise funds for charitable organisations. The charity market had recently become extremely competitive in Ireland because: (1) there was substantially less funding available from the public and private sectors to give to charities; (2) there had been a sharp decline in philanthropic activity because the wealth of high-worth individuals had been badly hit by the recession; and (3) there was also a large increase in the number of not-for-profit organisations seeking to secure funding. David also faced an additional challenge that few other entrepreneurs have to face: he has cerebral palsy. Cerebral palsy is generally characterized by an inability fully to control one's motor functions, particularly muscle control and co-ordination. While David had a very positive attitude to life, he wondered if organizing expeditions was a good business choice for someone with his condition. He also thought about getting a business partner as people frequently changed their behaviour when they met him and saw his disability. He had arranged a meeting with his business mentor in seven days' time, and David decided that he needed to consider all of the positive and negative aspects to his personal and business situation in preparation for this meeting. This analysis would help him determine the next step in the development of his business idea.

THE BUSINESS CONCEPT

David's idea involved establishing a not-for-profit business called Charity Voyage. Through this business he would arrange hill-walking/mountain-trekking events which would allow people to raise money for a charity of their choice. The idea is that each person that takes part in one of the events will have to raise a minimum amount of money; some would go to Charity Voyage to cover the cost of organising the event and the remainder would go to the chosen charity. This form of fundraising had become very popular in recent years, enabling individuals to undertake a personal challenge while simultaneously raising substantial sums of money for charities across the country. Indeed, the idea had become so popular that a number of commercial businesses had been established in Ireland to organize such events and the scale, type and location of activities had grown substantially. A quick browse of the Internet had shown David that a person could now participate in a challenge in many countries across the world, in many different activities, and almost for any charity. David wanted to maintain the charitable nature of the activity and so he decided to establish a not-for-profit organization rather than a commercial business. He also decided to stay focused on organizing events in Ireland and that the only activity offered would be hill-walking and mountain-trekking. He envisaged four types of events:

1 'Six of the Best' – climb six mountains within three days
2 'Six of the Best (Deluxe)' – climb six mountains within three days in comfort
3 A two-day event
4 A one-day event

---

[1] This case is written with thanks and respect to the late John Butler of Century Management.

The 'Six of the Best' would be his main event and the one which he would expect to be the most popular. In this, participants would take part as teams of three to five members and climb six mountains around the island of Ireland (including Carrantuohill and Slieve Donard). However, he recently started having second thoughts about how to organize this event and considered instead that it should be made up of 20 individual members all doing it for their own charity and they would only have to pay the cost of doing the event. Instead of paying a minimum sponsorship fee, each member would decide with their own charity how much money they needed to raise in advance of the event. David needed to clarify these options.

FINANCES

Like any business, David understood that there would be costs involved in managing Charity Voyage. He was fortunate in that he could start the business from his mother's house. He would, however, have to pay for insurance, promotional activities, telephone, petrol, etc. He estimated that his mobile-phone calls would cost €80 a month and that this would include personal and business phone calls. For the running of the business, he allocated no more than 75 per cent of the total bill to be spent on business calls, although his business mentor had argued that his phone bill could be higher, particularly if one takes Internet charges into account.

In addition to these ongoing costs, David intended to promote the business initially by sending an introduction package to the 270 charities that he identified in his analysis of the Irish charity market. This package would include a letter explaining the background of Charity Voyage and its business philosophy, an events brochure, details of the website and a business card with David's contact details. He had not gathered any projected costs for the promotional materials and support activities, but he estimated that €5,000 would be a minimum requirement.

As he began to prepare projected costs for each individual trip, David knew that keeping budgets very tight would be critical to the success of his business. Basing his figures on challenges in which he had previously participated, he estimated that the costs for the Deluxe version of the 'Six of the Best' would be as shown in Table 1.

TABLE 1 ESTIMATED COSTS OF 'SIX OF THE BEST – DELUXE'*

Item	Unit	Cost
Hotel @ 25pn pp	Two nights	€2,200
Petrol	1 bus	€200
Mountain leaders	360	€1,080
Water	480 litres	€160
Tea	1 box	€4
Coffee	1 box	€4
Sandwiches	€5 per head × 3 days	€660
Stew	€5 per head × 3 days	€660
Apples	1 box of 100	€20
Oranges	1 box of 100	€20
Bars	2 boxes of 48	€45
	Total	€5,713

* Based on 40 participants and 4 mountain leaders.

However, after a brief review of the figures, an accountant friend highlighted that the table did not include the cost of hiring the bus, that the cost of the mountain leaders on a daily basis seemed very low (€90 per person per day), and that for a Deluxe model he was offering very little comfort. He also highlighted that, based on a minimum sponsorship fee of €4,500 with 40 per cent going to Charity Voyage, each participant would be contributing €1,800 to the organisation of the event. Given the figures that David was presenting, it suggested that if he had 40 people on the trip then Charity Voyage would make a gross profit on each event of €66,287 (€72,000 – €5,713). The accountant suggested that either this was a really exciting business opportunity or that David needed to re-examine his figures again.

David had been frugal with his money over the years and had managed to save €5,300. He had made some enquiries to the local Enterprise Support agency regarding the possibility of securing financial support for his business and had discovered that there were no soft loans or grants for which he was eligible. In the current economic climate, he would have great difficulty in persuading a bank manager to give him a loan on such a risky business proposition, particularly when he had no collateral which he could offer as security against his loan. His family had always been very supportive of him and it seemed his only real hope of raising money was through them. He estimated that, at best, he might get €6,000 from his family, which potentially left him with a maximum investment of €11,300. He did not know if this would be enough to get him started.

CONCLUSION

David felt that he was making good progress with his business planning. However, he was not fully confident about the viability of his idea, particularly when the accountant asked him to reconsider the figures. He was also uncertain about the funds required to get the business started and where further funding might be sourced. David also needed to think more about the organizations and participants he should target as customers, how much he should spend on website development and promotional materials, and the transport and accommodation he should provide. More importantly, he wondered if he should find a partner because of his disability (although he felt that it would be for the sake of others rather than for his own). Maybe he could find a partner who would bring experience and money to the business. As David was preparing for the meeting with his mentor, he received a phone call from the manager of the mentoring programme giving him terrible news. His mentor had died unexpectedly on the previous day leaving behind a wife and a young family. His mentor was a successful businessman in his early fifties who had recently begun to enjoy the fruits of many years of hard work. It came as a terrible shock to David and it reminded him that he needed to make the most out of life as one never knew what might happen next!

3 FAMILY BUSINESSES

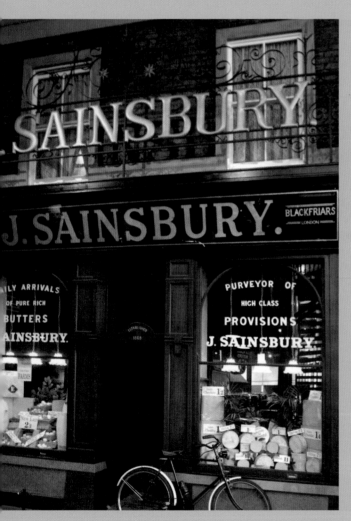

Chapter contributed by Dr Laura Galloway and Professor William Keogh, Heriot-Watt University

> ## LEARNING OUTCOMES
>
> At the end of this chapter you should be able to:
>
> - Discuss the importance of family businesses in the modern economy.
> - Describe the potential range of family stakeholders in the family firm.
> - Discuss the advantages and disadvantages of starting and developing a family business.
> - Discuss the issues often pertinent in family firms.
> - Describe the problems of succession planning in the family business.
> - Describe the main elements involved in a succession plan for a family business.

INTRODUCTION

The SME sector in most countries includes a preponderance of family firms.[1; 2] According to Peter Drucker[3] (p. 45): 'The majority of businesses everywhere – including the United States and all other developed countries – are family-controlled and family-managed.' Certainly this is true in the UK, where the Association of Chartered Certified Accountants (ACCA) estimates that three out of four businesses are family owned,[4] and in Australia where a Boyd Partners survey estimated that family businesses account for two-thirds of the total firms.[5] In developing countries the proportion of businesses that are family concerns is even higher, including Latin America, Southeast Asia and Africa.[1]

Family firms range from the small lifestyle firm to those with high entrepreneurial growth potential, as discussed in Chapter 10. Between these two poles, like other SMEs, there is infinite variety. Since many family firms span several generations, family firms have the potential to prevail for many years:[1] amongst the oldest surviving family businesses are the Zildjian Cymbal Company, now American, but founded in Constantinople (Istanbul) in 1623, and Waterford Wedgewood of Dublin, founded in 1759. Intergenerational family firms may have gone through various stages of development, from establishment and sustainability through to periods of high entrepreneurial growth. Most often these intergenerational changes are borne of variation in the external conditions in which the firm operates and the attitudes and ambitions of different owners through the generations. The stereotype of 'rags to riches and back again in three generations' is not entirely without foundation, but there are also many examples of family firms that once established by the founder have gone from strength to strength as a result of second and third (and more!) generational entrepreneurship.[6] An example of this is given later in the chapter in the box on the Fiat Legacy.[7]

DEFINING THE FAMILY BUSINESS

Family businesses are all around us and influence our lives in many ways. Most often they are defined as firms in which the ownership is controlled by the family unit, either having been started by two or more members of the same family, or having been passed from an original founder to next generations of the family. Elsewhere, family firms are defined as those that have a significant family presence such as ownership and management, but not necessarily both.[2] Nordqvist and Melin[1] point out that family can include immediate family, extended family (cousins, uncles, aunts), and family by marriage. Thereafter different generations of these various branches can be involved. If business ownership is shared between and amongst some combination of these, we tend to refer to their firm as a family firm. The family firm is therefore a somewhat amorphous concept.

THE PREVALENCE OF FAMILY BUSINESS

As noted in the introduction to this chapter, many family firms are small and lifestyle in orientation; local businesses passed on through one generation or more, such as carpenters or even a family farm. There is also, however, impressive precedent for the demonstration of entrepreneurship within family firms throughout the world; some of the most innovative and entrepreneurial firms are family-controlled.

Family Business Magazine[2] provides a compilation of the world's 250 largest family businesses, i.e. those with annual revenue of $1 billion or more. The list includes data from 28 countries, and within it a wide variety of industries are represented. 130 of these top family firms are based in the USA, with France having 17 and Germany 16. Korea has three companies in the 250 (Samsung, LG Group and Hyundai Motor), all of which are in the top 20 with 2 in the top 10. It was made clear in the report that data had been missed from the compilation because many companies operate through complex holding companies (particularly in Asia and Europe), therefore it is reasonable to conclude that this list represents a conservative account of the impact of the top-performing family firms.

FAMILY BUSINESS RESEARCH

Despite the importance of family-owned entrepreneurial businesses in modern economies, they have been the subject of comparatively little academic research. The practitioner community on the other hand, has a long tradition of profiling successful family firms and issues most often encountered in them. For example, in his book on leadership in family firms, Nicholson[8] identifies three main areas of particular concern:

- Succession
- Insularity
- Family conflict and governance.

Thus there is an opportunity for academic researchers to investigate family firms in a robust and systematic way, and indeed, there is a recent and emerging research literature using the family firm as a unit of analysis. Amongst these, notable developments include recent special editions in respected journals such as *Entrepreneurship and Regional Development*[9] and the *Journal of Family and Economic Issues*[10] on family business. Issues identified in these and other recent publications that are peculiar to, or at least most pertinent in, family firms include relationships within the family, intergenerational changes and succession and sustainability.[1] The interested reader is encouraged to examine the recommended reading for additional issues and insights into the areas of research in family-owned businesses. It is a potentially rich area that deserves ongoing further investigation by researchers in the entrepreneurship field.

CHARACTERISTICS OF FAMILY FIRMS

Family firms are said to have advantages and disadvantages that are unique to them, or at least more pertinent, than non-family firms. These can be felt in the firm during every stage of its development.

At the business start-up phase, dependence on family for support is a common occurrence and comes with advantages as well as disadvantages. The advantages include the fact that the family members know the would-be entrepreneur and their characteristics. They may also be prepared to make any loan at low or zero interest and the time limit for returning the funds may be elastic. There may also be advice and support from family members who have business experience. On the downside, there may be some unwanted interference regarding the way the business is run, particularly where family has been used as a funding source.

Support from family is found to be an important part of the start-up phase for entrepreneurs generally.[11] While most investigation of family firms includes focus on the founder, the role of family as an ongoing resource is often overlooked. In the literature on the influence of women in family firms in particular, both popular accounts of business and the academic literature have been criticized for placing too much focus on the formal structure of the business and the official owner.[12] This is discussed more fully in the section 'Other Considerations in Family Firms' later in this chapter.

As a business grows and becomes established, there are a number of issues that can more acutely affect a family firm compared with a non-family firm. Most prevalent amongst these are the company culture, relationships between owners and other family stakeholders and succession. The very same elements that can be the making of a family firm can also be the undoing. In this section we will look at the issues specific or pertinent to family firms and investigate how these can impact positively or negatively on the firm and on the family.

COMPANY CULTURE

For successful family firms the implicitly understood company culture can comprise advantage. Family firms can exhibit a 'sense of future' that comes from passing the organization through generations. Often the entrepreneurial passion of the founder is spread through the family and subsequent generations. Learning from past experiences also increases the store of knowledge, know-how and networks that the family operates in. Family involvement may also influence the adoption of a long-term view for the organization and the industry it is in. As reputation grows over the long term, so standards expected from the business and its employees also develop. There are many examples of family firms having generated strong businesses on the back of a shared culture and co-operation, long-term vision and established reputation. Marshall B. Paisner[13] (pp. 2–4), a family firm veteran himself, emphasizes in his book on managing family firms that the business culture in the family can be built by involving family members from a young age in what the business is all about by talking about it at the dinner table. This develops in family members deep and detailed knowledge of the business, its products, contacts and markets and this knowledge along with emotional ties to the firm can comprise significant advantage; it can drive focus on value and success. The 'family' ethos can also be extended to staff who are not family members: for example, John Spedan Lewis made staff partners in the John Lewis family firm invoking shared company values and commitment to the development of the firm.[14]

The culture in a family firm is borne of the firm comprising the sum of individuals who have shared business aims and are bonded by emotional ties. While collective vision and activity are important in all firms it is more likely to be more impactful in family firms because it is strengthened in many cases by family relationships and bonds. The complex relationship dynamics in family firms can also often be detrimental too. Nordqvist and Melin[1] maintain that conflicts can include:

> sibling rivalry, perceived unfairness in the division of ownership among family members, children's wishes to differentiate themselves from their parents, and marital discord.
>
> (p.223)

So, while family can strengthen a business, it can also be a divisive force, and it is to the importance of family relationships in the family firm context that we now turn.

FAMILY RELATIONSHIPS

Taking part in a family business can perhaps be summed up by this statement from Carol Kennedy[14] (p. 1) in her account of three of the UK's most well-known family firms: Sainsbury, Cadbury and John Lewis: 'Being part of a family is a universal human experience, at once suffocating, infuriating, comforting and supportive.'

Peter Leach,[15] (p. 1) expands on this idea. He claims that the entwined relationships – as family and as business associates – are complex and require that those involved manage them effectively for the benefit of the family and of the firm:

> As well as making the right decisions on the commercial problems that beset all enterprises, family business people have to be able to analyse the special dynamics that surround their businesses and their families.

If members of the same family start a firm, or if a firm owned by one family member employs other family members, there are often major issues to be dealt with. Many of these stem from the relationships within the family group. As well as the organizational structure,[16] issues of survival and/or success can depend on how individuals work together.[17] Lank investigated stakeholders with interests in family businesses and found that these parties have key roles to play if their goals are aligned with the business.[18] The parties associated with the family may be fairly broad-ranging, but one would expect that the group may include, in the direct line, parents, children and grandchildren. Also the group may include spouses, siblings and even cousins.[19] As a business develops over time, and particularly through generations, the complexity increases: for example, in 1990 there were 300 members of the Cadbury family with shares through trusts set up by previous generations.[14] For many firms, relationships have to be managed: family relationships and business relationships are not the same and there can be conflict in terms of prioritizing the family as a unit or the business as a unit.[1] The Stepek family case study at the end of this chapter illustrates some of the problems a family can face from internal and external pressures on the business and the family.

The favouring of family from a business perspective can be highly detrimental to a firm: employing family members can cause much friction amongst non-family staff, particularly where the family appoints inept or less able family members in senior positions, or where inequitable reward systems based on family status are applied. In turn these kinds of issues can act as barriers to recruitment of talented staff from outside.

Where relationships between family members are not good, further problems can arise and issues brought into the organization can become difficult to deal with. Sibling rivalry can cause major areas of concern such as in-fighting, jealousy and power struggles.[20; 21; 22] Fleming[23] identifies seven deadly sins, including sibling rivalry, that can destroy a business and one cause of this can be that the children have not resolved critical issues from their childhood.

Growing concerns associated with the business in its initial stage are likely to be dealt with by the founder and their immediate colleagues (family, siblings or partners) and, just as firms pass through stages similar to or the same as those identified by Churchill and Lewis[24] (see Chapter 10), the family firm may experience periods of stress that have a bearing on their relationships both as business associates and as family. In larger organizations, tensions can become public knowledge and cause possible harm. For example, the relationship between Henry Ford and his son Edsel was known to be fraught with problems and Henry was often seen to over-rule, dominate and humiliate Edsel publicly. Despite this, Edsel's contribution to the Ford business was significant during his short reign of the firm (Edsel died early leaving the firm in the hands of his son Henry Ford Jr). He developed the firm from production of the original Model T through to the introduction of other cars as the industry developed commercially and competitively.[25]

Relationships in family firms can impact the business, and in turn, business can impact family relationships. These can be horizontal relationships between siblings and spouses, or vertical relationships through generations as illustrated by the Ford example. It is to these intergenerational issues that we now turn.

FAMILY FIRMS THROUGH THE GENERATIONS

The proportion of family firms surviving through to the third generation and beyond is small and figures from Leach and Bogod[26] show that only 24 per cent of family businesses survive to the second generation and that only 14 per cent survive to the generation after that. Similar is found by Smyrnios and Walker in Australia[5] in which it is estimated that around 67 per cent of firms are family-owned businesses with approximately 55 per cent surviving the first generation and 28 per cent the second. French data covering much of the twentieth century[27] show that the proportion of managers at the second generation or beyond never exceeded 35 per cent. In part, this was seen as being caused by the difficulties in the transmission of ownership of the firm within the family group; that is, the succession of ownership, which will be discussed in the next section of this chapter.

It is difficult enough, in today's economic climate, to grow and develop a business and keep control. For example, firms in high-technology niche markets may well have competitors or customers trying to buy them out for their knowledge and expertise.[28] Alternatively, they may attract investors who offer development funds for a share in the firm. Thus, the business may not exist for long enough to be passed down through the family.

Although the large majority may not survive to the third generation, some of the survivors go on to become major international players. In fact, many of the big businesses emerging from families are household names such as Levi-Strauss, Mars, Wal-Mart Stores and Michelin. In Italy, the Agnelli family has become renowned because of the vast power and influence acquired that spans industry, politics, finance, the press, culture and society. The family owns the Fiat industrial complex, which not only makes cars, but a wide range of other

THE FIAT LEGACY

Fiat is one of Europe's largest companies with interests in many different industries including transportation, bio-engineering and financial services. As well as manufacturing automobiles, the company is also involved in commercial vehicles, engine components and tractors. The company was founded in 1899 by Giovanni Agnelli and other businessmen in Turin in Italy. The company began manufacturing automobiles and engine parts in the early part of the twentieth century and an early aim of the business was to control better the manufacturing process by reducing dependence on other suppliers. With the help of Vittorio Valletta from 1921, the company began to grow and diversify. Agnelli set up a holding company in 1927, Industrial Fiduciary Institute (IFI), which is now owned and operated by Agnelli's heirs. In 1945, with the death of Giovanni Agnelli, Vittorio Valletta took over as President and Managing Director. In 1966 he was succeeded by Giovanni Agnelli III, the founder's grandson. A merger was struck with Ferrari in 1969 and they also took control of Lancia. By 1999 they owned 90 per cent of Ferrari. Umberto, Giovanni's brother, a talented salesman, became second-in-command in 1972. Over the years the company has endured turbulent times at home and abroad as a result of competition and economic fluctuations. These also afforded the firm opportunities, however: for example, the company thrived in developing markets such as eastern Europe and South America. In the late 1970s the company reorganized and modernized its manufacturing processes including the use of assembly robots. Output per worker increased by over 60 per cent.

Giovanni Agnelli III died in 2003 and his brother Umberto became Chairman until he died in 2004. Luca Cordero di Montezemolo was named as Chairman, and Agnelli's heir John Elkann became Vice Chairman.[7; 29] See also www.fiatgroup.com.

products such as defence equipment (see box on the Fiat legacy).[29] Another family business to make it on the international scene (and also Italian) is Benetton. This family business has developed a brand which has been extremely adept at inventing and reinventing itself.[30]

Other intergenerational issues for entrepreneurial family firms include those associated with the development of the firm as it passes through growth and other entrepreneurial phases and ownership changes as a result of both family and business developments. For many family firms, particularly those that experience entrepreneurial growth, the role of the family changes as the organization develops.[15; 23] Ownership and control may change over time as shareholders and professional management are brought in and difficulties can be experienced; for example, in investment, direction and expansion. Family ownership may begin to move from total control to a diluted holding through the introduction of private shareholders or public shareholders. The life cycle of these development phases generally begins from the entrepreneurial owner-managed firm and this is passed through to the new generation after training and the development of the individuals. The next phase of the development generally coincides with changing direction for the business that involves the inflow of new partners or shareholders. Overall, if handled successfully, this results in a power transfer from the family through to professional management. However, it is common that, although the large shareholding is no longer with the family, the name of the family and key individuals are retained because of their importance to shareholders and the market. A famous British example of this is Cadbury. Sir Adrian Cadbury was still Chairman of the Board while his family held only 2 per cent of the shares.[14] In fact, from 1962 the Cadbury-Fry family held 50 per cent of Cadbury following the flotation of the company and this has been diluted over the years, including trustees of the family trusts diversifying portfolios into other areas following the change away from family ownership.

On the flip side of this, some previously successful family firms can experience periods of (sometimes serious) contraction or even failure as a result of either or both the business environment during subsequent generations and the style, ambitions and abilities of proceeding generations of owners. An example of this is given in the case study McGonagall Hats later in this chapter, whereupon the heir was unable to sustain the success of his father's firm. Similarly, the case study on Stepek at the end of this chapter illustrates that the complexities of family relationships, often amongst post-founder generations, can result in business failure, as family attention to business is distracted by rivalries and in-fighting.

SUCCESSION

Birley et al. found in their study of family firms that from 208 respondents, 45 per cent were children of the founder and 27 per cent were grandchildren.[31] Research conducted by Harvey[4] on family firms' succession practices identifies the following types of firm transition.

- Having one heir, 'the crown prince' – however chosen. A good example of this is Samsung where the founder chose his successor from the family (see box on the entrepreneurial global family firm).
- Having a 'sibling partnership', where roles are enacted according to the talents of the family – such as Baxters (see below).
- The 'cousin consortium', where the family ownership means that some members are active at senior levels while others are working their way up the organization. Some may also be passive shareholders.
- The 'stop-gap manager', who holds the fort until the next generation is ready. In part this was the case at Fiat, but Vittorio Valletta was more than this and held the top position for 21 years.
- Family ownership and professional managers. In this situation the family may not have anyone who could run the business, or who wanted to run the business, so professionals are brought in while the family retains ownership.

- A management buy-out.
- Selling the business in the marketplace.
- Disposing of the organization as an asset sale; that is, liquidating assets to get cash.

Succession in family firms can prove difficult for a number of reasons including the different ambitions and attitudes of the next-generation family members.[32]

While the original aim of the founder may have been to pass the firm on to future generations, this may not always be the best course of action for the firm. Where a business is passed to an heir, resentment can prevail amongst staff, especially where the heir is less able, is ill-qualified or ill-equipped to lead the organization. To a non-family member, who may well have much-needed knowledge or skills, this can cause great frustration as demonstrated in the case of McGonagall Hats later in this chapter. Over and above this, there are well-documented cases of autocratic or paternalistic styles of management within the family dynasty: Henry Ford, for example, was known to micro-manage and dominate the firm even after his son had officially taken over leadership.[25] Other issues involve sibling rivalry, as illustrated in the Stepek case. This type of rivalry can be an amplification of established family rivalries. Audrey Baxter, of the Baxter Foods family, outlined the importance of the roles with her siblings[33] (p. 15) when she succeeded her father as CEO: 'We are three very different people but our reasons for being in the company are the same.' She also explained that she and her siblings made a point of communicating much and often in order to keep everyone informed about company activities.

ENTREPRENEURSHIP IN ACTION

Byung-Chull Lee and Samsung

The Samsung Commercial Company was incorporated by Byung-Chull Lee in 1938. He had moved to Taegu in south-eastern Korea in 1936 and established a rice mill, using an inheritance to do so. Between 1936 and 1938 he traded in a wide range of products including wool and textiles. By 1938 the company employed 40 staff and began to expand into Manchuria and China. Today, Samsung's flagship division, Samsung Electronics, is one of the world's largest makers of computer memory chips – after Samsung became involved in 1980 with the purchase of the Korea Telecommunications Company. The division also manufactures a wide range of commonly used electronic products such as mobile phones and microwave ovens. Other divisions in the group deal in heavy industries, life insurance, securities and trading. Before his death in 1987, Byung-Chull Lee chose his third son, Kun-Hee Lee, as his successor and gradually relinquished control to him. This is regarded as unusual, as the eldest son is normally in this position, but it is believed that Byung-Chull Lee felt that Kun-Hee Lee was most capable of operating the company. Samsung Electronics (2007) is listed at 46 in the Fortune Global 500 (Electronics, electrical equipment) with revenues of $89 476 million, and 138 000 employees.[7] See also www.samsung.com.

Succession is not only a difficult issue for family firms: it affects all privately owned businesses. Succession is most often thought of in terms of retirement of the business owner, but in fact it is brought about for a variety of reasons. The report *SME Ownership Succession* by Martin et al.,[34] for the former Small Business Service (SBS), cites harvesting, personal reasons or retirement as the three most common inducements to succession, most often when owners are in their late fifties or early sixties. New owners of the business may come from external buyers or a continuation of the business from inside.

The research for the former SBS [34] was conducted in three regions of England and business advisers interviewed during the course of the study were concerned about the high proportion of ageing owners who were making no provision for the succession or continuity of their businesses when they withdrew. Owner-managed firms without a distinct management team and having between 10 and 50 employees were seen as being particularly vulnerable to succession failure. The SBS's statistics suggest that some 54 000 small firms in the UK (based on 35 per cent of owners exposed to age-related issues and representing around 1 million jobs) were at risk of succession failure.

Succession in family firms can be problematic for a variety of reasons. First, business growth can often be personal to the owner who might have difficulty relinquishing control.[34] They may believe that their successor is not good enough to do the job or they may take exception to a change in vision and direction of the organization their successor is planning. This can present some difficulties, but diplomacy and discussion are essential in order to bring both visions into line for the future of the organization. Also problematic are circumstances where successors are dependent upon the original owner/manager making decisions or cannot or will not take full control while the founder is still alive – even where he or she might have officially exited the firm. Other problems arise where there is no natural internal successor and the founder has to continue until such time as an heir comes of age or experience or an alternative manager can be found. In many cases an owner ignores the need for succession altogether. Fleming[23] suggests that in some family firms the succession issue is avoided because it can raise unpleasant family problems and issues that cause pain and conflict; the issue of succession forces the parent(s) to confront their own mortality and they may fear a loss of personal control in the business.

The report, *Leadership in Family Business*[8] by Nigel Nicholson of London Business School, found that from a sample of approximately 150 UK companies, the average age of board members was over 50. While 30 per cent of the sample had actually gone beyond the third generation, more than half of the companies were unable to state what kind of succession they would be looking for in the future; that is, from a family member or from someone from outside the business. Nicholson highlighted that loyalty was ranked very highly, in the top three of the important qualities sought by the boards. Perhaps significantly, 60 per cent of the sample did not have a non-executive director on their board – showing that these family businesses were still dominated by the family.

For many family firms though, over time family ownership may begin to move from total control to some degree of a diluted holding. This occurs through the introduction of private or public shareholders. The succession phase may well coincide with a change of business development and can coincide with a change in direction for the business. With the inflow of new partners or shareholders, a power transfer from the family through to professional management may be the result. This leads to a number of key questions relating to the personal qualities of CEOs; that is, the way to choose a successor and the involvement of the outgoing owner(s).

Robert Heller[35] outlines instances of disaster for family succession and he gives advice that fits all types of business, including promotion on merit and promoting talent in the organization. He also suggests the use of elder states-people to guide the younger managers – similar to the use of mentoring in entrepreneurship. Crucially, like business guru Tom Peters,[36] he advocates keeping close to the customer base. Successful succession in a family business requires an understanding of the situation, and appropriate training and experience of the successor. Failure to implement a successful succession may be due to reasons related to members of the family wishing to exit from the business, for example where the immediate heirs are seeking to establish themselves in different careers. Planning for succession is vital and a number of approaches and guides are available from sources, such as the ACCA[4] and BDO Stoy Hayward.[37; 38] Guides such as these most often identify the following issues as critical for succession:

- Plan for succession early
- Develop a written succession plan, involving relevant family and business colleagues
- Make use of outside help
- Establish a training process for the next generation

The importance of succession in business cannot be underestimated, particularly if incoming investors are involved, who not only wish to protect their investment but also want to see a successful business achieve its potential. The timing of succession and the departure by either the founder or chief executive of the company is not trivial. It is not just about age; it is also associated with the individual's energy and his or her willingness to push ahead with the things they are attempting to achieve.

McGONAGALL HAT FACTORY[1]

Contributed by Dr John Sanders, Heriot-Watt University

BACKGROUND

McGonagall Hat Factory was established in the early 1900s by Angus McGonagall to fill a growing demand for headwear in New Zealand. New Zealand has a largely temperate climate, but the weather can change unexpectedly, average rainfall is high and evenly spread throughout the year, and the level of solar ultraviolet radiation is very harsh, particularly during the summer months. As a consequence, immigrants demanded high quality hats that were durable enough to survive New Zealand's climatic conditions.

Up until the early 1960s nearly every New Zealander wore a hat, so hat-making thrived. However, during the mid-1960s, hat-wearing went out of fashion and the industry went into rapid decline. The hat-making companies that survived, including McGonagall Hat Factory, got into manufacturing cotton and straw hats requiring big production runs that kept operations viable. These surviving hat-makers were also helped by supplying a demand that was very heavily protected by import licensing which kept out overseas products. However, with deregulation of the New Zealand economy in the early 1980s, the company had to compete with an influx of cheap overseas, imports. In 1986, due to declining earnings and profits caused by low-cost hats from overseas, the great-grandson of Angus McGonagall sold the company to the clothing wholesaler Ben Harris and Sargood, a company that had acquired other hat-makers during the demise of the hat trade during the 1960s.

ALF PERKINSON

Eighteen months after Ben Harris and Sargood's acquisition of McGonagall Hat Factory, they sold the company along with a number of other clothing-related businesses due to debt problems. In a management buyout, Alf Perkinson, who managed hat operations for Ben Harris and Sargood, successfully purchased the McGonagall Hat Factory. Alf had been in the hat business for 30 years. He mortgaged his house and invested all of his savings to acquire the company. Along with the factory the purchase also included

---

[1] The case study McGonagall Hats is based on a firm in New Zealand. Names and some details have been changed.

around 500 hat blocks (some hat blocks were decades old). Hat blocks are essential for shaping either felt or straw into the specific style of hat required by the hat-maker. The number of hat blocks owned by the company gave it the greatest variety of hat styles and head sizes available in Australasia.

Alf's first decision as the new owner of the McGonagall Hat Factory was to focus on making up-market hats. This meant ending the factory's low-cost hat production. He also started to make branded hats (i.e. hats featuring organisational logos and names) for new customers like large companies, schools and sporting bodies.

One of the challenges for Alf was to find ways to sell hats. Most of Alf's stocks ended up in major department stores in both New Zealand and Australia. But what really gave his business a big boost was when the company began making hats under licence. In the late 1980s he began to make hats for the likes of the All Blacks, New South Wales and English rugby league teams and Canterbury International. Licensing work was secure as long as quality was maintained.

MELANOMA SCARE

The company received a further boost in sales due to the high incidence of the skin cancer known as melanoma in New Zealand, the deadliest of the known types of skin cancer. It appears that years of enjoying the sun during the warmer months without wearing a hat had taken its toll on New Zealanders' health. Between 1960 and 1990 the number of cases of melanoma in New Zealand doubled. Publicity surrounding melanoma caused a big surge in demand for casual hats.

With the return of the hat there was a rapid increase in the number of competitors making them, but they were mainly small boutique and designer operations, not volume producers like McGonagall Hat Factory. By the early 1990s the McGonagall Hat Factory was making more than NZ $4 million worth of head gear per year and producing about 350,000 hats annually in Auckland and Wellington. At this point it had become the largest hat-making company in the country. The company made almost 800 different styles, everything from bush hats, felt and wool hats, beach straws and sport caps, to ladies high fashion.

ALF PASSES AWAY

In early 2006, aged 70, Alf had a stroke and died suddenly. Control of the company passed to his son, Craig. Forty-three-year-old Craig had been a senior civil servant so had very limited knowledge and experience of the factory's operations or business in general. Craig's management style was in some respects like Alf's, as they both had a preference for being autocratic in their decision-making. However, the difference between the two is how they applied this preference. Alf in many ways behaved as a father figure to the workers; he was interested in their welfare, but still perceived that it was his exclusive right to make every decision. Most of the employees tolerated Alf's management style because he had saved their jobs back in 1986 and then he had gone on to improve company performance. Craig's management style on the other hand was much less subtle. He was dictatorial in terms of how operations should be run, and he expected absolute obedience. He closely supervised and controlled workers in all of their tasks, and was known as a micro-manager. Over time his style of management demotivated the highly skilled and experienced workforce and created a 'him and us' organisational culture. Craig did not seem to realise that he could not afford to alienate his workforce, because their individual skills were extremely valuable and would be difficult to replace if they decided to leave in large numbers. Craig was also seen as an interloper who had been given responsibility of the company via birth rather than merit.

Craig's objectives for the firm were exclusively about increasing output. In an effort to improve factory layout and utilisation Craig sold or dumped over 100 of the hat blocks Alf had tenderly cherished.

Performance standards procedures were implemented to maximise production from the workforce. Added to this, high-quality suppliers had been replaced in favour of low-quality and cheap providers. Quality problems started to emerge throughout each stage of the production process, i.e. via checks of hat finish, shape, body and feel. Quality was not a feature of either management strategy or workforce commitment. Craig believed that financial performance would be maintained and growth could be accomplished by refocusing on cheap bulk outputs.

CASH CRISIS

In 2007, the company confronted a number of major problems. First, declining quality standards had seen the departure of several key customers (i.e. Air New Zealand, the army, the police and the fire service) to its major competitor in New Zealand, Hills Hats Ltd. Second, within 12 months the company's good mix of customers and good debtors' book had shifted to a focus on fewer customers and a debtor book less well spread. Third, in February 2007, without any notice, its last remaining major customer went into liquidation. The demise of this customer meant McGonagall's faced a large bad debt problem. A tax payment was due to compound McGonagall's cash-flow problems as well. After more than 100 years of operations, McGonagall Hat Factory was in crisis.

DISCUSSION QUESTIONS

1 Having worked in the millinery industry all his life Alf Perkinson jumped at the chance to buy McGonagall Hat Factory. Since 1986 he steered the business through turbulent times and treated it as a labour of love. Without being aware of it, Alf made several mistakes though, and these contributed to the eventual crisis McGonagall Hats faces now. What were the mistakes he made?

2 What could Alf have done to avoid the mistakes you identified for Question 1?

3 What are the problems with Craig Perkinson's management of McGonagall Hats?

4 Describe the changes you would need to make to ensure the survival of the McGonagall Hat Factory.

OTHER CONSIDERATIONS IN FAMILY FIRMS

As with most studies of entrepreneurship and business the most common research focus is at the level of the founding entrepreneur or the business as a unit of analysis. Several researchers have questioned the extent to which this is a valid and appropriate means by which to investigate the complexities and nuances of most business ownership and operation.[12] The family firm is a very good example of a business entity that does not easily 'fit', in many cases, the traditional means of inspecting much of the activities and function of firms and the issues that affect them.

In Chapter 4 of this book women's entrepreneurship and the fact that much female entrepreneurship is 'hidden' by the fact that many firms are co-owned with men by women (and therefore are not usually included in the 'women's entrepreneurship' count) are discussed. Many family firms are started by a husband and wife team – sometimes this team is formally structured and in other cases the arrangement is less formal, whereby the husband 'owns' the firm but is supported, assisted and sometimes even employs (paid or unpaid) the owner's wife (as was the case for Jan Stepek detailed at the end of this chapter). Marshack[39] refers to women in business with their husbands as 'copreneurs' and certainly, businesses that are co-owned or that employ people related by birth or marriage to the owner are well within the definition of family firms. The role of women in family firms is an under-researched area; however, Hamilton[40] provides some insights. Findings from Hamilton's research demonstrate the complexity of family firms – that no two are the same and that a wide variety of management and operational styles can be observed. The research also implicates the role of family support – emotional and operational – as a significant factor in business success in many cases. Critically, Hamilton's study refutes the idea, common in entrepreneurship research, that firms are started and developed by the 'heroic male' stereotype and she demonstrates that control, decision-making and management are not always exclusively the domain of the male 'head of family' in family firms. Indeed she provides an example of a firm in which the male owner appears to customers, suppliers and stakeholders the dominant partner, but in fact this bears no relation to the power, control and operations internal to the business. In this case, it is the wife who runs the firm and the presentation to the outside world is a deliberate strategy on the part of the family in response to common perceptions amongst the business community about who *should* be in charge (p. 267).

The complexity of family firms reflects the ongoing business and family relationship and resource dynamic. Yilmazer and Schrank[11] identify that the extent to which the family is used as a business resource, and indeed the extent to which family resources and business resources are indiscriminate for families with firms, is not well understood. It is likely that the role of family members, especially women, and the appropriation and use of resources in family firms merits more investigation from researchers. Indeed, the suggestion is that it would afford a better understanding of entrepreneurship generally, that takes into account the infinite variation and complexity of roles and functions of different actors within firms.

EXITING THE FAMILY FIRM

There are many reasons for a family wishing to exit from a business. Amongst these is business failure: the 'rags to riches and back again in three generations' phenomenon. Failure may occur through the lack of innovation, a lack of investment, or disinterest from the family. If the company stagnates, through lack of innovation in its products or services, it may become outmoded or outdated and require substantial investment to rectify. Other considerations include family members seeking new pastures and different areas in which to work. It may be that the family members do not want to be involved in the family business and wish to pursue their own business and careers. Most of us will have some knowledge of a business where the founder and owner-manager has developed, in some cases, a multimillion-dollar business, only to find that family members do not wish to stay with the business and have hopes and aspirations for other careers they wish to pursue. A 2004 study featuring a sample of minority ethnic business owners for the Scottish government, illustrated that first-generation immigrants may have started a business in sectors such as retailing and catering, but problems now exist in transferring succession due to the different aspirations of the second generation. Their children were not willing to accept the long hours of work associated with running such businesses.[41] While this was observable amongst this group within the context of identifying issues for specific ethnic minorities, the sentiment can be representative of any family firm – many children of entrepreneurs have no desire to be involved in the family business. In other cases, passing a business on to a family member who is not sufficiently capable or devoted to the success of the firm can spell disaster and can be a source of much frustration to non-family members who might have been better equipped to take control, as in the McGonagall Hats case.

Failure is not the only way family firms experience cessation, however. From the founder's point of view, succession may be their first option, but there are other alternatives such as selling the business altogether[42] – thus becoming a one-generation organization. They may allow a management buy-out based on the workforce they built up or a management buy-in where an external group of managers would take over the firm. As mentioned earlier, in some cases the firm as a family organization need not disappear; family may keep shareholdings while external management run it, as was the case with Cadbury-Fry. Yet another alternative is to sell the business to other relatives.[43]

CONCLUSIONS

The importance of the family business cannot be understated. Although a large number of these organizations come and go, some achieve great growth, influence and contribution to the economy. The attrition rate is high and research from around the world indicates that few family-owned buinesses make it to the third generation and beyond.

Although family businesses may have problems, such as internal family politics and the normal rivalries that exist between siblings, the family business has played an enormous role in building the society in which we live. A great deal of support can come from the family and company culture and values are seen as important. New generations of family members need to fill an appropriate role and situations can arise that warrant the inclusion of professional senior managers – for example, where family members are not experienced enough or sufficiently qualified to take on senior positions.

The question of succession in family firms is vital and occupies a great deal of the research available on family-owned businesses. The obvious successor need not necessarily be the oldest family heir and planning the succession process is vital for ensuring success. Planning early is important and ensuring that stakeholders are involved will aid success of the plan – setting up a family group or council may be the best way forward. Formal education and training are vital ingredients for the execution of the plan. Although the succession issue can arise through death or retirement, there may be other reasons such as ill health or the founding entrepreneur wishing to move on to a new project.

In some instances the heir to the business may not come from the family, for example where a senior manager fills a stop-gap role until the family member is ready to assume a senior role. There may also be management buy-out situations where the family will sell their shares to an experienced internal management group and, in this instance, venture capitalists may become involved by providing funds, expertise and even a new CEO.

The role of the outgoing CEO is important and he or she may act as an adviser or mentor to the new CEO. It may also be difficult for them to accept the position they are in and part of the planning process has to include aspects of acceptance and change. At the heart of a business it is all about people, and family businesses also cope with the relationships, good and bad, that exist between family members.

The case study, 'Stepek', illustrates some of the key issues in family-owned businesses.

SUMMARY

PROBLEMS OF MANAGEMENT IN FAMILY BUSINESSES

- Family positions, either their role in the business or the various stances they may take over decision-making. For example, individuals may find themselves in a proactive role when they feel they are not qualified for it or even want to take on the role. Situations like this can occur due to the death of a parent.

- Politics within family factions can arise. For example, due to the role given to a family member's heir, i.e. not the CEO, or in the shareholding allocation to family members.

- The decision-making process may prove difficult because of the dominance of certain family members and a lack of objectivity, or because the business's best interests are not central. It may also be that the family involvement is so broad that it is difficult to get consensus.

- Sibling rivalry can result from many things including jealousy on almost any basis, e.g. company position, earnings, shareholding and potential prospects.

- Conflict can arise from the above as well as from external sources such as a rival wishing to buy the business.

- Nepotism can occur through the appointment of family members over those outside the family who have greater experience and qualifications for the position they are given. This can give rise to discontent in the workforce and the loss of very able members of staff.

- Flotation of the business can bring many problems (as well as benefits) for the family. Initially they will lose the amount of shareholding and control they have, external directors will be appointed and some members may be removed from their positions in favour of qualified individuals.

ENTREPRENEURSHIP IN ACTION

Jan and Martin Stepek and the Stepek family business[2]

INTRODUCTION

Polish-born Jan Stepek had a turbulent youth. He lost his mother to starvation, had endured slavery in a Soviet gulag, and as a Polish Navy radar operator had survived hunger, typhoid, dysentery, malaria, the invasion of Sicily and the Normandy D-Day landings during the Second World War.

In 1945 he was demobbed from the Navy in Plymouth and headed for Glasgow to study Engineering at the Royal College of Technology (now University of Strathclyde). Using his navy and engineering skills he became self-employed and repaired radios at people's houses, while his wife kept the business books. His good name and reputation grew and he opened the first shop in 1953 and formed a limited company in 1957. By 1960, he had built the business to a chain of six shops. The business grew into television rental and sales of electrical goods, where they competed against big High Street names in Scotland. As the business grew, so did the Stepek family: Jan and his wife had ten children. The oldest son, John, joined the firm in 1968, straight from school, followed between 1975 and 1983 by the other children – some more suited to business than others. By 2000 company turnover was £12 million.

THE FAMILY/BUSINESS SITUATION

It seemed like a good idea at the time, so right, so clever. Make maximum use of legal loopholes to reduce tax by giving your children shares in the family business stage by stage, in trusts. It appeared simple: ten kids, each to inherit 10 per cent of the shares each. Nice round numbers, no decimal points, no need even for a calculator. Coupled with this was investment in pensions. In good years, the idea was to contribute to

---

[2] We are grateful to Martin Stepek for the 'Entrepreneurship in Action' box on the Stepek family business.

the family pension scheme as much as possible, in each of the names in the group, up to the legal maximum. The business had the finest lawyers and accountants and followed their sage advice.

Some 20 years later and the motley crew of young men and women who were the Stepek siblings had become adults in their thirties, forties and fifties. All were now married, nine of the ten siblings had children of their own, and of course spouses. Ten spouses for 10 siblings, 20 children for 20 married husband and wives – and all those shares and pension funds. Sounds like a ball, does it not? Problem – whose ball was it? And whose rules were the Stepeks to play by?

Unfortunately, the financial plan did not turn out the way it had been planned. Because of those ingenious schemes to avoid tax, by 1999 one brother had over 15 per cent of the shares in his family, while the youngest had about 3 per cent. And those pension contributions? Well, they did not really reflect normal salaried levels of pension contributions so over the decades they were skewed. They were in fact more like profits than standard 10 or 12 per cent of salary pension schemes.

The family reviewed the history of the pensions contributions and reasoned as follows:

If they were actually more like profits, shouldn't they be considered quasi-dividends? Well maybe, but what's in a label? Dividend, pension contribution, it's all just money, isn't it? Except, dividends get paid according to how many shares you owned, while pensions are supposed to reflect salary or effort or something like that.

Of course, *some* of the pension money was *actual* pension money and that could be worked out retrospectively by calculations. But what about all the extra contributions? The thinking was that they could be called dividends retrospectively too. So the family could start to redistribute the excess pension holdings and share it equally among the 10 siblings. Aware that shareholdings were not distributed by the 10 per cent per individual that was supposed to happen, the first step was to redistribute the shares first to 10 per cent apiece, *then* redistribute the pension holdings that – maybe – was dividend. This would mean it would be all sorted the way Mum and Dad wanted, the whole wealth distribution would reflect equal ownership and individual sweat equity and the family could get back to running the business again. Except – family issues reared to the fore!

Well, says one sibling – or two, or ten, it does not matter who said what now in hindsight – I have my own kids to worry about and my spouse says why do we need to redistribute anything anyway? After all it was all done legally and agreed at the time, and anyway, we were just kids, it was Dad who chose to do it this way; and yes, I know we have a lot more than 10 per cent of the shares and six times your pension pot, but well I have my own spouse and kids to consider. Of course if it was just the 10 of us brothers and sisters it would be easy...

Meanwhile, the business had been going very well until a change in fiscal policy in the year 2000. The government increased IPT (insurance premium tax) from 4.5 per cent to VAT levels. The problem for the Stepeks was that they had tens of thousands of rental televisions and videos all with IPT. The key issue was that if they passed on the cost to the customers, all those old televisions and videos would come piling back into the warehouse because their competitors, Radio Rentals and Granada, had sufficient reserves to maintain their rental rates. This loss of customers would severely affect the company's cash flow. Potentially, income would dwindle to the extent that the company could go bust. So the Stepek family directors decided to maintain their rental rates. The result of this decision meant that they lost over £1 million from the bottom line which ultimately put them in the red – to the tune of £500 000.

THE END GAME

The in-fighting about the distribution of dividends and pensions started to drain the much-needed energy required for running a family business. Interminable board meetings to try to unravel all of the family issues went on year after year, leaving little energy or family unity to focus on the fast-changing electrical retail market. The family could not resolve their issues and the business suffered from a lack of energy and will to continue. The company went bust in 2002. Three hundred and fifty employees lost their jobs. A household name in Lanarkshire, well respected, with a unique culture of real care for their customers, was gone. A major part of the loss was that family issues had impacted the management and operations of the firm to the extent that business and market focus was lost. Comments Marin Stepek:

> If we had focused on the business, the family would have come crashing down. So we focused on the family and the business came crashing down. With sound advice and deep training in family business issues we'd have avoided most of this and handled what remained.

The demise of the business was not entirely due to family matters: some management mistakes had been made and the firm had suffered also from bad timing, ill-luck, and increased competitiveness in the electrical retail sector. By the time the company folded, they had reached around £12 million turnover and had returned to profit. Sound plans were developed, but just too late. In hindsight, perhaps without the incessant family issues they would have made the necessary decisions and transitions in time and survived, even grown.

COMMENT AND EXERCISE

This case illustrates some key issues of family and business and the complexity of relationships within them, and there are many lessons to be learned. In this story, the business goes down – but not the family! As Martin Stepek, CEO of the Scottish Family Business Association (SFBA), says:

> Still, I'm glad it was the business that went down rather than the family. I still have my seven brothers, two sisters, infinite in-laws and nephews and nieces and they're what matters ultimately. You can be very happy and successful without a family business. I've found that out. You can't be happy if you have the most successful business in the world but you've alienated your family. But it would have been best if we could have managed to keep family and business.

REVIEW QUESTIONS

1 How would you define a family firm?
2 What are the advantages of owning and developing a family business?
3 What are the drawbacks to owning and developing a family business?
4 Assume that your father was the founder of the family firm. What problems might you face in taking over as CEO?
5 What are the options available to the founder if no one in the family wishes to succeed him/her?
6 What are the key elements in managing succession?
7 Why do family businesses need a succession plan?
8 What are the founder's options if his or her heirs are not yet old enough or not yet suitably qualified or experienced to take over the family firm?
9 What characteristics and attributes would you look for in a member of a management buy-out?
10 When do you think the family business is most vulnerable?

SUGGESTED ASSIGNMENTS

Using the case study provided of the Stepek company:

1 Identify the key family issues in the case

2 How would you resolve the family/business issues outlined in this case?

3 What advice would you have given to them?

4 How would you organize succession of your firm if you had ten children?

REFERENCES

1 **Nordqvist, M. and Melin, L.** (2010) 'Entrepreneurial families and family firms', *Entrepreneurship and Regional Development*, vol. 22(3–4), pp. 211–39.

2 www.familybusinessmagazine. com; www.familybusinessmagazine.com/topglobal.html (accessed at February 2011).

3 **Drucker, P.** (1995) *Managing in a Time of Great Change*, BCA, London.

4 **Harvey, D.** (2004) *Keeping it in the Family*, ACCA, London.

5 **Smyrnios, K.X. and Walker, R.H.** (2003) *The Boyd Partners Australian Family and Private Business Survey*, RMIT University, Melbourne.

6 **Lumpkin, G.T., Brigham, K.H. and Moss, T.W.** (2010) 'Long-term orientation: Implications for the entrepreneurial orientation and performance of family businesses', *Entrepreneurship and Regional Development*, vol. 22(3–4), pp. 241–64.

7 **Derdak, T.** (ed.) (1988) *International Directory of Company Histories*, St James Press, Chicago, IL and London.

8 **Nicholson, N.** (2003) *Leadership in Family Business*, London Business School, London.

9 (2010) *Entrepreneurship and Regional Development*, vol. 22, no. 3-4.

10 (2010) *Journal of Family and Economic Issues*, vol. 31, no. 4.

11 **Yilmazer, T. and Schrank, H.** (2010) 'The use of owner resources in small and family owned businesses: Literature review and future research directions', *Journal of Family and Economic Issues*, vol. 31(4), pp. 399–413.

12 **Howarth, C., Tempest, S. and Coupland, C.** (2005) 'Rethinking entrepreneurship methodology and definitions of the entrepreneur', *Journal of Small Business and Enterprise Development*, vol. 12(1), pp. 24–40.

13 **Paisner, M.B.** (1999) *Sustaining the Family Business*, Basic Books, New York.

14 **Kennedy, C.** (2000) *The Merchant Princes*, Hutchinson, London.

15 **Leach, P.** (2007) *Family Businesses*, Profile Books, London.

16 **Barry, B.** (1975) 'The development of organisation structure in the family firm', *The Journal of General Management'*, vol. 3, no. 1. pp. 42–60.

17 **Alcorn, P.B.** (1982) *Success and Survival in the Family-Owned Business*, McGraw-Hill, London.

18 **Lank, A.** (1997) 'Making sure the dynasty does not become a Dallas', in S. Birley and D.F. Muzyka (eds), *Mastering Enterprise: Your Single-source Guide to Becoming an Entrepreneur*, Pitman, London.

19 **Poutziouris, P.** (1994) 'The development of the family business', in A. Gibb and M. Rebernick (eds), *Small Business Management in New Europe*, and Procedings of 24th ESBS, Slovenia.

20 **Levinson, H.** (1971) 'Conflicts that plague family businesses', *Harvard Business Review*, March–April, pp. 90–8.

21 **Miller, W.D.** (1998) 'Siblings and succession in the family business (case study)', *Harvard Business Review*, January–February, pp. 22–9.

22 **Kellermans, F.W. and Eddleston, K.A.** (2004) 'Feuding families: when conflict does a family firm good', *Entrepreneurship Theory and Practice*, vol. 28, no. 3, pp. 209–28.

23 **Fleming, Q.J.** (2000) *Keep the Family Baggage Out of the Family Business*, Simon & Schuster, New York.

24 **Churchill, N.C. and Lewis, V.L.** (1983) 'The five stages of small

business growth', *Harvard Business Review*, May–June, pp. 30–50.

25 **Collier, P. and Horowitz, D.** (1987), *The Fords*, Collins, London.

26 **Leach, P. and Bogod, T.** (1999) *The Stoy Hayward Guide to Family Business*, Kogan Page, London.

27 **Lescure, M.** (1999) 'Small and medium industrial enterprises in France 1900–1975', in K. Odaka and M. Sawai (eds), *Small Firms, Large Concerns*, Oxford University Press, Oxford.

28 **Keogh, W., Stewart, V. and Taylor, J.** (2001) 'Developing strategies for growth in HTSFs: looking beyond survival in an increasingly competitive marketplace', in W. During and R. Oakey (eds), *New Technology-Based Firms in the New Millennium*, Pergamon, London.

29 **Friedman, A.** (1988) *Agnelli and the Network of Italian Power*, Harrap, London.

30 **Mantle, J.** (1999) *Benetton: The Family, the Business and the Brand*, Little, Brown, London.

31 **Birley, S., Ng, D. and Godfrey, A.** (1999) 'The family and the business', *Long Range Planning*, vol. 32, no. 6, pp. 598–608.

32 **Le Breton Miller, I., Miller, D. and Steier, L.P.** (2004) 'Towards an integrative model of effective FOB succession', *Entrepreneurship Theory and Practice*, vol. 28, no. 4, pp. 305–28.

33 **Smith, M.** (1996) *Great Scots in Family Business*, report for Scottish Enterprise, Lang Syne, Glasgow.

34 **Martin, C., Martin, L. and Mabbett, A.** (2002) *SME Ownership Succession*, Small Business Service, Sheffield.

35 **Heller, R.** (1998) *Goldfinger: How Entrepreneurs Grow Rich by Starting Small*, Harper-Collins Business, London.

36 **Peters, T. and Waterman, R.H.** (1982) *In Search of Excellence: Lessons from America's Best-Run Companies*, Harper Collins, New York.

37 **BDO Stoy Hayward** (2004) *The Family Business Rulebook*, BDO Stoy Hayward LLP, London, www.bdo.co.uk.

38 **BDO Stoy Hayward** (2004) *Focusing on Business Families*, BDO Stoy Hayward LLP, London, www.bdo.co.uk (accessed at February 2011).

39 **Marshack, K.J.** (1994) 'Copreneurs and dual-career couples:
Are they different?' *Entrepreneurship Theory and Practice*, vol. 19(1), pp. 49–69.

40 **Hamilton, E.E.** (2006) 'Whose story is it anyway? Narrative accounts of the role of women in founding and establishing family businesses', *International Small Business Journal*, vol. 24(3), pp. 253–71.

41 **Deakins, D., Ishaq, M., Smallbone, D., Whittam, G. and Wyper, J.** (2004) *Minority Ethnic Enterprise in Scotland: A National Scoping Study*, Scottish Executive, Edinburgh.

42 **Niedermeyer, C., Jaskiewicz, P. and Klein, S.B.** (2010) 'Can't get no satisfaction? Evaluating the sale of the family business from the family's perspective and deriving implications for new venture activities', *Entrepreneurship and Regional Development*, vol. 22(3–4), pp. 293–320.

43 **Grisanti, D.A.** (1984) 'The agony of selling out to relatives', in D.E. Gumpert (ed.), *Growing Concerns: Building and Managing the Smaller Business*, Harvard Business Review Executive Book Series, John Wiley & Sons, New York.

RECOMMENDED READING

Entrepreneurship and Regional Development (2010) vol. 22, No. 3–4, special edition on Entrepreneurial Families and Family Firms.

Fleming, Q.J. (2000) *Keep the Family Baggage Out of the Family Business*, Simon & Schuster, New York.

Harvey, D. (2004) *Keeping it in the Family*, ACCA, London.

Hoy, F. and Sharma, P. (2010) *Entrepreneurial Family Firms*, Prentice Hall, New Jersey.

Journal of Family and Economic Issues (2010) vol. 31, no. 4, special edition on Family Business.

Leach, P. (2007) *Family Businesses*, Profile Books, London.

Martin, C., Martin, L. and Mabbett, A. (2002) *SME Ownership Succession*, Small Business Service, Sheffield.

Nicholson, N. and Björnberg, Å. (2005) *Family Business Leadership Enquiry*, London Business School, London.

Poutziouris, P.Z., Smyrnios, K.X. and Klein, S.B. (eds) (2007) *Handbook of Research on Family Business*, Edward Elgar, London and Northampton, MA.

Ward, J.L. (2004) *Perpetuating the Family Business: 50 Lessons Learned from Long-lasting, Successful Families in Business*, Palgrave Macmillan, Basingstoke.

4 DIVERSITY IN ENTREPRENEURSHIP: THE ROLE OF WOMEN AND ETHNIC MINORITIES

LEARNING OUTCOMES

At the end of this chapter you should be able to:

* Discuss the differing importance of men, women and ethnic minorities in entrepreneurship.

* Discuss factors that affect the importance and diversity of such roles.

* Describe key characteristics of female entrepreneurship.

* Describe recent policy initiatives to support women's enterprise in the UK.

* Discuss and account for the differing importance of Asian and African-Caribbean entrepreneurs.

* Describe the untapped potential of development that still exists with African and Caribbean entrepreneurs.

* Discuss why the issue of 'break-out' has become important for the future development of ethnic minority entrepreneurs.

INTRODUCTION

This chapter picks up some of the themes introduced in Chapter 1, where we noted that there are different rates of participation in entrepreneurial activity in different regions, in different environments and in different groups of society. For example, we have noted that some ethnic minority groups have high rates of participation in entrepreneurship, despite operating in inner-city environments that might have limited resources and markets. Tables 4.1 and 4.2 indicate the demographic importance of ethnic minorities in the UK; however, they have a greater importance in entrepreneurial activity than their relative importance by population might indicate. Taking self-employment as a proxy for participation in entrepreneurship, Figure 4.1 illustrates some of the variation and diversity in self-employment for ethnic minority groups. Although UK national data are available on the number of small businesses,[1] a breakdown by gender or ethnicity is not available, therefore self-employment data are used as proxy for gender and cultural diversity in entrepreneurship in the UK. Figure 4.1 shows that a number of sectors in society in the UK are under-represented, whereas others are over-represented. For example, Black Africans and Caribbeans are under-represented, whereas the highest rates of self-employment are attained by Pakistanis at over 20 per cent, who easily exceed the rates of self-employment by the next highest ethnic groups who are Chinese and White Irish respectively at around 16 per cent. These rates compare to a national average of 13 per cent, with fewer than 10 per cent from a mixed or black ethnic group. However, the pattern of ethnic minority groups is changing, with more recent immigrants increasing the diversity of the demographics of the UK population.

Ethnic minority owned businesses are vital to the prosperity of the UK economy. According to a recent UK Government report (p. 5):[2]

BAME led businesses are vital to the UK economy. There are an estimated 310,000 ethnic minority SMEs in the UK, contributing an estimated £20 billion to the UK economy per year – approximately 5% of total SME Gross Value Added (GVA).

(BAME here refers to Black and Minority Enterprise)

This chapter reviews recent evidence on the barriers that such groups face in participation. Equality of opportunity in society should be available to all groups, yet, in certain cases, barriers may exist due to institutional

TABLE 4.1 POPULATION ESTIMATES FOR ETHNIC MINORITY GROUPS IN THE UK

	Population	Percentage of UK population	Percentage of ethnic minority population
White	54.15 million	92.1	n/a
Mixed	6.77 million	1.2	14.6
All ethnic minorities	4.6 million	7.9	100.0
Indian	1.05 million	1.8	22.7
Pakistani	0.75 million	1.3	16.1
Bangladeshi	280,000	0.5	6.1
Other Asian	248,000	0.4	5.3
Caribbean	566,000	1.0	12.2
African	485,000	0.8	10.5
Other black	98,000	0.2	2.1
Chinese	247,000	0.4	5.3
Other	231,000	0.4	5.0
All UK population	58.8 million		

Source: *Annual Population Survey, January 2004 to December 2004*, Office for National Statistics, London. Crown Copyright material is reproduced with the permission of the Controller of HMSO and the Queen's Printer for Scotland.

practices that naturally favour men over women, or white business-owners over ethnic minority business-owners. Access to resources, such as finance, or access to markets, may be more limited due to formal institutional practices that favour specific groups in society. For example, formal business networks such as local chambers of commerce may be male dominated, with an influence on agendas that reflects such a biased membership. This can limit women's ability to access local business networks. We review recent evidence on the importance of such barriers in this chapter.

Recent data on population estimates put the UK population as approaching 62.3 million (2010 data) with population growth increasing with increased net in-migration.[4] According to the Office for National Statistics (ONS): 'Since the late 1990s – net international migration into the UK from abroad has been an increasingly important factor accounting for 45 per cent of total change.'[3] This indicates that 'new' migrants, for example from eastern Europe, are among some of the most recent waves of new in-migration forming increasingly important 'new communities' as illustrated in Figure 4.2.[5]

The UK population is predicted to increase to 65.6 million by 2018 and to over 70 million by 2029, with an average annual growth rate of 0.7 per cent. Much of the increase in population will come from the increasing ethnic diversity of the UK's population.[6]

We examine some of the known features of female entrepreneurship and then ethnic minority entrepreneurship in the rest of this chapter, including factors affecting start-up, growth and diversity, illustrated with appropriate case examples.

TABLE 4.2 POPULATION SIZE BY ETHNIC GROUP FOR ENGLAND & WALES (000s, 2007 DATA)

	Population	Percentage of total E&W population
White	47976.5	88.7
Mixed	893.8	0.17
Asian or British Indian	1329.6	2.5
Asian or British Pakistani	916.7	1.7
Asian or British Bangladeshi	360.4	0.7
British or Other Asian	344.1	0.6
Black or Black British Caribbean	602.9	1.1
Black or Black British African	736.6	1.4
Black or Black British Other Black	118.5	0.2
Chinese or Other Ethnic Group Chinese	408.8	0.8
Chinese or Other Ethnic Group Other	384.1	0.7
All England & Wales	54072	

Source: Office for National Statistics.

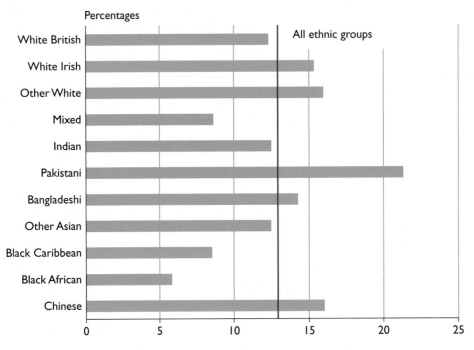

Percentages

FIGURE 4.1

Self-employment as a percentage of all in employment: by ethnic group, 2004

SOURCE: Ethnicity & Identity Employment Patterns: Annual Population Survey.

FEMALE ENTREPRENEURSHIP

by Dr Laura Galloway, Heriot-Watt University

INTRODUCTION

Throughout the world the female business start-up rate is substantially lower than that for males: often around half in a typical European or equivalent mature economy.[7; 8] The volume of female-owned firms is similarly low compared to those of men: for example, in the UK the Women's Enterprise Taskforce reports that female-owned businesses account for only 15 per cent of British business stock, and Harding reports for the Taskforce that women's business ownership is just 33 per cent of the rate of male business ownership.[9] However, Carter and Shaw[10] contend that if the definition of 'female-owned' is extended to include those with equal co-ownership 'it is estimated that between 34.1 per cent and 41.2 per cent of the UK business stock is included' (p. 6). These female business-owners are often termed 'hidden' entrepreneurs, in that, as co-owners with male(s), their firms are often not defined as female owned. Forson[11] argues that estimates of women's contribution to small-firm ownership are limited by this problem with definition and statistics; indeed, qualitative studies such as Marshack,[12] who refers to women in business with their husbands as 'copreneurs', and Hamilton,[13] who studies women in family firms, have found that co-owning females can have as much influence in a firm as their male partners (see Chapter 3 for a full discussion of family firms, and in particular, women's roles in them).

While the number of firms owned by women may be much greater than statistics reveal, Carter and Shaw find that where UK firms are wholly or majority owned, women still comprise a substantially lower proportion of business owners than men.[10] This is reflected throughout the developed world.[14] In the twenty-first century, however, female entrepreneurship has been growing at a higher rate than male entrepreneurship, especially in sectors such as education and community services.[15] This is seen as a positive trend and governments are keen to support and increase this trend in order to contribute to the economic base, provide employment[14] and particularly female employment.[16]

Despite the increased rate of start-up, Morris et al. find that women's firms are more likely to be smaller or sole proprietorships than male-owned firms.[17] Carter and Shaw also note this and that self-employment is nearly twice as likely among women as business ownership.[10] Similar characteristics of women's enterprise can be found elsewhere.[18]

FEMALE BUSINESS-OWNERS?

Carter[19] identifies that studies of female entrepreneurship have 'presented a prima facie picture of business women with more similarities than differences to their male counterparts' (p. 328). However, variation is observed also. These include that women business-owners are more likely than men to have close family in business;[20; 21] the greatest proportion are older than 35;[13] they are less likely than male business-owners to take up training;[20] and most are comparatively highly educated,[13] though often are not trading in their educational area.[22] Despite these general trends, there is much consensus that women entrepreneurs do not comprise a homogeneous group[20; 19; 11] and represent instead 'a diverse and complex group with varied backgrounds, circumstances and world views' according to Sarri and Trihopoulou[16] (p. 29). There is, thus, much variation in the types of firms women own, and as much variation in the type of woman who starts or owns a firm as there is among men. Just as there are exceptional male business-owners who add spectacularly to the value of the firms they create, and to the economic base, so too are there women whose experience of value-adding business success is exceptional, especially compared with other women of similar circumstances. For example, male entrepreneurs such as Richard Branson are highly exceptional in having created and driven a brand as successful as the Virgin Group. There are examples also of women who stand out as spectacularly successful, such as Anita Roddick of The Body Shop. More generally, though, it is claimed that business opportunity and success are less available to, and less experienced by, women compared with men.

FEMALES' FIRMS

In terms of the firms females own, various similarities have been found by empirical studies. The most prevalent of these is that while male-owned firms are represented in all industries, women-owned businesses tend to be concentrated in the retail and services industries.[9; 23; 24; 14; 25] Schmidt and Parker[29] contend that this is 'the logical extrapolation of highly gendered educational routes and vocational choices' (p. 433), therefore, the more lucrative manufacturing, engineering etc. sectors are dominated by males who have a long tradition of education in these areas. However, McClelland et al.'s contention that women with vocational education choose not to pursue businesses in their profession[22] suggests that the under-representation of women in traditionally male-dominated education only partly explains the retail and services concentration of female entrepreneurs.

Other trends found for women-owned firms include that most often their markets are local, with a small minority involved in export[18] and they are often smaller scale than male-owned firms.

Many researchers have found that female-owned firms are more likely than male-owned firms to be under-capitalized at start-up.[26] Carter and Shaw[10] report that 'there is unequivocal evidence that women-owned businesses start with lower levels of overall capitalisation, lower ratios of debt finance and are much less likely to use private equity or venture capital' (p. 9), and they link this to the retail/services sector preferences of women leading to smaller firms that are perceived as requiring less external funding. Other reasons for under-capitalization include that women as a group have less financial wealth than men; Carter and Shaw note that full-time female workers in the UK earn 17 per cent less than full-time male workers and claim that 'one consequence of earning less is that women have less financial capital with which to initiate business ownership' (p. 8). Carter[19] contends that undercapitalization 'has a long-term effect on business survival and success' (p. 322), and Carter and Shaw[10] note that 'undercapitalisation at start-up restricts future business growth and development' (p. 8).

It is known that compared with male-owned firms, female-owned firms are less likely to grow.[27] Schmidt and Parker[20] note that women's firms are said to 'under-perform on most of the key performance measures' (p. 431). One could argue that standard measures of success in firms do not allow for entrepreneurial diversity: if success is measured by growth, then women's firms can only be seen as underperforming. Similarly, female-owned firms have a higher cessation rate than male-owned firms.[10] This is often assumed to be failure. In fact there is no basis on which to assume that business cessation always implies business failure. Further, what Martin and Wright call 'deficiency' studies, comprising investigations of underperformance, lack of confidence and under-representation across specialisms and sectors compared with men,[28] have been criticized by many researchers.[13; 12; 10] Morris et al.[17] contend that lack of growth can be a 'deliberate and legitimate choice of women' (p. 224). They go on to claim that 'studies attempt to ascertain how men and women conform to male institutional standards, while failing to investigate uniquely female perspectives and contexts' (p. 226). Thus, they claim standard success measures are inappropriate in studies of female entrepreneurship as these measures reflect institutionalized male standards. If success is redefined as achievement of aims and ambitions, any variation between males' and females' aims and ambitions must result in different measures of success. This variation may be associated with reasons for being in business, reasons for staying in business, ambitions for the business, and include reasons for exiting business ownership.

WHY DO WOMEN START AND OWN FIRMS?

Negative reasons for female entrepreneurship have been identified in some studies, including lack of opportunity to advance or underemployment in the working environment.[20] This is often referred to as the 'glass ceiling', particularly where it refers to professional women.[21] Several writers extend this and claim that a male-dominated culture in some workplaces also contributes to female dissatisfaction with employment.[21; 23] Smith-Hunter and Boyd[24] apply Disadvantage Theory to this contention, citing from Weber that 'those from the mainstream economy because of discrimination will often turn to business ownership as an alternative to the labour market' (p. 20). The problem with the application of this theory is that it assumes that conditions in self-employment are better than in employment, but there is no evidence to suggest that the prevailing culture in the business community is any different from the prevailing culture in the workforce. Certainly, in their empirical study McClelland et al. found few negative factors motivating female business-ownership.[22]

Most often recent research has found that motivations for starting a firm are similar among men and women, and they involve desire for independence, achievement and challenge.[21] In her study of UK Asian businesses, Dhaliwal finds an additional motivator of status accorded by business ownership, which is found to be a 'driving force' for men but not for women.[29] It may be the case that this variation is not restricted to the Asian community. Flexibility in terms of working hours particularly has been found to be an additional, concurrent, motivator for women to a greater extent than for men.[21; 17; 10] This most often is put down to women generally having coexisting priorities of domestic responsibility and responsibility for generating income, where males have been found to tend to have income generation as a prioritized responsibility. Thus, the argument here is that some women are, in part, motivated to business ownership as a means of managing two time-demanding roles. In their comparative study of females in the workforce and females in business, Parasuraman and Simmers[30] concede that this may be a motivator, but the reality for women entrepreneurs, and particularly those with families, is that they experience more, not less, work–family conflict despite their 'autonomy and schedule flexibility' (p. 566). This is further discussed below.

The 'Entrepreneurship in Action' study included in this section on female entrepreneurship serves to illustrate the experiences of business start-up and ownership by a young woman in a dynamic and fast-changing sector, the creative music sector.

IDENTIFYING BARRIERS TO ENTREPRENEURSHIP AND ISSUES FOR BUSINESSWOMEN

One of the barriers commonly attributed to low rates of female entrepreneurship involves confidence. For example, in the UK a recent report by PROWESS cites lack of confidence as one of the main issues affecting women in terms of potential for business ownership and for business growth[31]. Morris et al.[17] contend that the

> socialisation process throughout women's lives may critically affect their self-assessments about being ill-prepared with regard to firm creation – even when outsiders evaluate skills and needs as being equal to those of men.
>
> (p. 222)

This perceived lack of skills has been found in many social science studies: in his study of perceptions of educational ability among males and females Steele finds that females consistently report their ability lower than do males, though whether this suggests that women under-report or men over-report confidence in their ability is not determined.[32] Certainly Verheul finds that female business-owners are less likely to apply the word 'entrepreneur' to themselves than male business-owners,[33] and Langowitz and Minniti in their multinational study of female entrepreneurship find that perceptual, subjective variables have a large impact on women who might start firms whereby women perceive that they are less equipped and that the environment is less favourable for business start-up than do men.[7] The other side of this coin is proposed by Ljunggren and Kolvereid.[23] They find in their study of Scandanavian women business-owners that those who start firms are more likely to have garnered extensive social support and have higher confidence in their entrepreneurial abilities than men, as evidenced in the case of Georgia Train in the 'Entrepreneurship in Action' example. Ljunggren and Kolvereid suggest that perhaps women do more self-screening and place higher requirements on themselves than do men, and this, in part, explains the lower rate of female entrepreneurship generally.

Women have a long history of economic subordination, and even in the most legislatively equal societies they have sociocultural roles and expectations that are different from those of men, and the effect of these on female entrepreneurship rates and performance permeates the literature. Verheul et al.[33] note that 'employment rates for women are still lower than for men in most OECD countries' (p. 154). Hundley[25] argues that women can opt out of economic activity, therefore there is a less prevalent culture of work and economic ambition for some, compared with men, and in turn this is likely to contribute to the under-representation of female entrepreneurs. Despite this, Smith-Hunter and Boyd[24] claim that there is more to it: 'the literature on women's business ownership suggests that … women are more disadvantaged than men' (p. 19). Carter and Shaw concur, though they point out that this disadvantage owes less to direct discrimination and more to indirect, knock-on effects of the prevailing social divisions and expectation of men and women.[10] It is impossible to divorce the sociocultural environment from understanding of women's business activity. Commentators such as Morris et al.[17] claim that 'culturally imposed attitudes regarding gender remain barriers to women in achieving higher financial rewards and status in the business world' (p. 224). Orhan and Scott[21] include general 'discomfort with a dominant masculine business culture' (p. 233) as one of the most significant barriers, and while this can be interpreted as generalized and implying that women are entirely subjugated, rather than culpable in terms of current socio-economic variation in men's and women's circumstances, there is much evidence that lack of access to traditional male-dominated business networks does comprise a substantial barrier to women.[19] In fact, Schmidt and Parker claim that women's lack of confidence is in part brought about and exacerbated by lack of inclusion in business culture and specifically business networks.[20]

Schmidt and Parker note that women do use networks for business, but that they tend to be informal networks, such as the use of family (including spouse) for business activities such as book-keeping, accounting, fixtures and support.[20] McClelland et al.[22] claim informal and formal networks have different value to an organization: informal networks are generally less likely to be value-adding in the same sense that formal business networks can be. For example, 'a reluctance to participate fully in existing financial networks'[20] is borne out by the common research finding that women are less likely than men to use external business finance,[10; 28] thereby contributing to the undercapitalization problem. Lack of use of formal networks has been considered by many researchers and explanations such as discrimination, exclusion and socialization of the genders have been suggested. In response to these, in several countries measures to improve businesswomen's access to formal networks have been taken, in some cases, by creating women-specific groups, such as the Women's Enterprise Forum, established in 2010 in the UK with a view to contributing to the rate of high-growth female-led ventures.[9] Despite this, for most women entrepreneurs there exists the problem of priority versus time. McClelland et al.[22] claim that 'women often do not have as much time for networking, particularly formal networking' (p. 88), and as Hundley[25] puts it: 'individuals have finite stocks of human energy' (p. 97). The responsibility for family and domestic life exists for many women alongside responsibility for business, the former affecting the latter (and vice versa).

FEMALE ENTREPRENEURS AND THE FAMILY

Family responsibility has been identified by most research as a significant issue, particularly in terms of explaining the lower rate of female entrepreneurship compared with men, lower value and growth of female-owned firms compared with male-owned firms and itinerant issues such as motivations and definitions of success.

For both men and women, family has an impact on business ownership. According to Verheul et al. this is most often negative: for both men and women it is riskier financially than employment and for women there is the additional issue of sufficient time to commit to both.[33] As already mentioned, women's firms tend to grow less than men's firms. One explanation given is that women deliberately keep their businesses small within the context of having to manage their business and domestic priorities in tandem.[17] Hundley[25] finds empirically in his quantitative study that self-employed men earn more, and self-employed women less, as family increases, and he postulates (albeit by generalizing) that if a woman is self-employed she is 'less constrained . . . in [her] allocation of effort between household and market work' (p. 97). Hundley also finds, however, that 'increased family size increases the probability that an employed woman will be self-employed' (p. 103). Therein lies the paradox: apparently family is a barrier to female business value and growth; however, it seems also to act as a catalyst to start-up.

Other writers have suggested that while men's firms are profit orientated, women's firms can involve a social orientation also, instead of pure profit pursuit.[21; 22] While Harding notes in the PROWESS report that the gap between the sexes in terms of social enterprise start-ups is far narrower than it is for profit-oriented businesses,[15] there is no evidence to suggest that women's for-profit firms are any less profit-driven than men's. Albeit arbitrarily attributed to those who are married, Hundley identifies that women can have three levels of economic participation: work, self-employment and non-participation. If men take on the greater part of the responsibility for income, women – including businesswomen – are less compelled to have the same focus. This generalization may contribute to the tendency for women's firms to be smaller than men's. Indeed, it could go some way to explaining why the rate of female business start-up is lower than that for males.

While it is important to remember that accounts of women's roles are generalized, there is some consensus that family/domestic responsibility is both a motivator to start and a limiter to growth for women's firms. There is also substantial evidence that despite the perceptions about flexibility, there is much role conflict for female entrepreneurs.[30; 34] Dhaliwal's analysis of Asian women in family firms includes that the time-consuming nature of owner-management is a source of regret and guilt about neglecting family, and especially childcare, activity.[29] Forson[11] claims that there is 'increasing policy recognition of the importance of child-care as a barrier for self-employed women' (p. 428). More specifically, Shelton[34] recommends that 'appropriate work–family management strategies will improve venture performance for women-owned businesses' (p. 292), and that this should be considered upon business start-up. While sensible, this raises further issues: in the face of evidence that suggests concern among women about access to a male-dominated business culture, to admit to role conflict from start-up might for many women comprise the implication that they are not fully committed to their firm. In fact, it suggests an honest appreciation of the realities of business ownership for many women, but may not be what banks and other external agents want to hear as it deviates from the pure-profit orientation of the traditional male-ownership model with which they are familiar and which they understand to be the norm.

Thus, the issues associated with women's business start-up and ownership are complex and are often inextricably linked to the sociocultural environment that incorporates different experiences, expectations and circumstances for women and men and between women. So to support women's business and improve the female start-up rate, policy must acknowledge and understand the complexity of the agenda. It is not simply a case of 'remedying' underperformance issues, such as improving confidence or networking skills (neither of which is inherently implicated as deficient, but rather as *different* in expression).

FEMALE BUSINESS SUPPORT AND POLICY

In the UK the government launched a Strategic Framework for Women's Enterprise in 2003,[35] which aimed to 'create an environment and culture that encourages women to start and grow businesses' (p. 6). The document stated that since women comprise a diverse group, 'effectively segmenting the market is crucial to providing effective support and services' (p. 16). Following this, the Women's Enterprise Taskforce was set up, with a three-year remit to increase the quantity and scale of women's entrepreneurship in the UK.[8] Thus diversity among women is acknowledged, as is the central truth that women are not men. While again it is important to make explicit that women-specific business needs and issues are generalizations and do not affect all would-be and actual women business-owners to the same extent, there are several areas in which research has identified commonality amongst women entrepreneurs. For example, women have been identified as doing less planning for business compared with men. An obvious intervention would be to improve business-planning support; however, women also are known to be less inclined to take up support where it is available.[11] Schmidt and Parker[20] suggest that lack of diversity at the support level is responsible, contending that 'increased diversity within an organization is a proven method by which that organization can increase diversity of those it seeks to serve' (p. 436). This is commonly identified in management and marketing literature[36] and there is no reason why it would not apply within the business support context. Carter[19] discusses the type of training and support available through agents as another reason for lack of uptake: 'women are expected to conform to male models and standards of behaviour' (p. 331). She claims that while many female entrepreneurs are 'dismissive of women-only start-up services and training, women who have participated are overwhelmingly supportive of such schemes' (p. 332). Similar has been found in other studies,[37] and in fact, in many countries the trend is increasingly moving towards business support market segmentation. For example, in the UK, it is one of the key recommendations made by the Women's Enterprise Taskforce[9] and is the rationale behind the UK women's business network PROWESS which seeks to develop 'an effective women-friendly business support infrastructure and enterprise culture'.[31] The type of support must reflect the realities of women's business ambitions and expectations for it to be useful though. One commonly identified means of providing this is through role models[20; 31] and peer mentoring,[19; 31] i.e. using more women to advise, support and provide examples of achievement for women entrepreneurs.

The need for specific support has been identified as required not only for start-up but also for continuation and for growth,[16; 15] if growth is sought. Harding notes that in the UK, PROWESS report that very little is known about how women's businesses grow and correspondingly it is very difficult to establish the reasons for lack of growth among female businesses and to identify appropriate support.[15] The reasons why many women do not seek to grow their firms are undoubtedly, however, linked to some extent to greater societal differences between women and men. To increase the rates and value of female businesses, there is a strong argument for policy that addresses the greater sociocultural issues that generate divisions between the genders in terms of educational trajectory, labour value and role experiences and expectations, all of which contribute to differences in economic potential and opportunity.

A NEW IDENTITY

Compared with at least 2000 years for men, economic activity among women is relatively new. Within this context 'deficiency model' understanding of women's economic activity and entrepreneurship in particular has been prevalent. Recent research and policy in many western countries are beginning to identify a new perception of and among women entrepreneurs. For example, there is evidence that among female motivations to start firms, is the desire to define one's own working environment.[23] Similar has been found by the current author among male gay entrepreneurs.[38] In their empirical study, Orhan and Scott[21] identify a category of women entrepreneurs they call 'new women' who have 'shifted [their] efforts from a desire to achieve along the same patterns as men, towards the recognition of [their] own identity regardless of gender stereotypes' (p. 235). Morris et al.[17] state that 'the feminist movement itself may have catalyzed the formation of ventures with specific intentions to overcome the typical masculine organization and the capitalist society that supports it' (p. 227). While this suggests a highly deliberate and politicized rationale and, as such is probably overstated, there is a growing body of evidence that suggests the idea that perceptions about women's economic activity are maturing away from the secondary and subordinate model towards a more independent one. 'Different' from male economic activity models is becoming increasingly prevalent and economically viable.

General conclusions on diversity in entrepreneurship are provided at the end of the chapter. We now turn to a section on ethnic minority entrepreneurship for the remaining parts of this chapter.

ENTREPRENEURSHIP IN ACTION

Georgia Train
by Zuleika Beavan, Manchester Metropolitan University

Georgia Train is not just an up-and-coming singer with her band Bitter Ruin, she is also a businesswoman. She has to be if she is going to succeed in the highly competitive and fast-moving music business.

Right from the start Georgia, and band-mate and fellow song-writer Ben Richards, saw Bitter Ruin as a business. They constituted it as a company, set up a business account and kept all the proceeds from gigs and music sales in the band. In the early days, they weren't even paying themselves a wage, so Georgia was living off the fees from giving music lessons.

As a self-managing band with no record label, they have also in effect had to set up their own label and PR operation to record, promote and distribute their music. When releasing an album, they plan for a six-month run-up and for six months of promotion afterwards. To separate out the creative and commercial side of what she does, and to give the impression that the operation is bigger than it is, Georgia sometimes uses a pseudonym when dealing with the business side of the band. And she is very aware, as a woman in the music industry, of the need to stand her ground, saying 'you need to prove even more than a man that you are determined!' Bitter Ruin recently extended their business activity and began to promote their own gigs. This means taking the financial risk on booking venues and selling their own tickets and has led to a significant increase in the income from touring which now allows them to take a wage from the band. It also means the occasional loss-making show.

Contacts and networks are crucial, and Georgia is always willing to draw on the experience of more established artists whenever she can. The decision to begin self-promoting their tours is an example of this, and came from advice from members of a band that Bitter Ruin supported on tour during 2010. A further source of inspiration for Georgia has been watching her father run his gardening business; she sees many similarities between what they do day to day. And with fans important for viral marketing, Georgia and Ben have established a network called The Ruined to strengthen the relationship. For the launch of their second album in 2011, The Ruined helped with a Twitter campaign which drew celebrity endorsements including Matt Lucas, Tim Minchin and Stephen Fry.

◀   Georgia is frank about all this; it is very hard work and it means she has to struggle to find the time for song-writing. She notes wryly: 'We end up spending more time trying to get ourselves known than actually making music.' So Georgia dreams of being signed by a label and having a professional team behind her, but she has no intention of rushing into this if it means a bad deal. Although she has been approached by potential managers and record labels, Georgia has drawn on what she learnt during her music degree, carefully to check contracts and evaluate what is being offered. She feels it is easy to be flattered into signing a poor deal and knows it is important to keep a cool head during negotiations. And as she hasn't been happy with anything offered so far, she continues to work as what she calls a DIY artist while looking out for a better deal.

DISCUSSION QUESTIONS

1   What have been the advantages to Georgia of business ownership?

2   What are the challenges that she has faced as a female business-owner in the creative-music sector?

3   What are the key factors that have contributed to her success?

ETHNIC MINORITY ENTREPRENEURSHIP

In Britain's history, ethnic immigrants have traditionally been of crucial importance to economic development, a tradition that goes back to groups such as the Huguenots. These ethnic groups have been willing to accept new practices or bring new skills that facilitate significant economic developments. The tradition continues to be significant in the modern economy where Asian entrepreneurs were the first to open retail outlets on Sundays, pre-dating a modern movement towards Sunday opening in most retail sectors. Ethnic entrepreneurs have also been willing to develop in areas that are shunned by 'mainstream' or white entrepreneurs – for example, economically marginal inner-city areas. Location in these inner-city areas has significant implications for ethnic minority entrepreneurs. Not only does location often limit the available market to the ethnic enclave, it also makes the acquisition and availability of resources (especially finance and insurance) difficult or expensive. Further discussion on the importance of location and environment, *acknowledging context*, is given later in this chapter.

AGE DISTRIBUTION OF ETHNIC GROUPS

Although Table 4.1 shows the demographic importance of the main ethnic groups in England and Wales, the potential of ethnic minorities in economic development can be highlighted further by demographic analysis of the 2001 Census data, which shows that one of the features of ethnic minorities is their considerably younger age profile. For example, in 2001 the census showed that 32 per cent of the African minority population were under 16 years of age compared with less than 20 per cent of the white population.[39] By contrast, 9 per cent of the Caribbean minority were aged 65 and over, compared with 16 per cent for the white group (which was the largest proportion of any group). Further illustration of the dramatic differences in age profiles of minority ethnic groups for the UK is illustrated in Figure 4.2. This has indicated that the changing demographic profile and entrepreneurial potential of ethnic minority groups is crucial to the future economic development of significant areas in Britain.[40]

Figure 4.1 indicates that the rates of self-employment in ethnic minority groups in the UK, although high, do vary, indicating diversity in entrepreneurial activity. Taking the five main ethnic minority groups in the UK, the highest rates are for South Asians, particularly Pakistanis and Bangladeshis, at 22 per cent and 13.5 per cent respectively, and for Chinese, who have self-employment rates of 16 per cent. However, the rates

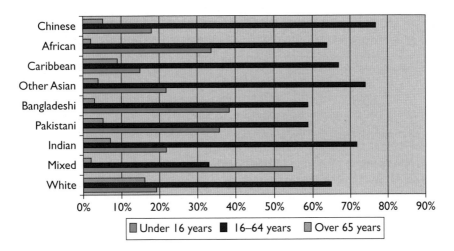

FIGURE 4.2

UK age distribution by ethnic group

SOURCE: Office for National Statistics, London. Crown copyright material is reproduced with the permission of the Controller of HMSO and the Queen's Printer for Scotland.

for Black Africans and Caribbeans are much lower, being only 6 to 8 per cent, but the dynamics of these patterns are changing, illustrating further diversity. For example, there are higher rates of those who have recently become self-employed in Black African and Black Caribbean ethnic groups compared to South Asian ethnic groups.[41]

ISSUES IN ETHNIC MINORITY ENTREPRENEURSHIP

The literature on ethnic minority enterprise development has focused on three main issues: *accessing resources*, notably finance and labour, *accessing markets* and *motivation*. Earlier literature focused on the cultural and additional forces that led early-stage immigrant labour into self-employment and high rates of participation in entrepreneurship. For example, Light stressed the importance of cultural minority status that produced a strong sense of social solidarity in immigrant and ethnic enterprise in North America.[42] Bonacich et al.'s study of Koreans in Los Angeles identified access to resources and informal support networks as two of the key factors that accounted for the success of this ethnic minority group in entrepreneurship.[43] Some writers have pointed to the success of ethnic groups despite difficult trading conditions, with survival achieved through piecing together a living from semi-legal activities.[44; 45] Light identified particularly the difficulties of black entrepreneurs in North America due to limited access to resources.[42] Models of such ethnic enterprise development – for example, those of Waldinger, and Waldinger et al.[46; 47] – reflect these issues and focus on how the entrepreneurial attributes of different ethnic groups determine their ability to access resources and markets to achieve entrepreneurial success.[48; 49]

Accessing resources

The first of the three issues has concerned the ability of ethnic minority entrepreneurs to generate or access resources. In some cases, writers have claimed that the advantages of informal networks have given ethnic minorities in business an advantage due to access to resources of finance and family labour.[50; 51; 52] Waldinger also pointed to the importance of informal networks as a key factor in successful entrepreneurial development of ethnic immigrants in New York.[46] Ethnic minority entrepreneurs' relationship with banks has also attracted research. For example, Curran and Blackburn's study of Bangladeshis, Greek-Cypriots, and Black African and Black Caribbeans in the UK highlighted the problems of the latter two ethnic groups in accessing bank finance.[53]

Previous research by the author has supported the findings of Curran and Blackburn,[53; 54] which show that small firms owned by ethnic minority entrepreneurs are no different from white-owned small firms in being heavily dependent on the banks for external finance. However, they found that reliance on bank finance was much less significant for Black African and Black Caribbeans, a finding also confirmed by the author's research.[55] A Bank of England report,[56] which reviewed the previous research at the time, indicated that there was a perception by ethnic minority entrepreneurs of prejudice by the banks, but concluded that problems perceived by ethnic minority entrepreneurs may be due to sectoral concentration of ethnic groups rather than any discrimination and called for more systematic research. For example, the report commented:

> There are a number of possible explanations as to why ethnic minority businesses encounter difficulties, including risk aversion behaviour by lenders, sectoral concentration of ethnic businesses, failure rates and lack of business planning.
>
> (p. 7)

The largest UK study on ethnic minority entrepreneurs and access to finance and business support, by Ram et al.,[57] was established as a result of the issues identified in the Bank of England report. This study suggests that reasons for differences in the pattern of access to finance are complex. For example, their report included in the conclusions that, 'The issue is complex, reflecting a preference for informal sources of finance in some cases, yet strong perceptions of discrimination on the part of the banks in others' (p. 116).

This study involved a demand-side baseline survey of the five main ethnic groups with a white control group, longitudinal case studies and an extensive programme of supply-side interviews with bank mangers and support agencies.[57] The demand-side research has confirmed particular problems of access to finance for Black African and Black Caribbeans.[58] The supply-side findings reflect variety in practice in bank managers' dealings with ethnic minority applications, despite proactive policies towards ethnic minority entrepreneurs by all the banks.[59]

There is evidence of diversity of experience of the business owners from different minority ethnic groups. In the Ram et al. study,[57] comment was made on different experience: 'The survey evidence in particular clearly demonstrates the diversity of experience that exists between ethnic minority groups with respect to raising external finance' (p. 7).

The study goes on to comment that the ability to raise formal sources of finance such as bank finance is significantly higher in Chinese-owned businesses, while significantly less in Black African- and Black Caribbean-owned businesses. Reliance on informal finance was more significant in South Asian-owned businesses. This diversity of experience will be further affected by differing experiences of ethnic minority entrepreneurs in traditional and emergent sectors.

Diversity of experience is compounded by variety in practice with relationships between ethnic minority entrepreneurs and their funders. Ram et al.[57] also comment that, 'There was variation in practice in the level and intensity of bank manager experience of ethnic minority businesses' (p. 118). Good practice was evident where bank managers had built up trust through stable relationships and close involvement with their local minority community, leading to a better understanding of the way that ethnic minority business owners conducted their business.

The importance to ethnic businesses of the use of family and co-ethnic labour has been highlighted by studies such as Wilson and Portes, whose research on Cubans in Miami pointed to the importance of ethnic preferences in hiring labour, which allowed this ethnic group to thrive where native whites did not, even where the native population had superior access to resources.[60]

Accessing markets

The second issue has stressed the reliance of ethnic minorities in business on co-ethnic markets.[61; 62] While this may be a deliberate strategy,[47] Light has argued that, in the case of Black Americans, their concentration in ethnic enclaves traps them in a potentially disadvantaged cycle from which it is difficult to break into the mainstream of officially registered businesses.[42] Studies in the UK have stressed the importance of the need for successful break-out into mainstream white-dominated markets,[63; 64] an issue that we would expect to be more important where markets are limited and peripheral. The related issue of location and the geographical characteristic of concentration of ethnic businesses in inner-city areas has further highlighted problems of break-out.

In the UK, the success of ethnic minority entrepreneurs has been officially recognized in the past – for example, with reports from the Ethnic Minority Business Initiative (EMBI)[65] – but the constraints that such entrepreneurs have overcome have not always received the same recognition. Their success has been achieved in marginal economic environments of the inner city and with limited access to either resources or mainstream markets. Debate on developing the need for break-out, led to the view that the success of ethnic minority businesses can only be secured through the development of more diversification into different sectors with discussion about the best way to secure strategies to move away from dependence on ethnic market niches.[53; 64] The ability of ethnic firms to achieve successful break-out has been shown to depend on successful integration of a holistic strategy involving marketing, finance, human resources and 'key' contacts with mainstream markets.[66]

Motivation

Attempts in the literature to explain the importance of ethnic minority entrepreneurs concentrate on the relative primacy of 'negative' or 'positive' factors in the motivations and development of ethnic minority small-firm owners – for example, Ward and Jenkins.[48] The debate surrounds whether or not the discrimination faced by ethnic minorities in the labour market was the predominant motivating factor in business ownership and entrepreneurship, or whether positive factors, such as a group's background experience of business ownership, were more important in the motivation decision. Although Curran and Blackburn[53] have indicated that motivational factors such as 'independence' were significant in entry to entrepreneurship, there is little doubt that a history of disadvantage and discrimination has led to the concentration of ethnic minority firms and entrepreneurs in marginal areas of economic activity. A national scoping study in Scotland, led by the author with colleagues, found contrasting experience of ethnic minority business owners, with some growth businesses in global markets, but some businesses trading in marginal economic environments, which were subject to particular problems associated with high crime rates, incidences of racism and high levels of insurance premiums.[67]

Curran and Blackburn[53] found in their study, perhaps surprisingly, that positive factors associated with the desire to be independent were higher than expected, and they claim that this was on similar levels to white-owned businesses. To some extent, the strong motivational factors were confirmed by our research with African and Caribbean entrepreneurs in UK cities, and with Asian entrepreneurs in Scotland.[55; 67] Over 80 per cent of Black African-Caribbean and Asian entrepreneurs agreed with positive statements concerning ambition and control of their environment. Yet, for a significant minority, negative factors associated with the lack of opportunity elsewhere were also important. Over 40 per cent (for both groups) agreed that they had faced discrimination in previous employment. In such circumstances, discrimination and the lack of opportunities in the labour market are significant 'push' factors. Evidence from these studies showed that such entrepreneurs were often more highly qualified than equivalent white entrepreneurs, a result confirmed by the more recent UK study for the British Bankers' Association (BBA).[57] Analysis of motivation factors with Black African and Black Caribbean entrepreneurs showed that a 'mix' of positive and negative factors were important in start-up and motivation. Negative factors included the lack of employment opportunities (although this may also be a significant factor for white entrepreneurs) and the lack of career opportunities when in employment. It may be that African and Caribbean entrepreneurs have the characteristics we would expect of white entrepreneurs. However, evidence of discrimination and frustrated career ambitions was found to be a factor with some Black African and Black Caribbean entrepreneurs.

Although a number of issues remain unresolved in motivation, such as the low participation rate of Black African and Black Caribbeans in entrepreneurship, attention has shifted from start-up to enterprise development issues. For example, ethnic minority entrepreneurs are perceived to be located in ethnic niche markets, such as Asian clothing firms supplying the needs of the Asian community or Caribbean hairdressers supplying a service that meets the needs of their community. The issue of 'break-out' from this reliance upon ethnic niche markets has been recognized as a policy issue for ethnic minority entrepreneurs; policy issues are explored later.

Some of the issues with ethnic minority and female entrepreneurs can be explored and discussed in the 'Entrepreneurship in Action' case that follows.

ENTREPRENEURSHIP IN ACTION

Perween Warsi and S&A Foods
by Dr Spinder Dhaliwal, University of Surrey, updated 2011

PERWEEN WARSI

Perween Warsi is the dynamic woman behind the Derby-based S&A Foods, named after her sons Sadiq and Abid. Perween was born and brought up in Bihar, Northern India and, from the age of four, she was in the kitchen helping to prepare special dishes for family occasions. She later married and moved to the UK before finally settling in Derby. Increasingly dissatisfied with the quality of Indian products already on the market, Perween decided to take the plunge and started her own business using her own family recipes. She was soon in great demand and made a major breakthrough when she won a contract to supply the major supermarket chain Asda in a blind food-tasting competition. The rest, as they say, is history. Since then, the business has enjoyed a meteoric rise and now employs several hundred people.

Perween has always been a rebel: 'I wanted to challenge the food industry. I found supermarket food to be boring, tasteless and poor value for money.' Her mission was to provide better tasting food: 'I am passionate about this,' she affirms.

In 1986, with the support of her family and friends Perween decided to create a business using her own recipes. She started off with a tiny cottage industry working from her own kitchen. Her first step was to produce Indian finger food for a local restaurant. She was soon in great demand and began to market herself more effectively and the orders poured in.

Perween extended her kitchen and began to employ a number of women. Most of these women were of Indian descent and many of them did not speak English.

Not content with a small business, Perween had aspirations to grow and hounded the supermarkets. Asda finally agreed to a blind tasting of Perween's foods alongside other samples. 'Our products got the thumbs-up and it was the best day of my business life.' Although luck played a part in her success, thanks to her persistence it was no accident that Asda was her big break.

This success, however, presented her with a problem. As S&A Foods became increasingly more successful, larger premises were needed to accommodate the growing business. Perween needed to expand rapidly in order to meet the orders and access to finance was proving to be difficult. Financiers were cautious and were looking for at least a three-year track record. Her few months of experience in her own kitchen did not leave them feeling comfortable about the venture. After some deliberation she joined forces with the Hughes Food Group, a local company, in order to generate funds to build a factory. A purpose-built factory was designed specifically to produce chilled Indian ready meals. By 1989 the first S&A Foods factory was built in Derby, creating over 100 jobs for the area. Her husband quit his job as a GP and joined the business full time.

The business flourished. Perween introduced a greater variety of dishes, as well as innovations in packaging such as the meal sold in its own wok when the balti craze hit Britain. However, she was soon to face a new challenge. Three years later saw the Warsi family fighting to regain control after the Hughes Food Group went into receivership and after a long drawn-out battle, Perween and her husband completed a management buy-out in November 1991 with the backing of the venture capitalists, 3i. This was a very difficult period not only because of the legal troubles. The company also faced stiff competition. Many food manufacturers were competing for a share of the lucrative ready-meal business. Perween began diversifying into Thai, Malaysian, Chinese and American food to keep ahead of the game. But the loss of control has not been forgotten – Perween plans to 'keep the business in the family' rather than float on the stock market.

Perween eventually regained 100 per cent ownership of Derby-based S&A Foods with the acquisition of the shareholding of venture capitalists, 3i. Perween believes firmly in building a team of highly qualified people around her and in developing a strong 'family' culture amongst employees who are encouraged to challenge their personal and professional boundaries and strive for excellence.

Success has been hard fought and well earned. What can we learn? First you do something you believe in, something you really care about. Second, you treat your people as people. People are assets so take care of them, get them involved. Perween is passionate about innovation and high standards when it comes to food and she encourages everyone in the business to get involved. From the CEO to the shop floor, no one is exempt from the responsibility of coming up with new ideas, be they in design, packaging or processing. In an industry which demands innovation, this is a company where it is expected from everyone. She attempts to instill a family culture within the company and is 'hands on'. She keeps abreast of daily events and is concerned about the welfare of her workers.

S&A Foods employs over 600 people and produces over 1.5 million ready-made meals per week, with ASDA as one of its clients. Perween has picked up many awards and honours including an MBE and CBE and various doctorates.

DISCUSSION QUESTIONS

1 What entrepreneurial attributes does Perween Warsi demonstrate?

2 What role did her family and community play in the business?

3 What role did access to finance play in the business?

4 Are there any lessons to be learned from this female entrepreneur?

Acknowledging context

One of the issues that has received attention in the literature on ethnic minority businesses (EMBs) has been the relative importance of the socio-economic and political environment compared with the ability of such EMB owners to access resources and markets. One approach that has gained popularity, led by a group of Dutch researchers, argues that it is important to acknowledge the wider environment within which EMB owners operate, including socio economic environment and the important political institutions. This is known as the 'mixed embeddedness' approach;[68] it recognizes the importance of context in the light of resources, such as human, social and financial capital, that can be drawn upon by EMB owners.

DIVERSITY IN LOCATION: URBAN V. RURAL ENVIRONMENTS

The importance of context and the environment can be illustrated by work undertaken by the author and colleagues with EMB owners in contrasting urban and rural localities.[69] Theoretically it is arguable that EMB owners in rural localities compared with urban, would face greater resource 'poverty' issues, have limited social networks and hence restricted access to human, financial and social capital, and therefore be relatively self-reliant. We could also hypothesize that such resource limitations would provide greater constraints and difficulties for such owners in achieving business growth.

For example, in terms of accessing resources, we found that accessing advice was noticeably absent from EMBs in the non-city urban and rural locations in Scotland. Even relatively successful EMB owners in such localities had bypassed support agencies. In rural localities there was evidence of some contact with the support agencies and intermediary bodies such as multicultural associations; nevertheless, there was a high degree of isolation and no contact with, or support from, agencies by EMB owners in such localities. For example, one EMB owner from the Highlands complained that he felt his business had suffered from a lack of support; in commenting on the barriers he faced, he stated that there was: 'A lack of confidence in me and support from the local enterprise advisers.' Accessing finance was also seen to be problematic by EMB owners in non-city localities as, although an issue with some in city localities, there was less of an alternative of informal finance which was the main source of finance for EMB owners in city localities.

In many cases, outside city localities, EMB owners were often in sectors that faced increased competition and declining demand, yet without access to advice or resources that might help them achieve diversification, although there was also evidence of some successful survival strategies in the face of such difficulties. For example, the owner of one convenience food store in a central locality commented that 'turnover had declined' due to increased presence of 'big supermarkets', yet he still found that customers were retained because of the nature of their immediate catchment area. Taking the experience of a Bangladeshi convenience store owner from a rural area in the south of Scotland, a similar picture emerges of 'declining demand', yet they were still resourceful enough to introduce measures that had enabled some expansion despite increased competition: 'We are always looking at improving things, we have a salad bar, we are always looking for ideas to change things and expand.' The rural location meant that 'convenience' still provided a survival strategy, in the face of increased competition.

In localities outside the main city locations, a lack of established networks compounded the limited access to resources. This contrasts with a more common experience in city localities of a network of informal advice. There was evidence that sources of social capital in city localities were still important for second generation and young company owners, although the source of social capital or sources of advice may well be different in nature, because of different, if overlapping, networks.

A characteristic of EMB owners in rural areas, in dealing with business problems, was that these had to be solved in isolation. Allowing for the context of the rural environment with a greater dispersed pattern of numbers of small firms, this feature of relative isolation, with no apparent networks to tap into, was particularly apparent. The experience of EMB owners in rural localities of 'doing business in isolation' reinforces the notion of resource poverty. A lack of family, social and business networks to turn to for advice bears out an initial hypothesis that such EMB owners are relatively isolated and relatively invisible, after taking into account the context of the rural environment. It was clear that they adopted coping strategies based on loyalties of local customers in sectors of declining demand, but lacked access to standard sources of advice and networks.

In emergent sectors such as leisure, computing and telecommunications, the larger markets of city localities, with greater access to resources such as finance, provided a better platform for achieving growth. Achieving business growth in some areas outside the main cities meant resorting to innovative networking and using opportunities to diversify. A typical experience, especially in a traditional sector, was maintaining income in the face of declining overall demand. It was noticeable that barriers to achieving growth were more significant and perhaps more difficult to deal with due to the more limited access to resources that characterized such localities.

Some EMB owners in rural and non-city localities admitted that it was 'more difficult to do business', but approached this with a stoic acceptance that such attitudes were only to be expected and that they had to work harder to achieve success because of such barriers. It was in the nature of dealing with customers or suppliers where different forms of racism materialized. In a small number of cases, reference was made to the effect of changing a name on doing business and the beneficial effect of removing the perception, for example, of dealing with an Asian business.

The combination of these barriers and difficulties meant that for some EMB owners, in some localities, the realities of doing business, of their experience and their everyday lives, meant that they were forced to adopt coping strategies, adjusting to different markets, to greater costs and to surviving rather than achieving successful diversification and growth, an experience that was more typical of non-city environments, that is in the central and more rural localities.

DIVERSITY IN LOCATION: 'SUPER DIVERSITY'

It is arguable that in some city and urban areas of the UK, it is no longer feasible to discuss ethnic groups as 'minorities'. Rather, because of increasing diversity, there are many ethnic groups that are represented so that discussion of a small number of minority ethnic groups is no longer feasible. This notion of 'super' or 'hyper' diversity is an increasing feature of our urban areas as we move into the second decade of the twenty-first century.[70] It has resulted from increased migration from many different nations into the UK and into other European nations, whether from North Africa, South America or South-East Asia. Our urban demographics are rapidly changing with 'super diversity' now a key feature of the main UK cities. Although this gives great complexity, it is also a tremendous asset as super diversity is directly linked to increased creativity. For example, the city of London based its successful bid for the 2012 Olympics with the slogan 'The world in one city'. Terms such as 'global village' are now coined to capture this super diversity in one city. This is true not just of London, but of other major cities across the world and in the UK, including New York, Birmingham and Manchester to give just a few examples.

The role of immigrants has not only benefited the UK in creating such modern diversity and severe restrictions can be counter-productive. One of the most successful growth companies in modern times, Yahoo, was founded by a migrant entrepreneur, Jerry Yang, who was ten years old when his family migrated to the USA from Taiwan. He later went on to Stanford University where he developed the concept for Yahoo.

ETHNIC MINORITY ENTREPRENEURSHIP: POLICY

It is arguable that similar principles to those of support for women's enterprise apply to support for ethnic minority enterprise owners. For example, Ram and Smallbone, in their review,[71] considered good practice to include: instruments or initiatives that are focused on the distinctive support needs of EMBs, or specific subgroups; delivery approaches that are based on engagement and interaction with ethnic minority communities; culturally sensitive delivery methods; and approaches that include strategies for drawing EMB owners into mainstream support. In a review of support for five cities, arising from the UK study for the British Bankers' Association,[72] it was found that each of the localities had a different pattern and mix of mainstream agencies, specialized ethnic business-focused enterprise agencies, intervention by local authorities and EMB associations. In both England and Scotland, mainstream agencies have inclusivity as an important objective, yet the main issue has been a lack of engagement by ethnic minority entrepreneurs with support agencies.[72]

A lack of engagement

It is now well established, from previous research, that ethnic minority entrepreneurs are reluctant to access mainstream enterprise support provision.[73] For example, in a survey for Humberside Training and Enterprise Council (TEC) of 292 EMBs, of which 45 per cent were Chinese owned, only 4 per cent had used business support previously, compared with 66 per cent of all businesses. Moreover, nearly three-quarters of EMBs had never used any form of business support, compared with 32 per cent of all firms.[74] In London, one study suggested that the low level of use of mainstream support provision was related to the EMB owner's general perception of the support environment, misgivings about the support that is offered, confusion caused by the continued fragmentation of the support infrastructure and a failure of agencies to deliver 'one-stop' support in practice.[75]

The relative failure of mainstream support provision to reach ethnic minority enterprise owners has contributed to the development of specialized enterprise support agencies, based on funding from a variety of sources and initiatives, which have tended to change over time, thereby contributing to changing fortunes for individual agencies. However, instead of being complementary and well co-ordinated with mainstream provision, many of these specialist agencies have operated alongside existing mainstream agencies such as Business Links rather than working closely with them, although there are exceptions. For example, Ram reported a lack of integration between specialized and mainstream provision in his study of enterprise support for African-Caribbeans in different city locations in the UK.[76] In practice, the pattern of enterprise support for EMBs varies between cities, depending on the mix of mainstream and specialized agencies.

Another issue concerns the language and forms of communication used by mainstream business-support providers to communicate with potential EMB clients, which could be improved through a greater use of ethnic-based media, such as radio and newsletters, to disseminate information on business support issues. In one study involving the author, we found that one of the gaps in enterprise support strategy in Glasgow, at the time, was limited use of ethnic-based media. Such factors help to explain the low level of use of formal sources of external advice and assistance by EMBs, particularly at start-up.[77]

It could be that the low take-up of business support from formal agencies reflects a low level of perceived need, or a lack of interest, by ethnic minority entrepreneurs in receiving external assistance, which is a more extreme form of the apathy shown by many small-business owners (regardless of their ethnicity) towards business support providers. However, there is evidence to suggest that the low level of use of mainstream business support agencies cannot be put down to the lack of interest on the part of the business owners[78; 79] since both studies found their South Asian samples receptive to appropriate business support. The reliance on social networks, which are embedded in ethnic communities, may provide strong social capital, but it may also militate against accessing mainstream sources of support and advice.[80]

The principal obstacles for support agencies, therefore, can be associated with identifying and reaching ethnic minority entrepreneurs. Ram and Smallbone suggest that when this is linked to often inadequate databases, together with the inappropriateness of the 'product-oriented' approaches used by support agencies, it may not be surprising that formal support is bypassed by EMB owners.[71]

Finally it has been suggested that ethnic minority entrepreneurs' needs are different from those of other small businesses, which Ram and Jones have indicated are associated with their sector, size and geographic distributions.[73] In terms of sector, South Asians are strongly represented in the catering, clothing and food retailing sectors,[81] Chinese in catering,[82] and African and Caribbeans in construction.[83] Although our research has shown that new-generation EMB owners are favouring emergent sectors,[77] traditional sectoral concentrations remain important and, therefore, have to be taken into consideration when formulating support policies for ethnic minority entrepreneurs.

CONCLUSIONS

This chapter has celebrated the diversity of enterpreneurship through a focus on women and ethnic minority entrepreneurs. Even within these categories, however, diversity is a key theme. Diversity in entrepreneurship will always provide an issue for policy because it is not possible to treat any group of entrepreneurs as being homogeneous; the needs of business-owners will vary and their needs will depend as much on the characteristics of their businesses (on their size, on their sector and on their location) as on whether they are owned by women, men or ethnic minorities. However, from the evidence that has been reviewed in this chapter, it is possible to identify the distinctive experiences of ethnic minority and women entrepreneurs. It is noticeable that the evidence does suggest that some ethnic minority entrepreneurs – especially, for example, Black African and Black Caribbean – do have very different experiences when accessing bank finance than do other entrepreneurs.

Diversity is important too for women's firms. Much of the discussion of female entrepreneurship has focused on the issues associated with business ownership and family responsibility. However, many females do not have families; many potential and actual female entrepreneurs have circumstances, including education, opportunity, wealth etc., similar to those of men. As such we might expect them to be less 'deficient' or less 'different' in terms of business outlook and ambition. For some this will be the case, for others not. Additionally, over time the socio-economic circumstances of women may vary considerably. For female entrepreneurs, therefore, the perceived value, utility and purpose of their businesses may well vary over time as their other circumstances change. Thus diversity in entrepreneurship for women can include not only diversity among women, but diversity of the business experience for each female entrepreneur. Such is the complexity of the entrepreneurship phenomenon. Emerging trends in research reflect this. Howarth et al.[84] point out that entrepreneurship is 'a field characterised by dynamism, ambiguity, discontinuity, uniqueness and innovation' (p. 25). The 'deficiency model' of female self-employment and business ownership is therefore itself deficient if we are to understand properly the complexity and value of female (and any non-standard, minority) entrepreneurship.

Ethnic minority enterprise development has succeeded largely outside mainstream support and largely without access to special support. For example, in some areas, success has been achieved through entrepreneurs and other community leaders taking individual action and setting up their own initiatives, using ethnic literature to ensure that firms and entrepreneurs are engaged.

The diversity of ethnic minority enterprise is increasing and it is arguable that it is no longer appropriate to use 'minority' groups as a term; rather, 'super diversity' characterises ethnic businesses. Generational issues have not been explored in this chapter, yet new young Asian and other ethnic minority entrepreneurs are entering entrepreneurship from very different backgrounds than those of their parents and grandparents. While the family experience and tradition are still important in the Asian community, many of these new young ethnic minority entrepreneurs may have a family background that does not have the tradition of business ownership. It is these new entrepreneurs that are forging the future of ethnic minority enterprise development in the UK. They have different expectations, are often highly educated and enter entrepreneurship against a background of high family expectations not to follow a career in self-employment.

Women are also increasing their participation in entrepreneurship, yet policies, such as the Strategic Framework,[32] still take a piecemeal approach to support and assume that women entrepreneurs have homogeneous needs, when, in practice, diversity characterizes their experience. In the case of both women and ethnic minority entrepreneurs policies continue to defy the variety of their experience, participation and activity.

Further case studies on ethnic-owned business can be found in the students' online learning centre.

REVIEW QUESTIONS

1 Why do official participation rates for women in business tend to underestimate their importance?
2 Why might women face higher start-up barriers than do men?
3 How does the pattern of self-employment in ethnic minorities in the UK illustrate diversity?
4 How might this diversity be changing?
5 Commercial banks and mainstream support agencies may be seen by ethnic minority entrepreneurs as 'white' institutions. This can be overlain with perceptions of prejudice in such institutions against them. What could the banks do to reduce such perceptions in order to improve access to formal bank finance? Similarly, what could support agencies do?

6 Why are ethnic minority entrepreneurs important to Britain's future prosperity in the twenty-first century?

7 Which ethnic groups appear to be the most under-represented in entrepreneurship? What factors might account for this?

8 Give examples of factors that would be regarded as positive and negative motivations for ethnic minority entrepreneurs.

9 How would you expect motivations to differ between new-start business-owners in different ethnic minority groups?

10 In the past, problems of accessing resources may have caused some ethnic minority entrepreneurs to enter sectors that have low barriers to entry – for example, clothing manufacture, retailing and wholesaling. How is increased competition in these sectors likely to affect such ethnic minority businesses today?

11 Why has policy on support for women in enterprise become important?

12 Why is the issue of mainstream v. specialized support relevant to both ethnic minority and women's enterprise support policies?

13 What factors may explain the lack of engagement and the low take-up of support by ethnic minority entrepreneurs?

SUGGESTED ASSIGNMENTS

1 There has been considerable research effort into understanding characteristics of ethnic minority entrepreneurs, the issues that they face, and their potential in economic regeneration and recovery. Using material from this chapter, discuss the potential reasons for this attention, focusing on Asian entrepreneurs.

2 Critically discuss the nature of recent support initiatives for women's enterprise in the UK.

3 You are a business adviser to a new women's enterprise, seeking to start up in the UK. Explain the relevance of recent policy initiatives, and recommend networks that they may consider joining as a form of advice and information (see www.prowess.org.uk (accessed July 2011)).

REFERENCES

1 **Small Business Service** (2004) *A Government Action Plan for Small Businesses: The Evidence Base*, SBS/DTI, London.

2 **Department for Business, Innovation and Skills** (2009) *The Government's Response to the Ethnic Minority Business Task Force*, BIS.

3 **ONS** (2007) *Population Estimates*, Office for National Statistics, London.

4 **ONS** (2011) *Population Estimates*, Office for National Statistics, available at http://www.statistics.gov.uk (accessed at November 2011).

5 **Ram, M. and Jones, T.** (2007) 'Ethnic minority businesses in the

UK: A review of research and policy developments', report for the ESRC, paper presented to an ESRC/CRE/DTI/EMDA seminar, February, London.

6 **ONS** (2009) *National Population Projections 2008-based*, Office for National Statistics, London.

7 **Langowitz, N. and Minniti, M.** (2007) 'The entrepreneurial propensity of women', *Entrepreneurship, Theory and Practice*, vol. 31, no. 3, pp. 341–64.

8 **Women's Enterprise Taskforce** (2009a) *The Women's Enterprise Taskforce (2006–2009)* available at http://www.womensenterprisetask-force.co.uk (accessed at July 2011).

9 **Women's Enterprise Taskforce** (2009b) *Greater Return On Women's Enterprise*, Women's Enterprise Taskforce, available at http://www.womensenterprisetaskforce.co.uk/download/b2eba531bd89 2522226d1da6b68187aa.html (accessed at July 2011).

10 **Carter, S. and Shaw, E.** (2006) *Women's Business Ownership: Recent Research and Policy Developments, Report to the Small Business Service*, available at www.berr.gov.uk/files/file38330.pdf (accessed at July 2011).

11 **Forson, C.** (2006) 'The strategic framework for women's enterprise: BME women at the margins', *Equal Opportunities International*, vol. 25, no. 6, pp. 418–32.

12 **Marshack, K.J.** (1994) 'Copreneurs and dual-career couples: are they different?', *Entrepreneurship Theory and Practice*, vol. 19, no. 1, pp. 49–69.

13 **Hamilton, E.E.** (2006) 'Whose story is it anyway? Narrative accounts of the role of women in founding and establishing family businesses', *International Small Business Journal*, vol. 24, no. 3, pp. 253–71.

14 **Verheul, I., van Stel, A. and Thurik, R.** (2006) 'Explaining female and male entrepreneurship at the country level', *Entrepreneurship and Regional Development*, vol. 18, pp. 151–83.

15 **Harding, R.** (2007) *State of Women's Enterprise in the UK*, PROWESS, Norwich.

16 **Sarri, K. and Trihopoulou, A.** (2005) 'Female entrepreneurs' personal characteristics and motivations: a review of the Greek situation', *Women in Management Review*, vol. 20, no. 1, pp. 24–36.

17 **Morris, M.H., Nola, M.N., Craig, W.E. and Coombes, S.M.** (2006) 'The dilemma of growth: understanding venture size choices of women entrepreneurs', *Journal of Small Business Management*, vol. 44, no. 2, pp. 221–44.

18 For example in the USA: **National Women's Business Council** (2007) *Study of Women-Owned and Led Businesses: An Overview of the Data in NWBC's Special Tabulations*, Small Business Administration National Women's Business Council/Concentrance Consulting Group, Washington, DC.

19 **Carter, S.** (2000) 'Improving the numbers and performance of women-owned businesses: some implications for training and advisory services', *Education and Training*, vol. 42, no. 4/5, pp. 326–33.

20 **Schmidt, R.A. and Parker, C.** (2003) 'Diversity in independent retailing: barriers and benefits – the impact of gender', *International Journal of Retail and Distribution Management*, vol. 31, no. 8, pp. 428–39.

21 **Orhan, M. and Scott, D.** (2001) 'Why women enter into entrepreneurship: an explanatory model',

Women in Management Review, vol. 16, no. 5, pp. 232–43.

22 **McClelland, E., Swail, J., Bell, J. and Ibbotson, P.** (2005) 'Following the pathway of female entrepreneurs: a six country investigation', *International Journal of Entrepreneurial Behaviour and Research*, vol. 11, no. 2, pp. 84–107.

23 **Ljunggren, E. and Kolvereid, L.** (1996) 'New business formation: does gender make a difference?', *Women in Management Review*, vol. 11, no. 4, pp. 3–12.

24 **Smith-Hunter, A.E. and Boyd, R.L.** (2004) 'Applying theories of entrepreneurship to a comparative analysis of white and minority women business owners', *Women in Management Review*, vol. 19, no. 1, pp. 18–28.

25 **Hundley, G.** (2000) 'Male/female earnings differences in self-employment: the effects of marriage, children, and the household division of labor', *Industrial and Labor Relations Review*, vol. 54, no. 1, pp. 95–114.

26 **Carter, S. and Rosa, P.** (1998) 'The financing of male and female owned businesses', *Entrepreneurship and Regional Development*, vol. 10, no. 3, pp. 225–41.

27 **Hirisch, R.D. and Brush, C.C.** (1983), 'The woman entrepreneur: management skills and business problems', *Journal of Small Business Management*, vol. 22, no. 1, pp. 30–7.

28 **Martin, L. and Wright, L.T.** (2005) 'No gender in cyberspace? Empowering entrepreneurship and innovation in female-run ICT small firms', *International Journal of Entrepreneurial Behaviour and Research*, vol. 11, no. 2, pp. 162–78.

29 **Dhaliwal, S.** (2000) 'Entrepreneurship – a learning process: the experiences of Asian female

entrepreneurs and women in business', *Education and Training*, vol. 42, no. 8, pp. 445–52.

30 **Parasuraman, S. and Simmers, C.A.** (2001) 'Type of employment, work–family conflict and well-being: a comparative study', *Journal of Organisational Behaviour*, vol. 22, pp. 551–68.

31 **PROWESS** (2011) 'About PROWESS' available at http://www.prowess.org.uk/about/about.asp (accessed at July 2011).

32 **Steele, C.** (1997) 'A threat in the air: how stereotypes shape intellectual identity and performance', *American Psychologist*, vol. 52, no. 6, pp. 613–29.

33 **Verheul, I., Uhlaner, L. and Thurik, A.R.** (2002) *Entrepreneurial Self Perception and Gender*, Erasmus Research Institute of Management Report.

34 **Shelton, L.M.** (2006) 'Female entrepreneurs, work–family conflict, and venture performance: new insights into the work–family interface', *Journal of Small Business Management*, vol. 44, no. 2, pp. 285–97.

35 **DTI/Small Business Service** (2003) *A Strategic Framework for Women's Enterprise*, Department for Business, Enterprise and Regulatory Reform, London.

36 For example **Pollitt, D.** (2005) 'Diversity is about more than observing the letter of the law', *Human Resource Management International Digest*, vol. 13, no. 4, pp. 37–40.

37 **Watkins, J.M. and Watkins, D.S.** (1984) 'The female entrepreneur: her background and determinants of business choice – some British data', *International Small Business Journal*, vol. 2, no. 4, pp. 21–31.

38 **Galloway, L.** (2010) 'The experiences of male gay business owners in the UK', *International Small Business Journal.*

39 **Office for National Statistics** (2003) *Report on Ethnicity in the UK*, ONS, London.

40 **Scottish Government** (2004) *Analysis of Ethnicity in the 2001 Census – Summary Report*, Office of the Chief Statistician, Scottish Government, Edinburgh.

41 **SBS** (2004) *A Government Action Plan for Small Business: The Evidence Base*, SBS/DTI, London.

42 **Light, I.** (1984) 'Immigrants and ethnic enterprise in North America', *Ethnic and Racial Studies*, vol. 7, no. 2, pp. 195–216.

43 **Bonacich, E., Light, I. and Wong, C.** (1977) 'Koreans in business', *Society*, vol. 14, pp. 54–9.

44 **Light, I.** (1980) 'Asian enterprise in America', in S. Cummings (ed.), *Self-help in Urban America*, Kennikat Press, New York, pp. 33–57.

45 **Glasgow, D.** (1980) *The Black Underclass*, Jossey-Bass, San Francisco, CA.

46 **Waldinger, R.** (1988) 'The ethnic division of labor transformed: native minorities and new immigrants in post-industrial New York', *New Community*, vol. 14, no. 3, pp. 318–32.

47 **Waldinger, R., Aldrich, H., Ward, R. and associates** (eds) (1990) *Ethnic Entrepreneurs*, Sage, Newbury Park, CA.

48 **Ward, R. and Jenkins, R.** (eds) (1984) *Ethnic Communities in Business*, Cambridge University Press, Cambridge.

49 **Waldinger, R., Aldrich, H., Ward, R. and associates** (1990) *Ethnic Entrepreneurs*, Sage, Newbury Park, CA.

50 **Light, I. and Bonacich, E.** (1988) *Immigrant Entrepreneurs*, California University Press, Berkeley, CA.

51 **Werbner, P.** (1990) 'Renewing an industrial past: British Pakistani entrepreneurship in Manchester', *Migration*, vol. 8, pp. 7–41.

52 **Ward, R.** (1991) 'Economic development and ethnic business', in J. Curran and R. Blackburn (eds), *Paths of Enterprise*, Routledge, London.

53 **Curran, J. and Blackburn, R.** (1993) *Ethnic Enterprise and the High Street Bank*, Kingston Small Business Research Centre, Kingston University, Survey.

54 **Ram, M. and Deakins, D.** (1995) *African-Caribbean Entrepreneurship in Britain*, University of Central England, Birmingham.

55 **Deakins, D., Hussain, G. and Ram, M.** (1993) *The Finance of Ethnic Minority Entrepreneurs*, University of Central England, Birmingham.

56 **Bank of England** (1999) *The Financing of Ethnic Minority Firms in the UK: A Special Report*, Bank of England, London.

57 **Ram, M., Smallbone, D. and Deakins, D.** (2002) *Ethnic Minority Businesses in the UK: Access to Finance and Business Support*, British Bankers' Association, London.

58 **Smallbone, D., Ram, M., Deakins, D. and Baldock, R.** (2003) 'Access to finance by ethnic minority businesses in the UK', *International Small Business Journal*, vol. 21, no. 3, pp. 291–314.

59 **Deakins, D., Ram. M., Smallbone, D. and Fletcher, M.** (2003) 'Ethnic minority entrepreneurs and the commercial banks in the UK: access to formal sources of finance and decision-making by their

bankers', in C.H. Stiles and C. Galbraith (eds), *Ethnic Entrepreneurship: Structure and Process*, Elsevier, Oxford, pp. 293–314.

60 **Wilson, K.L. and Portes, A.** (1980) 'Immigrant enclaves: an analysis of the labor market experiences of Cubans in Miami', *American Journal of Sociology*, vol. 86, pp. 295–319.

61 **Reeves F. and Ward, R.** (1984) 'West Indian business in Britain', in R. Ward and R. Jenkins (eds), *Ethnic Communities in Business*, Cambridge University Press, Cambridge.

62 **Jones, T., McEvoy, D. and Barrett, J.** (1992) 'Raising capital for the ethnic minority small business', paper presented for the ESRC Small Business Research Initiative, University of Warwick, September.

63 **Ram, M.** (1993) *Managing to Survive: Working Lives in Small Firms*, Routledge, London.

64 **Ram, M. and Hillin, G.** (1994) 'Achieving break-out: developing a strategy for the ethnic minority firm in the inner city', paper presented to the Ethnic Minority Small Firms Seminar, UCE, Birmingham, March.

65 **Ethnic Minority Business Initiative** (EMBI) (1991) *Final Report*, Home Office, London.

66 **Ram, M. and Hillin, G.** (1994) 'Achieving break-out: developing mainstream ethnic minority businesses', *Small Business and Enterprise Development*, vol. 1, no. 2, pp. 15–21.

67 **Deakins, D., Ishaq, M., Smallbone, D., Whittam, G. and Wyper, J.** (2005) *Minority Ethnic Enterprise in Scotland: A National Scoping Study, Final Research Report*, Scottish Government, Edinburgh.

68 **GEM** (2001) *Executive Report*, Kauffman Center for Entrepreneurial Leadership, Babson College, Boston, MA.

69 **Deakins, D., Ishaq, M., Whittam, G. and Wyper, J.** (2010) 'Diversity in ethnic minority business from rural and urban localities', *International Journal of Entrepreneurship and Small Business*, vol. 9, no. 2, pp. 177–92.

70 **Vertovec, S.** (2007) 'Super diversity and its implications', *Ethnic and Racial Studies*, vol. 30, no. 6, pp. 1024–54.

71 **Ram, M. and Smallbone, D.** (2004) 'Policies to support ethnic minority enterprise: the English experience', *Entrepreneurship and Regional Development*, vol. 15, no. 2, pp. 151–66.

72 **Deakins, D., Ram, M. and Smallbone, D.** (2003) 'Addressing the business support needs of ethnic minority firms in the UK', *Environment and Planning C; Government and Policy*, vol. 21, no. 4, pp. 843–59.

73 **Ram, M. and Jones, T.** (1998) *Ethnic Minorities in Business*, Small Business Research Trust, Milton Keynes.

74 **Humberside TEC** (1999) *Other Ethnic Businesses in Humberside*, Research Briefing no. 14, Humberside TEC.

75 **GLE/CEEDR** (2000) *Review of Business Support for Ethnic Minority Owned Businesses (EMBs) in London, Final Report*, May, Greater London Enterprise, London.

76 **Ram, M.** (1998) 'Enterprise support and ethnic minority firms', *Journal of Ethnic and Migration Studies*, vol. 24, no. 1, pp. 143–58.

77 **Deakins, D., Majmudar, M. and Paddison, A.** (1997) 'Developing success strategies for ethnic minorities in business: evidence from Scotland', *New Community*, vol. 23, no. 3, pp. 325–42.

78 **Marlow, S.** (1992) 'Take-up of business growth training schemes by ethnic minority owned firms', *International Small Business Journal*, vol. 10, no. 4, pp. 34–46.

79 **Ram, M. and Sparrow, J.** (1993) *Supporting Asian Businesses*, University of Central England Business School, UCE, Birmingham.

80 **Flap, H., Kumcu, A. and Bulder, B.** (1999) 'The social capital of ethnic entrepreneurs and their business success', in J. Rath (ed.), *Immigrant Businesses: The Economic, Political and Social Capital*, London, Macmillan.

81 **Curran, J. and Burrows, R.** (1988) *Enterprise in Britain: A National Profile of Small Business and the Self-employed*, Small Business Research Trust, Milton Keynes.

82 **Song, M.** (1997) 'Children's labour in ethnic family businesses: the case of Chinese takeaway businesses in Britain', *Ethnic and Racial Studies*, vol. 20. no. 1, pp. 690–716.

83 **Curran, J. and Blackburn, R.** (1993) *Ethnic Enterprise and the High Street Bank*, Kingston Business School, Kingston University, Surrey.

84 **Howarth, C., Tempest, S. and Coupland, C.** (2005) 'Rethinking entrepreneurship methodology and definitions of the entrepreneur,' *Journal of Small Business and Enterprise Development*, vol. 12, no. 1, pp. 24–40.

RECOMMENDED READING

Department for Business, Innovation and Skills (2009) *The Government's Response to the Ethnic Minority Business Task Force*, BIS, London.

Ram, M. and Jones, T. (2007) 'Ethnic minority businesses in the UK: a review of research and policy developments', report for the ESRC, paper presented to an ESRC/CRE/DTI/EMDA seminar, February, London.

Ram, M., Smallbone, D. and Deakins, D. (2002) *Ethnic Minority Businesses in the UK: Access to Finance and Business Support*, British Bankers' Association, London.

Vertovec, S. (2007) 'Super Diversity and its Implications', *Ethnic and Racial Studies*, vol. 30, no. 6, pp. 1024–54.

5 SOCIAL ENTREPRENEURSHIP

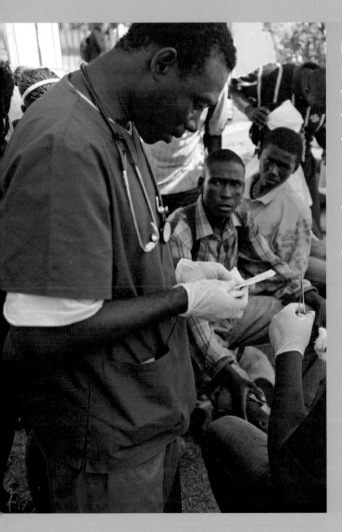

Chapter contributed by Dr Kean Birch, York University, Toronto and
Geoffrey Whittam, University of the West of Scotland

LEARNING OUTCOMES

At the end of this chapter you should be able to:

- Discuss the relevance of social entrepreneurship to society.

- Describe the differences between the third sector, social economy, social enterprise and social entrepreneurship.

- Describe the role and extent of social entrepreneurship in the modern economy.

- Discuss why social entrepreneurship has become popular with policymakers.

- Discuss the potential problems with social entrepreneurship in the delivery of services and goods.

- Discuss the importance of recent policy initiatives for their impact on social entrepreneurship.

- Describe examples of good practice within the field of social entrepreneurship.

INTRODUCTION

In 2006 the Nobel Peace Prize was jointly shared by Muhammad Yunus and the micro-finance organisation he founded, Grameen Bank. The bank was established to provide small loans to people – mainly women – in order to alleviate poverty in Bangladesh and was based on the concept of mutual trust in lending.[1] An 'Entrepreneurship in action' case study is discussed on Muhammad Yunus and the Grameen Bank in Chapter 11. The award of the Nobel Prize illustrates the growing importance placed on finding solutions to social and economic problems that are not constrained by free-market thinking and policies. In particular, the interest in finding social solutions to *socio-economic* problems such as poverty and global warming has stimulated numerous projects and initiatives that combine economic, social and ecological goals into a 'triple bottom line'.[2]

Increasingly such concerns with socio-economic problems and solutions have been 'mainstreamed' into government policy as evident in the UK over the last decade or so.[3] New Labour's (1997–2010) policy agenda, ably dissected by Haugh and Kitson,[4] sought to encourage social enterprise and social entrepreneurship.[5] Similarly, the new Coalition government (2010) has sought to position social entrepreneurship at the centre of an emerging 'Big Society' agenda championed by the Prime Minister. In a speech he gave in Liverpool in July 2010, David Cameron outlined the Big Society as:

> . . . about a huge culture change where people, in their everyday lives, in their homes, in their neighbourhoods, in their workplace don't always turn to officials, local authorities or central government for answers to the problems they face but instead feel both free and powerful enough to help themselves and their own communities.[6]

These various government agendas and policies can be criticised for positioning the social economy and social entrepreneurship as 'flanking mechanisms', designed to shore up a tottering free-market economic system by relieving the state of its responsibility for social welfare and shifting public service delivery to voluntary or charitable groups.[7] What has become worrying recently in light of the Big Society agenda and the knock-on effects of massive public-spending cuts is the threat that government policy neuters critical voices within the social economy, both in terms of the critique of government policy and the creation of alternative visions of socio-economic development.[8; 9]

Despite all this popular policy and scholarly interest, however, there is still considerable confusion over the definition of social entrepreneurship and its relationship to the third sector, social enterprise and social economy. Furthermore, there are questions about the extent of the third sector and what social entrepreneurship actually contributes to our societies and economies. As a consequence there has been a considerable amount of new research and studies of social entrepreneurship that has sought to reduce this confusion and provide a clearer picture of social entrepreneurship and its socio-economic impacts.[10] Despite the growing interest, however, Helen Haugh still argues that 'research in social entrepreneurship ... is hindered by the lack of standard and universally acceptable definitions'.[11]

Due to the continuing ambiguity around social entrepreneurship, it is important to maintain a critical stance when discussing the scholarly and political motivations behind conceptual definitions as well as empirical research and policy initiatives. An array of activities, organisations and individuals can be used as examples of social entrepreneurship, including corporate social responsibility (CSR),[12] fair trade,[13] and even events like *LiveAid*, although they all represent very different types of activity. In light of this, it is useful to keep in mind that the key feature of social entrepreneurship is the pursuit of a social goal using entrepreneurial or business-based methods. The first section of this chapter will clarify these definitional ambiguities, while the following sections will cover the extent of social entrepreneurship in the UK; the impacts of social entrepreneurship on socio-economic development; and the implications of recent policy agendas and initiatives in the UK.

ORIGINS OF SOCIAL ENTREPRENEURSHIP

The terms *social economy* and *third sector* are used to refer to social entrepreneurship in a general sense. The term social economy has a long pedigree stretching back to the early twentieth century and refers to changes (e.g. poverty, inequality) brought about as a consequence of the Industrial Revolution in the eighteenth and nineteenth centuries. In the English-speaking world the preferred term in academic debate, until relatively recently, was voluntary, or not-for-profit, sector. In France, and some other continental European countries, the term social economy has been in wide use for well over a century. The differences between Anglo and French organisational forms explains this difference, with the former more closely tied to charitable causes and communities while the latter are based on the notion of political liberty and free association. *Social entrepreneurship* itself was not used until the 1970s; since then it has become an increasingly popular term, promoted by the likes of Bill Drayton of Ashoka and the commentator Charles Leadbeater. More recently the term *social enterprise* has been coined to refer to organisations that pursue social objectives through business methods, while *third sector* is increasingly used to cover the whole gamut of such activities.

DISCUSSION QUESTIONS

1 What is social entrepreneurship?

2 How does social entrepreneurship contribute to socio-economic development?

3 Why has social entrepreneurship become popular amongst policymakers?

THREE KEY CONCEPTS

As mentioned above, social entrepreneurship can refer to many types of activity, organisation and people. Seelos and Mair [14] highlight this when they distinguish between at least three types of research on social entrepreneurship. It has been used, for example, to define the activities of non-profit organisations that are trying to diversify their funding sources so that they are less dependent upon grants from governments or private foundations – something which is increasingly important in light of public-spending cuts. It has also been used to define individuals who seek to solve a specific social problem. Finally, it has also been used to define commercial businesses which undertake socially responsible initiatives. From this diversity it is evident that the definition of social entrepreneurship has ranged from organising a community group through to incorporating corporate social responsibility into business decision-making; it is therefore important to delineate clearly between different concepts.

There are three core concepts underpinning the discussion of social entrepreneurship. All three are connected with one another, but they are also distinct (see Figure 5.1). The first concept is the social economy, which represents the organisations that pursue social goals not undertaken by either government or commercial businesses. However, it excludes the household and informal economies because the social economy consists of organisations with more formal structures and institutions. The second concept is that of social enterprise. This can be best represented as the activity of pursuing social objectives through entrepreneurial, business means and is therefore a sub-set of the social economy. Finally, social entrepreneurship is a concept that covers the individual motivation and leadership behind the pursuit of social objectives.

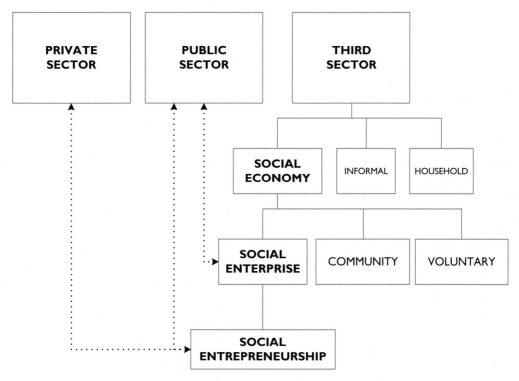

FIGURE 5.1

The third sector

SOURCE: Adapted from Birch and Whittam (2008).[10]

THE SOCIAL ECONOMY

The social economy is characterised by both specific organisational forms and organisational principles (see Table 5.1). The central feature is the pursuit of social objectives through reciprocal (as opposed to market or distributive) relationships between people and organisations.[15] The particular stress on non-profit and not-for-profit organisational forms contrasts with the private sector and, to some extent, with social enterprise. These principles mean that the social economy is made up of organisations which primarily seek to (and are often legally required to) reinvest any profits they make into the organisation itself and to serve public or social interests.[16] Some organisations, such as workers' co-operatives, are not required to serve the public interest – although they may do so – and can distribute profits amongst their members rather than to external stakeholders.[17] All these organisations are characterised by democratic decision-making, their independent status and mixed financing of activities. Consequently the means to achieve the social objectives of the organisation are as important as the social goals because some activities may contradict the underlying principles.[18] For example, an organisation that seeks to alleviate poverty could not be considered as part of the social economy if it involved the exploitation of workers or the degradation of the local community or environment. Thus the social economy represents the organisational structures and institutional environment in which social entrepreneurship is encouraged and promoted.

SOCIAL ENTERPRISE

It is possible to distinguish between three main groups within the social economy. These include *community groups* such as civic or neighbourhood societies and associations; *voluntary groups* like charities or housing associations; and *social enterprise groups* like the new Community Interest Company in the UK.[4] The last of these, social enterprise groups, represents the second core concept relevant to social entrepreneurship. In some definitions social entrepreneurship is regarded as the establishment of social enterprises;[19] however, this definition produces a rather simplistic perspective that does not address the motivation behind social entrepreneurship or explore the wider activities it involves. Social enterprise is better defined as the derivation of a significant proportion of organisational income – usually between 25 and 50 per cent – from trading activities.[20; 5] It can therefore represent a particular point in the life-cycle of an organisation; that is, when it achieves a level of financial sustainability that means it is no longer reliant upon grant-based funding.[21] It is the activity of social enterprise, rather than the creation of a particular organisation, that sets social enterprise apart from other elements of the social economy and wider third sector. Thus the extent to which trading dominates an organisation represents a useful means to define social enterprise.[22]

SOCIAL ENTREPRENEURSHIP

The preceding two concepts help to differentiate social entrepreneurship from the wider debates around the third sector. Social entrepreneurship does not necessarily rely upon specific organisational forms as is arguable

TABLE 5.1 ORGANISATIONAL FEATURES OF THE SOCIAL ECONOMY

Organisational form	Organisational principles
Not-for-profit / non-profit	Social objective (e.g. unmet needs)
Democratic	Voluntary (e.g. involvement by choice)
Mixed financing	Sustainable
Independent (e.g. non-state)	Mutual

TABLE 5.2 DEFINITIONS OF SOCIAL ENTREPRENEURSHIP

Leadbeater (1997)	Individuals whose social capital enables them to promote social value through innovation.[27]
Brinckerhoff (2000)	Individuals who take risks on the behalf of other people.[28]
Thompson et al. (2000)	Individual who combines vision, values and resources to address an unmet need.[29]
Dees (2001)	Individuals who act as 'change agents' in society.[30]
Institute for Social Entrepreneurs (2002)	Obtaining both a financial and social return on investment.[31]
Mort et al. (2003)	Individuals whose leadership and personal credibility can generate commitment to a social goal in others.[32]
Haugh (2005)	Activities connected to the creation of social value and organisations to pursue those social values.[11]
Mair and Marti (2006)	Focus on creating social value over creating economic value.[33]
Nicholls (2006)	Combination of accountability, effectiveness and impact.[22]
Peredo and McLean (2006)	Aim to create social value; vision of an opportunity to create value; innovation; accept risks; and resourceful.[19]

with the social economy. Nor does it necessarily entail specific types of activity as is, again, arguable, with social enterprise. Rather it concerns the motivation and leadership that underpins the commitment to pursuing social goals. In many ways it is similar to the idea of the 'public entrepreneur'[23] or the 'social' or 'civic' entrepreneur,[24] because there are no specific organisational forms or activities that need to underpin social entrepreneurship. Instead, social entrepreneurship concerns more ephemeral characteristics (for definition see Table 5.2.) For example, Nicholls and Cho[25] argue that social entrepreneurship has three dimensions: *sociality* or the intentional pursuit of social goals; *innovation* to change society; and *market orientation* to search for financial resources. In a more famous definition, Dees[30] describes social entrepreneurs as people who act as 'change agent[s] in the social sector' by adopting a mission, pursuing new opportunities, innovating and learning, avoiding limits on resources, and being concerned with accountability. Similarly, Bornstein[26] defines social entrepreneurs as 'people with new ideas to address major problems who are relentless in the pursuit of their visions'. What comes across in these descriptions is the crucial importance of a 'vision' to social entrepreneurship alongside the combination of both imagination and evangelism to pursue this vision. Thus social entrepreneurship is characterised by the willingness to seek new paths and to find others who will follow that path.

THE EXTENT OF THE THIRD SECTOR

There are several difficulties with measuring the extent of the third sector and social entrepreneurship. The first concerns the definition of third sector organisations (TSOs), which can range from charities through to workers' co-operatives. The second related problem is that because there is no standard definition, data on TSOs have not been collected in a systematic fashion by a single agency. Finally, and most importantly here, social entrepreneurship can be found throughout the three sectors of the economy – public, private and third – making it particularly difficult to calculate.

Despite these difficulties, there have been a number of attempts in the last few years to collect systematic data on TSOs and social entrepreneurship. For example, ECOTEC[34] estimated that there were 5,300 social enterprises in the UK. However, since then a report by IFF Research[35] for the former DTI's *Small Business Service* identified 15,000 social enterprises, which has since been revised to 55,000 – or 5 per cent of all businesses – two years later.[36; 37] It is reasonable to assume that the difference between these numbers illustrates the problems in defining the third sector rather than showing an explosion in TSO numbers. The difference also illustrates the extent to which the third sector has become an important policy agenda because there has been a drive to produce creditable data. Recent research by the new *Third Sector Research Centre*, established in 2008, illustrates some of the difficulties in defining and measuring the third sector.[38] It also represents a very useful resource base when studying or researching social entrepreneurship.

As well as numbers of TSOs, it is important to take into consideration the size of the third sector workforce and extent of volunteering. This is because the size of the workforce is more likely to reveal the extent of social entrepreneurship, as opposed to the overall third sector, since the number of social enterprises only covers certain organisations. In Britain, the voluntary sector employed around 600,000 people in 2005, or 2 per cent of the British population,[39] which has risen to 668,000 people in 2008/09.[40] Between 1996 and 2008/09 then, there has been a 38 per cent rise in people employed by the voluntary sector although the proportion of the total population has largely remained the same over these intervening years (see Table 5.3). Furthermore, the number of people who volunteer at least once a month has been estimated at 11.6 million or the equivalent of around one million full-time employees.[41] Considering this information it is evident that the voluntary sector contributes significantly to British society in terms of both employment and the social impact that volunteering can make to people's lives.

Despite the large increase in the voluntary sector workforce in the last ten years, the sector has mainly kept pace with other sectors rather than growing disproportionately to them. More specific assessments of social entrepreneurship, such as those by the Global Entrepreneurship Monitor (GEM), estimate that 1.2 million people or 3.2 per cent of the British population was engaged in social entrepreneurship in 2005.[41] This would suggest that the voluntary sector does not cover the whole gamut of social entrepreneurship and that there is still a need to develop clearer definitions and evidence of social entrepreneurship.

Despite these misgivings, it is useful to also consider the geographical distribution of the third sector and social entrepreneurship because it shows that they are both concentrated in specific areas (see Figure 5.2). This figure shows that they are regionally concentrated in places like London and the south-west and north-west of

TABLE 5.3 THE BRITISH WORKFORCE BY SECTOR, 1996–2005 (THOUSANDS/PER CENT)

	1996	1999	2002	2005
Voluntary sector	483 (2)	544 (2)	567 (2)	611 (2)
Public sector	6,135 (24)	6,112 (23)	6,441 (24)	6,978 (25)
Private sector	18,517 (74)	19,680 (75)	20,536 (75)	20,536 (73)
Total	25,141	26,339	27,231	28,130

Source: Adapted from Clark (2007), p. 8.[39]

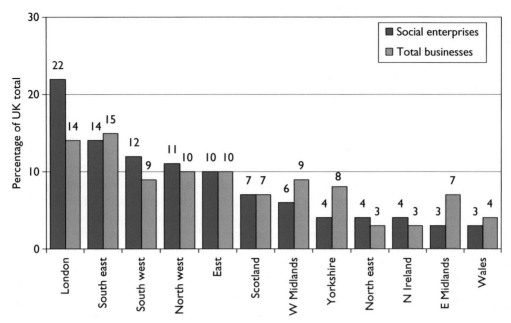

FIGURE 5.2

Regional spread of the British third sector

SOURCE: Adapted from IFF Research (2005), p.11.[35]

England, as well as being located in deprived areas and in urban areas.[35; 41; 42] More recent data also illustrate a particular geography to the third sector; for example, Figure 5.3 shows a clear connection between the number of voluntary organisations in a region and the relative economic performance of a region. The regions with the most voluntary sector organisations are those with the best GDP performance, like London, south east, south west and east England, and Scotland.

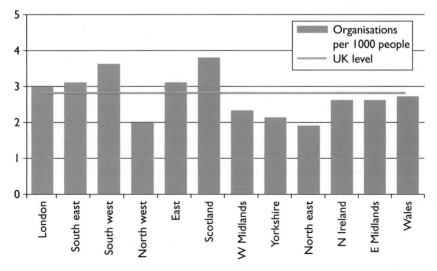

FIGURE 5.3

Regional spread of the British voluntary sector

SOURCE: Adapted from Clark et al. (2010).[40]

THE SOCIO-ECONOMIC IMPACTS OF SOCIAL ENTREPRENEURSHIP

One of the main reasons that the third sector and social entrepreneurship are receiving increased academic and policy attention in recent years is because of the perceived contribution that they can have to social and not just economic development. It is for this reason that it is useful to consider what *socio-economic* impacts the third sector and social entrepreneurship have. The policy and academic debates on social entrepreneurship have emphasised the important role that it has with regard to the creation and embedding of *social capital*.[28; 36; 37] The concept of social capital is itself complex and has also received considerable attention in recent years (for definitions see Table 5.4).[43; 44; 45] A number of different types of social capital have been identified, each of which performs different functions not all of which are socially beneficial. The importance of the third sector and social entrepreneurship in both producing and reproducing social capital is therefore difficult to identify definitively. However, it is possible to consider how social entrepreneurship might both contribute to its development as well as depend upon different forms of social capital.[10; 46] A discussion of the role of social capital in entrepreneurship is also provided in Chapter 1.

TABLE 5.4 SOCIAL CAPITAL DEFINITIONS

General definition	The reciprocal relationships in a social network that produce trust, shared norms and access to information[44]
Bonding social capital	The intra-community bonds that produce social norms and cohesion
Binding social capital	The network of extra-community ties that connect different groups to one another producing trust between groups
Linking social capital	The links between disparate groups with diverse and different norms that enable access to new information
Holding social capital	The holders and builders of social bonds, networks and links who act as change agents

SOCIAL ENTREPRENEURSHIP AND THE CREATION OF SOCIAL CAPITAL

It is important to remember that social entrepreneurship does not clearly relate to either a set of outcomes or a simple process, but rather to individual motivation and leadership. As such, social entrepreneurship concerns the ability of people to perceive opportunities (e.g. vision of an unmet social need), their capacity to seize those opportunities (e.g. their knowledge and skills), the resources they have available (e.g. financial and social capital) and the social change that they engender in their immediate social group and further afield (e.g. institutional transformation).[30] All these features of social entrepreneurship to some extent depend upon the social capital that individuals or groups of individuals currently have. In turn, they lead to the creation of new social capital.[10]

Social entrepreneurship, in this context, entails more than the ability of a person to earn income or develop innovative strategies in pursuit of a social goal. This is for at least two reasons. First, an income-earning focus would ignore the importance of shared norms such as reciprocity and co-operation in the social economy. Furthermore, it would also ignore a whole swathe of individuals involved in a range of activities from corporate social responsibility (CSR) and corporate philanthropy[47] through to 'anti-preneurs' in the global justice movement or non-mainstream groups.[48] Thus any understanding of the impact of social entrepreneurship needs to take into account the social value that is produced, especially in the form of social capital.

Second, innovation as a process of social value creation could entail the destruction of existing social relations, social institutions and communities and their replacement with new social structures. Thus innovation could destroy potentially beneficial social capital as much as it creates new, beneficial forms of social capital.

Taking these two issues seriously means that social entrepreneurship involves more than merely the achievement of financial independence or the introduction of new ideas in pursuit of social value. Social value already exists in the form of social capital and social entrepreneurship entails the strengthening and extension of this social capital. Social entrepreneurship can achieve these aims because of the unique position it has in social change. First, it engenders collaboration between a diverse range of individuals and groups, linking them together in the pursuit of a common social goal. For example, the 'Entrepreneurship in Action' case study of *Kibble Education and Care Centre*, in the box below, shows how the shift from grant-funding to earned-income depended upon the establishment of new working-relationships between Kibble and local authorities in Scotland to provide services for excluded young people. Second, such collaboration means that social entrepreneurship promotes and develops new social networks by bringing different individuals and groups together. For example, to provide opportunities for excluded young people, Kibble has spun out a number of new social

ENTREPRENEURSHIP IN ACTION

Kibble Education and Care Centre

A social enterprise working with young people, a model for the future . . . an enterprise from the past.

The Kibble Centre in Paisley is a social enterprise working with young people who have a complex mix of social, emotional, educational and behavioural problems, and with over 400 employees and a turnover of over £15 million is one of Scotland's largest social enterprises. Kibble has had its success recognised by a host of awards, such as The Social Enterprise of the Year 2004, Enterprising Solutions, and Young Social Enterprise 2005, and is known particularly for its social innovation. Kibble has a long history, founded in 1857 by a charitable bequest from Miss Elizabeth Kibble who came from a wealthy Paisley textile family. In her last will and testament of 1840 she laid down that the money be used to 'found and endow in Paisley an Institution for the purpose of reclaiming youthful offenders against the laws'. This same charitable mission is still at the core of all that Kibble does; however, there have been many challenges and changes in the over 150 years of Kibble's existence.

Over the period Kibble has changed status from Reformatory to Industrial School to Approved School to List D School and from 1 April 1996 to Kibble Education and Care Centre. It is the latter change which posed the greatest challenge to Kibble. 1996 marked the change from Kibble being maintained and run by grants from local authorities to having to become a 'self-financing business'. While ownership was still the responsibility of local trustees they had little understanding of how services could be sold. Additionally, managers had come through the public service route and were now being asked to commercialise their work and furthermore, staff had followed policies and worked to local authority guidelines and procedures. There was a stark choice: close the centre or develop a new form of organisation.

The trustees and staff chose the latter strategy, so a new company was formed to become the organisation's trading arm, limited by guarantee but still with charitable status. The new company would operate

▶

with its mission at its heart, as a social business still owned and governed by the local community. The bank was convinced of the viability of the business plan and agreed to provide overdraft facilities over the critical early months.

The new way of working also required a new way of thinking for Kibble's main customers, the local authorities. Many local authorities in the west of Scotland appeared to be opposed to outsourcing their services; much of the controversy centred on what charges should be paid for services. The local authorities believed that they had the right to set the price and Kibble should then simply make a budget fit whatever it was given by each of Scotland's 32 local authorities. However, after a period of approximately six years, good working relationships were established between local authorities and Kibble, and the organisation has grown from a turnover of £1.4m and about 60 staff with fewer than 50 people being looked after at the facility to a turnover of over £15m, employing over 400 staff, accommodating over 100 young people.

In an interview with Graham Bell, the CE of Kibble said the success of Kibble is based on 'the decision to build the strategy on the mission, as opposed to building the mission on the strategy'.[1] Furthermore, a decision was also taken to be 'future thinking' around its social mission, which has led to Kibble identifying market niches. In the early days this involved exploiting the social reform process, which had been developing. 1997–98 saw 'an emphasis on firstly reducing the number of young people in residential care, and secondly increasing community support for young people in need. Kibble's strategy was built on meeting both of these reforming trends.' In other words, Kibble sought to provide services that local authorities were obliged to provide but are unwilling or unable to do so. A further aspect of the forward-thinking strategy involved making greater use of the campus, utilising it for non-residential use, for youth training, care leavers' services and outreach support services etc. This had the further advantage of maintaining solid links with the local community. This strategic thinking was based on a large amount of research undertaken by the staff of Kibble, which meant visiting similar organisations at home and abroad and discovering 'best practice'. The links established at this time have continued to be developed and Kibble has a worldwide reputation for education and caring support for vulnerable young people.

Kibble also operates *Kibble Works*: social enterprise companies where many of the young people at Kibble, who are at risk of being classed as MC2 (young people requiring More Choices, More Chances, formerly described as NEET not in employment, education or training), are given an opportunity to work and learn within a commercially viable and sustainable social enterprise. Each year since 1996 new services equivalent to two new small social businesses have developed under the Kibble umbrella. The Kibble Works enterprises make Kibble a social enterprise incubator and the spin-out businesses include warehousing and distribution, recycling, trades, marketing, catering, print solutions, ICT, vehicle maintenance and administration.

Kibble, with 93 per cent of turnover coming from fee income, has moved a long way since 1996 and 100 per cent dependency on grant income.

Further information: http://www.kibble.org/index.php

enterprises through its trading arm, *Kibble Works*. These enable young people to work and learn new skills in a commercial setting making them directly relevant to employers elsewhere.

As well as the beneficial features of social entrepreneurship, it is important to consider the possible downsides of social entrepreneurship. In particular, there is a possibility that the visions driving social value creation are unaccountable to democratic decision-making because they depend upon a single driving agent (e.g. an individual or a group). Disparities in power between the social entrepreneur and the group or community they seek to help may mean that it is the social entrepreneur rather than the group or community that defines the social value of a particular project.[49] Furthermore, the social entrepreneur's capacity to operate between different groups means that they can position themselves at crucial points to ensure that it is their vision that inspires the different groups rather than the visions of the different groups themselves. The social entrepreneur can utilise their social capital to strengthen their own social capital without strengthening that of the groups they are helping. In order to alleviate this problem, social entrepreneurship could adopt a *stakeholder* model of organising that both provides legitimacy for the social entrepreneur[50] as well as an avenue for the groups they seek to help to make their wishes known.[51]

POLICY INITIATIVES AND THEIR IMPLICATIONS

Social entrepreneurship and the third sector have engendered considerable policy interest and support within the EU in the last few years.[52] Policy support has been particularly evident in Britain with both the recent Labour government (1997–2010) and the new Coalition government (2010). For example, an early indication of the Labour government's endorsement of social entrepreneurship was the 1998 launch of the *Compact* between the government and the third sector,[53] which sought to formalise the relationship between the two sectors.[3] Subsequent policy agendas and initiatives have reinforced this relationship. These include the establishment of the Active Communities Directorate (ACD) in 1999 at the Home Office and a Social Enterprise Unit (SEU) in 2002 at the DTI. The SEU quickly produced a social enterprise strategy, also in 2002, whose central aims were to:

- Create an enabling environment
- Make social enterprises better businesses, and
- Establish the value of social enterprise.[5]

Another objective was to establish ways to measure the extent of social enterprise and social entrepreneurship which led to a 2003 report by ECOTEC identifying 5,300 social enterprises.[34] The Social Enterprise Coalition also arose out of this agenda and now represents the 'voice of the sector'.[54]

Since then there have been a raft of policies designed to encourage and stimulate the third sector. For example, the 2004 *Futurebuilders* programme was set up to provide capital investment for TSOs, while other initiatives like the Community Development Finance Institutions (CDFI) and Community Interest Company (CIC) have also been established to encourage social entrepreneurship.[55; 4] The latter are a new type of company introduced in 2005 that is designed to provide community benefit and to lock company assets so that they are used for this goal. Since 2005 around 1500 CICs have been set up. In 2006 the government set up the Office of the Third Sector (OTS) in the Cabinet Office, bringing together the ACD and SEU in one department.[56] Under the auspices of the newly created OTS, the government established the Community Asset Fund (CAF) in 2007,[57] which was designed to refurbish local authority buildings before their transfer to TSOs.

More recently, in 2010 the Coalition government's Big Society agenda has led to the dismantling of the OTS and its replacement with the Office for Civil Society (OCS). The OCS works:

. . . across government departments to translate the Big Society agenda into practical policies, provides support to voluntary and community organisations and is responsible for delivering a number of key Big Society programmes.[58]

The recent Big Society agenda illustrates another example of the 'mainstreaming' of the third sector (or civil society) into public policy, which Kendall[3] argues started under the previous Labour government; this was and still is an unprecedented move with regard to the relationship between the state and the third sector. The implications of this mainstreaming are most obvious in relation to public service reform during the Labour administration – which has been tied to the financial sustainability of the third sector[59] – and the potential effects of public spending cuts and austerity measures under the Coalition.[9] The idea of a self-sustaining third sector has become intrinsically linked to public-sector reform and public spending because third sector organisations (TSOs) and social entrepreneurship are seen as key vehicles for the delivery of public services since they are supposed to be more attuned to the needs of service users.[60] One example of this was the Labour government's support for the building up of TSOs' capacity for service delivery through *Futurebuilders*, while the third sector *Compacts* made it clear 'that public funding is provided on the basis of its contribution to government "policy priorities"'.[61]

The shift to a contract-based relationship between TSOs and the government, from the previous grants-based one, has had a significant impact on the third sector. Firstly, the increasing reliance of the third sector on government contracts, rather than grants, has been highlighted as a concern because it concentrates resources in the largest TSOs which have a greater capacity to both bid for contracts and to administer them when granted.[62; 63] Secondly, despite the claimed benefits of third sector involvement in service delivery, there have been reports that question the effectiveness and responsiveness of the third sector.[64] Thirdly, there have been concerns about the general ability of TSOs to become self-financing.[65] Finally, and in light of the public-spending cuts pursued by the Coalition, it is likely that the third sector, including many community, voluntary and charitable organisations, faces up to £5 billion worth of cuts over the next few years[66]; the impact of this funding loss is incalculable, raising fears about the decimation of not only the third sector but also civil society generally.[9] What all this means for social entrepreneurship is unclear since the policy initiatives undertaken by the last two governments could both release individuals with visions for social change from existing constraints, yet at the same time establish new constraints to deal with.

Some policy issues are highlighted in the following 'Entrepreneurship in Action' box on Surrey Docks Farm.

ENTREPRENEURSHIP IN ACTION

Surrey Docks Farm, Rotherhithe, London

Surrey Docks Farm is a working farm on the Thames Path in Rotherhithe, central London, two miles downstream from Tower Bridge.

Its 2.2-acre site has an orchard with beehives and geese, a farmyard with goats, sheep, turkeys and chickens, there are pigs, two cows, two donkeys and a pony. There are rabbits, guinea-pigs and ferrets. The farm also has vegetable and fruit growing areas, allotments, a herb and dye garden, a duck pond, a wildlife area and more.

The farm is an educational charity whose mission is . . .

> To run a working farm that is a community asset: to provide educational and practical opportunities for all people in the local area and beyond, for them to learn about and experience farming, food production, animal care, horticulture, crafts, cooking, nutrition and any other relevant matters.

We promote equal opportunities, teamwork, responsibility, respect for people and nature, sustainability, health and recreation.

The farm is very much part of the local community. It is run by a Management Committee that is elected each year by members of the farm's Provident Society – membership of that is open to all at £1 a year.

The farm is open to visitors seven days a week. During the week, it is visited by many organised school parties who are given hands-on workshops and tours by the farm's Education Officer.

The farm's New Leaf and Cow Pat projects are designed to give adults with learning difficulties choice-based experience and therapy with plants, produce and animals. Those adults arrive through local Social Services departments and several charities.

The farm increasingly provides placements for school-age students who might be home-educated, between schools, having problems at school or in trouble.

Visitors to the farm are encouraged to feed the animals and learn about them. The farm produces meat, fruit and vegetables for eating and sells that produce, and honey, jams, etc. and crafts too. The farm encourages participation for all in those processes through volunteering, allotment holding and, for example, the Have a Go Horticulture and Young Farmers clubs. It's a rural experience in the city and one of the farm's key partners is the Worshipful Company of Farmers.

The farm has an 8-tonne lorry that is its Mobile Farm; it takes a variety of animals to schools, fairs and special events and sets up a small farmyard there.

The farm encourages volunteering in every aspect of its work, with the animals, with horticulture, with repairs and maintenance, and in the office. Around ten corporate teams from banks etc. held team-building days at the farm in 2010. The farm's multi-ethnic and hugely varied team of volunteers represents the rich diversity of the area. The farm has an excellent reputation for taking on troubled and withdrawn volunteers and helping them to develop and make new contacts.

Much work is done with the London Probation Service. Their Community Payback scheme sends minor offenders to the farm to help with a wide variety of work.

The excellent farm café is open five days a week (Wednesday–Sunday). The farm's blacksmith has done recent work for Hampton Court Palace and the Tower of London. There are regular open-to-all yoga, sewing, pottery, beekeeping, floristry and massage sessions at the farm. The farm is a huge local community asset that is providing more and more local services.

The farm costs around £300,000 a year to run and has five paid members of staff. It earns 80 per cent of its income and Southwark Council provides the other 20 per cent. The farm is always looking for ways to broaden and increase its income streams.

Please see video clip of the mobile farm: http://www.youtube.com/watch?v=JzWsCz8X91A.

DISCUSSION QUESTIONS

1   How has policy supported this example of social enterprise?

2   What are the benefits to local communities?

3   What are the arguments for and against policymakers supporting social enterprises?

CONCLUSIONS

In this chapter we have explored the meaning of social entrepreneurship and its importance to socio-economic development. Social entrepreneurship has a long and somewhat convoluted history from its origins in the nineteenth century through to the present day when it has assumed growing importance in academic and policy circles. Social entrepreneurship can be defined as the pursuit of a vision of social change that necessitates the enrolment of others into the cause. As such it not only involves the creation of social value as well as economic value, but also an awareness of opportunities and innovative solutions to problems, accountability to a greater good, and an element of risk-taking.

It has been estimated that over one million people in the UK are involved in social entrepreneurship[41] and that there are over 50,000 British social enterprises.[36] However, despite the growth in the voluntary sector, social enterprises and social entrepreneurship, two points need to be emphasised. First, the sector as whole has largely kept pace with both the public and private sectors over the last decade or so in the UK.[39] Second, the distribution of the third sector is highly uneven across Britain with certain places like London and south-west England having higher proportions of social enterprises than other regions.[35]

Consequently, there may be limitations to the role that social entrepreneurship can have in socio-economic development.[10] Despite this caveat, we can argue that social entrepreneurship has a significant impact on the development of communities through the encouragement of social capital. The chapter defined social capital as the reciprocal relationships in a social network that produce trust, shared norms and access to information.[44] It also highlighted how it is important to differentiate between types of social capital in order to understand the impact of social entrepreneurship. Furthermore, it is crucial to consider the possible negative effects of social entrepreneurship such as the unaccountability of certain visions due to power disparities and the need to spread social capital rather than concentrate it in one individual or organisation.

Finally, the chapter has outlined recent British government policy agendas designed to encourage the third sector and social entrepreneurship. It is evident that the third sector has become an important policy tool for the delivery of public services following the 'hollowing out' of the state during the 1980s and 1990s. A number of policy initiatives have been particularly important, including the introduction of a new type of company designed specifically to operate as a social enterprise: that is, the Community Interest Company. Further initiatives include the voluntary sector 'compact' to encourage cooperation between the state and third sectors and the *Futurebuilders* programme to enhance the capacity of third sector organisations to deliver public services. However, despite this encouragement of social entrepreneurship, a number of worrying issues remain. For example, does social entrepreneurship represent the best way to deliver services and goods to vulnerable groups in society? What does the 'mainstreaming' of the third sector mean for the future of social entrepreneurship? How will the third sector retain its distinctive features in a society that is dominated by the private and public sectors? What impact will the public-funding cuts have on the third sector? Despite these concerns, social entrepreneurship remains an exciting opportunity and a fulfilling experience for many people who want to change the world.

REVIEW QUESTIONS

1 What is social capital and how does it contribute to socio-economic development?
2 What is the relationship between social entrepreneurship and social capital?
3 What are the problematic features of social entrepreneurship? Discuss whether and how these issues can be alleviated.
4 What has driven third sector policy in the UK?
5 Has third sector policy in the UK helped to encourage social entrepreneurship?
6 What impact does the policy shift from grant funding to contract funding have on social entrepreneurship?

SUGGESTED ASSIGNMENTS

1 Students are split into groups and asked to define the key terms: third sector, social entrepreneurship, social economy and social enterprise. In particular students should identify the key characteristics of social entrepreneurship identified in the recommended readings.

2 Students discuss the relationship between social entrepreneurship and social capital. Why is it important to consider the social *and* economic impacts of entrepreneurial activity?

3 Students discuss why social entrepreneurship has become so popular in policy circles. Identify some key problems which social enterprises may face in the future.

4 Go to the following web-site: http://www.skollfoundation.org/ and you will find nine examples of projects started by social entrepreneurs posted on YouTube. View one of these postings and identify similarities and differences between your example and the 'Entrepreneurship in Action' case study of *Kibble* in this chapter.

REFERENCES

1 **Grameen Foundation**, http://www.grameenfoundation.org.
2 **Elkington, J.** (2004) 'Enter the triple bottom line', in A. Henriques and J. Richardson (eds), *The Triple Bottom Line*, Earthscan, London.
3 **Kendall, J.** (2000) 'The mainstreaming of the third sector into public policy in England in the late 1990s: whys and wherefores', *Policy and Politics*, vol. 28, pp. 541–62.
4 **Haugh, H. and Kitson, M.** (2007) 'The Third Way and the third sector: New Labour's economic policy and the social economy', *Cambridge Journal of Economics*, vol. 31, pp. 973–94.
5 **DTI** (2002) *Social Enterprise: a strategy for success*, Department of Trade and Industry, London.
6 **Cameron, D.** (2010) *Big Society Speech*, Monday 19 June 2010, Liverpool (http://www.number10.gov.uk/news/speeches-and-transcripts/2010/07/big-society-speech-53572, accessed February 2011).
7 **Graefe, P.** (2007) 'Social economy policies as flanking for neoliberalism: transnational policy solutions, emergent contradictions, local

alternatives', in S. Lee and S. McBride (eds), *Neo-liberalism, State Power and Global Governance*, Springer, Netherlands, pp. 69–86.

8   **McMurtry, J.J.** (2004) 'Social economy as political practice', *International Journal of Social Economics*, vol. 31, pp. 868–78.

9   **Toynbee, P.** (2011) 'Big society's a busted flush, but who will admit it first?', *The Guardian*, Monday 7 February 2011 (http://www.guardian.co.uk/commentisfree/2011/feb/07/big-society-is-not-working, accessed February 2011).

10   **Birch, K. and Whittam, G.** (2008) 'Critical survey: The third sector and the regional development of social capital', *Regional Studies*, vol. 42, pp. 437–50.

11   **Haugh, H.** (2005) 'A research agenda for social entrepreneurship', *Social Enterprise Journal*, vol. 1, pp. 1–12.

12   **Trebeck, K.** (2008) 'Exploring the responsiveness of companies: corporate social responsibility to stakeholders', *Social Responsibility Journal*, vol. 4, pp. 349–65.

13   **Reed, D.** (2009) 'What do corporations have to do with fair trade? Positive and normative analysis from a value chain perspective', *Journal of Business Ethics*, vol. 86, pp. 3–26.

14   **Seelos, C. and Mair, J.** (2005) 'Sustainable development: How social entrepreneurs make it happen', IESE Business School Working Paper No. 611, University of Navarra.

15   **Amin, A., Cameron, A. and Hudson, R.** (2002) *Placing the Social Economy*, Routledge, London.

16   **Moulaert, F. and Ailenei, O.** (2005) 'Social economy, third sector and solidarity relations: A conceptual synthesis from history to present', *Urban Studies*, vol. 42, pp. 2037–53.

17   **Lindsay, G. and Hems, L.** (2004) 'Sociétés cooperatives d'intérêt collectif: The arrival of social enterprise within the French social economy', *Voluntas: International Journal of Voluntary and Nonprofit Organizations*, vol. 15, pp. 265–86.

18   **Eikenberry, A. and Kluver, J.** (2004) 'The marketization of the nonprofit sector: Civil society at risk?', *Public Administration Review*, vol. 64, pp. 132–40.

19   **Peredo, A. and McLean, M.** (2006) 'Social entrepreneurship: A critical review of the concept', *Journal of World Business*, vol. 41, pp. 56–65.

20   **OECD** (1999) *Social Enterprises*, Organisation for Economic Co-operation and Development, Paris.

21   **Arthur, L., Scott Cato, M., Keenoy, T. and Smith, R.** (2003) 'Developing an operational definition of the social economy', *Journal of Cooperative Studies*, vol. 36, pp. 163–89.

22   **Nicholls, A.** (2006) 'Playing the field: a new approach to the meaning of social entrepreneurship', *Social Enterprise Journal*, vol. 2, pp. 1–5.

23   **Waddock, S. and Post, J.** (1991) 'Social entrepreneurs and catalytic change', *Public Administration Review*, vol. 51, pp. 393–401.

24   **Hockerts, K.** (2006) 'Entrepreneurial opportunity in social purpose business ventures', in J. Mair, J. Robertson and K. Hockerts (eds), *Social Entrepreneurship*, Palgrave Macmillan, London.

25   **Nicholls, A. and Cho, A.** (2006) 'Social entrepreneurship: The structuration of a field', in A. Nicholls (ed.), *Social Entrepreneurship: New Models of Sustainable Social Change*, Oxford University Press, Oxford, pp. 99–118.

26   **Bornstein, D.** (2005) *How to Change the World: Social Entre-preneurs and the Power of New Ideas*, Penguin Books, New Delhi, p. 1.

27   **Leadbeater, C.** (1997) *The rise of the social entrepreneur*, Demos, London.

28   **Brinckerhoff, P.** (2000) *Social Entrepreneurship*, John Wiley & Sons, New York.

29   **Thompson, J., Alvy, G. and Lees, A.** (2000) 'Social entrepreneurship – a new look at the people and the potential', *Management Decision*, vol. 38, pp. 328–38.

30   **Dees, J.G.** (2001) 'The Meaning of "Social Entrepreneurship"', online paper available at http://www.fuqua.duke.edu/centers/case/documents/dees_SE.pdf.

31   **The Institute for Social Entrepreneurs** http://www.socialent.org.

32   **Mort, G., Weerawardena, J. and Carnegie, K.** (2003) 'Social entrepreneurship: Towards conceptualisation', *International Journal of Nonprofit and Voluntary Sector Marketing*, vol. 8, pp. 76–88.

33   **Mair, J. and Marti, I.** (2006) 'Social entrepreneurship research: A source of explanation, prediction, and delight', *Journal of World Business*, vol. 41, pp. 36–44.

34   **ECOTEC** (2003) *Guidance on Mapping Social Enterprise: Final Report to the DTI Social Enterprise Unit*, Department of Trade and Industry, London.

35   **IFF Research** (2005) *A Survey of Social Enterprise Across the UK*, Small Business Service, London.

36   **HM Treasury and Cabinet Office** (2006) *The Future Role of the Third Sector in Social and Economic Regeneration: Interim Report*, HM Treasury, London.

37   **HM Treasury and Cabinet Office** (2007) *The Future Role of the Third Sector in Social and Economic Regeneration: Final Report*, HM Treasury, London.

38 **Lyon, D., Teasdale, S. and Baldock, R.** (2010) *Approaches to Measuring the Scale of the Social Enterprise Sector in the UK*, Working Paper 43, Third Sector Research Centre.

39 **Clark, J.** (2007) *The UK Voluntary Sector Workforce Almanac*, National Council for Voluntary Organisations, London.

40 **Clark, J., Kane, D., Wilding, K. and Wilton, J.** (2010) *UK Civil Society Almanac 2010*, National Council for Voluntary Organisations, London.

41 **Harding, R.** (2006) *GEM Social Entrepreneurship Monitor: United Kingdom 2006*, London Business School, London.

42 **Buckingham, H., Pinch, S. and Sunley, P.** (2010) *The Regional Geography of Social Enterprise in the UK: a Review of Recent Surveys*, Working Paper 35, Third Sector Research Centre.

43 **Putnam, R.** (2000) *Bowling Alone*, Simon & Schuster, London.

44 **Woolcock, M.** (1998) 'Social capital and economic development: Toward a theoretical synthesis and policy framework', *Theory and Society*, vol. 27, pp. 151–208.

45 **Fine, B.** (2001) *Social Capital versus Social Theory*, Routledge, London.

46 **Evans, M. and Syrett, S.** (2007) 'Generating social capital? The social economy and local economic development', *European Urban and Regional Studies*, vol. 14, pp. 55–74.

47 **Trebeck, K.** (2007) *Private Sector Contribution to Regeneration: Concepts, Actions and Synergies*, CPPR Working Paper 9, University of Glasgow, Glasgow.

48 **Adbusters**, http://adbusters.org/metas/politico/antipreneur/forum.

49 **Baron, S.** (2004) 'Social capital in British politics and policy making', in J. Franklin (ed.), *Politics, Trust and Networks: Social Capital in Critical Perspective*, Families & Social Capital ESRC Research Group Working Paper 7, South Bank University, London.

50 **Dart, R.** (2004) 'The legitimacy of social enterprise', *Nonprofit Management and Leadership*, vol. 14, pp. 411–24.

51 **Tracey, P., Phillips, N. and Haugh, H.** (2005) 'Beyond philanthropy: Community enterprise as a basis for corporate citizenship', *Journal of Business Ethics*, vol. 58, pp. 327–44.

52 **EU**, http://ec.europa.eu/enterprise/entrepeneurship/coop/index.htm.

53 **Voluntary Sector Compact**, http://www.thecompact.org.uk.

54 **Social Enterprise Coalition**, http://www.socialenterprise.org.uk.

55 **Community Interest Company**, http://www.cicregulator.gov.uk.

56 **The Office of the Third Sector**, http://www.cabinetoffice.gov.uk/third_sector.aspx.

57 **OTS** (2007) *Consultation on the Community Asset Fund*, Office of the Third Sector, London.

58 **Office of Civil Society**, http://www.cabinetoffice.gov.uk/big-society.

59 **Wallace, B.** (2005) 'Exploring the meanings(s) of sustainability for community based social entrepreneurs', *Social Enterprise Journal*, vol. 1, pp. 78–89.

60 **OTS** (2006) *Partnership in Public Services: An Action Plan for Third Sector Involvement*, Office of the Third Sector, London.

61 **Fyfe, N.** (2005) 'Making space for "neo-communitarianism"? The third sector, state and civil society in the UK', *Antipode*, vol. 37, pp. 536–57 at p. 543.

62 **Wittenberg, B.** (2007) 'Under the thumb of the state', *The Guardian*, 6 June.

63 **Burdett, R.** (2007) 'Industrial disease', *The Guardian*, 17 October.

64 **Hopkins, A.** (2007) *Delivering public services: Service users' experiences of the third sector*, National Consumer Council, London.

65 **Casselman, B.** (2007) 'Why "social enterprise" rarely works', *The Wall Street Journal*, 1 June.

66 **Joy, I**. (2010) *Preparing for Cuts*, New Philanthropy Capital, London.

RECOMMENDED READING

Dees, G. (2001) *The Meaning of 'Social Entrepreneurship'*, online paper available at: http://www.fuqua.duke.edu/centers/case/documents/dees_SE.pdf.

DTI (2002) *Social Enterprise: A Strategy for Success*, Department of Trade and Industry, London, available online at: http://www.cabinetoffice.gov.uk/third_sector/social_enterprise/action_plan.aspx.

Harding, R. (2006) *GEM: Social Entrepreneurship Monitor: United Kingdom 2006*, London Business School, London, available online at: http://www.london.edu/gem.html.

Jones, D., Keogh, B. and O'Leary, H. (2007) *Developing the Social Economy: Critical Review of the Literature*, Communities

Scotland, Edinburgh, available online at: http://www. communitiesscotland. gov.uk/stellent/groups/public/ documents/webpages/PIR_ DEVELOPINGTHESOCIAL ECONOMY.hcsp?&sitemap=1.

Leadbeater, C. (1997) *The Rise of the Social Entrepreneur*, DEMOS, London, available online at: http://www.demos. co.uk/publications/ socialentrepreneur.

Peredo, A. and McLean, M. (2006) 'Social entrepreneurship: A critical review of the concept', *Journal of World Business*, vol. 41, pp. 56–65.

6 CORPORATE ENTREPRENEURSHIP

LEARNING OUTCOMES

At the end of this chapter you should be able to:

- Identify the importance of entrepreneurship within existing firms.

- Discuss the various forms of corporate entrepreneurship and describe the factors that may affect their success.

- Describe the components of an entrepreneurial orientation and the importance of a balanced pursuit of these.

- Discuss the environmental changes that are driving the focus upon corporate entrepreneurship.

- Outline emerging empirical patterns of intrapreneurship and appreciate the importance of quantification.

INTRODUCTION

As Chapter 1 detailed, there is a great variety of approaches to defining entrepreneurship, reflecting varying perspectives. However, common in many of them, and common in public conceptions of entrepreneurship, is the pursuit of opportunity with limited resources. This is entrepreneurship as manifest in most new-venture creation activities, where market opportunities are identified and exploited in the face of resource constraints.[1] How then can we make sense of corporate entrepreneurship? In a world where, when compared to most of the new and small firms we encounter, corporations appear to have an abundance of resources. They appear well endowed with human, financial and physical capital; they frequently enjoy brand equity, which helps them launch new products and services; and, of course, they usually have, at least some, successful products or services (with the associated income streams). In this light, the phrase 'corporate entrepreneurship' seems a curious juxtaposition or contradiction in terms.[2] Yet, longstanding evidence[3; 4] appears to suggests that the process of identifying and exploiting opportunities in large established firms is subject to a similar bundle of risks as those faced by new ventures and smaller enterprises.[1]

Perhaps more importantly, while the study of corporate entrepreneurship is not new, there is a growing belief in an increasing entrepreneurial imperative for large corporations.[5] This imperative is being driven by turbulence in the various environments in which corporations operate. In these terms Morris, Kuratko and Covin[6] talk about the 'embattled corporation', facing dramatic changes in the way they must do business. These authors identify four dimensions through which environmental turbulence has created a need for new management practices, in general, and in corporate entrepreneurship in particular:

- Through *customers* – where increasingly fragmented markets do not permit a 'one size fits all' approach to serving diverse customer groups and where rising customer expectations place greater emphasis on costly customization (including investments in relationships and in more elaborate support functions)

- Through *competitors* – where competitors' new products tempt existing customers away and place an additional burden on new product development, where the speed of innovation and imitation has improved (and intellectual property becomes less easy to protect), and where technology changes have permitted small niche players to encroach on the more profitable markets of large diversified firms

- Through *technology* – where technological advances in information search and management, but also in customer management, production, sales, logistics and inventory management, and, perhaps most crucially, in the technologies of innovation, have raised new challenges for executives in large firms

- Through *legal, regulatory and ethical standards* – where increasing oversight has resulted in greater accountability to a wider group of stakeholders, growing litigation has raised the stakes on liability, more stringent regulatory environments have limited choice and forced companies to learn new ways to compete, and, most recently, rising affluence in home countries has seen priorities shift amongst some stakeholder groups, leading to more public attempts to hold companies accountable for the social and environmental consequences of their actions.

Of course, these four domains are not entirely independent. For instance, much of the increased oversight has been afforded by new media technologies. Similarly, new niche competition is a result, at least in part, of market fragmentation. Neither is the idea of enacting entrepreneurial strategies in turbulent environments a new one. Indeed, it harks back to the classic work of Burns and Stalker[7] on organic and mechanistic firms and to Miller and Friesen[8] on innovation in conservative and entrepreneurial firms. One of the shared theses of these is the contingent role played by the environment in strategy formulations. In other words, while firm strategy and organizational structure must 'fit', both must also fit with the firm's environment. That is, while organic firms pursuing entrepreneurial strategies may prosper in turbulent environments, conservative firms with mechanistic structures are better suited to stable environments. Our contention, and the impetus behind much of the renewed interest in corporate entrepreneurship, is that there are very few stable environments remaining where conservatism will win the day. At best, large firms can aim for ambidexterity, through which the superintendence and administration of existing business is carried out in parallel with the search for new business.[9; 10] To employ March's classic terminology:[11] the former may be thought of as 'exploitation', while the latter is 'exploration'.

In the current chapter we attempt to further delineate what is meant by corporate entrepreneurship and to look at some of the forms it takes. We also look, in large, at corporate entrepreneurship as strategy. What does it mean and what does it require at the organisational level to have an entrepreneurial strategy or to be open to corporate entrepreneurship? What limitations might be suggested by the existing work and the corporate entrepreneurship thesis? We conclude the chapter by recounting some recent empirical evidence on one particular form of corporate entrepreneurship – 'intrapreneurship'.

DEFINITIONS AND FORMS OF CORPORATE ENTREPRENEURSHIP

As the earlier allusion to ambidexterity hints, corporate entrepreneurship is often modelled as a learning process through which firms sequentially engage in exploration and exploitation.[1] That is, opportunity search activities are followed by the exploitation of resulting discoveries. However, what seems to be becoming more common is an emphasis on the concurrency of exploration and exploitation. This 'true' ambidexterity, wherein firms simultaneously explore potential new opportunities while also exploiting existing products, services, markets and so on, raises greater challenges around, for instance, the allocation of resources and is at the core of striving to pursue corporate entrepreneurship as strategy. Before we turn to this, however, it is important to stress that corporate entrepreneurship is not homogeneous in form.[12]

A fairly typical definition of corporate entrepreneurship is offered by Sharma and Chrisman[13] as: 'the process whereby an individual or group of individuals, in association with an existing organization, create a new organization or instigate renewal or innovation within that organization'. In this we can see the common distinction between the creation and pursuit of new venture opportunities and strategic renewal.[14] The former, following the work of Gifford Pinchot in the 1980s,[15] is normally labelled 'intrapreneurship' since it refers to [almost] classical entrepreneurial activities within existing firms. The latter, in contrast, is often captured under the term 'strategic entrepreneurship',[16] which has been defined as 'involving the identification and exploitation of opportunities, while simultaneously creating and sustaining competitive advantage'.[1; 17] Broadly, it may involve such activities as strategic renewal, organizational rejuvenation, sustained regeneration, business model reconstruction and domain redefinition.[18] Stopford and Baden-Fuller[19] go a step further, noting that 'the strategy literature identifies three types of corporate entrepreneurship...':

1　Individual: the creation of new businesses within existing organizations – what is called 'intrapreneurship' or 'corporate venturing' (e.g. 3M's development and introduction of Post-it Notes is a classic account of intrapreneurship[20]).

2　Renewal: the transformation or renewal of existing organizations – that is, 'strategic entrepreneurship' (IBM's reinvention of its core business in the 1990s is perhaps one of the more dramatic recent examples of corporate renewal).

3　Framebreaking: where an enterprise changes the 'rules of competition' for its industry (Dell's direct selling and mass customization approach to computers is one such example[14]).

However, these 'types' are not unrelated or wholly independent (see below). As Stopford and Baden-Fuller note,[19] 'most authors accept that all types of entrepreneurship are based on innovations that require changes in the patterns of resource deployment and the creation of new capabilities to add new possibilities for positioning in markets' (p. 522). Following this, two common themes appear to underscore almost all definitions of corporate entrepreneurship: a focus on innovation; and an indication of the centrality of the innovation activity to the overall activities of the firm.[21]

Yet, notwithstanding these common themes, there is considerable variety in how companies approach corporate entrepreneurship – not least as the scope of corporate entrepreneurship is widening to organizations and contexts not previously thought to be fertile ground for entrepreneurship (such as the public and third sector organizations). To this end Wolcott and Lippitz[22] provide a useful framework for simplifying and understanding the bases of heterogeneity in approaches to corporate entrepreneurship.

These authors contend that there are two dimensions falling under the control of management that consistently differentiate the approach companies take towards corporate entrepreneurship:

Organizational ownership – 'who, if anyone, within the organization has primary ownership for the creation of the new business? (Note: responsibility and accountability ... might be focused in a designated group or groups, or it might be diffused across the organization)' (p. 76)

Resource authority – 'is there a dedicated "pot of money" allocated to corporate entrepreneurship, or are new business concepts funded in an ad hoc manner through divisional or corporate budgets?' (p. 76)

The potential independence of these two dimensions allows the authors to draw a 2 x 2 matrix, which serves to outline four 'dominant' models (Figure 6.1). For instance, the combination of diffused ownership of corporate entrepreneurial activities and ad hoc funding is styled the 'opportunist' approach, while more focused ownership and dedicated resources is associated with the 'producer' approach. The basic premise of the framework is that the different approaches are likely to be more or less suitable for different environments. This idea that one size is unlikely to fit all is intuitively appealing and accords with the acknowledged heterogeneity of corporate entrepreneurship – if not with the casual use of the term.

In more detail: the authors suggest that most companies begin with the *opportunist* model. As we will discuss below, unstructured individual entrepreneurship typically precedes more structured and pervasive

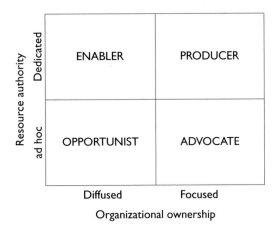

FIGURE 6.1

A typology of approaches to corporate entrepreneurship

SOURCE: Adapted from Wolcott and Lippitz (2007).[22]

organization-wide entrepreneurship.[19] In the absence of dedicated resources or designated ownership, corporate entrepreneurship relies upon 'the efforts and serendipity of intrepid "project champions"' (p. 76). Of course, it may not happen at all. The *opportunist* approach is only likely to work in high-trust environments, with extensive social networks underlying the formal organizational hierarchy. In such environments, multiple executives are liable to be in a position to encounter and endorse new venture proposals. In environments where these are absent, ideas are likely to fall through the cracks or be insufficiently supported.

Following one or more unstructured successes, organizations are likely to become more considered in their approach to pursuing organic growth through corporate entrepreneurship. A diffused, ad hoc, approach is unlikely to be one which promises easy reproducibility. As such, the *opportunist* model is positioned as a starting point from which companies evolve to the more premeditated models that occupy that top and right of Figure 6.1. Again, the suitability of the various models is contingent upon the fit with the organizational environment. The *enabler* model, for instance, is proposed for organizations where concept development and experimentation are relatively inexpensive (e.g. consultancies and technology organizations).

As Wolcott and Lippitz note, Google is the poster child of the *enabler* model. At Google, employees are permitted to spend up to 20 per cent of their time exploring concepts, building prototypes, selling their ideas to colleagues and building teams to champion them. Project teams form themselves, based on their own terms. If, and when, the team believes it has a commercially viable opportunity it approaches the Google Product Council (which includes the company founders and senior executives) for funding. Successfully funded projects receive further assistance from the Google Product Strategy Forum (e.g. in business modelling and in setting milestones). While there is a dedicated source of funds (and other resources), entrepreneurial activity is open to, and encouraged in, all employees. Crucial to this openness is the principle that the Google Product Council applies no predetermined criteria or hurdle rates on projects. As long as there is demonstrated promise and employee interest, projects may continue.

Of course, Google is not a typical company. Its entrepreneurial culture, the fast-paced technology and market environments it inhabits and its access to capital make it a difficult company to imitate. However, Wolcott and Lippitz point out that other organizations, such as Boeing and Whirlpool, have also found that 'dedicated funds for innovation combined with clear, disciplined processes for allocating those funds can go a long way to unlocking latent entrepreneurial potential' (p. 77). The basic premise of the *enabler* model is that employees, from across the company, will be prepared to develop new ideas if they are given enough support. Importantly, this support is not simply financial. The *enabler* model also requires strong personnel development and executive engagement if it is to succeed. In Google, the former is manifest in creative and elaborate recruitment activities (see Figure 6.2) that are designed to ensure that new employees are a fit for Google's culture. The latter, however, is equally important in ensuring trust in the organization's commitment to corporate entrepreneurship.

There is also a danger that access to such dedicated pools of resource may encourage 'bowling for dollars' – i.e. the pursuit of projects that should fall within ordinary business-unit activity or projects that the employees are not seriously committed to championing. An alternative approach, which avoids this danger, is the *advocate* model. In the *advocate* model, funding is not at issue. Rather, the company assigns ownership of corporate entrepreneurial activity to a dedicated group who act as evangelists and advisers to other parts of the organization. Where projects are pursued, the funding comes largely from existing business-unit budgets. As an example, Wolcott and Lippitz cite DuPont's Market Driven Growth initiative. In 1999, having determined that DuPont had reached a 'stall point', CEO Chad Holliday asked executive Bob Cooper to develop and implement an initiative that would help reinvigorate company growth. The result was the company-wide launch of the Market Driven Growth initiative in 2000 (see also http://marketdrivengrowth. blogspot.com). The initiative provides DuPont employees with a range of help and advice on activities from idea generation to commercialization. New-venture project teams work with a facilitator from the programme to prepare a business plan that is subsequently presented to business-unit leadership. Successful ventures act as signals to other parts of the organization and have helped build a multi-billion dollar growth portfolio at DuPont. Importantly, use of the programme is not mandated by senior executives and tangible support is fairly modest (Wolcott and Lippitz report that it is staffed by five full-time employees). Indeed, Bob Cooper is recorded as saying: 'I thought I'd spend most of my time helping design and build new businesses … Instead, I spent at least half my time advocating' (p. 78).[22] This *advocacy* model has proven particularly adept at promoting the growth of established business through the introduction of new ideas. It also helps prevent 'turf wars' between old and new business by allowing the 'old' some ownership of the 'new'. It is, however, less likely to be accommodating of more radical forms of corporate entrepreneurship or innovation.

While established business units are unlikely sponsors of disruptive innovation and change, a *producer* model which vests both resources and ownership in a unit with dedicated responsibility for corporate entrepreneurship may be more permissive. A well-resourced, independent initiative will be better placed to provide the co-ordination necessary where complex technologies are involved or where projects require competences that are spread across different parts of the organization. Wolcott and Lippitz cite IBM, Motorola and Cargill as examples of companies pursuing a *producer* model, but elaborate on Cargill's approach: the Emerging Business Accelerator (EBA). They quote David Patchen (the unit's founder and managing director): 'Prior to the EBA we lacked a clearly defined process for pursuing opportunities that fell outside the scope of existing business units and functions' (p. 78).[22] The EBA was founded in 2004 to complement the activities of the outward-looking corporate venture arm: Cargill Ventures. However, the EBA is not about innovation in existing businesses (Cargill has a Chief Innovation Officer structure that is separate from the EBA); rather, it is concerned with the development of new business. The group funds new business opportunities that have the potential to become new business units for Cargill. The ideas

FIGURE 6.2

Google engineer recruitment advert, 2004

underpinning these opportunities may come from within the organization or from outside. The example given by Wolcott and Lippitz relates the development of de-icing technology: Cargill's established de-icing business identified a new de-icing technology that inhibited ice formation. Given cost and performance considerations, the new technology was to be marketed and sold to road builders for critical applications such as bridges. However, Cargill's existing de-icing business was positioned in a commodity market, selling in volume to the United States Department of Transport. While the technology originated in the established business unit, the business model required to commercialize it was unfamiliar. Accordingly, the new technology was transferred to the EBA to bring it to market.

The EBA positions itself as a 'global clearing house for new concepts and value propositions across Cargill' (p. 79).[22] It gathers promising opportunities, builds executive teams, conducts due diligence, provides capital and monitors performance.

Of course, the *producer* model is not without challenges. Clearly, to be pursued on a similar scale to Cargill, it requires the commitment of considerable resource. It also entails the initial separation of promising projects and the eventual reintroduction of successes. Neither of these is easy, and jealousy and anxiety must be guarded against. For the *producer* model to work, organizations must build credibility and trust in their corporate-venture activities.

In summary, the archetypes suggested by Wolcott and Lippitz (2007) are a simplifying device. While corporate entrepreneurship activities in some companies may resemble one of the four ideal forms more than others, the two dimensions are more usefully thought of as continua with any individual organization's position reflecting as a tendency towards more or less focused ownership and more or less dedicated resources. Indeed, Wolcott and Lippitz[22] suggest that very large companies may be able to pursue multiple approaches to corporate entrepreneurship, noting within IBM the coexistence of an *advocate* model (Thinkplace and the innovation jams – e.g. https://www.collaborationjam.com) and a hybrid *producer-advocate* model in the form of the Emerging Business Opportunities programme. Indeed, like an *enabler*, IBM also supports corporate entrepreneurship at the divisional level and has developed a corporate culture that, through distributed power bases, may represent aspects of an *opportunist* model. Ultimately, however, the message is clear:

> Unless a company is blessed with the right culture – and few are – corporate entrepreneurship won't just happen. It needs to be nurtured and managed as a strategic, deliberate act. The traditional, isolated 'skunkworks' project is no longer the primary option for companies pursuing the creation of new businesses. Indeed, as IBM, Google, DuPont and others have shown, corporate entrepreneurship does not have to rely solely on serendipity and the grassroots efforts of a few 'project champions'.[22]
>
> (p. 82)

CORPORATE ENTREPRENEURSHIP AS STRATEGY

The idea, then, is that while corporate entrepreneurial initiatives may frequently appear as the unplanned byproducts of an organization's day-to-day (deliberate and spontaneous) actions,[23] this is likely to be insufficient. Such outcomes may speak to the ubiquity of corporate entrepreneurship, but are unlikely to be the basis of a sustainable strategy. Rather as Ireland, Covin and Kuratko[24] suggest, corporate entrepreneurship as strategy 'implies a level of purposefulness and intentionality with respect to entrepreneurial initiatives that is anything other than inevitable' (p. 21).

The starting point for this appears to be a commitment to innovation and entrepreneurship amongst the senior executives in an organization. In their study of a select number of large, European domestic appliance producers, Baden-Fuller and Stopford[19] observed that individual entrepreneurship 'especially amongst those who hold power' (p. 534) paved the way for more persistent organization-wide entrepreneurship: 'Sustainable progress did not start until the top team was committed to a common direction and was prepared to undergo the pain of reexamining their fundamental values' (p. 530).

This is a common theme. Ireland, Covin and Kuratko[24] talk in terms of 'pro-entrepreneurial cognition', noting that it is essential in top managers if a corporate entrepreneurship strategy is to be introduced and to prevail. While important, the pro-entrepreneurial cognition of other employees is likely to be a function of the extent to which the organization's incentive system encourages entrepreneurial activities such as opportunity recognition and exploitation – and this will be shaped, in large part, by the executive team.

While these authors define pro-entrepreneurial cognition as positive attitudes to entrepreneurship that are independent of context, there is a clear parallel with the more familiar concept of 'entrepreneurial orientation' (EO). Evidence suggests that EO, which has been shown to associate with stronger performance,[25] is found in organizations where senior executives and organizational culture demonstrate a strong disposition towards innovation, through risk taking and the pursuit of opportunity.[26] Indeed, Dess and Lumpkin[14] are quite blunt: 'Firms that want to engage in successful CE need to have an EO' (p. 147). Entrepreneurial orientation is the driving force for corporate entrepreneurship.

ENTREPRENEURIAL ORIENTATION

What then is entrepreneurial orientation? Adapted from Dess and Lumpkin,[14] Table 6.1 outlines the dimensions of EO typically elaborated in the research literature.

Often these attributes are presented entirely in a positive light. As Dess and Lumpkin themselves note, those that advocate the acquisition of a strong entrepreneurial orientation display a 'normative bias'. In other words, they implicitly favour the pursuit of exploration and adaptation over the efficient allocation and exploitation of the organization's existing resources. Accordingly, and following Dess and Lumpkin, we attempt a more balanced elaboration of the dimensions listed in Table 6.1:

Autonomy – While 'top down' approaches to supporting corporate entrepreneurship, such as those discussed in the previous section, are characteristic of the more entrepreneurial organizations, it nonetheless appears true

TABLE 6.1 DIMENSIONS OF ENTREPRENEURIAL ORIENTATION

Dimension	Definition
Autonomy	Scope for independent action by individuals or groups in pursuit of a business opportunity
Innovativeness	A willingness to pursue novelty through investments in experimentation and creativity. Novelty may be manifest in many aspects of the business
Proactiveness	Opportunity orientation. The efforts an organization makes to identify and seize opportunities. Often characterized as foresight or a 'forward-looking' perspective
Competitive aggressiveness	A willingness to 'do battle' with competitors. Refers to an organization's efforts to outperform or out-compete rivals
Risk-taking	The willingness to make decisions and commit resources to projects or ventures whose outcomes cannot be known with certainty in advance

Source: Dess and Lumpkin, (2005).[14]

that many of the best ideas come from the 'bottom up'. For these ideas to become adequately defined and to gain impetus, a product (or project) 'champion' is often required. These champions busy themselves with resource acquisition and advocacy and, in this, require considerable freedom of action or discretion in decision-making.

The primary danger that may result from too much autonomy is one of co-ordination. In the absence of co-ordination there is considerable danger of inefficiency through duplication of effort and insufficient oversight. Clearly, as we will see with all dimensions of EO, a balance must be struck. Part of striking this balance is about defining a clear sense of purpose, and we return to this below.

Innovativeness – As noted earlier in the chapter, innovativeness is perhaps the only consistent theme in the literature on corporate entrepreneurship. Without doubt, innovativeness is a central component in an entrepreneurial strategy. Importantly, as discussed elsewhere in the text, innovation is not simply a technological phenomenon. While new products or production processes may be the source of increased revenues or reduced costs, competitive advantage is as likely to arise from new ways of doing business involving, for instance, new ways of serving markets or new ways of organizing resources (e.g. consider Dell's direct selling model and its impact on the PC industry).

Of course, an innovation strategy is essentially speculative, with returns unknowable in advance. Innovators run the risk of wasted resources if investments (in R&D, training, marketing and so on) don't yield the hoped-for results. Even if the innovation is successfully developed, the risks of imitation are often very high. Nonetheless, alertness to and investment in new ways to create and capture value are the clearest characteristics of organizations pursuing a corporate entrepreneurship strategy.

Proactiveness – Related to innovativeness, proactive organizations 'monitor trends, identify the future needs of existing customers, and anticipated changes in demand or emerging problems that can lead to new venture opportunities' (p. 150).[14] It is not, of course, simply about spotting patterns, but must also be accompanied by a willingness to act on the new intelligence. Successful proactiveness confers first mover advantages on organizations, and requires that competitors devote resources to responding. The benefits to being a first mover include: premium pricing (with a period where there is no competition to drive down prices); brand building; and channel selection (e.g. the best suppliers or distributors).

However, there are also costs to pioneering and not all first movers are successful. For instance, in addition to direct development costs, first movers with new technologies and new products typically have to bear the costs of educating or convincing sceptical customers. These initial costs, and a commitment to original processes, often result in persistently higher costs that allow followers to underprice leaders. Similarly, early followers may also learn from the mistakes and successes of their predecessors which serves to reduce their own investment requirements and risks. Recent evidence supports this ambivalent picture, suggesting that while there is often a sales premium to pioneering, this may be outweighed by cost disadvantages.[27; 28] As before, a delicate balancing act that weighs costs and benefits is required.

Competitive aggressiveness – Refers to the efforts an organization makes to outperform its rivals. Often this involves leveraging the resources made available through past successes (as a result of innovativeness or proactiveness). Common manifestations of aggressiveness include entering new markets with dramatically lower prices than incumbents (often sacrificing profitability to achieve market share) or pre-announcing new products or technologies to discourage competitors (in addition to informing customers). Despite the apparent contradiction in terms, competitive aggression may also be defensive, such that 'firms need to be forceful in defending the competitive position that has made them an industry leader' (p. 151).[14] And copying the practices and techniques of successful competitors is common.

However, more aggressiveness is not always positive. Companies may damage their reputation and lose goodwill by being too aggressive. Dess and Lumpkin give Microsoft and its consequent antitrust travails as an example of this. They conclude that 'competitive aggressiveness is a strategy best used in moderation' (p. 152).

Risk-taking – Risk-taking relates to an organization's readiness to pursue opportunities despite uncertainty around the eventual success. That is, 'to act boldly without knowing the consequences' (p. 152).[14] Like innovation, risk-taking is central to contemporary (and casual) definitions of classical entrepreneurship. Successful corporate entrepreneurship typically involves investments far in advance of anticipated returns. And, equally typically, the scale of these anticipated returns will be unknowable. Dess and Lumpkin identify three types of risk that organisations and their executives face in pursuing entrepreneurial activities:

1   Business risk – associated with activities such as entering new markets or supporting unproven technologies
2   Financial risk – relating to the financial exposure required and the risk/return profile of any new venture. That is, to engage in entrepreneurial activities, organizations may have to borrow heavily or commit large proportions of their resources
3   Personal risk – refers to the reputation effects of success or failure for executives leading the new venture. Success in the new venture can give executives considerable influence over the future direction of the organization (as well as significant pecuniary and status rewards). Failure, of course, can have the opposite effects

In this way, risks are not something that organizations seek out for their own sake. Rather, as Drucker argued, entrepreneurs (corporate or classical) are not typically risk seekers.[29] Like most rational individuals they take steps to minimize risk. A corporate entrepreneurship strategy may involve a higher tolerance for risk, but the calculation of risks is a crucial activity.

Following this, in discussing the dimensions of entrepreneurial orientation, as the basis of corporate entrepreneurship, we have indicated in all instances the need for 'balance'.

As noted above, there is danger that discussions of corporate entrepreneurship take on too normative a tone such that innovation is good, more innovation is better, or risk-taking is good, more risk-taking is better. Given the consequences of unsuccessful innovation, risk-taking and so on, this would certainly be foolish. Firms must, it is suggested, 'strike a balance'. But how is the right balance to be found? Is there an algorithm or scoresheet which may be used?

Clearly the answer to this final question is 'no'. However, in avoiding ill-considered imperatives to pursue entrepreneurship we believe that organizations may usefully think about why they exist. While some might argue that, at least, private-sector organizations exist to make money, it makes more sense to think of organizations existing to create value. Money is made only to the extent that value is created, communicated and priced. Organizations that fail to create sufficient value rarely persist. Accordingly, any strategy that the organization pursues should aim at creating more value or reducing the costs of value creation – the aim being to maximize the difference between value and costs. A focus on 'value' ought to help in balancing, by requiring organizations to examine the motivations for pursuing new opportunities and providing a basis for estimating costs and benefits. Moreover, as Dess and Lumpkin conclude,[14] 'whatever form CE efforts take, the key to successfully creating value is viewing every value chain activity as a source of competitive advantage'. Or, at least, as a potential source of competitive advantage.

QUANTIFYING CORPORATE ENTREPRENEURSHIP

We opened this chapter by noting growing interest in corporate entrepreneurship and a growing belief in its importance as a competitive strategy for firms and organizations. However, whether this increasing attention reflects an increasing incidence of entrepreneurial activities within these firms and organizations is more difficult to say. While the extent of classical entrepreneurship, in the form of new venture creation, is often proxied by government-collected data on business start-up rates or self-employment figures, there is no equivalent data source for corporate entrepreneurship. Indeed, most studies of corporate entrepreneurship involve a few case studies (often exclusively concerned with successful firms) or, rarely, limited surveys. As such, it is difficult to say with any confidence how commonplace or widespread is corporate entrepreneurship. Certainly, our *intuition* is that it is on the increase in line with changing environmental and competitive pressures. However, this is hardly satisfactory and a key challenge remains acceptably quantifying the level of corporate entrepreneurship.

To this end an intriguing recent project is reported in a paper by three Dutch economists, Neils Bosma, Erik Stam and Sander Wennekers.[30] As an extension of the Global Entrepreneurship Monitor, and using a similar framework, these authors report the levels of **intrapreneurship** in 11 countries.[a] The authors stress that their study is exploratory and we should certainly be careful in drawing conclusions from it. However, the initial findings are intriguing.

In the first instance, it is important to recall that 'intrapreneurship' is only part of what we have discussed as corporate entrepreneurship. However, it is an important part and is most closely aligned with notions of classical entrepreneurship. In their study, Bosma, Stam and Wennekers operationalize intrapreneurship as 'employees developing new business activities for their employer, including establishing a new outlet or subsidiary and launching new products or product-market combinations' (p. 4). From this, they further distinguish 'narrow' and 'broad' definitions, where the latter includes individuals engaged in *either* idea development for new business *or* preparation and exploitation of these activities. The former (i.e. the narrow definition) requires that individuals be involved in both idea development and the exploitation of opportunities. Here, the parallel with our early discussions of exploration and exploitation is clear.

Regardless of whether intrapreneurship is defined narrowly or broadly, the headline figures are quite clear: intrapreneurship is a minority activity. On the basis of the narrow definition, Bosma and colleagues report intrapreneurship rates (as percentage of employees) ranging from 0.6 per cent in Iran to 4.2 per cent in Norway. Adopting the broader definition inevitably increases the rate of intrapreneurship – from 1.2 per cent (again, in Iran) and 7.4 per cent (again, in Norway). These figures are far lower than those for classical entrepreneurship (using the GEM's Total Entrepreneurship Activity rate – recall Chapter 2), though it is important to note that the simple number of individuals involved in these activities is unlikely to be a very good indicator of the relative economic impact of intrapreneurship and classical entrepreneurship.

Beyond simple frequencies, the authors also highlight some interesting patterns in the data. For instance, there appears to be an inverted U-shaped relationship between employee age and intrapreneurship prevalence rates, with the lowest rates recorded for employees aged 18–24 and 55–64. Perhaps unsurprisingly, intrapreneurship increases with firm size; it is more than double in companies employing in excess of 250 compared to those employing fewer than 10. Women also seem less likely to be intrapreneurial than men, especially in high-income countries. Indeed, in contrast to the U-shaped relationship observed between economic development and classical entrepreneurship (recall Chapter 2), the data suggest a simpler positive relationship between the wealth of a country (measured by GDP per capita) and intrapreneurship rates.

While the relationship is far from perfect (with low-income Chile recording a higher intrapreneurship rate than high-income Spain), the data displayed in Figure 6.3 are strongly suggestive of increasing intrapreneurship with increasing economic development. By way of potential explanation, Bosma and colleagues note that higher education levels, higher employee autonomy and higher share of employees in multi-person organisations are likely factors. However, they are keen to stress the smallness of their sample and the need for further work.

In other interesting analyses, the authors sketch the relationship between intrapreneurship and independent entrepreneurship, using both the GEM's TEA and owner-management of independent young businesses (this

---

[a] Brazil, Chile, Ecuador, Iran, Republic of Korea, Latvia, the Netherlands, Norway, Peru, Spain and Uruguay.

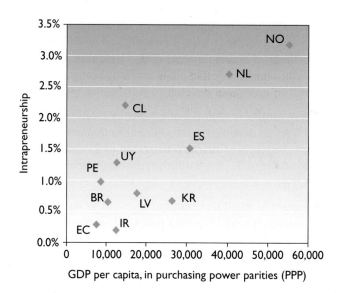

FIGURE 6.3

Intrapreneurship (narrow definition) and economic development

SOURCE: Bosma et al. (2010).[30]

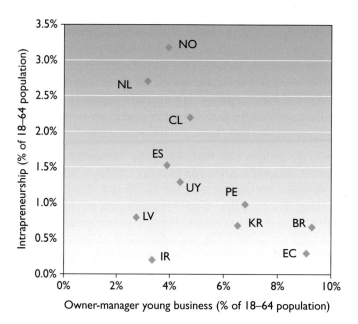

FIGURE 6.4

Intrapreneurship and owner management

SOURCE: Bosma et al. (2010).[30]

latter is shown in Figure 6.4). In both instances the data indicate a negative relationship. That is, while their evidence suggests that at the micro-level intrapreneurship begets entrepreneurship (i.e. intrapreneurs record higher entrepreneurial intentions than other employees, with the differences highest in high-income econo-mies), at the macro level intrapreneurship may substitute for independent entrepreneurship.

Again, the authors are keen to stress the exploratory nature of their study but, rightly, point to the far-reaching implications if further research were to support their findings. In trying to understand this relationship, they speculate on the role of economic development. That is, the positive effect of economic development on the presence of large firms and the consequent negative effect on the prevalence of independent entrepreneurship. And, relatedly, that higher levels of economic development (manifest in higher personal incomes) raise the opportunity cost of entrepreneurship, acting as a disincentive and depressing levels of independent entrepreneurship. In summary, they note that:

> Given a 'supply of entrepreneurial talent', it might then depend on various contextual determinants, such as the level of economic development, the institutional framework (e.g. employment protection) and management styles within organizations (possibly related to national culture), whether entrepreneurial individuals exploit their entrepreneurial tendencies within a business or choose to start up for themselves.
>
> (p. 23)

At the very least, there would be important implications for economic development policy or for educational practice that viewed independent entrepreneurship as the only legitimate expression of 'entrepreneurial tendencies'. Regardless, Bosma, Stam and Wennekers don't claim too much from their work to date. We include it here as a novel attempt to quantify intrapreneurship and to relate it to a variety of important structural and demographic factors. The results, while tentative, are intriguing and we look forward to future developments.

CONCLUSIONS

In this chapter we have tried to outline the nature of corporate entrepreneurship and understand the bases for an increasing entrepreneurial imperative within established and larger firms. Ireland, Covin and Kuratko[24] suggest that corporate entrepreneurship or 'an entrepreneurial strategic vision' (p. 28) is the rational response to the existence of three inter-related environmental conditions: competitive intensity, technological change and emerging or fragmenting product-market domains. The essence of all three is 'dynamism'. That is, openness to corporate entrepreneurship, in some form, has become progressively more important as the rate of change in organizational environments has increased. This change is driven by a variety of factors, but prominent amongst these has been the accelerated development of information and communication technologies; the globalisation of production and of markets; and rising standards of living. All serve to give a growing number of more demanding customers greater choice, while simultaneously placing a downward pressure on prices.

We closed the chapter with a look at some recent, if limited, evidence on one form of corporate entrepreneurship: intrapreneurship. The picture painted should temper the discussion of corporate entrepreneurship somewhat. At least from the perspective of employees, intrapreneurship is a minority activity and its incidence is far less than that of classical entrepreneurship (though this does not imply that its economic impact is less). Importantly, as with classical entrepreneurship (see the discussion in Chapter 2), intrapreneurship – and, quite possibly, corporate entrepreneurship more generally – appears to vary with economic development. In other words, there is likely to be an institutional contingency underpinning levels of corporate entrepreneurship, which speaks to incentive structures within a society. Intriguingly, classical entrepreneurship and intrapreneurship appear to substitute for one another. Of course, given the exploratory nature of this early work, more needs to be done to establish these patterns.

REVIEW QUESTIONS

1   What is driving the increasing interest in corporate entrepreneurship?
2   In what dimensions of the environment might firms perceive turbulence?
3   What is meant by ambidexterity in the context of organizational strategy?
4   What are Stopford and Baden-Fuller's three forms of corporate entrepreneurship?
5   On what dimensions do Wolcott and Lippitz believe approaches to corporate entrepreneurship may vary?
6   What are the different approaches identified by Wolcott and Lippitz?
7   Are any of the case studies in this book engaged in corporate entrepreneurship? Which form or approach have they taken?
8   What are the dimensions of entrepreneurial orientation?
9   How might organizations approach the difficult task of balancing the dimension of entrepreneurial orientation?
10 What is the incidence of intrapreneurship in the countries studied by Bosma, Stam and Wennekers?
11 What appears to be the relationship between intrapreneurship and independent entrepreneurship?

SUGGESTED ASSIGNMENTS

1   Working in groups, ask students to identify a large organization that they believe to be entrepreneurial. Require each group to justify its selection.

2   In teams, ask the students to debate the implications of a trade-off between independent entrepreneurship and corporate entrepreneurship as hinted at by the work of Bosma, Stam and Wennekers.

REFERENCES

1   **Phan, P.H., Wright, M., Ucbasaran, D. and Tan, W. L.** (2009) 'Corporate entrepreneurship: Current research and future directions', *Journal of Business Venturing*, vol. 24, no. 3, pp. 197–205.

2   **Stevenson, H.H. and Jarillo, J.C.** (2007) 'A paradigm of entrepreneurship: Entrepreneurial management', in A.C. Garcia, D. Ribeiro, and S. Roig, (eds) *Entrepreneurship: Concepts, Theory and Perspective*, Springer, NY, pp. 155–70.

3   **Burgelman, R.A.** (1983) 'A process model of internal corporate venturing in the diversified major firm', *Administrative Science Quarterly*, vol. 28, no. 2, pp. 223–44.

4   **Grinyer, P. and McKiernan, P.** (1980) 'Generating major change in stagnating companies', *Strategic Management Journal*, vol. 11, pp. 131–46.

5   **Kuratko, D.F.** (2010) 'Corporate entrepreneurship: An introduction and research review', in Z.J. Acs and D.B. Audretsch (eds), *Handbook of Entrepreneurship Research*, Springer New York, New York, NY, pp. 129–63.

6   **Morris, M.H., Kuratko, D.F. and Covin, J.G.** (2010) *Corporate Entrepreneurship & Innovation*. Cengage Learning, Cincinnati, OH.

7   **Burns, T. and Stalker, G.M.** (1961) *The Management of Innovation*, Tavistock, London.

8   **Miller, D. and Friesen, P.H.** (1982) 'Innovation in conservative and entrepreneurial firms: Two models of strategic momentum', *Strategic Management Journal*, vol. 3, no.1, pp. 1–25.

9   **Tushman, M.L. and O'Reilly III, C.A.** (1996) 'Ambidextrous organizations: Managing evolutionary and revolutionary change', *California Management Review*, vol. 38, no. 4, pp. 8–30.

10 **Duncan, R.B.** (1976) 'The ambidextrous organization: Designing dual structures for innovation', *The Management of Organization Design*, vol. 1, pp. 167–88.

11 **March, J.G.** (1991) 'Exploration and exploitation in organizational

learning', *Organization Science*, vol. 2, no.1, pp. 71–87.

12 **Narayanan, V.K., Yang, Y. and Zahra, S.A.** (2009) 'Corporate venturing and value creation: A review and proposed framework', *Research Policy*, vol. 38, no.1, pp. 58–76.

13 **Sharma, P. and Chrisman, S.J.J.** (2007) 'Toward a reconciliation of the definitional issues in the field of corporate entrepreneurship', in A.C. Garcia, D. Ribeiro and S. Roig (eds) *Entrepreneurship: Concepts, Theory and Perspective*, Springer, NY, pp. 83–103.

14 **Dess, G.G. and Lumpkin, G.T.** (2005) 'Research edge: The role of entrepreneurial orientation in stimulating effective corporate entrepreneurship', *The Academy of Management Executive (1993)*, vol. 19, no.1, pp. 147–56.

15 **Pinchot, G.** (1985) *Intrapreneuring: Why you don't have to leave the corporation to become an entrepreneur*, Harper & Row, New York.

16 **Kuratko, D.F. and Audretsch, D.B.** (2009) 'Strategic entrepreneurship: Exploring different perspectives of an emerging concept', *Entrepreneurship Theory and Practice*, vol. 33, no. 1, pp. 1–17.

17 **Ireland, R.D., Hitt, M.A. and Sirmon, D.G.** (2003) 'A model of strategic entrepreneurship: The construct and its dimensions',

Journal of Management, vol. 29, no. 6, pp. 963–89.

18 **Covin, J.G. and Miles, M.P.** (1999) 'Corporate entrepreneurship and the pursuit of competitive advantage', *Entrepreneurship Theory and Practice*, vol. 23, pp. 47–64.

19 **Stopford, J.M. and Baden-Fuller, C.W.F.** (1994) 'Creating corporate entrepreneurship', *Strategic Management Journal*, vol. 15, no. 7, pp. 521–36.

20 **Fry, A.** (1988) 'Lessons from a successful intrapreneur', *The Journal of Business Strategy*, vol. 9, no. 2, pp. 20–6.

21 **Kazanjian, R.K., Drazin, R. and Glynn, M.A.** (2002) 'Implementing strategies for corporate entrepreneurship: A knowledge-based perspective', in M. Hitt, R.D. Ireland, S.M. Camp and D. Sexton (eds), *Strategic Entrepreneurship: Creating a New Mindset*, Wiley-Blackwell, Oxford, pp. 173–200.

22 **Wolcott, R.C. and Lippitz, M.J.** (2007) 'The four models of corporate entrepreneurship', *MIT Sloan Management Review*, vol. 49, no.1, pp. 75–82.

23 **Burgelman, R.A.** (1983) 'A process model of internal corporate venturing in the diversified major firm', *Administrative Science Quarterly*, vol. 28, pp. 223–44.

24 **Ireland, R.D., Covin, J.G. and Kuratko, D.F.** (2009) 'Conceptualizing corporate entrepreneur-

ship strategy', *Entrepreneurship Theory and Practice*, vol. 33, no. 1, pp. 19–46.

25 **Rauch, A., Wiklund, J., Lumpkin, G.T. and Frese, M.** (2009) 'Entrepreneurial orientation and business performance: An assessment of past research and suggestions for the future', *Entrepreneurship Theory and Practice*, vol. 33, no. 3, pp. 761–87.

26 **Memili, E., Lumpkin, G.T. and Dess, G.G.** (2010) 'Entrepreneurial orientation: the driving force for corporate entrepreneurship', in P. Mazzola and F. Kellermanns (eds), *Handbook of Research on Strategy Process*, Edward Elgar, Cheltenham, p. 326.

27 **Boulding, W. and Christen, M.** (2003) 'Sustainable pioneering advantage? Profit implications of market entry order', *Marketing Science*, vol. 22, pp. 371–92.

28 **Boulding, W. and Christen M.** (2008) 'Disentangling pioneering cost advantages and disadvantages', *Marketing Science*, vol. 27, no. 4, p. 699.

29 **Drucker, P.F.** (2006) *Innovation and Entrepreneurship*, Harper Paperbacks.

30 **Bosma, N.S., Stam, F.C. and Wennekers, A.R.M.** (2010) *Intrapreneurship: An International Study*, SCALES working paper, http://www.ondernemerschap.nl/pdf-ez/H201005.pdf.

RECOMMENDED READING

Sharma, P. and Chrisman, S.J.J. (2007) 'Toward a reconciliation of the definitional issues in the field of corporate entrepreneurship', *Entrepreneurship*, pp. 83–103.

Ireland, R.D., Hitt, M.A. and Sirmon, D.G. (2003) 'A model of strategic entrepreneurship:

The construct and its dimensions', *Journal of Management*, vol. 29, no. 6, pp. 963–89.

Phan, P.H., Wright, M., Ucbasaran, D. and Tan, W.L. (2009) 'Corporate entrepreneurship: Current research and future directions',

Journal of Business Venturing, vol. 24, no. 3, pp. 197–205.

Bosma, N.S., Stam, F.C. and Wennekers, A.R.M. (2010) *Intrapreneurship: An International Study*, SCALES working paper, http://www.ondernemerschap.nl/pdf-ez/H201005.pdf.

PART THREE
STRATEGY AND THE SMALL FIRM

In this part of the text we move from the domains of entrepreneurship into the strategic decision-making areas of entrepreneurship. Strategic decision-making is required for entrepreneurs to achieve the recognition and exploitation of opportunities. Experienced entrepreneurs often comment that they come across opportunities all the time, for new uses of products, to do things differently or to apply technology in different ways or to exploit now markets. However, only few opportunities will be exploited because to do so require strategic decisions on accessing finance, on undertaking innovation and change, and particular strategies are required for achieving growth and exploiting international markets.

The chapters in Part 3 examine such decision-making in more detail. Chapter 7 examines issues in raising finance and discusses entrepreneurial strategies with bank finance from the perspective of small firms. Chapter 8 examines the strategies and issues in raising venture capital. Risk is inherent in entrepreneurial decision-making, but this is examined from the perspective of both the entrepreneur and the supplier of funding, whether a banker or a venture capitalist.

Chapters 9 and 10 examine two closely related areas in which strategic entrepreneurial decision-making is crucial achieving growth and achieving internationalization. In some cases these are symbiotic, such as with technology based small firms who are automatically in international markets, and in some they are more defined but still linked where entrepreneurial growth occurs first in domestic markets which are then used as a base to establish international markets. In both chapters, issues in such strategic decision making are examined and explored, examining both theoretical concepts and 'Entrepreneurship in Action' case studies and evidence. The section concludes with a chapter on innovation in small firms. Chapter 11 attempts to explore both why small firms matter for innovation and why innovation matters for small firms.

BEYOND PRODUCTS

by Sophie Manigart
Vlerick Gent Management School and Ghent University

It was a sunny afternoon in May 2005. Despite the heat, Peter Van Riet was thinking of snow, snowboards and snowboard bindings. It took three years of his life and all of his savings to develop a revolutionary model of snowboard bindings. Having been a semi-professional snowboarder as a teenager, he sensed that the market was waiting for his ultimate snowboard binding. But he urgently needed money to start up a company, develop a first prototype, test it on snow, and start sales and production, providing he wanted his first sales to happen before the winter season of 2006–2007. Four business angels were interested in his project. Together with his financial partner, Peter was considering how much dilution he would have to face for a proposed investment of €300,000 by a group of business angels.

BACKGROUND

Peter Van Riet used his knowledge of snowboard bindings and his training and experience as a product developer to design a completely new snowboard binding. His new binding combines extreme ease of use with the same freestyle feeling as traditional strap bindings. The current snowboard bindings are either strap bindings, where the boot is sealed by two straps, or step-in bindings, which can be compared to traditional alpine ski bindings. While being very versatile and adaptable to a large range of boots, a significant draw-back of the strap binding is the fact that it is rather cumbersome to take on. To overcome this disadvantage, the step-in binding has been developed. The major disadvantage of the step-in binding is that it must be used with hard boots, which experienced snowboarders dislike, and it is more expensive than strap bindings. Snowboard addicts feel that soft boots are essential for the perfect feeling that is so important in freestyle; moreover, it improves the comfort of the snowboarders. Due to the disadvantages, the newer step-in binding has never taken over the dominant position of the strap binding. Meanwhile, a new company called Flow, which was established in 1996, introduced a different type of hybrid binding. Despite its non-natural way to step in and its limited ways to adapt the binding to the snowboarder, Flow rapidly became successful. The success of Flow suggests that the market is ready for a new product.

PRODUCT DEVELOPMENT

A snowboarder is typically offered a choice of bindings separately from boards. A sport-apparel shop sells both boards and bindings, assembling them on the site as to the customer's choice. There is hence no urgent need to team up with a snowboard manufacturer: marketing and sales of bindings occur separately from that of boards. The average consumer price for a strap binding is €165, but prices range from €100 to €400 for top models. Flow sells its hybrid bindings from €170 to €340, with an average model costing €200. The average snowboarder becomes more demanding with respect to quality, design and comfort, making the top bindings more attractive.

The new hybrid binding developed by Peter combines the ease of use of the step-in binding with the comfort of soft boots, without the disadvantages of the Flow concept. He further improved the comfort and flexibility of the binding through intensive co-development efforts with Italian and Belgian engineering companies, and with a major American chemicals company for the composite materials. This resulted in a hybrid binding, with the positive features of both the traditional strap and the step-in bindings. A first

Benelux patent was filed in 1997 and expanded to the main winter sports countries in Europe, the USA and Canada in 1998. No patent has been filed in Japan due to the high translation costs involved. The intellectual property protection expires in 2018. A first real test came when the hybrid concept was presented at the important yearly ISPO trade fair in Munich in February 2001. Reactions were generally favourable for the new design and the concept proved to be on the right track.

Given that further development required more money than Peter possessed, he decided to involve a financial partner as a shareholder. However, the development proved to be rather slow and the financial partner eventually stepped out of the project, losing his initial investment. The product was further developed to the current 'strap-in' binding that is now ready for full testing and, if technically successful, for commercialisation. He also sought coaching for the development of his business plan, something which he knew nothing about until then, by participating in a business-plan competition, Bizidee. Not only did he win the competition in 2004, but he also found an experienced business partner with complementary financial and accounting skills willing to invest some money towards further product and business plan development. Together with the money, it was important that the new partner was willing to work part-time for the company.

Peter now feels that the business idea is sufficiently developed to start up a company, Beyond Products, which should be aimed at developing and commercialising the new snowboard binding. He has invested approximately €350,000 from his own, his first and his second partner's savings and time in the project up to now: €207,000 for the product development, €81,000 patent costs, and the remaining for miscellaneous costs such as marketing expenses (mainly the trade fair). While the patent and marketing costs were out-of-pocket expenses, a large part of the product development costs consisted of his time. He estimates that Beyond Products needs €300,000 cash to get up and running, and to develop and test a prototype that could then be presented at the next ISPO trade fair in January 2006. This is essential, as orders for the 2006–2007 snow season are generated during the fair.

WHAT NEXT?

A syndicate of four business angels is interested in an equity investment of €300,000 in Beyond Products. This, together with a small bank loan, should allow Beyond Products to reach June 2006, when new cash (€500,000) will have to be raised in a second investment round. If the prototype works well in the 'on-snow' test and if reactions are positive at the ISPO fair, then the new financing round could be done at much better valuations than now, as uncertainty will have been reduced significantly. Peter plans to transfer the IP rights, which are now in his personal name, to the company. Peter and his partner are currently considering how many shares the business angels could get for their €300,000 investment. One of the key issues that they cannot resolve is what equity percentage would be fair to the business angels, without diluting the founders' position too much while also compensating them honestly for their efforts until now.

7 SOURCES OF FINANCE: OVERVIEW OF ISSUES AND BANK FINANCE

LEARNING OUTCOMES

At the end of this chapter you should be able to:

* Discuss the importance of alternative sources of finance for entrepreneurs and SMEs.

* Describe why entrepreneurs and SMEs are at a disadvantage compared with large firms in financial markets.

* Discuss the problems that face the providers of finance to the SME sector.

* Compare survey results and known national characteristics on the importance of sources of finance for entrepreneurs and SMEs and whether these have been affected by the post global financial crisis.

* Account for the importance of bank finance as a source of external finance for entrepreneurs and SME owners.

* Discuss the factors that affect lending by bank managers to owners of SMEs.

* Describe the factors that affect the bank manager relationship with owners of SMEs.

INTRODUCTION

This chapter is concerned predominantly with sources of finance for entrepreneurs and small and medium-sized enterprises (SMEs), taking the definition of SMEs as that given in Chapter 2. Thus for many small firms certain sources of finance are not available due to entry barriers. For example, many entrepreneurs and SMEs are automatically excluded from some financial sources, such as the London Stock Exchange, and face difficulties raising some types of finance, such as long-term loans, because of the automatically higher risk associated with firms that have little equity in the form of share capital. In the majority of cases the only equity is that of the proprietors. This chapter gives an overview of the sources of finance, but its focus is on bank finance. Chapter 8 will examine sources of venture finance. However, some time is spent here on the theoretical issues that provide the foundation for an examination of this important area.

It is worth making a distinction between the theoretical basis of entrepreneurs' and SMEs' finance and what we know about the sources of finance they actually use. It is easy to hypothesize, from what has been said above, about the difficulties facing entrepreneurs and small firms: that they are likely to rely heavily on personal savings and equity for long-term finance and perhaps trade credit for short-term finance. However, these hypotheses need to be balanced against known evidence on sources of finance. We will also consider the impact of the global financial crisis (GFC) in 2008/09 and its effect on the ability of entrepreneurs and small firms to access finance. The current economic environment is sometimes referred to as the post-GFC economy.

There is a variety of sources of finance available to the entrepreneur and small and medium-sized firms. A simple way of classifying these sources is shown in Figure 7.1. This figure shows sources of finance classified as internal and external.

Internal sources of finance include the personal equity of the entrepreneur, usually in the form of savings, remortgage, or perhaps money raised from family and friends. This is sometimes referred to as the '3Fs' of small firm start-up finance – that is, the founder(s), family and friends. After the initial start-up of the firm, retained profits and earnings provide internal capital. Usually, within a small firm, it is normal for internal sources to provide the major proportion of the firm's capital and financial structure. External finance can be

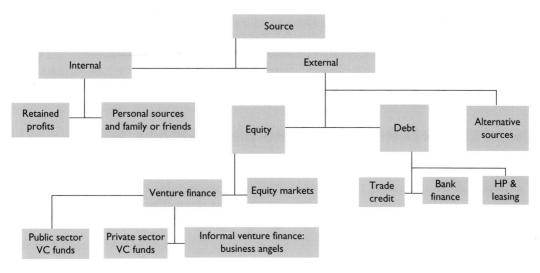

FIGURE 7.1

Sources of finance for entrepreneurs and small firms

drawn from a number of sources. As shown by Figure 7.1, the principal sources for the entrepreneur are advances from banks, equity from venture capitalists and informal investors, and short-term trade credit. Other external sources may include leasing, hire-purchase and factoring (or invoice discounting). In the UK the small-firm entrepreneur may qualify for grants or 'soft loans' from public-sector bodies such as the Enterprise Direc-torate of the Department for Business, Innovation and Skills or Enterprise Capital Funds (ECFs), or may qualify for other schemes such as Enterprise Finance Guarantee (EFG) (previously, the Small Firms' Loan Guarantee Scheme). Local government may also provide loans and grants and there are a number of agencies that have attempted to set up their own financing schemes for small firms. These may include venture capital and loans from enterprise agencies, Business Links and Local Economic Development Agencies such as, in Scotland, the Local Enterprise Companies (LECs).

Whether entrepreneurs face real difficulties in raising external finance can be disputed, but the concern with this area on the part of policymakers has given rise to the range of assistance that is now available to small firms and entrepreneurs. In particular, small-scale, community-based funds have been the subject of recent initiatives through funds established via the Enterprise Directorate of the Department for Business, Innovation and Skills, such as funds and schemes supported from the Phoenix Fund.[1] Small-scale loan schemes or micro-credit schemes have been established in the more deprived areas where it can be difficult for potential entrepreneurs to raise external finance because of limited wealth and personal savings. Start-up firms in such localities may also be seen by potential funders as having greater risk than those in other localities and may pay higher interest rates as a result. For example, the Bank of England has commented in one report[2] that evidence suggests that 'businesses in deprived areas represented on average a somewhat greater credit risk than those elsewhere in the country' (p. 14). In a review of the need for schemes to provide additional sources of external finance for small firms, the former Small Business Service concluded that some start-up firms and small businesses faced diffi-culties in accessing the debt finance they required.[3]

Whether schemes such as those supported through the Phoenix Fund are effective is an issue we touch upon later, but they have arisen at least in part because of theoretical concerns that small firm entrepreneurs will be at a disadvantage in raising finance compared to large firms. In particular, concern has centred on whether entrepreneurs face finance gaps, and whether these have become more acute in the post-GFC environment, due to the fact that the supply of relatively small amounts of finance required by small firms (less than £250,000) can be uneconomic to provide and subsequently monitor for financial institutions (especially when considering sources of equity capital). Following the GFC, there has been concern that bank finance has become very restrictive as banks seek to reduce their risks and exposure. We now consider these issues in more detail.

ISSUES FOR ENTREPRENEURS AND SMALL FIRMS

FINANCE GAPS

If gaps arise they do so because of mismatches between supply and demand. The existence of a finance gap will arise because demand from small firms is greater than the willingness of financial institutions to supply the finance at current market conditions. For finance such as bank loans, these gaps may be termed credit rationing.

A gap may exist such as that illustrated by Figure 7.2, where demand exceeds the available supply at current market rates of interest. In Figure 7.2, the total advances that small firms would like to take up are given by *ob*. However, the amount that banks are willing to supply is given by *oa*. Hence the existence of a debt gap given by the distance *ab*. Governments can attempt to close this gap by shifting the supply curve of (debt) finance to the right by the introduction of schemes such as the EFG; this allows the banks to provide additional loanable funds.

The discussion so far is an oversimplification of the market for small-firm entrepreneurs' finance. For example, we are assuming that all propositions from small firms that banks receive are homogeneous. This will patently not be the case and we would expect some propositions to be treated more favourably than others. An equally important point arises about whether the 'good' propositions receive finance and the 'poor' propositions do not. This is the problem of adverse selection that is discussed in more detail below.

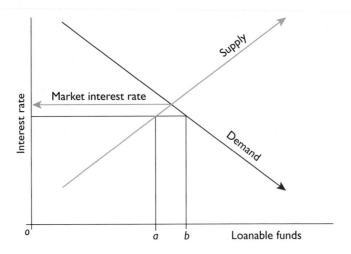

FIGURE 7.2

Demand and supply for bank credit

NOTES: (i) The market interest rate is likely to be established below the equilibrium level due to Bank of England regulation.

   (ii) The demand for loanable funds is assumed to consist of homogeneous and 'good' propositions seeking bank finance implying a 'gap' which could be met by rationing.

Finance gaps, however, have been recognized for over 80 years. They were first highlighted by the Macmillan Report of 1931[4] and subsequently termed the 'Macmillan gap'. Macmillan found, at the time, that small businesses and entrepreneurs would find it difficult to raise amounts of less than £200,000, equivalent to £5 million today. The London Stock Exchange required a minimum figure of this amount to allow the trading of equity capital in a firm. There is little doubt that this gap has been substantially narrowed with the development of the venture capital industry in the UK. However, various official reports and other researchers have pointed to the continued existence of an equity gap in the UK[5] and the Enterprise Directorate review of evidence[3] suggested that 'Small businesses find it difficult to obtain modest amounts of private equity finance'. This has been confirmed with a further review (the Rowlands Report) of SMEs' access to growth capital post GFC.[6] This report concluded that (p. 5): 'A gap exists for companies looking for between £2m and £10m in growth capital'. Although, as discussed in the next chapter, there have been important developments in the promotion of sources of informal venture capital, the announcement by the Bank of England that it was no longer concerned with the production of its annual report on the finance of small firms (the last year that the Bank produced its annual report was 2004) would suggest that the official view is that there are no longer significant issues for the majority of small firms in raising finance.[7] However, as suggested by the Rowlands Report,[6] it is arguable that an equity gap for entrepreneurs and small firms still exists because of the factors discussed below.

REASONS FOR THE CONTINUED EXISTENCE OF EQUITY GAPS

1 It is not economic to issue shares for relatively small amounts of equity on the Stock Exchange (e.g. commission costs are high for small issues of less than £1 million).

2 Difficulties can exist in getting a listing on the Stock Exchange. The development of the Alternative Investment Market (AIM), however, has provided a successful alternative stock market to the London Stock Exchange, particularly for smaller and medium-sized firms to gain a listing.

3 It is not economic for venture capitalists to provide relatively small amounts of equity capital. The reasons for this are that venture capital companies will want to monitor the performance of the company closely, because they supply equity – not debt – capital and are consequently not guaranteed a return. Furthermore, the costs of arranging the finance and the appraisal of propositions are generally fixed costs.[8] A full discussion of venture capital is given in the next chapter.

4 Venture capitalists require high rates of return because they are assuming higher risks than the banks. Only certain high-performing entrepreneurs and firms, the high-growth firms, will be able to achieve the high rates of return required by venture capitalists who have in turn to satisfy the requirements of the shareholders in the venture-capital fund. As a consequence of this, venture capitalists tend to concentrate on certain sectors of the economy only, or on certain types of finance, such as management buy-outs (MBOs) (see Chapter 8). Recent figures on the formal venture-capital industry continue to show that the majority of the sector's funds are invested in MBOs and management buy-ins (MBIs),[9] so that the importance of this sector for the finance of entrepreneurs and small firms is limited.

5 Venture capitalists will apply a 'due diligence' procedure to any proposition that is being considered for investment. This will take a considerable period of time and only a small proportion of applications for formal venture capital eventually receive funding after the due diligence procedure. Typically, less than 3 per cent of applications for such formal venture capital will receive funding from this sector. It is worth noting that, for a time, due diligence was short-circuited during the Internet 'bubble' of 1999–2000, with the need to secure venture finance in 'days' rather than 'months'. Well-publicized Internet companies' problems since then have seen such short-circuit mechanisms largely decline – for example, the relative demise of First Tuesday, a networking market mechanism for Internet entrepreneurs and venture capitalists that was popular in terms of attendance during the Internet company (dotcom) boom. [10] The Skype case, in Chapter 1, illustrates some of the stages or 'rounds' of venture capital required which was launched at a time when venture-capital funds were looking for Internet firms as investments.

6 Venture capitalists will also require an exit route for the sale of their shareholding after a period of time with their investment in the entrepreneurial venture. The normal method of seeking an exit route for such a holding will be to seek an initial public offering (IPO) on the Stock Exchange or AIM. Thus, venture capitalists will seek high-growth entrepreneurial concerns that can be turned within a short period (say five years) into public companies and provide an IPO as an exit route for their holding and their funds.

7 Venture capitalists will also seek to take an active part in the management of the company in order to safeguard their investment. They will seek to add value to their investment through an active role in the management and use their networking capabilities to open up additional opportunities for the growth of the entrepreneurial concern. The extent to which venture capitalists can add value to the management of investee companies has been one of the concerns in the venture-capital sector.

Informal venture capital, which has seen important developments in recent years, has considerable potential to reduce equity gaps for small firms and is discussed in more detail, together with a full discussion of the formal venture-capital industry, in the next chapter. For the rest of this chapter we focus on the banks as a source of entrepreneurial finance.

ENTREPRENEURIAL FINANCE AND THE BANKS

For the entrepreneur, banks are easily accessible (through high-street branches) and provide short-term debt finance that in theory is attractive; the entrepreneur does not give up control and debt may be provided at times to suit the entrepreneur. However, banks, theoretically, face issues in assessing propositions from entrepreneurs. These issues arise in any investment situation where providers and borrowers have different sets of information. However, for banks we get two problems: adverse selection and moral hazard.

ADVERSE SELECTION

Adverse selection occurs when either the bank provides finance for a venture that subsequently fails or the bank refuses finance for a venture that would have been successful. It may occur because the bank does not have all the available information or the information is imperfect. The difficulty here is that the information required by the bank to assess perfectly the risk of the proposition is not costless to obtain. However, it can be argued that banks should over time reduce the mistakes they make, since they should have the skills and resources necessary to increase the frequency of correct decisions.

MORAL HAZARD

Moral hazard is more difficult for the bank to control. Once an entrepreneur has raised the bank loan, there is no guarantee that he or she will act in the best interests of the bank. Therefore, moral hazard is a monitoring problem for the bank and, for relatively small amounts of finance, it is not economic for banks to monitor performance closely. For this reason banks will usually require security. This contributes to the problems facing entrepreneurs. Those entrepreneurs without substantial equity and with insufficient security will fall into the debt gap.

Bank assessments of small firm applications for loan finance are examples of decision-making under uncertainty incorporating asymmetric information for the provider and the client. The foundations of analysis of possible mismatches between supply and demand that can occur under these conditions have been laid down by Akerlof's seminal 1970 paper.[11] Writers have developed the significance of these conditions for finance theory using a principal–agent framework.[12; 13; 14] The relevance of these insights is limited when considering the finance of entrepreneurs and small firms who have restricted access to financial markets. Concepts of moral hazard and adverse selection, however, are still important and have been further refined by later writers.[15; 16; 17]

Stiglitz and Weiss have shown that the problems of moral hazard and adverse selection are likely to produce credit rationing, insufficient credit available for all sound propositions.[18] However, de Meza argues that (equally) credit is oversupplied because over-optimistic entrepreneurs exaggerate returns and bankers will fund proposals that may fail.[19] Recent surveys, post-GFC, confirm that access to bank finance is still a problematic issue for some SMEs, especially in some sectors, such as manufacturing.[20; 21] The review by the former SBS on the evidence for access to debt finance by small firms, although pre GFC, supports the view that some entrepreneurs and small firms face difficulties in accessing debt finance.[3] At the time of writing, we have enjoyed a period of remarkably low interest rates (by historical standards), a period in which interest rates have been declining. Post GFC there seems to be evidence that conditions for accessing and acquiring debt finance have deteriorated as banks, in the UK, have initially restricted lending and raised short-term interest rates.[22]

ENTREPRENEURS, SMALL FIRMS AND THE BANKS

Previous research by the author[23] on the risk assessment practices of banks in the UK has suggested that adverse selection could occur with UK banks. Some results from this research are discussed in the students' Online Learning Centre. Since this earlier research was conducted, it is recognized that bank manager practices have changed and are now supported by techniques of financial modelling and credit-scoring.[2] These are discussed below in the context of recent research involving the author. An additional factor, from a demand-side perspective, is the theory of discouraged borrowing:[24] that some entrepreneurs are discouraged from approaching the banks because of a perception that they will be unsuccessful or a perception that they will not have the information and good credit history that it is perceived that banks require. For example, there is some evidence that some ethnic minority entrepreneurs may be discouraged due to perceptions held of institutional bias against their proposals[25] and other work has suggested that women seeking to start up businesses may also form a category of discouraged borrowers.[26]

The effect of discouraged borrowing was also a factor in recent research involving the author conducted on SMEs' access to bank finance in Scotland.[27] The research investigated in depth the importance of issues reported by 25 per cent of SMEs from an annual survey of 1000 SMEs in Scotland.[28] These were SME owners involved in an annual small business survey conducted in Scotland as part of a larger UK survey (the results on the importance of sources of finance for the UK study are discussed later in the chapter). From this information, five case study 'scenarios' were developed for participating bank managers. These consisted of a narrative description, anonymized by the researchers, but reflecting real case examples together with projected financial information. Three of the main commercial banks in Scotland participated in the research which allowed the researchers to use protocol analysis for each of the five case-study scenarios by the bank managers. Four of the five cases had extensive financial information, with one provided as a narrative only. Eight bank managers from the three participating commercial banks took part in this research. The protocol analysis involved inviting each of the bank managers to talk through how each case would be dealt with, the processes involved and to give their views on the strengths and weaknesses of each case. A second part of the interview discussed more general factors with the bank managers. The findings demonstrated that all the commercial banks in the UK segment of the SME market use credit scoring for smaller funding applications (in some cases for credit proposals of less than £100,000) with relationships managed by a local bank manager and use more sophisticated financial modelling for larger applications, with relationships managed by an area manager or more senior bank manager. Interested readers can find more information provided in the students' Online Learning Centre.

The research revealed the following conclusions:

BANK MANAGER DISCUSSION OF SME CASE PROPOSALS

- Bank managers place heavy reliance on personal relationships and knowledge of SME business-owners, building up relationships over a period of time. They are prepared to invest considerable time, visiting premises and becoming familiar with businesses. A primary requirement for any proposition from either existing or new business customers is to understand the nature of the proposition and the serviceability and sustainability of the proposed venture. Thus, although bank managers have targets for new business, it is easier for existing business customers to seek funding, particularly where this might fall outside established 'norms', such as, for example, highly geared propositions, or relatively large credit facilities compared to the size of the firm and turnover.

- Banks have standard financial 'models' that are followed in terms of financial requirements, although there may be considerable discretion exercised by individual bank managers, dependent on seniority. In addition, it was clear that bank managers would, as far as their discretion allowed, seek to support established businesses with which they have an established personal relationship. The financial modelling process produces a result which indicates the category for the strength of the proposition in terms of risk/reward, but with latitude for bank managers to use discretion. However, given the segmentation applied by the banks, it will be easier for larger SMEs to obtain funding. Although how the SME market is segmented varies, and this does not apply to all the banks, micro and small firms are likely to have their propositions credit-scored (reducing the extent of bank manager discretion and flexibility). This is likely to make propositions from small firms that differed from bank 'norms', such as highly geared propositions with limited security, difficult to accept, especially if there were any issues with credit history and the trading track record.

- A number of factors can affect the financial modelling process and hence the extent of latitude and discretion of managers. Entrepreneurs seeking to start new businesses will find it more difficult because of the lack of any trading history. In such circumstances, previous experience, age and credit history of the entrepreneur will be important. These propositions are likely to be credit-scored which may limit the flexibility that bank managers have, especially as such proposals are referred for final approval to a central credit department. Propositions that do not match bank preferences and modelling requirements will be difficult to support.

- Additional factors include location and sector. Although no sectors are excluded by the banks, SMEs in competitive sectors may find it difficult to raise finance, especially if they are operating in ways that do not fit the banks' own internal guides on benchmarking for the sector. A similar comment can be made on location. Rural locations can be difficult environments for SMEs, having limited local markets and limited networks and resources. For example, large areas of Scotland, the Highlands and Islands and the south of Scotland qualify as rural under Scottish government definitions; SMEs in such localities seeking to grow and raise finance may find it difficult to raise bank finance, especially if reliant on local and regional markets.

- Security was a secondary factor, but nonetheless important. Established SMEs with limited security will find it difficult to raise finance for propositions that contain higher risk or do not meet banks' financial modelling requirements. Changes to the former Small Firms' Loan Guarantee Scheme, now the EFG, under the Graham Review, have meant that the banks have in some cases reduced their use of the Scheme.

- With advent of relationship banking, an alternative conceptual framework is required similar to that shown in Figure 7.3. This illustrates that the role and importance of the entrepreneur–bank manager relationship in the decision-making process of banks in the twenty-first century, and in the post-GFC period, will have become more important.[29]

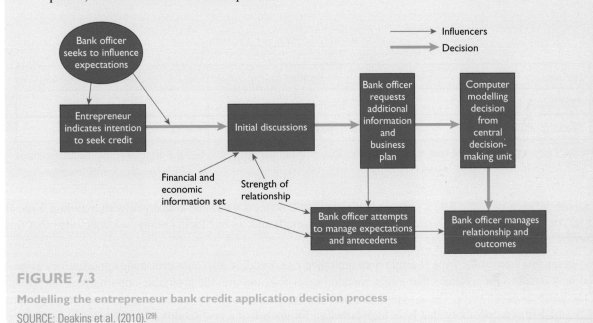

FIGURE 7.3

Modelling the entrepreneur bank credit application decision process

SOURCE: Deakins et al. (2010).[29]

THE ROLE OF SECURITY

The establishment of relationship banking, illustrated in Figure 7.3, means that bank officers will manage the frequent monitoring of information to reduce moral hazard. However, a cost-minimization approach will also include using methods that ensure commitment on the part of the entrepreneur. We would expect collateral (assets that may be pledged as security) to have an important role because it can ensure commitment and also provides a fail-safe method for the bank to recover losses. In conditions of uncertainty, security can signal commitment and, following Spence,[30] the importance of signalling commitment has also been recognized.[31] Thus liquidity constraints and uncertainty combine to encourage the provider of finance to require security when this is available. Also Chan and Kannatas have pointed out that the type of security provided by the entrepreneur can offer information to the provider.[32]

Collateral, however, is not without costs and its own problems; for example, there are valuation problems, there might be depreciation to consider and it might be necessary to revalue collateral at intervals. The taking of collateral, then, needs to be balanced against the costs of management for the bank. Also the taking of collateral does nothing to reduce adverse selection. It merely provides a method for the bank to recover (some) potential losses where it considers risks to be high. In practice the development of relationship banking has overtaken the need to provide security with many credit applications. However, if we assume that bank managers are risk averse, we can expect that collateral will be required where risks are perceived to be high – for example, with technology-based entrepreneurs or with propositions that have high gearing. Security, in practice, will often be a critical requirement where risk is perceived to be high.

Theoretically, adverse selection should not occur if the bank has perfect information and can rely with certainty on cash-flow predictions. Following Altman,[33] we have argued that it is necessary to define two different categories of adverse selection. First, the bank could approve a proposition that turns out to be a business failure. Second, the bank could refuse to accept a proposition that turns out to be a business success. As illustrated in Table 7.1, we define these categories as Type II and Type I errors respectively.

TABLE 7.1 POTENTIAL OUTCOMES FROM DECISION-MAKING ON A PROPOSITION

Outcome	Funded	Not funded
Proposition successful	Correct decision	Type I error
Proposition fails	Type II error	Correct decision

Note: The reader may like to note that this classification of potential errors reverses the original Altman classification.

As can be seen in Table 7.1, it is more likely that bank officers would be concerned with avoiding Type II errors (partly because Type I errors will not be discovered) and, in our earlier study, we concluded that this contributed to adverse selection.[34]

Systems that control for Type II errors may minimize risk, but they also miss profitable opportunities associated with business propositions that might contain higher risk, but provide profitable opportunities for growth in the business of the bank. These hypotheses provide theoretical explanations of why bank officers may turn away small-firm propositions that have high potential for growth and profitability.

RAISING ENTREPRENEURIAL FINANCE

The role of security and the Enterprise Finance Guarantee Scheme

Many developed economies (although not all) have a state-sponsored loan guarantee scheme with the main objective being to assist those entrepreneurs with little security to raise bank finance. The state accepts that bankers will require security, although the importance of this is changing for some bankers (see the section on credit-scoring, below).

In the UK, the Enterprise Finance Guarantee Scheme (EFG), which replaced the former Small Firms' Loan Guarantee Scheme (SFLGS) in January 2009, provides a vehicle for those entrepreneurs with little security, with, at the time of writing, the government guaranteeing up to 75 per cent of the loan. The EFG opened up the SFLGS to include a wider number of businesses and was, in part at least, a response to the tighter credit conditions following the early impact of the GFC in 2008. In the UK's 2010 budget the government announced an additional £200m extension funding allocated to the new EFG to support up to £700m of credit funding for SMEs until March 2011 and a 20-day limit on lenders to process applications under the Scheme. In the UK, take-up rates under both Schemes have been variable,[35] but an evaluation of the former SFLGS concluded that the economic benefits outweighed the costs of the Scheme.[36] One of the key findings from this report was that (page 5):

> SFLG has created a level playing field for credit constrained businesses allowing them to achieve performance levels on a par to otherwise unconstrained businesses.

To qualify for the Scheme, propositions have to be put forward to the Enterprise Directorate by bankers, although decision-making is delegated to bankers. Under the early operation of the Scheme, in the 1990s, default rates were high, but in more recent years these have improved, as have take-up rates.[5] The Scheme is intended to be self-financing, and the entrepreneurs who qualify pay a premium interest rate (currently set at 2 per cent).

The former SFLGS has in previous years excluded some sectors. From a study involving the author, on access to finance by ethnic minority businesses (EMBs),[37] it was suggested that the Scheme may disadvantage EMBs due to concentrations of EMBs in retailing, a sector that was excluded. It was recommended that the former SBS should review the operation of the Scheme in the light of difficulties faced by EMBs. Following review by the then DTI (now BIS), the SFLGS was changed in 2003 to include additional sectors, but the target SMEs were defined as those established for less than five years.[38] Under the EFG established businesses facing previous credit restrictions can now apply.

THE GRAHAM REVIEW

The Graham Review of the former SFLGS in 2004[39] identified a number of weaknesses in the operation of the scheme and proposed some reforms that have been operated since December 2005. A significant change was to give full delegation on decision-making on lending to the banks, allowing integration and more streamlined decision-making. Three main changes were implemented:

- The scheme was restricted to start-up and early-stage SMEs, up to five years old (since extended to established businesses by the EFG in 2009)

- The eligibility criteria were simplified

- Bank lenders became responsible for decision-making

KEY FEATURES OF EFG

Following the Graham Review, and the renaming of the Scheme in 2009, the main features of EFG are:

- A guarantee to the lender covering 75 per cent of the amount; the borrower pays a 2 per cent per annum premium

- Loans can be up to £250,000 for up to 10 years

- Lending can be for a total of £1,000 up to £1 million

- Applies to firms with turnover of up to £25 million

- Applications must be processed by lenders within 20 working days

It is still relatively early to make any comment on these changes, especially those introduced under the EFG, but widening the criteria to include additional sectors and delegation of decision-making to bank managers are positive improvements in the EFG.

FINANCIAL MODELLING AND CREDIT-SCORING

The advent of computerized credit-scoring for personal customer loan applications has been mirrored with the introduction by some banks of credit analysis systems of applications for credit by business customers, or a form of credit-scoring for smaller applications and more sophisticated financial modelling for larger applications. The last Bank of England report suggested that the trend towards credit-scoring techniques for business loan applications has become increasingly prominent.[2] Credit-scoring relies upon the application of predictable variables for an individual's credit rating, such as occupation, postcode of home address, family commitments and previous payment record. Scores are attached to each of the criteria, which will lead to an automatic acceptance/rejection decision issued by computer, effectively disenfranchising the bank officer of any responsibility to make subjective judgements about individual applications. Financial modelling requires trading history and more qualitative information and produces a risk-return outcome against a categorized scale, indicating the strength of a proposition. When such systems are applied to business applications, in theory, the potential for variation in bank manager decisions should be reduced to a minimum. However, this also means that individual bank-manager discretion to use local knowledge and local information about the entrepreneur may also be reduced, perhaps leading to automatic rejections that, before the advent of quantitative analytical credit-scoring, would have been carefully considered by the banks. However, the research conducted with bank managers in Scotland did reveal that considerable discretion was still enjoyed by more senior bank managers, particular where the SME owner was an existing customer of the bank and had built up a good relationship with the manager. The Bank of England has reported[2] that, 'Qualitative techniques [of decision-making] based around a manager's judgement are increasingly being supported or even supplemented by computer-based quantitative analysis' (p. 13).

In the UK, each of the main commercial banks – Barclays, HSBC, Lloyds TSB, NatWest/RBS – operates different systems for credit applications from entrepreneurs. Three of the banks have adopted a centralized system where the role of the bank manager has become a purely relationship role, with credit applications referred to a central credit risk unit.[40] The manager still has a role in preparing the application, but has no discretionary powers in decision-making on the application, which is credit-scored by the central risk unit. The other two commercial banks have adopted a form of credit-scoring for business applications, but have retained local discretion in decision-making. However, all new start-up business propositions have to be referred for central approval.

Credit-scoring and financial modelling has brought costs and benefits for banks and entrepreneurs. It may automatically rule out some applications (which would otherwise be successful) because of the credit history of the entrepreneur or because of previous credit judgments (for example, a county court judgment, which will automatically result in a reject decision), but it has also meant that bank manager discretion can be increased and it has reduced the extent of security levels required.[40]

It can be argued that some entrepreneurs are disadvantaged by bank managers' formal methods of risk assessment, whether operating qualitative and heuristic-based decision-making or more quantitative, credit-scoring techniques. For example, the former SBS has argued in its Strategic Framework for Women's Enterprise, that 'traditional credit-scoring systems discriminate against women, who tend to have a less detailed and more fragmented financial track record' and claims outright that female entrepreneurs suffer 'prejudice on the part of lenders'.[41] The author's involvement in research studies with ethnic minority entrepreneurs and their access to finance has produced reports that suggest some entrepreneurs from different ethnic groups may also be disadvantaged.[42] However, rather than some prejudice, as suggested by the former SBS's Strategic Framework document, in reality it is different and highly variable practices by bank managers that account for differences in treatment of different groups of entrepreneurs. For example, one of the ethnic minority studies suggested that good practice by bank managers, where they were involved in local ethnic minority communities, led to a greater understanding of business practices and familiarity with propositions from the ethnic minority community, allowing them to influence decision-making practices favourably even where these were centralized.[40]

THE IMPACT OF THE GLOBAL FINANCIAL CRISIS OF AUTUMN 2008

In a momentous period of just a few days in September 2008, one major US investment bank, Lehman Brothers, filed for Chapter 11 bankruptcy, being effectively allowed to collapse; Merrill Lynch was forced into a merger with Bank of America; and a rescue deal was announced for the American insurance giant, AIG. This was followed by dramatic falls in the share prices of UK commercial banks, especially the HBOS Group, and the UK government hastily brokered a deal between Lloyds TSB and HBOS, which effectively meant the takeover of HBOS by Lloyds TSB. Economic and financial commentary at the time indicated that this takeover would never normally have been allowed by the Competition Commission due to the complex monopoly that exists in the commercial banking sector in the UK. Despite these unprecedented measures, the financial crisis became global in extent by October 2008, with commercial banks across Europe in difficulties in raising capital and liquidity and with Icelandic banks failing altogether. As we have mentioned earlier, the subsequent period has been referred to as the post-GFC economic and financial environment. The UK government announced a special range of measures in an attempt to restore confidence on 8 October 2008, combined with a cut in the Bank of England base rate. The main part of the package was to provide capital to the banks via part nationalization and to offer guarantees for inter-bank lending. Following the collapse in the HBOS share price, the RBS share price had also fallen dramatically and further falls in both Lloyds TSB and HBOS had threatened to terminate the special deal that had been brokered by the government. The government effectively owned 60 per cent of RBS Group and 40 per cent of the combined Lloyds Banking Group. These measures were followed by similar measures (part nationalization and guarantees for liquidity) in other European countries and across the Atlantic in the USA, illustrating the global impact of the GFC.

Although these were seismic events, it should be noted that they do not affect the principles of bank lending to entrepreneurs and small firms, which have been explained in this chapter. Indeed the GFC had arisen because traditional banking principles of lending in the American mortgage market had been abandoned, with evidence that bank mortgage lending in the domestic personal sector had ignored normal risk-lending practices.

Further research undertaken with the UK commercial and wholesale banks by the author at the time of the crisis, autumn 2008, suggested that the GFC was affecting the more marginal cases and that entrepreneurs with poor track records, or in certain categories, were more likely to face difficulties. Bankers interviewed at the time still had funds to lend to SMEs with good proposals. There was a view expressed that the effects on UK banking would still be temporary, although with structural adjustments, and that the basic principles of sound bank lending to business customers were still in place. However, surveys of small businesses since then have suggested a restricted credit market with increases in the costs of obtaining credit for entrepreneurs in the UK.[22] The introduction of the expanded EFG in 2009 and additional funding announced in 2010 represented a recognition by the UK government that access to finance for entrepreneurs and small firms had become much more restricted post GFC. There is little doubt that the post-GFC period has seen greater regulation and control by the government on the financial banking sectors and similar increased controls across Europe and other developed nations.

SOME EMPIRICAL EVIDENCE

In terms of empirical research, it is known from various sources that entrepreneurs and small firms are highly dependent on internal sources of finance, as might be expected to follow from our earlier discussion in this chapter. Empirical evidence from a number of different surveys indicates that bank finance is by far the most important source of external finance for entrepreneurs and small firms. The most comprehensive survey of SMEs in the UK are the Small Business Surveys (SBS), undertaken for the Department for Business, Innovation and Skills (BIS). The last survey was undertaken in 2010,[43] following a gap from the last Annual SBS (the ASBS) in 2007/08, since when only a smaller survey, the Business Barometer, has been undertaken.[44] For the 2007/08 ASBS report, although pre GFC, the findings are drawn from a survey of 7,783 SMEs in the UK.[45] The findings for the importance of different sources of external debt finance are shown in Figure 7.4. These indicate that 44 per cent of small-business owners used bank loans and a further 26 per cent used bank overdrafts. Other external sources of finance were of relatively minor significance, indicating that established SMEs relied heavily on banks for external debt finance.[45]

Those seeking leasing or hire-purchase was little changed at 10 per cent. These percentages are also shown in Figure 7.4, although it should be borne in mind that the sample sizes are different, with the latter figures being less reliable. Nevertheless, there is a notable increase in SMEs seeking short-term overdraft finance, which suggests that this has been one of the effects of the GFC and the continued recessionary conditions since the autumn of 2008. Further, the evidence from the smaller sample that was surveyed in 2010 confirmed that obtaining debt finance had become more difficult for SMEs post GFC. As commented on in the 2010 SME Business Barometer (p. 4),[44]

> the proportion having difficulty obtaining finance remains much higher than was the case in the 07/08 ASBS.

This trend has been confirmed with the larger survey, the 2010 SBS,[43] which undertook a survey of 4,580 SMEs. The 2010 survey indicated that, of those who sought funding in the past 12 months, the main categories sought were still dominated by bank finance, with bank loans at 40 per cent (down from 44 per cent in 2007/08), but those seeking bank overdrafts had increased to 35 per cent (from 26 per cent in 2007/08), confirming that post GFC more small firms were seeking short-term overdrafts to meet liquidity requirements in the global recession.

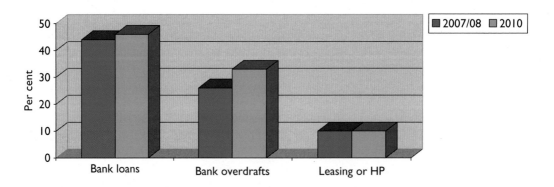

FIGURE 7.4

Importance of sources of external debt finance sought by UK SMEs, 2007/08 and 2010

SOURCE: *Annual Survey of Small Businesses 2007/08* and *Business Barometer 2010*.[43; 44]

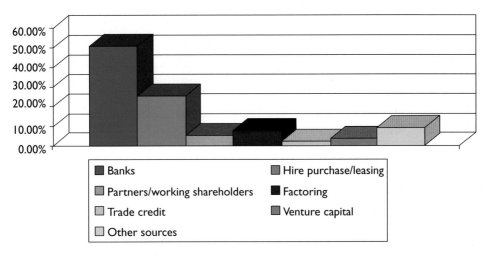

FIGURE 7.5

External sources of finance for small firms, 2000–02

SOURCE: ESRC Centre for Business Research (1992–2002).[46]

Similar findings have been demonstrated by research by Cambridge University's Centre for Business Research (CBR) (1992–2002).[46] Figure 7.5 gives its figures for the importance of external sources of finance received by small firms in the period 2000–02.

From research undertaken as part of a project on the financing needs of ethnic minority entrepreneurs, published data on the percentage accessing finance is shown in Table 7.2.[47] This shows that 39 per cent had attempted to raise finance in the previous year.

More recent data from the Minority Ethnic Group (MEG) boost to the 2010 SBS indicated that of the sample of MEG-led established businesses, 30 per cent sought to raise external finance (up from 22 per cent in the 2007/08 survey).[48] However, there is no breakdown given against different ethnic minority groups to compare with our earlier data.

TABLE 7.2 EXTERNAL FINANCE SOUGHT BY ETHNIC MINORITY BUSINESS OWNERS AT START-UP

Ethnic group	Proportion of business owners seeking source of finance
African-Caribbean	31%
Pakistani	35%
Indian	41%
Bangladeshi	34%
Chinese	51%
All ethnic business	39%

Source: Smallbone et al. (2001).[47]

TABLE 7.3 START-UP FINANCE FOR A SAMPLE OF 60 START-UP ENTREPRENEURS IN SCOTLAND

Source	Percentage of respondents	Importance (mean score)
Personal sources	80	4.2
Enterprise Allowance Scheme*	66	2.9
Local govt grant	50	2.1
Trade credit	44	1.7
Bank overdraft	37	1.5
Other public sector	29	1.2
Family and friends	20	1.1
Bank loan	22	0.9
Venture capital	7	0.2
PSYBT**	12	4.86
Other source	7	0.2

Note: * The importance of the EAS is accounted for by the large majority of respondents which were trading for less than one year.
** Prince's Scottish Youth Business Trust (applies to young entrepreneurs only, less than 26 years old).

It is likely that internal sources and the entrepreneur's equity will be very important for start-up finance. For comparative purposes, using our study of start-up small firms,[49] we report the results in terms of importance for sources of finance in Table 7.3. Although it shows that a high proportion of start-ups do use bank finance, a more significant feature is the comparative importance of personal savings, which are rated significantly higher than bank finance in importance as a source of finance.

MICRO-CREDIT: THE ROLE OF COMMUNITY DEVELOPMENT FINANCIAL INSTITUTIONS

In the UK, in recent years there has been the growth of alternative micro-credit schemes for entrepreneurs and SMEs that might be considered, at best, marginal propositions for the banks. They have often been located in socially deprived inner-city areas, although some of these early schemes have since expanded to cover much larger regional areas. One example is the former Glasgow Regeneration Fund (GRF), originally targeted at inner-city, social regeneration areas. GRF was wound up in 2001 and became the Strathclyde Fund and later the Western Scotland Regeneration Fund, which is now operated by DSL Finance (http://www.dsl-businessfinance.co.uk).

The principle of Community Development Financial Institutions (CDFIs) is illustrated by the model shown in Figure 7.6. Banks and other financial institutions provide wholesale funds at favourable interest rates, often long term. They effectively transfer the risk of lending to the CDFI fund which is managed independently, often by a community-based organisation. Small-business owners and entrepreneurs apply for relatively small credit advances, such as loans less than £5,000, to the CDFI. The fund is operated along commercial lines, but often the entrepreneur will receive support from a business adviser employed by the CDFI.

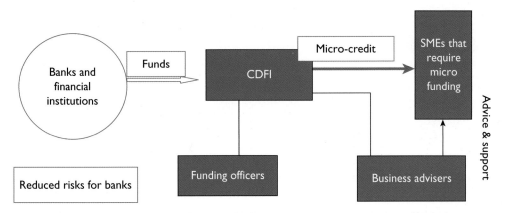

FIGURE 7.6

Micro-credit: The Community Development Financial Institutions model

In the UK, CDFIs have been closely associated with social enterprise and fostering start-ups in socially deprived areas, hence they have been seen as a vehicle for regeneration. The numbers of CDFIs have grown during the past decade after early schemes in inner-city areas such as those in Birmingham and Glasgow in the 1990s. An evaluation report in 2010[50] estimated that the numbers have now stabilised in the UK at 'somewhere between 70 and 80' (p. 7) with total capital reaching close to £600m. The evaluation report found that CDFIs had fulfilled an important function by providing funding to disadvantaged business-owners and had benefited the UK economy through additional business start-ups and retaining businesses that would otherwise not have been funded. The report stated that (p. i)[50]

> CDFIs continue to address the consistent market failure to reflect the economic and social benefits of lending in underserved markets, leading to reduced enterprise outcomes, particularly amongst disadvantaged groups and areas.

It is likely, however, that this hides considerable variety between CDFIs that perform very well and others that are less successful. From research conducted by the author, it became clear that running a successful CDFI required specific expertise and experience; although some are large and well known, such as the Aston Reinvestment Trust in Birmingham, others are known to have high default rates. CDFIs still have to apply credit-lending principles, and where there is not the financial expertise to apply these, problems of sustainability and high default rates may exist.

CONCLUSIONS

In this chapter, we have taken an overview of the important issues in the finance of entrepreneurs and small firms. Much of this discussion has centred on finance gaps and their implications for entrepreneurs and small firms. We have tried to show, theoretically, why these gaps might emerge, given problems of uncertainty and asymmetric information.

We have shown that entrepreneurs and small firms continue to be dependent on banks for external finance, despite schemes that attempt to improve the availability of equity capital. We have shown that some entrepreneurs also face problems in raising bank finance, that UK bank practices of risk assessment can be variable and that adverse selection (where potentially viable projects are not receiving finance) can exist through variability in bank-manager practice.

By now you should be able to discuss the advantages and disadvantages of the most important of these sources. You should also have an understanding of why small firms and entrepreneurs are at a disadvantage compared to larger firms in financial markets, as well as an appreciation of the problems that face providers of finance to entrepreneurs and small firms.

This chapter has focused on debt finance; the following chapter will examine in more detail sources of venture capital (including formal and informal sources) and some of the issues in raising equity. However, before the next chapter, we examine technology-based start-ups as a special case on raising entrepreneurial finance. An 'Entrepreneurship in Action' case study is included at the end of the chapter on raising bank finance: Skype Part II. This can be seen as a technology-based start-up and therefore falls within this special category for the finance of entrepreneurs and small firms. Other case material is available in the students' OLC and discussion is provided in the tutor's OLC.

RAISING ENTREPRENEURIAL FINANCE

Technology-based start-ups: a special case

Technology-based small firm (TBSF) start-ups can be seen as a special case[51] with distinct financing needs due to the following factors.

1 Extensive R&D periods for product development. This necessitates raising finance for R&D and the development of prototypes, known as seed capital.

2 Thus any start-up TSBF will face a lengthy period of negative cash flow and losses during the R&D period; this can vary from a few months (say with software providers) to ten years or more (say with bio-technology applications). Such technology-based entrepreneurs will exhaust private savings/internal sources and need to rely on raising external capital.

3 Although patents can be used to protect new products/processes, they are intangible assets and banks are unwilling to accept them as security.

4 Developing cash-flow forecasts for the business plan can be problematic since, with new-technology products, existing markets do not exist. Consequently banks are unwilling to lend against forecasts.

5   The new technology will need a technology appraisal to determine its viability and banks are not equipped to undertake such approaches.

The former government scheme to assist technology-based start-ups in the UK, the Small Firms' Merit Award for Research and Technology (SMART), has now been replaced in England and Wales by the Government Grant for Research and Technology, which has removed some of the competitive elements of the former SMART scheme. Four types of grant are available under this scheme at different levels, depending on the nature of the technology-based project, from micro (up to £20,000 grant) to exceptional developments (up to £500,000 for qualifying projects). At the time of writing, the SMART scheme still applied in Scotland.

For a recent survey and discussion of the issues in the financing of TBSFs in the UK, their growth performance and the impact on their financing of the post-GFC period, see a 2011 research report by Ullah, North and Baldock.[52]

ENTREPRENEURSHIP IN ACTION

Raising Bank Finance

SKYPE PART II

By 2002, the founders of Kazaa (Niklas Zennström and Janus Friis) had sold the Kazaa network, but were short of cash to invest in their new start-up project: Skype. They required investment funds and had embarked on a search for venture finance in 2002. However, having bank funds can help to lever in equity in the form of venture capital. At the time, Niklas Zennström and Janus Friis would have considered bank funding, yet Skype was unproven technology and would have been considered a technology-based start-up, even though the two entrepreneurs had previous business experience through their involvement with Kazaa.

Assume that they approached some of the main commercial banks for funding the next phase of development of Skype, which was as yet unproven technology:

DISCUSSION QUESTIONS

Assume that Niklas Zennström and Janus Friis are seeking to raise US$500,000. They have prepared a business plan which shows that no income is generated from customers as subscribers, only from advertising.

1   What information would you have required as a bank manager?

2   What questions would you have asked them as a bank manager?

3   How would you have tried to establish a relationship with them as technology-based entrepreneurs?

REVIEW QUESTIONS

1 What difficulties do entrepreneurs face in raising equity finance? How do you expect this to differ with start-ups and with established firms?
2 List the main sources of debt and equity finance for entrepreneurs.
3 Taking the bank manager–entrepreneur relationship:
   (a) What flows of information might exist between the bank manager and the entrepreneur?
   (b) What factors will affect the banker–entrepreneur relationship?
4 The empirical evidence in this chapter suggests that entrepreneurs have a preference for finance in a distinct order: personal sources, debt from banks and then venture-capital sources. This result has been called the Pecking Order Hypothesis and it is thought that entrepreneurs will seek finance in this order of preference. What factors would account for such a 'pecking order' of preference by entrepreneurs? (Hint: consider the obligations of entrepreneurs to debt and equity funders.)
5 What is the main purpose of the government-sponsored Enterprise Fund Guarantee Scheme? Do you consider that there is still a need for such a scheme?
6 What do you understand by credit-scoring?
7 What implications for entrepreneurs might exist from the advent of credit-scoring applied by the commercial banks to business applications?
8 What benefits might a Community Development Financial Institution (CDFI) scheme provide to its member small firms and entrepreneurs?
9 Why do CDFIs reduce the risks for banks in lending micro-credit to small business customers?
10 What are the special issues faced by technology-based entrepreneurs in accessing finance. Why are they likely to face security requirements from banks in credit applications?

SUGGESTED ASSIGNMENTS

1 Complete a report on the issues in the finance of start-up entrepreneurs.

2 Collect material on lending and services to small firms and entrepreneurs from the local high street banks, including charges.

   (a) Compare the services and discuss whether there are any differences in services or charges.

   (b) How do you expect the main commercial banks to compete for their small business customers?

REFERENCES

1 **Enterprise Directorate** (former SBS) (2001) *Phoenix Fund and Early Growth Fund*, Enterprise Directorate, BERR, London.
2 **Bank of England** (2004) *Finance for Small Firms: An Eleventh Report*, Bank of England, London.
3 **Enterprise Directorate** (former SBS) (2004) *A Government Action Plan for Small Business: The Evidence Base*, Enterprise Directorate, BERR, London.
4 **HM Government** (1931) *Report of the Committee on Finance and Industry* (Macmillan Report), CMND 3897, HMSO, London.
5 For example, **Bank of England** (1994–2001) *Finance for Small Firms Annual Reports*, Bank of England, London.

6 **Rowlands Report (**2009) *The Provision of Growth Capital to UK Small and Medium-Sized Enterprises*, Department of Business, Innovation and Skills, HMSO, London.

7 **Bank of England** (2004) Statement, Bank of England, London.

8 **Harrison, R. and Mason, C**. (1991) 'Informal investment networks: a case study from the UK', *Entrepreneurship and Regional Development*, vol. 3, no. 2, pp. 269–79.

9 **BVCA** (2003) *Venture Capital in the UK: Annual Report*, British Venture Capital Association, London.

10 **Bank of England** (2001) *Finance for Small Firms – an Eighth Report*, Bank of England, London.

11 **Akerlof, G.** (1970) 'The market for lemons: qualitative uncertainty and the market mechanism', *Quarterly Journal of Economics*, vol. 89, pp. 488–500.

12 **Mirrlees, J.A.** (1974) 'Notes on welfare economics, information and uncertainty', in M. Balch, D. McFadden and S. Wu (eds), *Essays in Economic Behaviour Under Uncertainty*, North Holland, Oxford.

13 **Mirrlees, J.A.** (1975) *The Theory of Moral Hazard and Unobservable Behaviour*, Nuffield College, Oxford.

14 **Jensen, M.C. and Meckling, W.H.** (1976) 'Theory of the firm: managerial behaviour, agency costs and ownership structure', *Journal of Financial Economics*, vol. 3, pp. 305–60.

15 **Harris, M. and Townsend, R.M.** (1981) 'Resource allocation under asymmetric information', *Econometrica*, vol. 49, pp. 33–64.

16 **Hellwig, M.** (1987) 'Some recent developments in the theory of competition in markets with adverse selection', *European Economic Review*, vol. 31, pp. 319–25.

17 **Magill, M. and Shafer, W.** (1991) 'Incomplete markets', in W. Hildenbrand and H. Sonneschein (eds), *The Handbook of Mathematical Economics*, vol. 4, North-Holland, Oxford.

18 **Stiglitz, J. and Weiss, A.** (1981) 'Credit rationing in markets with imperfect information', *American Economic Review*, vol. 71, pp. 393–410.

19 **De Meza, D. and Webb, D.** (1987) 'Too much investment: a problem of asymmetric information', *Quarterly Journal of Economics*, vol. 102, pp. 281–92.

20 **Aston Business School** (1991) *Constraints on the Growth of Small Firms*, DTI, HMSO, London.

21 **Forum of Private Business Biennial Survey Reports** (1996–2006) *Private Businesses and their Banks*, FPB, Knutsford.

22 **Federation of Small Business** (2010) *The FSB–ICM Voice of Small Business Annual Survey*, FSB, London.

23 **Deakins, D. and Hussain, G.** (1991) *Risk Assessment by Bank Managers*, University of Central England Business School, Birmingham.

24 **Kon, Y. and Storey, D.** (2003) 'A theory of discouraged borrowers', *Small Business Economics*, vol. 21, no. 1, pp. 37–49.

25 **CEEDR** (2007) *The Impact of Perceived Access to Finance Difficulties on the Demand for External Finance: A Literature Review*, Report for the Small Business Service, DTI, London.

26 **Roper, S. and Scott, J.** (2007) 'Gender differences in access to startup finance: an econometric analysis of GEM data', paper presented to 30th ISBE Conference, November, Glasgow.

27 **North, D., Deakins, D., Baldock, R., Whittam, G., Ekanem, I. and Wyper, J.** (2008) *Access to Bank Finance for Scottish SMEs*, Research Report for the Enterprise, Energy and Tourism Directorate, Scottish Government, Edinburgh.

28 **Scottish Government** (2007) *Annual Survey of Small Businesses: Scotland 2005*, Institute of Employment Studies for the Scottish Government, Scottish Government, Edinburgh.

29 **Deakins, D., North, D., Baldock, R. and Whittam, G.** (2008) 'SMEs' access to finance: Is there still a debt finance gap?' 30th ISBE National Conference, November, Belfast; ISBE best papers at: http://www.isbe.org.uk/BestPapers#Bel08 (accessed September 2011).

30 **Spence, A.M.** (1974) *Market Signaling*, Harvard University Press, Cambridge, MA.

31 **Crawford, V. and Sobell, J.** (1982) 'Strategic information transmission', *Econometrica*, vol. 50, pp. 1431–51.

32 **Chan, Y. and Kannatas, G.** (1985) 'Asymmetric valuations and the role of collateral in loan agreements', *Journal of Money, Credit and Banking*, vol. 17, no. 1, pp. 84–95.

33 **Altman, E.I.** (1971) *Corporate Bankruptcy in America*, Heath, Lexington, MA.

34 **Deakins, D. and Hussain, G.** (1994) 'Financial information, the banker and small business: a comment', *The British Accounting Review*, vol. 26, pp. 323–35.

35 **Deakins, D., Ram, M., Smallbone, D. and, Fletcher, M.** (2002) 'Decision-making and the development of relationships with ethnic minority entrepreneurs by UK bankers', paper presented to the 2002 Babson Entrepreneurship

Research Conference, June, Boulder, Colorado.

36 **Cowling, M**. (2010) *Economic Evaluation of the Small Firms' Loan Guarantee Scheme*, report for Department for Business, Innovation and Skills, London.

37 **Ram, M., Smallbone, D. and Deakins, D.** (2002) *Ethnic Minority Businesses in the UK: Access to Finance and Business Support*, British Bankers Association, London.

38 **Bank of England** (2003) *Finance for Small Firms – a Tenth Report*, Bank of England, London.

39 **HM Treasury** (2004) *The Graham Review of the Small Firms Loan Guarantee Scheme*, September, HM Treasury, London.

40 **Deakins, D., Ram, M., Smallbone, D. and Fletcher, M.** (2004) 'Ethnic minority entrepreneurs in the commercial banks in the UK: access to formal sources of finance and decision-making by their bank managers', in C.H. Stiles and C.S. Galbraith (eds), *Ethnic Entrepreneurship: Structure and Process*, Elsevier, Oxford.

41 **Small Business Service** (2003) *A Strategic Framework for Women's Enterprise*, Small Business Service, DTI, London.

42 **Smallbone, D., Ram, M, Deakins, D. and Baldock, R.** (2003) 'Access to finance by ethnic minority businesses in the UK', *International Small Business Journal*, vol. 21, no. 3, pp. 291–314.

43 **Department for Business, Innovation and Skills** (2011) *BIS Small Business Survey 2010*, IFF Research, Department for Business, Innovation and Skills, London.

44 **Department for Business, Innovation and Skills** (2010) *SME Business Barometer*, IFF Research, Department for Business, Innovation and Skills, London.

45 **Williams, M. and Cowling, M.** (2009) *Annual Small Business Survey 2007/08*, Report for the former Department for Business, Enterprise and Regulatory Reform, now Department for Business, Innovation and Skills, London.

46 **ESRC Centre for Business Research** (1992–2002) *The State of British Enterprise*, Reports, Department of Applied Economics, University of Cambridge, Cambridge.

47 **Smallbone, D., Ram, M., Deakins, D. and Baldock, R.** (2001) 'Access to finance by ethnic minority businesses in the UK',

International Small Business Journal, vol. 21, no. 3, pp. 291–314.

48 **Department for Business, Innovation and Skills** (2011) *BIS Small Business Survey 2010 Minority Ethnic Group (MEG) led Business Boost*, IFF Research, Department for Business, Innovation and Skills, London.

49 **Deakins, D., Graham, L., Sullivan, R. and Whittam, G.** (1997) *New Venture Support: An Analysis of Mentoring Provision for New Entrepreneurs*, Paisley Enterprise Research Centre, University of Paisley, Scotland.

50 **Department for Business, Innovation and Skills and the Cabinet Office** (2010) *Evaluation of Community Development Funding Initiatives (CDFIs)*, BIS, London.

51 **DTI** (1994) *An Evaluation of the Small Firms Merit Award for Research and Technology (SMART)*, DTI, London.

52 **Ullah, F., North D. and Baldock, R. (2011)** *The Impact of the Financial Crisis on the Financing and Growth of Technology-Based Small Firms in the United Kingdom*, Institute for Small Business and Entrepreneurship, London; available at http://www.isbe.org.uk (accessed September 2011).

RECOMMENDED READING

Rowlands Report (2009) *The Provision of Growth Capital to UK Small and Medium-Sized Enterprises*, Department of Business, Innovation and Skills, HMSO, London.

Ullah, F., North, D. and Baldock, R. (2011) *The Impact*

of the Financial Crisis on the Financing and Growth of Technology-Based Small Firms in the United Kingdom, Institute for Small Business and Entrepreneurship, London.

Bank of England Annual Reports (1994–2004) *Finance*

for Small Firms, nos. 1–11, Bank of England, London.

Bank of England (2001) *Financing of Technology-based Small Firms*, Bank of England, London.

8 SOURCES OF VENTURE FINANCE

INTRODUCTION

As the previous chapter makes clear, the bulk of academic and policy discussions regarding small-firm finance have tended to concentrate on the firm's ability to access bank debt; or, to rephrase, the extent to which small firms are 'credit rationed'.[1] This is as it should be. Studies have long concluded that, where such funding is sought, banks are significantly the most important source of external finance for the SME sector.[2] The recent UK survey of SME finance,[3] for instance, reported that around 56 per cent and 39 per cent of sample firms approached banks for overdraft or loan/mortgage financing during 2007 (of which, 90 per cent and 96 per cent, respectively, were successful in accessing at least some funds), while, in contrast, a mere 2 per cent of firms reported seeking access to equity finance in the same year (of which a remarkable 94 per cent claim to have to have been, at least partially, successful).

However, notwithstanding the dominance of banks as a potential source of finance – indeed, in many respects, as a result of it – there has been growing concern over the shortage of long-term risk capital, or equity, within the financial structure of many small firms.[4] Reliance upon bank debt to fund start-up or growth and development, may give rise to a number of problems. Among the most obvious of these is the imposed short-termism. Debt capital is not patient capital and term loans rarely exceed three to five years. However, perhaps more importantly, debt capital is seldom committed capital. As discussed in the previous chapter, debt may be secured (against either the business's or the owner's assets) and requires periodic repayment of interest and ultimate payment of the principal. This places the firm in an extremely exposed position in the event of a slump in sales or other pressures on profitability and, crucially, cash flow. In situations where firms default on debt repayments, and as a last resort, banks may either repossess assets or force the company into receivership (typically banks hold the assets of the firm or principals as security against default). Accordingly, and at least for those firms with significant growth potential, commentators argue that patient and committed risk capital, the returns to which will be contingent upon the success of the business, is more appropriately required.

The idea that there exists an 'equity gap', or deficiency in the provision of smaller amounts of risk capital, is not new. For example, in the UK the inability of small firms to access small-scale risk capital for either start-up or business development has been widely accepted since at least the 1931 Macmillan report,[5] and thereafter, in government terms, the 1971 Bolton report,[6] the 1979 Wilson report[7] and the 1989 Williams report.[8] This gap has traditionally been thought to fall somewhere between the resources that may realistically be provided by private individuals (such as the entrepreneur, family, friends and associates) and the capital required for stock market flotation (though this is clearly very wide, and a 'new equity gap' of between £250,000 and

£1,000,000 is now more commonly recognised). Accordingly, it is with reference to the amelioration of equity gaps, that the current chapter seeks to outline the potential and actual role played by venture capital.

THE NATURE OF VENTURE CAPITAL

So, what is venture capital? As the name suggests, sounding a little like 'adventure capital', it is capital that clearly involves a degree of risk. However, more specifically, venture capital may be defined, generically, as financial investment in *unquoted* companies, which have significant growth potential, with a view to yielding substantial capital gains in line with the additional risk and illiquidity of an investment that cannot be freely traded during the lifetime of the investor's commitment to the business. Moreover, venture capital is thought to provide the bridge between the levels of capital that may be provided by the founder, their family and friends, and private investors – which is often exhausted at the prototype or 'proof-of-concept' and start-up stages (if a technology-based entrepreneur) – and the significant amounts required for a stock market listing and to attract large-scale institutional investments (Figure 8.1).

 Classic venture capital assists young and growing firms with the potential for significant future growth, and is frequently a complement to debt finance. However, venture capital is fundamentally equity orientated. As Mason and Harrison[9] note:

> The objective [of venture capital] is to achieve a *high return* on the investment in the form of *capital gain* through an *exit*, achieved by the sale of the equity stake rather than through [interest or] dividend income. Exit is normally achieved either through an initial public offering (IPO), involving the flotation of the company on a stock market where its shares are traded freely, or through a trade sale in which the venture capital fund, normally along with all the other shareholders in the company, sell out to another company.
>
> (p. 15)

Within this broad framework, a number of 'types' of venture capital are commonly identified, as described below.

- Institutional venture capital (or formal venture capital) – investments in entrepreneurial ventures by firms of full-time professionals who raise finance from pension funds, banks, insurance companies and other financial institutions.
- Informal venture capital (or business angel finance) – investments by wealthy private individuals who are prepared to use their financial resources to make risk investments based upon their experience and interests.

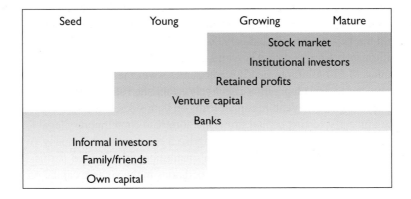

FIGURE 8.1

Stage model of finance

Business angels are often retired senior executives of large companies, or entrepreneurs who have sold their companies and now wish to use the money.

- Corporate venture capital (or corporate venturing) – minority investments made by large companies in smaller enterprises for a principally strategic (such as gaining a window on new technologies) rather than an exclusively financial motive. As McNally[10] notes, '[t]he combination of a small firm's know-how, inventive efficiency and flexibility and a larger firm's financial, production, marketing and distribution resources can provide opportunities for synergies that can contribute to both firms' competitive advantage' (p. 16).

- Public-sector venture capital – while government plays a role in encouraging private-sector venture capital – through policy instruments such as the Enterprise Investment Scheme (http://www.hmrc.gov.uk/eis/) or offering (primarily, capital gains) tax incentives – it may, more occasionally, act more directly as a provider of venture finance. The most visible examples of such direct public-sector activities, during the 1970s and 1980s, included the investment arms of the Scottish and Welsh Development Agencies.[11] However, the trend is emphatically towards hybrid, public–private partnerships.[12] In such cases (e.g. the Regional Venture Capital Funds), private- and public-sector capital is pooled, though fund management is undertaken along private sector (institutional) lines and follows a largely commercial imperative, rather than being bound by exclusively social or welfare considerations. Nonetheless, such funds aim at filling 'gaps', or alleviating deficiencies, in mainstream venture capital provision, by ensuring a more even spatial distribution of activity, or by directing a larger proportion of the fund towards higher-risk, early-stage and high-technology investments.

However, despite the growth in public-sector and corporate venturing, these 'types' of venture capital still account for a relatively small proportion of private-sector equity investments. The bulk of investment activity remains the province of institutional venture capitalists and business angels. Accordingly, these latter two form the basis of the current chapter.

Clearly, to the extent that it involves equity investment in smaller firms with a view to capital gain, venture capital is not a new phenomenon. Throughout history, wealthy private individuals have invested in smaller enterprises or ventures, sharing part of the risk, in return for a share in the outcome. However, in its formal, institutional guise, venture capital is largely a contemporary phenomenon, dating from the post-Second World War period.[13; 14] In the USA, the genesis of the institutional venture capital industry is typically traced to the founding of the American Research and Development Corporation (ARD) in 1946 and, in the UK, the founding of the Industrial and Commercial Finance Corporation (ICFC, now renamed 3i plc) by the Bank of England and the major clearing banks, in 1945. In both instances, these were probably the first firms, as opposed to individuals, dedicated to providing risk capital to new and potentially super-growth firms, principally in manufacturing or technology-based sectors. However, contrary to popular mythology, neither US industry nor, as is generally accepted, UK industry experienced much growth until considerably later. As Timmons[15] observes, 'the [US] venture capital industry did not experience a growth spurt until the 1980s, when the industry "went ballistic" – rising from approximately $0.5 billion, in 1977, to just over $4 billion in 1987' (pp. 441–43). Similarly, in the UK, venture capital investments rose from £66 million, in 163 companies, to £1.65 billion, in 1569 companies, over the period 1981–89.[16] However, notwithstanding the lag in activity, these early progenitors effectively established the 'rules of the game', which have served to determine the 'shape' of independent venture capital firms on both sides of the Atlantic. That is, in common with many of the more successful early venture capital firms, the dominant contemporary legal form is of a limited partnership.[a] Specifically, venture capital funds usually comprise a management company (whose directors are the general partners), which raises risk capital from financial institutions (the limited partners). The key issue here, however, is that venture capital firms are essentially intermediaries in the venture capital process (Figure 8.2).

---

[a] Though, as a matter of historical interest, ARD, as a result of institutional investor reluctance, was structured as a publicly traded, closed-end fund and marketed mostly to individuals.

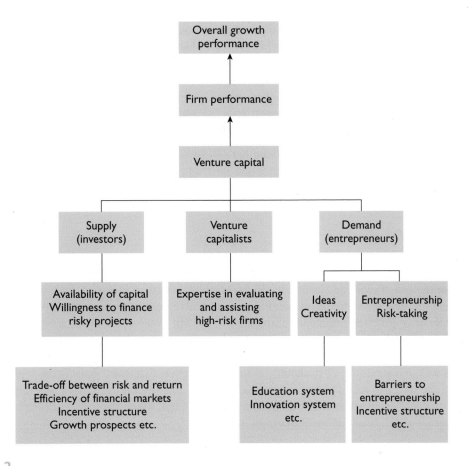

FIGURE 8.2

The nature of venture capital

SOURCE: Adapted from Baygan and Freudenberg (2000).[17]

As Figure 8.2 makes clear, the use and economic impact of venture capital is likely to be a function of a number of underlying supply- and demand-side framework conditions. On the demand side, it is clear that the flow of good entrepreneurial projects, allied to a willingness to share equity, is a necessary element of a successful venture capital system. This in turn is likely to be a function of the education and innovation systems, and of the prevailing culture in society, and will be facilitated, or hindered, by institutional framework conditions, such as the nature and level of taxation, legislation and regulation. On the supply side, the flow of venture capital funds will be determined by, among other things, the efficiency of financial markets and the availability of alternative investment opportunities, investor attitudes towards risk and return, the taxation system and the growth prospects of the economy as a whole. It is worth noting, however, that the relative efficacy of demand and supply mechanisms is not independent. It is surely no coincidence that those economies with comparatively low barriers to entrepreneurship also have more active venture capital industries and vice versa.[17] Countries with high-level venture capital activity and low barriers to entrepreneurship include the USA, the UK, Canada and Sweden. By contrast, countries such as France, Italy, Austria and Switzerland tend to have lower levels of venture capital activity and relatively higher barriers to entrepreneurship.

Notwithstanding the potential negative association between venture capital activity and barriers to entrepreneurship, the role of venture capitalists per se remains the same – that is, as intermediaries. In this model of the system, venture capitalists bring expertise in evaluating, assisting and monitoring high-risk firms. Entrepreneurs are in want of capital and investors are in want of expertise and knowledge. Venture capital firms encourage the former and provide the latter. In particular, their *raison d'être* concerns the ability to reduce the costs of information asymmetries (see below). As Amit et al.[18] note:

> Venture capitalists operate in environments where their relative efficiency in selecting and monitoring investments gives them a comparative advantage over other investors . . . [accordingly] . . . Venture capitalists should be prominent in industries where informational concerns are important, such as biotechnology, computer software, etc., rather than in 'routine' start-ups such as restaurants, retail outlets, etc. The latter are risky, in that returns show high variance, but they are relatively easy to monitor by conventional financial intermediaries.
>
> (p. 441)

So venture capital firms attenuate information asymmetries (i.e. reduce the costs of incomplete information), providing, as a minimum, finance and assistance to firms and expertise to investors. But, to what end? As Figure 8.2 intimates, the general supposition holds that the involvement of venture capitalists will lead to the superior performance of investee firms and, ultimately, to growth in the economy as a whole. Indeed, studies undertaken on behalf of the venture capital associations in the USA and Europe show that venture capital-backed companies have generally outperformed *Fortune* 500/FT-Excel 500 companies in terms of employment growth, exports and investment.[16;17] It should be noted, however, that since only firms with demonstrable growth potential are likely to received venture capital backing, this finding is perhaps less remarkable than it appears at first glance. Nevertheless, the European Venture Capital Association[19] describes venture capital-supported companies as 'engines for our economies' (p. 2).

THE SCALE AND SCOPE OF VENTURE CAPITAL

Now that we understand a little about the nature of venture capital, the next questions one might ask are: 'How much is there?', 'Where does it come from?' and 'Where does it go?' That is, what is the scale and scope of venture capital activity?

Figure 8.3 provides the answer to the first of these questions for Europe and the USA. After growing substantially in the closing years of the last century (with a particular surge from 1998–2000) the amount of venture capital invested peaked in 2000 at around US$500 billion and US$150 billion in the USA and Europe respectively. Thereafter, both the number of funds and the amount raised declined precipitously, bottoming out at US$91 billion and US$61 billion in 2003. That the decline in the US was much sharper and the subsequent recovery more pronounced probably says something about the relative make-up of the financial systems on either side of the Atlantic, allied to the nature of the crisis that precipitated the decline. Indeed, if one subtracts the UK from the European figures the differences become amplified. The dotcom, or 'new economy', bubble was largely an endogenous phenomenon from the perspective of capital markets. That is, it was driven by the unrealistic expectations of market participants regarding the value of information and media technologies and the companies that used them. When the bubble burst, the USA and UK suffered more.

Given the historical make-up of the financial systems within these countries, this is not surprising. Tylecote,[20] for instance, distinguishes between different capital market regimes. In historically 'stock exchange-based' economies (such as the USA and the UK), larger firms look to the stock market as a major source of equity and investment. Accordingly, banks play only a limited role in providing risk capital 'since their lending is *transactional*

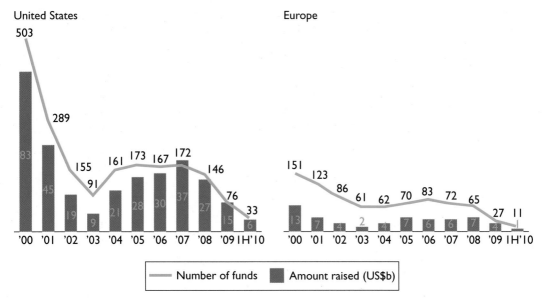

FIGURE 8.3

US and European VC fund-raising

SOURCE: Ernst and Young Venture Capital Insights and Trends Report 2010.

rather than relational' (p. 262). Each loan is considered a one-off, secured against collateral or against the scrap value of the firm's assets. In these economies, venture capital is viewed as an alternative source of risk for those firms that cannot bear the transaction costs associated with a market listing, but where the markets provide a possible exit route. By contrast, in 'bank-based' economies (e.g. Germany and Japan), comparatively few firms are 'listed' on the stock exchange and the market is not considered a major source of funds. Rather, firms rely on private (or occasionally state) banks as the principal source of external finance. Loans are no longer of a one-off nature and lending is relational rather than transactional:[20]

> seen as part of a long-term relationship in which the firm is bound to inform the bank fully as to its position and prospects and the bank is committed to support the firm through bad times, in return for influence over its policy and personnel.
>
> (p. 262)

In such instances, banks become adept at managing or alleviating information asymmetries and the opportunities for venture capitalists are limited. However, this historical distinction between stock exchange and bank-based financial systems has become somewhat blurred. For instance, many economies, formerly classed as 'bank-based' (such as Germany), have begun a drift towards occupying some middle ground between bank- and stock exchange-based systems (as evidenced by the blocked takeover of the London Stock Exchange by the Deutsche Börse in 2006 and the merger of Euronext – itself a merger of the Dutch, Belgian and French exchanges – with the New York Stock Exchange in April 2007), while UK banks, for instance, would undoubtedly argue that they have made a shift towards relationship-based, rather than transaction-based, lending.

Of course, the financial crisis that became evident when the imminent bankruptcy of Lehman Brothers was announced on 15 September 2008 has also led to sharp falls in venture capital activity in the EU and USA.

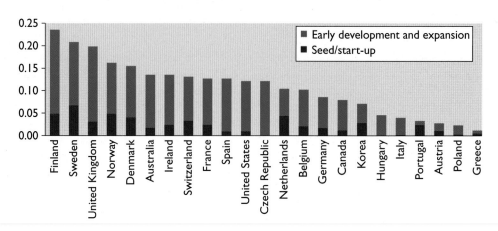

FIGURE 8.4

Venture capital investment as a % of GDP (2008)

SOURCE: OECD (2009), *Measuring Entrepreneurship: A Digest of Indicators*, OECD, Paris, based on the OECD Entrepreneurship Financing Database.

While the levels of 2000 were probably unsustainable, those of 2005–2006 were not. Viewed in this light, this recent fall has been more worrying and, at the time of writing, shows every sign of being at least as persistent – with EU funds raised in the first half of 2011 down 28 per cent from a year earlier. For some, the causes of this more recent crisis have been exogenous (i.e. a malfunctioning financial sector), and its effects more widely felt. The numbers of funds and amounts raised are far below the earlier lows that followed the bursting of the dotcom bubble. The immediate prospects are not clear, but one obvious consequence has been an increasingly prominent role for public funds (see http://www.nesta.org.uk/library/documents/Venture_Capital.pdf). While public funds hardly featured in the dotcom era, they now participate in 40 per cent of all UK venture capital deals and 56 per cent of early-stage deals.

Despite the falls, the figures still point to more vigorous venture capital activity in the USA, followed at some distance by the UK. Indeed, beyond simple numbers of funds and amounts raised, the USA and UK are considered the most 'vibrant' venture capital markets in the world. For instance, the *Global Venture Capital Attractiveness Index* (http://blog.iese.edu/vcpeindex/), developed by researchers at IESE Business School, ranks the USA first and the UK second in 'attractiveness of countries for investors in venture capital and private equity' in 2011, followed by Canada and Singapore.

Yet, if one controls for the size of the respective economies (see Figure 8.4), the USA no longer leads the way. Indeed, in the Nordic countries and in the UK, both 'seed/start-up' and 'development/expansion' venture capital investments were higher in 2008 as a proportion of GDP than in the USA. Interestingly, while latter-stage investments still dominate relative to classic early-stage venture capital, the ratio is smaller in many European economies than in the USA. Regardless, venture capture investment in many European countries remains low both as a proportion of GDP and absolutely. Recognition of this deficiency led the Committee of Wise Men to:

urge governments and the European institutions to pay particular attention to ensuring that there is an appropriate environment for the development of the supply of risk capital for growing small and medium sized companies, given the crucial importance of this sector for job creation.[21]

Beyond investment amounts, there is a sense of maturity in the US and European venture capital industries. Figure 8.5, for instance, tracks the number of active venture capital firms in the USA, Europe, China and India. The picture painted is one of broad decline from the highs of 2000. The overall number of venture capital firms actively making investments in the USA declined from 1338 to 885 over the period 2000–2009: a decline of 34 per cent. In Europe the decline has been even steeper at 38 per cent. In both cases the numbers of very active firms (those making four or more investments per year) has declined still further: 56 per cent in the USA and 66 per cent in Europe. Set against the declining numbers of active investors in these major venture capital markets, the emerging economies of China and India provide an interesting counterpoint. Though there has been some slowdown following the financial crisis of 2008, the broad trend is towards growth, albeit from a low base. In many markets the trend is towards later exits (http://www.nesta.org.uk/library/documents/Venture_Capital.pdf). In contrast, venture capital firms may more easily be able to identify opportunities for later-stage

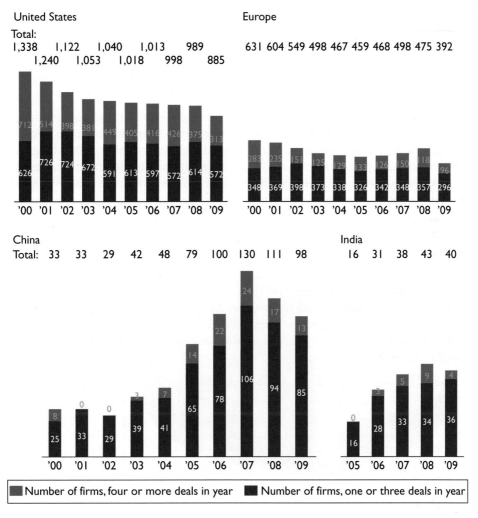

FIGURE 8.5

Number of active venture capital firms

SOURCE: Ernst and Young Venture Capital Insights and Trends Report 2010.

investments that allow them to realize faster returns. Since 2005, the number of venture capital firms making investments in Chinese companies has grown 24 per cent to 98; in India the growth has been some 150 per cent, from 16 to 40 companies.

Yet, notwithstanding this increasing interest in developing economies, the figures (e.g. Figure 8.4) paint a picture of a relatively strong venture capital market in parts of the EU. But where does the capital come from? As Figure 8.6 indicates (using UK data), the bulk of 'tracked' private equity, or formal venture capital, is raised from large institutional funds and from the portfolios of wealthy families – primarily pension funds, family offices and funds of funds. Other institutions, such as banks and insurance companies, appear to be playing less of a role following the 2008 financial crisis (banks' contribution, for instance, has fallen from 10 per cent in 2006 to 2 per cent in 2010). Regardless, venture capital represents only a small proportion of the portfolio of investments held by these funds and is, in this sense, a peripheral activity. Provided that these investors are holding diversified portfolios they will not be worried about the idiosyncratic risks of a single project, but only how the risk of the project contributes to the risk of their overall portfolio. Accordingly, the promise of very high returns offered by venture capital-backed companies may prove to be an attractive investment opportunity, for a limited proportion of the total fund, set against the risk–return profile of their other investments. Even during the boom years of the late 1990s, the amount invested in venture capital was consistently less than 1 per cent of annual institutional investment in the UK. This, in turn, may explain why most institutional investors are willing to allow independent venture capital companies to manage their limited exposure to this specialist activity rather than bringing the responsibility for investment in-house.

In contrast to institutional investors, academic institutions, government and private individuals make a limited contribution to 'visible', or formal, venture capital activity. Corporate investors appear to be playing an increasing role (13 per cent of all funds raised compared with 4 per cent in 2006). Indeed, in the case of corporate investors, and also private individuals, the data in Figure 8.6 undoubtedly under-represents their contribution. Corporate investors, for instance, often invest directly, while the greater proportion of investments by private individuals is 'informal', and indeed invisible, and so not covered by the methodology of the BVCA.

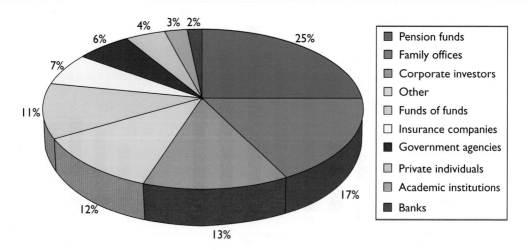

FIGURE 8.6

UK funds by source in 2010

SOURCE: BVCA Report on Investment Activity 2010.

NOTE: 'Other' includes such categories as overseas sovereign wealth funds, capital markets and family offices.

Finally, in this section, we turn to the destination of venture capital finance or, more specifically, the types of investment that are made. Typically, five broad types, or stages, of investment are distinguished,[22] as follows.

1 Seed financing – Aims to facilitate pre-market development of a business concept. It is an investment made very early in the business development cycle and is frequently concerned with research and development, the manufacture of prototypes, or business planning and market research activities prior to bringing a product to the market and commencing large-scale production. This is often called 'proof-of-concept' funding.

2 Start-up financing – Investment in those firms that have made few, if any, commercial sales. However, product development and market-research activities are complete and funding is required to support initial production and marketing activities.

3 Expansion finance – Capital provided to support the growth and development of an established company. Occasionally commentators discern a further three substages within the broad heading of expansion finance: *first stage* (when a firm has begun trading but requires further capital to materially increase production); *second stage* (when additional finance is required to increase production capacity and expand into new markets); *mezzanine finance* (which seeks to provide further expansion or working capital with a view to an initial public offering).

4 Replacement capital – The provision of finance[22] 'to allow existing non-private equity [here, venture capital] investors to buy back or redeem part, or all, of another investor's shareholding' (p. 18).

5 Buy-in/buy-out finance – Management buy-out (MBO) finance is provided to enable the current operating management to acquire a significant shareholding in the firm they manage. By contrast, management buy-in (MBI) finance enables managers from outside the company to buy into it. A less frequent occurrence, in this category, is the curiously named buy-in management buy-out (BIMBO), which allows the incumbent management to purchase the business they manage with the assistance of some incoming management.

Figure 8.7 illustrates the distribution of investment funds and investments among these stages for the UK. As the graph makes clear, the vast majority of venture capital is directed towards later-stage financing –

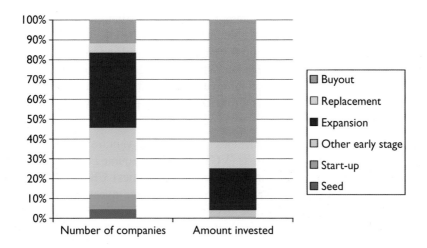

FIGURE 8.7

Stage distribution of UK investments in 2010

SOURCE: BVCA Report on Investment Activity 2010.

NOTE: These figures exclude a small number of large public to private and rescue/turnaround projects.

buyout, replacement and expansion projects. Indeed, recent European figures suggest that the trend is increasingly towards fewer, larger and later-stage (principally buy-out) investments (see www.evca.com). Given that information asymmetries, associated costs and risks are likely to be reduced in situations where firms have an established track record this is unsurprising. Moreover, and notwithstanding our belief in the ability of venture capitalists to manage information asymmetries more efficiently, one would anticipate that,[18]

> they will still prefer projects where monitoring and selection costs are relatively low or where the costs of informational asymmetry are less severe. Thus, within a given industry where venture capitalists would be expected to focus, we would also expect venture capitalists to favor firms with some track records over pure start-ups.
>
> (p.441)

Indeed, it is known that the transaction costs of venture investments are proportionately higher for smaller projects.[23] Thus, we would expect a higher proportion of funds and of deals to be directed to larger-scale expansion or buy-out projects. Yet, despite the logic of these trends, a number of concerns are rightly raised. In particular, both academic and policy sources[24; 25; 26] have long recorded the special problems faced by small high- and new-technology-based firms in accessing appropriate venture finance. In this, the general consensus holds that,[25]

> The distinctive requirement of technology-based firms at seed, start-up and early stage is for genuine risk capital. Amounts required may be relatively small, but investment horizons may be long . . . *Classic venture capital* should provide part of the answer, but the industry . . . has tended to focus less on early stage investments (especially in technology) and more on development capital and MBOs/MBIs.
>
> (p. 6)

Another concern, hinted at in the second line of the above quote, relates to the typical size of venture capital investments. In general, due to the disproportionate burden of transaction costs, very few venture capitalists are willing to invest less than £500,000, while the average investment is often in excess of £1 million.[27] Indeed, according to BVCA figures in 2010 the average amount invested in the UK was £9.153 million (http://admin. bvca.co.uk/library/documents/RIA_2010.pdf), up from around £5.5 million in 2009. Undoubtedly, this figure is skewed by a smaller number of extremely large later-stage investments. Nonetheless, the average early-stage investment was £789,000. Clearly, a predilection for investments of this scale necessarily excludes many promising small and early-stage entrepreneurial firms. From a supply-side perspective, this is believed to be the basis of the new equity gap discussed earlier.

One proffered solution to these observed deficiencies in institutional venture capital provision saw the launch, in the Finance Act 1995, of Venture Capital Trusts (VCTs). VCTs are quoted companies that aim to encourage investment in smaller, unlisted (unquoted and AIM-quoted companies) UK companies by offering private investors tax incentives on funds up to £200,000 in return for a five-year investment commitment. Certain types of activity, or 'qualifying firms', are ineligible for investment under the scheme. Generally, these activities are similar to those excluded under the Enterprise Investment Scheme (EIS) and, most notably, include land and property development. However, it is not yet clear to what extent VCTs may address the bias towards expansion and buy-in/buy-out finance. More generally, the evidence on their performance is mixed.[28] One other potential solution may be provided by the informal venture capital market. That is, as commentators have increasingly suggested, business angels may, in this context, be effective 'gap funders'.[29] Accordingly, we return to the role of informal investors later in this chapter.

ASYMMETRIC INFORMATION, ADVERSE SELECTION, MORAL HAZARD AND VENTURE CAPITAL

Although we have already discussed the nature and implications of asymmetric information, adverse selection and moral hazard in relation to bank finance (and for a discussion in relation to debt finance see Chapter 7), there are additional implications for venture finance. We have already noted a general belief in the function of venture capitalists as managers or attenuators of information asymmetries. Indeed, this viewpoint is fairly well established in the academic literature.[18; 30] Accordingly, it is worth briefly outlining what we mean by information asymmetry and its implications for the venture capital investment process. This can be compared with our discussion on the implications for bankers in the previous chapter.

In the economics literature, the classic exposition of the effects of information asymmetry on market efficiencies probably dates from Akerlof's[31] example of the market for used cars. In this illustration, sellers of used cars have private information about the quality of the cars they are selling, which is not available, *ex ante*, to potential buyers. Accordingly, as a result of the opportunistic behaviour of some sellers, poor-quality cars (or lemons, as Akerlof terms them) dominate, and the market selects 'adversely'. In other words, buyers demonstrate a preference for potentially not buying a good car rather than potentially buying a lemon. In this situation, the market collapses and few deals are done.

Adverse selection problems of this kind are likely to arise in most real-world contracting situations and, in the current context, it is generally held that, 'without such financial intermediaries [i.e. specialist venture capital firms], the market would tend to fail. This is because relatively poorly informed investors who were drawn into bad projects ("lemons") would subsequently cease to provide venture capital finance'.[30] In venture capital contracting relations, the investee firm is liable to have information not readily available to the potential investors. Moreover, firms have a clear incentive to 'talk up' or provide an optimistic view of their business history, current position or project potential.[32] Anyone who has watched television's *Dragons Den* can readily appreciate this truism. On the other hand, investors may find it prohibitively costly to determine the true nature of these. This is often characterised as a problem of 'hidden information' and, it is suggested, venture capital firms are sufficiently experienced and specialised in such high-risk investments to be able to cope with, or reduce, information asymmetries of this type. However, this is by no means to suggest that venture capitalists eliminate the potential for adverse selection. Indeed, since the proportionate costs of 'due diligence' (i.e. gathering the requisite information about a potential investee firm) are generally believed to be inversely related to firm size and age, adverse selection may still persist in the market for seed, start-up and early-stage investments. This, in turn, may partly explain the observed preference for later-stage, and larger-scale, expansion and buy-out/buy-in financing. Nonetheless, the key issue is that venture capitalists serve to reduce the *ex ante* information asymmetries that lead to adverse selection and ameliorate the problems of 'hidden information', which may deter institutional investors from direct involvement in venture capital activity.

As also discussed in Chapter 7, information asymmetries commonly occur *ex post*. Here, the general idea is that the (partial) separation of ownership and control creates scope for moral hazard. A firm that is insured, in part, against the risk of failure, through the sale of equity, may alter its behaviour in such a way as to act to the detriment of investors. To use the jargon of economics, the firm (agent) will seek to maximise its own utility irrespective of whether or not this coincides with the maximisation of the investor's (principal's) utility. This, in turn, leads to higher agency costs, as the investor firm is required to supervise and monitor the activities of the investee firm. At this point, agency problems (and the requisite agency costs) are thought to be highest when the level of *ex ante* information asymmetry is high (as noted above), when the agent has the incentive and ability to affect the distribution of income streams and when partial ownership permits agents to consume firm resources/assets at a lower cost than their value to the firm and/or the investor.[33] Such a situation commonly marks the small-firm–investor relationship. While the notion of adverse selection is fairly unproblematic (associated with problems of 'hidden information'), we may more clearly term moral hazard an 'asymmetry of interests' associating them with problems of 'hidden actions'.[34; 35] Moreover, high agency costs inevitably lead to higher direct and indirect funding costs for the innovative small firm. That is, institutional investors are likely to require a greater equity holding from small firms than from large, for a proportionately similar investment. One commonly suggested means to mitigate moral hazard, or minimise agency costs, is through staged investment, which creates the option to abandon the project and provides an incentive for the entrepreneurial firm to act 'appropriately'. In addition, syndication (i.e. co-ordinated investment by two or more venture capitalists) may be a further means to reducing the problems caused by information asymmetries.[36] Nonetheless, the most common means of reducing moral hazard is through tightly specified contracts, though clearly these are costly to enforce. Again, however, the key issue is that venture capitalists are better placed to manage *ex post* information asymmetries than the institutional investors they represent.

THE INVESTMENT PROCESS

Before outlining a 'typical' investment process, to the extent that such a thing exists, it is worth reiterating the low levels of venture capital use in the small-firm sector generally (studies invariably put the figure at between 2 and 4 per cent of firms). This, in itself, is hardly remarkable. Since we have long recognized that very few firms enjoy significant growth,[2] only a small number of firms will, in turn, represent sufficiently attractive investment opportunities to venture capitalists. Moreover, research suggests that venture capital firms[9] 'are seeking companies that can provide an internal rate of return of at least 30% in the case of established companies, rising to 60% or more for seed and start-up investments' (p. 15). Accordingly, it is likely that many of the best projects will eschew venture capital as too costly, choosing instead to leverage longer-term debt. For instance, it is suggested that, in addition to allowing individual entrepreneurs to maintain control, the acceptance of debt may act as a positive market signal[34; 37; 38; 39] – that is,[34] 'high-quality managers [of high-quality projects] will signal their quality by choosing a capital structure involving a large percentage of debt, that will not be copied by the low-quality manager' (p. 321). This debt cannot be assumed without a high degree of confidence in the profitability of the project and the ability of the firm to make periodic repayments. Further, acceptance of debt may also signal the entrepreneur's unwillingness to share in the expected gains from any investment. In part, the extent to which the requirement for returns in excess of 30 per cent acts as a disincentive to seeking venture capital may point to an additional asymmetry to those discussed above: an 'asymmetry of expectations'. Indeed, this asymmetry of expectations may go to the heart of the debate regarding the extent to which 'equity gaps' are a demand- or supply-side phenomenon. As Moore and Garnsey[35] noted, there exists a clearly established 'expectations gap between the owners of firms and venture capitalists, in terms of the scale of returns required and the size of the equity stake demanded' (p. 509).

However, notwithstanding the relative peripherality of venture capital, a growing number of (high-growth potential) firms are thought to be seeking it. Yet, of these firms, a very small proportion of applications that are assessed ever gain access to capital; and this does not include the great many applications that are not given more than the most cursory screening. For instance, a study of the Midlands Enterprise Fund[40] noted that, of 206 applications assessed, only three investments were made – i.e. an investment ratio of 1.46 per cent. While this fund was particularly specialised, in having both economic development and commercial imperatives, investment ratios of this magnitude are fairly standard. Accordingly, it is important that we have an appreciation of the process by which venture capitalists decide which projects to fund and which to discard.

To this end, a number of studies have sought to delineate the investment cycle, invariably describing it as a sequential process of between five and ten steps.[41; 42; 43] However, at the risk of oversimplifying things, these have largely served to extend Tybejee and Bruno's[44] early work, and have been broadly faithful to its essence. Tybejee and Bruno outline an ordered process, comprising five key steps: deal origination; screening; evaluation; deal structuring; and monitoring or post-investment activities,[44] as illustrated in Figure 8.8.

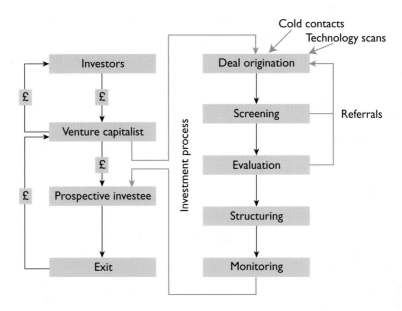

FIGURE 8.8

The venture capital process

We will now look at each of these five steps in detail.

1 Deal origination – Prospective investments may come from a number of sources, including unsolicited applications and technology scans. However, the most common means are either through an intermediary or by referral from another financial institution.

2 Screening – It is common to further subdivide this step – for example, into venture capital specific and generic screening.[43] However, the essence is much the same. Screening consists of an examination of the business plan in an attempt to identify features that warrant further investigation. Rather worryingly, UK studies[45] have suggested that the average first-reading time for an application is between 10 and 15 minutes.

3 Evaluation – In the first instance, this stage is likely to comprise a series of meetings between the venture capitalist and the managers/directors of the applicant firm. Thereafter, and crucially, due diligence is undertaken. As a minimum, this is likely to include: a thorough analysis of the financial viability of the proposition and the accuracy, or appropriateness, of financial projections; credit searches on the company and its owners; an appraisal of the firm's operating history.

4 Structuring – Having decided, in principle, to invest, this stage involves negotiations over the nature of the investment. At its simplest, the issue may be thought of as 'How much equity for how much money?' However, the provision of third-party equity is usually only one element in the final deal. Additional sources of finance may also include secured and unsecured debt from banks, loan notes and various convertible instruments. Clearly, this is liable to be the most sensitive stage in the investment process, as entrepreneurs become anxious over perceived inequities.

5 Monitoring – According to Boocock and Wood[40] 'One of the characteristics of venture finance is an *active* interest in the performance of investee companies . . . a combination of capital and consulting' (pp. 40–2, emphasis added). In general, as an agency problem, the emphasis is on effective communication and the flow of information. In this circumstance, the venture capitalist normally takes a non-executive seat on the board. However, more occasionally, the venture capitalist may assume a more 'hands-on' approach, where this course of action is deemed necessary.

The above process lays out, in simple terms, the role of venture capitalists in identifying, appraising, investing in, and subsequently monitoring and advising on business projects. It also makes clear the various points at which investment decisions are made. For instance, Murray[16] notes that approximately 80 per cent of applications are rejected at the initial screening stage, often for tangible reasons associated with the size of investment, or the industry or activity; although in the Boocock and Wood study,[40] 31 per cent of rejections were as a result of an 'incomplete plan'. Further rejections are likely to occur as a result of due diligence – finding 'skeletons in the closet' – or the inability to settle upon an agreed deal structure. For obvious reasons, though, rejections become less common as the investment process progresses. Notwithstanding this, the general objective of the process is to pare down the many applications to a few attractive investment opportunities.

Yet something is clearly missing from the preceding description. Though not part of the 'investment process' as outlined in Figure 8.8, *exit* is plainly an integral part of the venture capital process as a whole. As earlier discussions have made clear, the objective of the venture capitalist is to realise a capital gain through the sale of equity, rather than through interest or dividend income. The ultimate necessity of exit shapes every aspect of the venture capital decision-making process, from the sorts of investments made[46] to the amounts and timing of capital committed. Accordingly, some brief comments seem appropriate. To this end, it is common practice to identify five principal exit routes,[47] as follows.

1 *Initial Public Offering (IPO)* – In an IPO, the firm offers shares for sale to public investors. While the venture capitalist will ordinarily not offer all (or even part) of its equity stake immediately, common convention still holds an IPO as a form of exit, since it inevitably presages a full exit at some future date (note: Figure 8.9 distinguishes IPOs from the sale of quoted equity after flotation).

2 *Trade sale* – Sometimes known as an 'acquisition exit', in a trade sale the *entire* firm is sold to a third party. The purchaser is typically a business entity that is in the same, or similar, business to the selling firm (e.g. a competitor, supplier or customer). Following acquisition, the purchasing firm may choose to integrate the purchased firm into its own business, or allow continued operational independence in order to preserve the factors responsible for past successes. In either case, strategic access to products, markets or technologies is the primary motivation for the transaction.

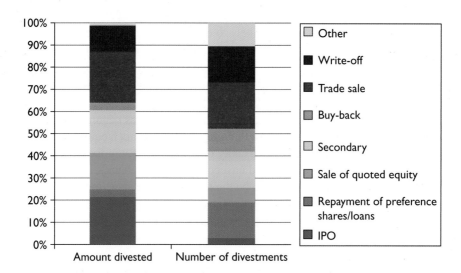

FIGURE 8.9

UK divestments in 2010

3 *Secondary sale* – A secondary sale differs from a trade sale in that only the venture capitalist sells to a third party. The entrepreneur(s) and other investors retain their stakes in the venture. Frequently, this involves selling to another venture capitalist or financial institution, where the purchaser exhibits greater confidence in the prospects of the venture, or believes that it can bring greater technological familiarity or a more relevant set of skills to bear. Alternatively, the purchaser may be a strategic acquirer (as above), seeking a window on the firm's technology, often with a view to 100 per cent acquisition at some later date.

4 *Buyback/MBO* – In a buyback, the entrepreneur(s) or management team will repurchase the shares held by the venture capitalist. In some instances, this will be prompted by the exercise of contractual rights ceded to the venture capitalist at the time of the initial investment. Such rights may include the power to 'put' its shares to the entrepreneur(s) after a stated period of time, or if certain performance targets are not met (e.g. the failure to go public).

5 *Write-off* – A write-off takes place when the venture capitalist walks away from its investment. Usually this will involve the failure of the investee company, and is sometimes equated with insolvency or bankruptcy. However, occasionally the venture capitalist may continue to hold shares in a barely profitable enterprise.

Figure 8.9 outlines recent data on venture capital divestments (i.e. exits) for the UK. Given the headlines devoted to it during the stock market booms of the late 1990s and mid-2000s, it is perhaps surprising that IPOs account for around one-fifth of divestment by value (though much more if one includes sales of quoted equity), and only 3 per cent of all divestments. Importantly, write-offs constitute 12 per cent of divestments by amount and 16 per cent by number of divestments. These proportions, which have been falling, may reflect the general trend towards larger and safer investments. Regardless, the most common form of divestment, both by amount divested and by number of divestments, is a trade sale: the BVCA reports 121 divestments through trade sale compared with only 15 though IPO in 2010.

Beyond these external factors, the choice of exit strategy is influenced by a variety of other concerns, including the company's financial performance and stage of development, industry and capital market condition, the venture capitalist's reputation, and the profile of partners in the venture capital syndicate.[48] However, just as the venture capitalist brings expertise to bear on the investment decision, and upon subsequent monitoring and assistance, so the venture capitalist exercises judgement in relation to the exit decision:[47] 'determining *when* and by *what means* and for *what consideration* the investment will be exited' (p. 8) – subject to prevailing constraints.

While the foregoing gives an idea of *when* the investment decision occurs, given low investment rates, it is important to also understand *why* the decision to invest is made, or not. To this end, a myriad of criteria are invariably identified by academic studies, many of which correspond with those employed by banks to assess lending proposals (see Chapter 7). On the whole, the approach tends to emphasise the balance between negative risk factors and positive return factors.[44] Specifically, these may include the attractiveness of the proposed market, the intended company strategy (e.g. level of product differentiation, existence of proprietary product), the size and stage of investment, the investors' technological or product market familiarity, the entrepreneur's own commitment, and the geographic location of the venture. However, as Murray[16] notes, there has been a surprising degree of convergence among the many academic studies in this area. To illustrate, he quotes Mac-Millan et al.,[49] such that:

> There is no question that irrespective of the horse (product), horse race (market), or odds (financial criteria), it is the jockey (entrepreneur) who fundamentally determines whether the venture capitalist will place the bet at all.

Clearly, certain baseline criteria must be established in respect of the 'horse', 'horse race' and 'odds'. However, the key point is that 'shortcomings of senior management' are the most commonly cited reason for failure in investment applications.

INFORMAL VENTURE CAPITAL AND BUSINESS ANGELS

Earlier in the chapter we hinted at the potential role business angels may play as 'gap-funders'. That is, there is a widely held belief that,[50]

> Business Angels fill the financing gap between founder, family and friends . . . and the stage at which institutional venture capital funds might become interested. Because of their high transaction costs, venture capital funds typically have a high minimum investment size, a minimum efficient overall fund size and a correspondingly restricted number of portfolio companies which can be evaluated, invested in and monitored . . . In the UK there are very few funds that are willing to invest less than £500,000, and the average investment by a venture capital fund in an early stage investment is over £1 million.
>
> (p. 137)

Business angels are private, high-net-worth individuals who make direct investments in unquoted companies with which they have no family connection. It has been assumed that the bulk of angels are 'cashed-out' entrepreneurs who seek to act as value-added investors, contributing commercial acumen, contacts and entrepreneurial skills. In this sense, informal venture capital may be thought of as 'smart money'.[50] However, a study of 144 business angels in Scotland found that the majority were not previous entrepreneurs but had careers in large firms and financial institutions.[51] Far more than institutional venture capitalists, business angels adopt a hands-on role providing an array of strategic, monitoring and supporting inputs. Research indicates that entrepreneurs who have raised finance from angels report their most valuable contribution is as a sounding board for management. Moreover, angels invest predominantly at seed and start-up stages and provide relatively small amounts of capital. For instance, while the average investment by a venture capital fund in an early-stage investment is over £1 million, business angels typically invest less than £100,000 (although larger amounts are possible in situations where deals are syndicated). However, given their hands-on involvement, business angels are fairly infrequent investors, managing only a few investments at a time.

Furthermore, it is important to understand that business angels are not philanthropists or altruists. They are motivated, first and foremost, by capital gain – typically in the region of 20 per cent per annum, over the life of the investment, though they may derive some 'psychological income' from being involved with a new business and helping to develop the next generation of entrepreneurs. Given that the primary reason for investing is pecuniary, it is hardly surprising to find that business angels are at least as selective as formal venture capitalists. For instance, one study of Canadian private investors[52] noted that 72.6 per cent of deals were rejected on the basis of 'first impressions', while a further 15.9 per cent were rejected after a detailed reading of the business plan. In other words, a cumulative 88.5 per cent were rejected without ever meeting the principals of the business. Moreover, given similarities in objectives and context, one should anticipate that the investment process would be broadly similar to that utilised in the case of formal venture capital, though perhaps with less attendant bureaucracy in the form of professional advisers and, crucially, over a shorter time frame. Mason and Harrison[53] have suggested that business angels, in deciding whether to invest, are primarily concerned to answer four key questions.

1   Is there a market for the product or service, is it growing and how competitive is it?

2   Will the product or service be competitive? Does it merely represent a 'me-too' product or service?

3   Is the entrepreneurial team credible? What is the experience and expertise of the management team?

4   What is the upside potential of the venture? Relatedly, why is the money being sought and to what use will it be put?

Again, the essence of these questions is not remarkable and simply paraphrases the criteria employed by other investors or providers of external finance. The key issue, however, is the private investor's ability to adequately assess these concerns. That is, since business angels frequently invest in areas where they have prior experience or a declared interest, one may anticipate that they will enjoy a comparative advantage in gauging the potential of a given opportunity.

However, irrespective of process, the consensus holds that private, or informal, investors are the primary source of external equity for new firms (i.e. for those seeking seed or start-up capital). Yet, this axiom relies heavily upon anecdotal evidence and upon speculation or estimation. As noted earlier, the bulk of informal venture capital is invisible and there is simply no way to accurately measure the scale of business angel activity. That is:[53]

> Most business angels strive to preserve their anonymity, although some have a high profile. There are no directories which list business angels and there are no public records of their investments. It is therefore impossible to say how many business angels there are, or how much they invest in aggregate.
>
> (p. 110)

However, despite these difficulties, attempts have been made to estimate the size of the informal venture capital market. For instance, Mason[54] recently noted that GEM estimates suggest that informal venture capital activity accounts for 60–90 per cent of all venture capital activity in the 18 countries where data were available. A previous attempt by the same author and Harrison[50] is more revealing. This attempt extrapolates from the visible proportion of the UK market ('the tip of the iceberg'). This visible proportion is represented by Business Angel Networks (BANs). BANs are essentially intermediary organisations that seek to reduce inefficiencies in the market by acting as an information conduit, or 'dating agency', bringing investors and entrepreneurs together. Taking BANs as a starting point, they estimated that, in 1999, private investors made at least 1800 *early-stage* investments involving a total investment of £220 million. When one contrasts this with the 241 investments, involving a total investment of £228 million, made by venture capital funds in the same period, then the considerable contribution, especially in the provision of smaller amounts of capital, made by business angels becomes clear. Moreover, while the authors admit that the evidence upon which this estimate is based is somewhat 'flimsy', they maintain that, at worst, it is likely to significantly understate the level of business angel activity.

The general implication is that, in situations where entrepreneurs are seeking less than £250,000, they may more appropriately direct their efforts towards the informal venture capital market rather than institutional venture capital funds.

CONCLUSIONS

This chapter has sought to outline the role of venture capital, as genuine risk capital, in supporting the start-up and development of high-risk, but high-growth-potential, new and small firms. Given the higher levels of information asymmetries, which are invariably associated with higher-risk projects, and the necessarily longer-term investment horizon, it is suggested that the sale of equity through venture capital intermediaries may be a more appropriate source of funding than bank debt. This is likely to be particularly true for firms in high- and new-technology-based industries.

However, the chapter also noted the formal venture capitalist's preference for later-stage and larger-scale investments. In light of the disproportionately high transaction costs associated with investments in smaller and younger firms, this is not in itself remarkable. Yet it has led to the identification, by many, of a 'new equity gap', impacting upon firms seeking relatively small amounts of 'classic' venture capital. In other words, formal venture capitalists are unlikely to be attracted by investments of less than £250,000 in firms with little or no track record, or in emerging but untested technologies. Clearly there is a role for public/private partnerships in ameliorating these concerns, and some positive signals are being sent, most notably by the development of regional venture capital funds in England – though, they may be falling short of the 'gap'.[12]

Accordingly, the 'gap' may more usefully, or more significantly, be met by independent or syndicated private investors, or business angels.[55] Notwithstanding the foregoing, it is important that we recognise that this is not merely a supply-side issue. Many venture capital funds and business angels bemoan the quality of proposals that come their way. Moreover, many entrepreneurs eschew equity funding, viewing it as dissolution of their control. If autonomy was central to the start-up decision this is understandable. However, it is important to educate entrepreneurs that it may be better to own part of an orchard rather than the whole of an apple.

Finally, with respect to the investment decision-making process, we detailed some of the myriad, and logical, factors that influence the investor's judgement. However, we noted the common finding that both venture capital funds and business angels invest, first and foremost, in people.

As a postscript, the chapter also noted a number of recent trends in venture capital funding; most notably, the diminishing role played by certain institutions (e.g. banks and insurance companies) and the general decline in venture capital funds raised following the financial crisis of 2008, with the implication being that this decline may be part of a more general readjustment. Venture capital levels have contracted to rates not seen since the mid 1990s. For some commentators, this is to be welcomed. Colin Mason,[56] for instance, quotes *The Economist* to the effect that 'although many venture capitalists have been outstanding at raising cash, they have been pretty lousy at investing it' (p. 281). In the USA, as the largest venture capital market, commitments to venture capital rose to above $70 billion in 2000, though they had never exceeded $10 billion prior to 1996. Of course, venture capital commitments dropped to under $10 billion during the bear markets of 2002–2003, but ranged from $25–$33 billion with a more robust stock market between 2005 and 2008. For Mason and others, the venture capital industry has simply gotten too large. Too much money is in the system and this is driving down returns. The venture capital model works where the general partners are able to identify 'good' ventures in which to invest the funds provided by the limited partners. With so much money swilling around, there are simply too few 'good' ventures that promise sufficient returns to justify the additional risk and illiquidity that investments in unquoted companies entail. Mason and others see a number of likely outcomes: firstly, a simple reduction in the number of venture capital companies; secondly, and more intriguingly, he suggests that:

> The choice facing individual VCs is either to become big and global or to be small and focused. As one commentator noted, 'get back to boutique . . . or figure out global. Only a few firms will thrive in between'.

(p. 283)

Some of this imperative may be reflected in the growing number of venture capital companies making investments in Chinese and Indian firms (recall Figure 8.5).

Unremarkably, not everyone believes that venture capitalism is 'broken'. Indeed, two leading commentators (Steven Kaplan and Josh Lerner) launched a recent defence of the US industry suggesting that, in historical terms, it is neither too large nor underperforming.[57] They argue that what we are seeing now is a normal part of the booms and busts of the industry: high returns in the past attracted greater capital that, in turn, depressed returns and attracted less capital that will lead to higher returns, and hence the beginnings of a new cycle (p. 11). For us, the question is open and we are sure that the second decade of the twenty-first century will be an interesting one for those interested in the supply of venture capital and the activities of venture capital firms.

REVIEW QUESTIONS

1 Review your understanding of the difference between venture finance and debt finance. What is classic venture capital?

2 Why are venture capitalists seen as financial intermediaries?

3 What factors might account for the explosive growth in the venture capital industry in the 1980s and 1990s?

4 How do venture capitalists reduce the costs of information asymmetries?

5 What amounts of finance can be considered within the size of the equity gap for entrepreneurial small firms seeking to raise venture finance?

6 From the discussion given in this chapter, why do you think that this equity gap arises?

7 What are the main sources of venture finance funds in the UK?

8 Why is the apparent gap between the UK and the USA for venture finance funds not as large as it might appear?

9 'There are only ever going to be a small number of firms suitable as venture finance investments.' Give reasons for this statement from demand and supply perspectives.

10 What are the main stages in the venture capital cycle? And why is it a cycle?

11 What are the major differences between business angel investors and venture capital companies?

12 What are the advantages of business angels (over venture capital companies) for an entrepreneur seeking to raise entrepreneurial finance?

13 How would you advise such an entrepreneur, seeking to raise venture finance, on the best ways to find a business angel investor?

SUGGESTED ASSIGNMENTS

1 Identify and interview an entrepreneur about his or her attitude toward sharing equity.

2 List the pros and cons associated with investing in the different investment stages.

3 As an entrepreneur, list the pros and cons associated with both formal and informal venture capital.

4 Visit the following websites and compile a report on the level of venture capital activity in the UK, the USA and Europe:

- www.bvca.co.uk
- www.evca.com
- www.nvca.com

REFERENCES

1 **Berger, A. and Udell, G.** (2005) 'Small business and debt finance', in Z. Acs, and D. Audretsch (eds), *Handbook of Entrepreneurship Research: An Interdisciplinary Survey and Introduction*, Springer, NY, pp. 299–330.

2 **Storey, D.** (1994) *Understanding the Small Business Sector*, Routledge, London.

3 **Cosh, A., Hughes, A., Bullock, A. and Milner I.** (2008) *Financing UK Small and Medium-sized Enterprises: The 2007 Survey*, A report from the Centre for Business Research, University of Cambridge, Cambridge.

4 **Oakey, R.** (2007) 'A commentary on gap in funding for moderate "non-stellar" growth small businesses in the United Kingdom', *Venture Capital*, vol. 9, no. 3, pp. 223–35.

5 **Macmillan** (1931) *Report of the Committee on Finance and Industry*, Cmnd 3897, HMSO, London.

6 **Bolton** (1971) *Report of the Committee of Inquiry on Small Firms*, Cmnd 4811, HMSO, London.

7 **Wilson** (1979) *The Financing of Small Firms*, Interim Report of the Committee to Review the Functioning of the Financial Institutions, Cmnd 7503, HMSO, London.

8 **Williams, P.** (1989) *Financing of High-technology Businesses: A Report to the Paymaster General*, HMSO, London.

9 **Mason, C. and Harrison, R.** (1999) 'Venture capital: Rationale, aims and scope', Editorial, *Venture Capital*, vol. 1, no. 1, pp. 1–46.

10 **McNally, K.** (1995) 'Corporate venture capital: The financing of technology businesses', *International Journal of Entrepreneurial Behaviour and Research*, vol. 1, no. 3, pp. 9–43.

11 **Doran, A. and Bannock, G.** (2000) 'Publicly sponsored regional venture capital: What can the UK learn from the US experience?', *Venture Capital*, vol. 2, pp. 255–86.

12 **Mason, C. and Harrison, R.** (2003) 'Closing the regional equity gap? A critique of the Department of Trade and Industry's Regional Venture Capital Funds Initiative', *Regional Studies*, vol. 37, no. 8, pp. 855–68.

13 **Bygrave, W. and Timmons, J.** (1992) *Venture Capital at the Crossroads*, Harvard Business School Press, Boston, MA.

14 **Wright, M. and Robbie, K.** (1998) 'Venture capital and private equity: A review and synthesis', *Journal of Business Finance Accounting*, vol. 25, pp. 521–70.

15 **Timmons, J.** (1999) *New Venture Creation: Entrepreneurship for the 21st Century*, McGraw-Hill, Boston.

16 **Murray, G.** (1992) 'A challenging market place for venture capital', *Long Range Planning*, vol. 25, pp. 79–86.

17 **Baygan, G. and Freudenberg, M.** (2000) *The Internationalisation of Venture Capital Activity in OECD Countries: Implications for Measurement and Policy*, STI WP 2000/7, OECD, Paris.

18 **Amit, R., Brander, J. and Zott, C.** (1998) 'Why do venture capital firms exist? Theory and Canadian evidence', *Journal of Business Venturing*, vol. 13, pp. 441–66.

19 **Bottazzi, L. and Da Rin, M.** (2002) 'Venture capital in Europe and the financing of innovative companies', *Economic Policy*, April, pp. 231–69.

20 **Tylecote, A.** (1994) 'Financial systems and innovation', in M. Dodgson and R. Rothwell (eds), *The Handbook of Industrial Innovation*, Edward Elgar, Cheltenham, pp. 259–67.

21 **Committee of Wise Men** (2001) *Final Report of the Committee of Wise Men on the Regulation of European Security Markets*, Brussels, available at http://ec.europa.eu/internal_market/securities/docs/lamfalussy/wisemen/final-report-wise-men_en.pdf (accessed at 28 October 2011).

22 **BVCA** (2004) *A Guide to Private Equity*, BVCA, London.

23 **Brouwer, M. and Hendrix, B.** (1998) 'Two worlds of venture capital: What happened to US and Dutch early stage investment', *Small Business Economics*, vol. 10, pp. 333–48.

24 **Carpenter, R. and Petersen, B.** (2002) 'Capital market imperfections, high-tech investment, and new equity financing', *The Economic Journal*, vol. 112, F54–F72.

25 **Bank of England** (1996) *The Financing of Technology-based Small Firms*, October, London.

26 **Lockett, A., Murray, G. and Wright, M.** (2002) 'Do UK venture capitalists *still* have a bias against investment in new technology firms?', *Research Policy*, vol. 31, no. 6, pp. 1009–30.

27 **BVCA** (2007) *Report on Investment Activity 2006*, BVCA, London.

28 **Cumming, D.** (2003) 'The structure, governance and performance of UK venture capital trusts', *Journal of Corporate Law Studies*, vol. 3, no. 2, pp. 191–217.

29 **Mason, C. and Harrison, R.** (1995) 'Closing the regional equity gap: The role of informal venture capital', *Small Business Economics*, vol. 7, pp. 153–72.

30 **Reid, G.** (1999) 'The application of principal-agent methods to investor–investee relations in the UK venture capital industry', *Venture Capital*, vol. 1, pp. 285–302.

31 **Akerlof, G.** (1970) 'The market for lemons: Quality uncertainty and the market mechanism', *Quarterly Journal of Economics*, vol. 84, pp. 488–500.

32 **Hall, B.** (2002) 'The financing of R&D', *Oxford Review of Economic Policy*, vol. 18, no. 1, pp. 35–51.

33 **Jensen, M. and Meckling, W.** (1976) 'Theory of the firm: Managerial behaviour, agency costs and ownership structure', *Journal of Financial Economics*, vol. 3, pp. 305–60.

34 **Goodacre, A. and Tonks, I.** (1995) 'Finance and technological change', in P. Stoneman (ed.), *Handbook of the Economics of Innovation and Technological Change*, Blackwell, Oxford, pp. 298–341.

35 **Moore, I. and Garnsey, E.** (1993) 'Funding for innovation in small firms: The role of government', *Research Policy*, vol. 22, pp. 507–19.

36 **Lerner, J.** (1994) 'The syndication of venture capital investments', *The Financier*, vol. 23, pp. 16–27.

37 **Ross, S.** (1977) 'The determination of financial structure: The incentive-signalling approach', *Bell Journal of Economics*, vol. 8, pp. 23–40.

38 **Myers, S. and Majluf, N.** (1984) 'Corporate financing and investment decisions when firms have information that investors do not', *Journal of Financial Economics*, vol. 13, pp. 187–221.

39 **Giudici, G. and Paleari, S.** (2000) 'The provision of finance to innovation: A survey conducted among Italian technology-based small firms', *Small Business Economics*, vol. 14, pp. 37–53.

40 **Boocock, G. and Wood, M.** (1997) 'The evaluation criteria used by venture capitalists: Evidence from a UK venture fund', *International Small Business Journal*, vol. 16, pp. 36–57.

41 **Silver, A.** (1985) *Venture Capital: The Complete Guide for Investors*, John Wiley & Sons, New York.

42 **Hall, G.** (1989) 'Lack of finance as a constraint on the expansion of innovatory small firms', in J. Barber, J. Metcalfe and M. Porteous (eds), *Barriers to Growth in Small Firms*, Routledge, London.

43 **Fried, V. and Hisrich, R.** (1994) 'Toward a model of venture capital investment decision making', *Financial Management*, vol. 23, pp. 28–37.

44 **Tybejee, T. and Bruno, A.** (1984) 'A model of venture capital investment activity', *Management Science*, vol. 30, pp. 1051–66.

45 **Sweeting, R.** (1991) 'UK venture capital funds and the funding of new technology-based businesses: process and relationships', *Journal of Management Studies*, vol. 28, pp. 601–22.

46 **Gompers, P. and Lerner, J.** (2001) 'The venture capital revolution', *Journal of Economic Perspectives*, vol. 15, pp. 145–68.

47 **Cumming, D.J. and Macintosh, J.G.** (2000) *The Extent of Venture Capital Exits: Evidence from Canada and the United States*, University of Toronto Law and Economics Research Paper No. 01–03.

48 **Nahata, R.** (2003) *The Determinants of Venture Capital Exits: An Empirical Analysis of Venture Backed Companies*, Vanderbilt University Working Paper, 900128.

49 **MacMillan, I., Siegal, R. and Subba Narishima, P.** (1985) 'Criteria used by venture capitalists to evaluate new venture proposals', *Journal of Business Venturing*, vol. 1, pp. 126–41.

50 **Mason, C. and Harrison, R.** (2000) 'The size of the informal venture capital market in the United Kingdom', *Small Business Economics*, vol. 15, pp. 137–48.

51 **Paul, S., Johnston, J., Whittam, G. and Wilson, L.** (2002) 'Are business angels entrepreneurs?', paper presented to the Small Business and Enterprise Development Conference, April, Nottingham.

52 **Feeney, L., Haines, G. and Riding, A.** (1999) 'Private investors' investment criteria: Insights from qualitative data', *Venture Capital*, vol. 2, pp. 121–45.

53 **Mason, C. and Harrison, R.** (1997) 'Business angels are the answers to the entrepreneur's prayer', in S. Birley and D. Muzyka (eds), *Mastering Entrepreneurship*, FT/Prentice Hall, London, pp. 110–14.

54 **Mason, C.** (2006) 'Informal sources of venture finance', in S. Parker (ed.), *The Lifecycle of Entrepreneurial Ventures*, Springer, NY, pp. 259–99.

55 **Mason, C. and Harrison, R.** (2004) 'Improving access to early stage venture capital in regional economies: A new approach to investment readiness', *Local Economy*, vol. 19, no. 2, pp. 159–73.

56 **Mason, C.** (2009) 'Venture capital in crisis?', *Venture Capital*, vol. 11, no. 4, pp. 279–85.

57 **Kaplan, S. and Lerner, J.** (2010) 'It ain't broke: The past, present, and future of venture capital', *Journal of Applied Corporate Finance*, vol. 22, no. 2, pp. 1–12.

RECOMMENDED READING

Ernst and Young (2010) *Back to Basics: Global Venture Capital Trends and Insight Report 2010* available at http://www.ey.com/Publication/vwLUAssets/VC_insights-and-trends-report_2010/$FILE/VC_insights-and-trends-report_2010.pdf (accessed at 28 October 2011).

BVCA *Private Equity and Venture Capital Report on Investment Activity 2010* available at http://admin.bvca.co.uk/library/documents/RIA_2010.pdf (accessed at 28 October 2011).

Oakey, R. (2007) 'A commentary on gap in funding for moderate "non-stellar" growth small businesses in the United Kingdom', *Venture Capital*, vol. 9, no. 3, pp. 223–35.

Mason, C. (2009) 'Venture capital in crisis?', *Venture Capital*, vol. 11, no. 4, pp. 279–85.

Kaplan, S. and Lerner, J. (2010) 'It ain't broke: The past, present, and future of venture capital', *Journal of Applied Corporate Finance*, vol. 22, no. 2, pp. 1–12.

9 INNOVATION AND ENTREPRENEURSHIP

> ## LEARNING OUTCOMES
>
> At the end of this chapter you should be able to:
>
> - Define innovation in the context of the entrepreneurship process.
>
> - Describe the advantages and disadvantages for small firms in the innovation process.
>
> - Describe factors affecting the nature of dynamics in the innovation process.
>
> - Discuss the importance for small firms of external linkages with the innovation process.
>
> - Describe the factors that affect innovative performance in different industrial sectors.
>
> - Discuss concepts that determine how designs are adopted and become dominant.

INTRODUCTION

Academics and policymakers rarely understate the importance of industrial innovation. The recent OECD Innovation Strategy,[1] for instance, holds that, 'innovation . . . will increasingly be needed to drive growth and employment and improve living standards' and that 'innovation is crucial' to solving such problems as climate change, food security or access to clean water (p. 9). At the level of the individual firm, Chris Freeman went further,[2] encapsulating a common sentiment in suggesting that 'not to innovate is to die' (p. 266). A growing body of empirical work appears to support Freeman's imperative, typically recording higher average performance (in sales or employment growth) on the part of innovating firms relative to their non-innovating peers.[3; 4; 5] However, an important caution is to note that innovating firms also display much greater volatility of performance. That is, while successful innovation may confer significant competitive and performance advantages, unsuccessful innovation can be fatal. An innovation strategy is inevitably a risky strategy.

In addition to this received wisdom regarding innovation and firm performance, it has gradually become clear that there is no firm size uniquely suited to innovation. That is, both large and small firms have significant and often complementary roles to perform in the process of technological development and innovation more broadly defined.[6] With this in mind, this chapter seeks to outline the distinct contribution made by smaller firms to innovation, and identifies some key enabling and constraining factors.

WHAT DO WE MEAN BY INNOVATION?

The clearest link between innovation and entrepreneurship, or innovation and small firms, may arguably be traced to the early work of Joseph Schumpeter.[7] With respect to the nature of innovation, Schumpeter identified five principal sources of 'creative destruction' (see box).

This conception is far broader than technical advance, narrowly defined, though Schumpeter was unambiguous in excluding merely marginal or aesthetic changes. Moreover, this more eclectic view is certainly attractive. For instance, in developing the idea of 'Hidden Innovation', the UK's National Endowment for Science Technology and the Arts (NESTA) noted that:[8]

We need a broad view of where innovation comes from and where it applies. In other words, we need to look beyond science and technological invention and the obvious forms of innovation that result in new materials or products. We need to think of innovation as a process that is of vital importance to all sectors of the UK economy, and build innovation policy that reflects this.

SCHUMPETER'S FORCES OF CREATIVE DESTRUCTION

- The introduction of a new good (or a significant improvement in the quality of an existing good)
- The introduction of a new method of production (i.e. an innovation in processes)
- The opening of a new market (in particular an export market in a new territory)
- The 'conquest of a new source of supply of raw materials or half-manufactured goods'
- The creation of a new type of industrial organization (i.e. an administrative innovation)

NESTA's plea is for a better balance between innovation policy and innovation practice. It often seems that innovation policy is little more than a subset of science policy, with its emphasis upon R&D expenditures, patent awards, or science and engineering graduates. Yet, in mature economies such as the UK, a greater part of innovation is not primarily technical, but includes new forms of organizing, new business models or new methods of reaching customers. NESTA's examples of 'hidden innovation' range from such initiatives as the UK's Community Legal Advice Centres[a] to the introduction of internet banking – neither of which is well captured by traditional 'innovation' metrics.

However, notwithstanding the attractiveness of this perspective, a narrow technological view of innovation continues to dominate academic and popular debate. A prime example is the influential pan-European Community Innovation Surveys (CIS), which are largely concerned with product and process innovations and with substantive changes in the technology underlying these. Undoubtedly, this is a little disappointing and will afford only a partial understanding of innovations and innovators – most especially in large sections of the small-firms sector. Indeed, perhaps the most worrying consequence of this approach is the almost inevitable conclusion that service firms are not innovative. While this is a long-held view in the economics literature, there is a growing body of work that points to considerable innovation within services (particularly organizational innovation) and the inadequacy of the narrow technical view.[9] In light of these 'new' insights, we offer some comment on services innovation towards the end of the chapter.

Unfortunately, however, the current chapter cannot hope to address the broader conception of innovation adequately. In part this is an issue of space; in part a function of how much we know. A great deal of work remains to be done to elaborate these broader patterns of innovation, most especially within services. In contrast, our understanding of technological development through product and process innovation is reasonably well developed. Moreover, while there may be some ambivalence with regard to the performance of individual firms (as noted, the evidence suggests that firms engaged in technical innovation will exhibit greater variety of

---

[a] Which, as a means of delivering legal aid, are an important part of the government's social inclusion agenda.

performance[4]), innovations of this type undoubtedly impact upon aggregate economic performance. To that extent, a narrow technical focus is not without merits. While the picture painted will be incomplete, it is nonetheless valuable. Indeed, one should note that Schumpeter's five forms of innovation are not mutually exclusive. Process innovations, for instance, are often accompanied by changes in workforce organization. Similarly, product innovations often serve new markets or require new methods of engaging with existing markets. Indeed, it is increasingly difficult to simply categorize innovations in accordance with Schumpeter's taxonomy. By way of illustration, is the firm that introduces an online stock-listing and order-processing service (e.g. Amazon) engaging in product, process, supply or market innovation?

Irrespective of the answer to this question, what is clear is that all kinds of innovation involve 'newness'. That is, innovation is fundamentally concerned with novelty. However, this is not to say that innovation is simply invention. Indeed, the evidence suggests that borrowing plays a larger role than invention in most successful innovations. Innovation incorporates both creation or discovery aspects and diffusion or utilization aspects. The difficulty, however, is that novelty is ultimately a relative concept. When we say that something is 'new', to whom do we mean it is new, and in what dimensions (e.g. new technologies or new combinations of existing technologies) do we measure this 'newness'? For example, was the first online travel agency innovative even though the medium and technology had previously been used successfully to sell books? Was the IBM 5150 personal computer (PC), which revolutionized the early personal computer market, an innovation, even though it was essentially an amalgam of existing technologies (e.g. television monitor, QWERTY keyboard, printed circuit boards, memory chips, semiconductors and so on)?

To this end, a number of simple models have been developed better to understand the 'domain of innovation'. Figure 9.1 outlines one of the most popular of these.[10] This model is commonly used in studies of small-firm innovation to distinguish levels of 'innovativeness' and has been central to the measurement of innovation in successive Community Innovation Surveys. These surveys explicitly ask firms whether they have introduced new products or processes in a given time period and whether these were new to the industry or new to the firm only. Implicit in the distinction is the existence of a hierarchy of innovation. Products or processes that are new to the firm, but not to the industry or market, are essentially imitations (though the term 'imitation' should not be understood pejoratively). In contrast, products or processes that are new to both the firm and the market fit more closely with Schmookler's[11] classic, if contended, definition of innovation:

> When an enterprise produces a good or service or uses a method or input that is new to it, it makes a technical change. The first company to make a given technical change is an innovator. Its action is innovation.
>
> (p. 3)

The empirical literature often labels these levels of innovation 'incremental' and 'novel', respectively. While the jargon is simply a matter of convenience, there is some evidence that firms introducing relatively 'novel' innovations (i.e. those that are new to the industry or market) differ from their less- and non-innovative peers along a number of dimensions, including the propensity to co-operate,[12] training,[13] access to finance[14] and performance.[4] Without doubt, the distinctions implied in Figure 9.1 are helpful in understanding and categorizing innovations and have contributed to both academic debate and policy formation. However, models of this type are concerned with innovation outputs and inevitably have less to say about the innovation processes.

To the extent that innovation is concerned with discovery through to diffusion, it is clear that understanding innovation involves understanding process as well as measuring output. One easy inference to draw from this is that innovation, as a commercial phenomenon, is somehow a linear process – beginning with basic science and ending in sales, or beginning with an articulated customer need, which is subsequently developed into a saleable product. Indeed, just such a conception dominated academic and industrial thinking from the 1950s up until the early 1970s; conceived of as either 'science-push' innovation (in which the emergence of new opportunities

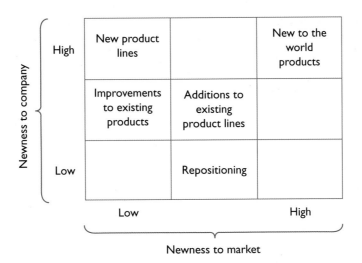

FIGURE 9.1

Classification of innovations

SOURCE: Cooper (1993).[10]

based upon new technologies drives the process; see Figure 9.2) or 'demand-pull' innovation (reflecting more stationary technology, an increase in the importance of marketing to firm growth and a 'needs'-driven innovation agenda; see Figure 9.3). Rothwell[15] termed these linear approaches the 'First-generation Innovation Process' and the 'Second-generation Innovation Process' respectively, and notes that systematic empirical evidence, available for the first time in the mid-1970s, had suggested that 'the technology-push or need-pull models of innovation were extreme and atypical examples of a more general process of *interaction* between, on the one hand, technological capabilities and, on the other, market needs' (p. 9, emphasis added). And despite recent, if limited, defence of the linear model,[16] it is this idea of interaction that underpins current thinking.

This view of innovation, as a process of complex links and feedback mechanisms, is most notably represented by Kline and Rosenberg's[17] 'chain-linked' model and by Rothwell and Zegveld's[18] 'coupling' model (Figure 9.4). In both these models innovation is conceived of as a network of inter-organizational and extra-organizational communication paths, linking the various in-house functions and allowing the firm to connect with both the marketplace and the wider scientific and technological community. At each stage of the development process, innovation endeavours may be informed by internal and external user constituencies and by the external technological state of the art. The principal difference between the models relates to the source of innovative ideas. In Kline and Rosenberg's model the process is seen as starting with the identification of a market need. Rothwell and Zegveld, however, are less prescriptive and allow for the interplay of markets and technology during the idea-generation process. Irrespective of these differences, the basic premise of bilateral interaction and feedback underpins both models. With a view to conceptualizing innovation, this is certainly a more satisfactory representation of the intricacy one would typically anticipate, given the degree of market and technological uncertainties involved. Moreover, persistent internal and external feedback mechanisms and reference points are likely to reduce waste and increase the speed of acceptance of the final product or process, thus contributing, ultimately, to innovation success.

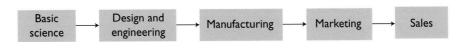

FIGURE 9.2

Science-push innovation (1950s–mid-1960s)

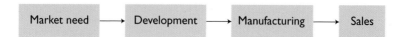

FIGURE 9.3

Demand-pull innovation (mid-1960s–early 1970s)

Rothwell[15] designated this the 'third generation' and proceeded to describe a further two generations: the fourth-generation 'parallel/integration' model (inspired by innovation practices at Nissan) and the fifth-generation 'systems integration and networking' model (with the emphasis on time/cost trade-offs). However, to the extent that the third generation represents innovation as a process of 'interactive learning and collective entrepreneurship'(p. 9),[19] it is broadly in line with contemporary thinking. Central to the third generation is the pervasive idea[20] that 'innovation by firms cannot be understood purely in terms of independent decision making at the level of the firm' (p. 73). Nor, realistically, is it likely to be confined to a series of simple phased, bilateral or dyadic interactions, as Figure 9.4 suggests. Rather, many commentators now hold that innovation is increasingly a matter of collective action. In other words, innovation may, more appropriately, be considered the product of networks of related actors, operating within systems of innovation. Tether[21] argues that, in consequence, 'the old debates about firm-size, market structure and innovation are becoming outmoded, as the boundaries of the firm are becoming increasingly "fuzzy"' (p. 947). While one may feel that this overstates the case, there is little doubt that the idea of 'innovation networks' and, more recently, the concept of 'open innovation' enjoy considerable favour in both policy and academic circles. Indeed, the benefits of innovation networking and 'openness' may be of particular relevance to small firms[22] and we return to these issues later in the chapter. In the meantime, our concern is, more directly, with the relationship between innovation and firm size.

INNOVATION AND FIRM SIZE

Before outlining some of the more popular approaches to considering the issue of firm size and innovation, it is worth revisiting Schumpeter's contribution to the debate and the influence it has had upon prevailing thought. In his initial deliberations, what one may term 'Schumpeter Mark I', Schumpeter[7] proposed that it was the

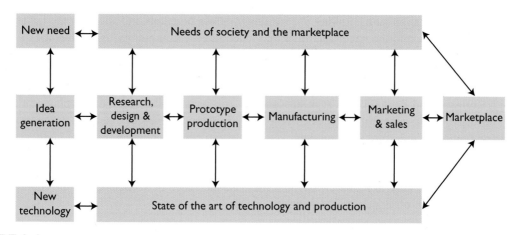

FIGURE 9.4

The 'coupling' model

SOURCE: Adapted from Rothwell (1991).[18]

exceptional creative drive of independent entrepreneurs that led to the introduction of radical new products and the creation of new industries, undermining the status quo and driving changes in market structures (see also Chapter 1). This is the Schumpeter who takes pride of place in many undergraduate entrepreneurship courses. However, in *Capitalism, Socialism and Democracy*, Schumpeter[23] adopts what appears to be a diametrically opposite position, arguing that:

> The monopolist firm will generate a larger supply of innovations because there are advantages which, though not strictly unattainable on the competitive level of enterprise, are as a matter of fact secured only on the monopoly level.
>
> (p. 101)

Essentially, this later Schumpeter ('Schumpeter Mark II') suggests that, since the process, or task, of innovation has become increasingly routinized (over the first half of the twentieth century), admitting increasing returns to scale, large firms are likely to possess advantages over smaller rivals. For instance, large firms may be able to spread the risk of innovation over a number of projects, adopting a portfolio approach, whereas smaller firms are often constrained to put 'all their eggs in one basket'. Moreover, if firms are liable to innovate only where positive post-innovation returns are anticipated, one may plausibly assume that a high degree of market power (i.e. the ability to set prices above marginal cost), frequently associated with larger size, would be the first best condition for innovation. Indeed, a belief in the importance of monopoly power in stimulating innovation underpins the international system of patents. At the risk of oversimplifying, successful patents, conferring exclusive rights to make and sell a given product, create fixed-term monopolies, preventing imitation and allowing firms to recoup research and development expenses. Importantly, Schumpeter was primarily concerned with how these market structure effects, rather than firm size per se, would impact upon the propensity to innovate. Yet, while a high degree of market power often implies larger size, the two are not inevitably associated. In contrast, J.K. Galbraith was more direct in his assessment of the relationship between innovation and firm size, noting that:

> There is no more pleasant fiction than that technical change is the product of the matchless ingenuity of the small man forced by competition to employ his wits to better his neighbour . . . Because development is costly, it follows that it can be carried on only by a firm that has the resources which are associated with considerable size.[24]
>
> (p. 86)

This view, that 'big is best', or that large firms are at the heart of the process of innovation and wealth and welfare creation, dominated academic and policy thinking through most of the second half of the twentieth century. However, in the last 25 years a 'new learning' has emerged.[25] Influential empirical studies in both the USA and the UK[26; 27; 28; 29] noted that,[30] subject to certain sectoral variations, 'small firms can keep up with large firms in the field of innovation' (p. 335) and, indeed, may more efficiently use R&D inputs to generate innovation outputs. In other words, rather than searching for some firm size uniquely and unequivocally optimal for innovation, it is vital that we recognize that small and large firms may fulfil different and often complementary roles – what Rothwell termed 'dynamic complementarity'.[6]

DYNAMIC COMPLEMENTARITY

In a much cited paper, Rothwell[6] suggested that the relative importance of firms of different sizes to innovation in a particular industry is likely to depend upon the *age* of that industry. In a related paper, Rothwell[28] drew upon Kaplinsky's[31] early studies of the computer-aided design (CAD) industry to illustrate the point (see Figure 9.5). In this industry, the early running was made by large, technologically advanced, mechanical engineering firms in the defence, aerospace and automotive industries (involving collaborations with mainframe computer manufacturers such as IBM). Importantly, development of the technology was primarily for 'own use', with little or no market for CAD beyond this. The second phase of the industry's evolution is characterized by a rapid diffusion of the technology to other sectors, principally electronics. The emergence of new, independent firms provided, in large part, the impetus for this diffusion. Many of these firms were established by software writers spinning off from firms with experience of CAD software in the aerospace and automotive industries. Others, from the electronics sector itself, were attracted by the obvious future potential of the CAD sector. As Kaplinsky[31] notes, 'The consequence was a variety of new firms, initially making digitising equipment and subsequently moving to the supply of complete turnkey systems' (p. 44), that is, systems supplied, installed, built and ready for immediate use.

In the third phase of the industry, CAD equipment began to penetrate manufacturing. The rate of diffusion proved so rapid that industry growth rates increased from 55 per cent per annum to 80 per cent per annum. All firms adopted a strategy of expanding their range of applications to comprehensively cover all industries. This diversification and expansion required financial resources beyond the scope of internal revenues and firms took recourse to debt, venture capital and the stock markets – in this way diluting ownership and independence. As firms grew in size, some came to hold more dominant positions. At the same time, large firms from other, CAD-using, sectors began acquiring specialist CAD firms, sparking a period of horizontal and vertical integration. In this way, and in addition to growing firm size, the third phase in the industry's evolution was marked by growing organic trends towards concentration and a tendency for formerly independent CAD firms to be swallowed up by existing multinationals. The final stage of the industry's evolution, termed 'maturity' by Kaplinsky, witnessed the emergence, once again, of small firms spun off from larger, older and established firms. These firms evolved to serve the lower ends of the market, that is, market segments characterized by demand for cheaper, lower-capability systems than those offered by established firms and demanded by established

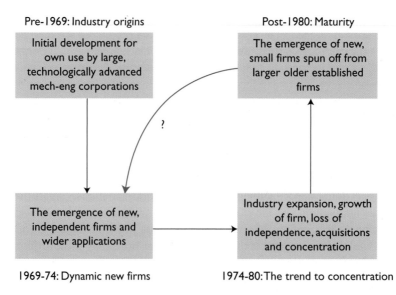

FIGURE 9.5

The evolution of the **CAD** industry

SOURCE: Kaplinsky (1983).[31]

customers. Thus, while the trend towards concentration continued in the existing industry, new entrants began to offer dedicated systems to new users, whose engineering data-processing requirements were less extensive and whose budgets were limited.

From the evolution of the CAD industry and his own work on the US semiconductor industry,[32] Rothwell[28] sketched some general patterns, as follows.

- In both industries, established large corporations played a crucial role in early invention and innovation. Importantly, however, initial development activity was geared to 'own use'.
- In both cases, much of the rapid diffusion and market growth resulted from the formation and expansion of new-technology-based firm (NTBFs).
- In both CAD and semiconductors, the technological entrepreneurs behind the NTBFs often emerged from established firms, bringing both technology and applications knowhow with them.
- In both instances, large corporations and venture capital played a significant role in funding the start-up and growth of NTBFs.
- In both cases, the industries rapidly became highly concentrated and the focus of external takeover activity.
- As both industries matured, scale economies became increasingly important and stable oligopolies formed, leaving only specialist market niches for new and small firms.

In other words, it is not that large or small firm size is uniquely and consistently 'fit'. Rather, it is that they may be suited to playing different roles at different stages of technology and market evolution.

THE DYNAMICS OF INNOVATION

Rothwell's specific observations tally reasonably well with more general models of the 'dynamics of innovation', perhaps the most compelling of which was initially developed by William Abernathy and James Utterback. [33] This model, subsequently elaborated in detail by Utterback,[34] holds that the rates of product and process innovation are related and vary over the course of the industry life-cycle. The early stage of the industry is characterized by considerable radical product innovation. Firms are said by Utterback[34] to be 'unencumbered by universal technical standards or by uniform products expectations in the marketplace [and] experiment freely with new forms and materials' (p. 81). In other words, firms are not sure what is technically possible and customers are unable clearly to articulate their wants. The consequence is considerable variety in the fundamentals of the various products producers bring to the market, and high rates of product innovation within individual producers as their products are refined through further R&D and exposure to customers and competition. At this stage, processes must be flexible enough to accommodate the flurry of product changes. As such, they tend to be crude and inefficient, relying upon general-purpose machinery and highly skilled labour. There are no specialized tools or machines and products are assembled in a series of, often skill-intensive, discrete steps.

However, this period of radical product innovation eventually ends with the emergence of a dominant design (see box). Producers become better informed about what is technically possible and customers are better able to judge how well the various alternatives satisfy their more settled expectations. Accordingly, the scope for radical product innovation diminishes and the emphasis shifts to manufacturing greater quantities of the dominant design at lower costs, to meet the demands of an expanding market. In other words, the emphasis shifts to cost-reducing process innovation and to exploiting emerging scale economies. Firms dedicate their research efforts to improving production techniques and developing specialized machinery (which often requires lower-skill, lower-cost labour), which serve, in turn, to further open up the market. By way of illustration, Utterback points to studies of the US automotive industry, which suggested that improvements in processes had reduced the time taken to manufacture a car from a pre-Model-A (i.e. the original Ford) 4600 man hours ('roughly the time required to build an average house') to approximately 20 man hours in 1990.

DOMINANT DESIGN

A dominant design in a product class is, by definition, the one that captures the allegiance of the marketplace, the one that competitors and innovators must adhere to if they are to command significant market following. The dominant design usually takes the form of a new product (or set of features) synthesized from individual technological innovations introduced independently in prior product variants . . .

. . . a dominant design embodies the requirement of many classes of users of a particular product, even though it may not meet the needs of a particular class to quite the same extent as would a customized design. Nor is a dominant design the one that embodies the most extreme technical performance. It is a so-called satisficer of many in terms of the interplay of technical possibilities and market choices, instead of an optimizer for a few . . .

A dominant design drastically reduces the number of performance requirements to be met by a product by making many of those requirements implicit in the design itself. Thus, few today would ask if a car had an electric starter and electric windshield wipers, or whether a typewriter could produce upper- and lower-case letters, or whether a computer had a built-in disk drive, though these were unique features in models that preceded the dominant design . . .

Source: Utterback,[34] pp. 24–6.

More importantly, for our current purposes, what are the implications of this model for the relationship between firm size and innovation? To this end, the model suggests initially few producers serving a small market of 'gadgeteers' or 'lead users' with highly differentiated and unsettled products. As a result of the smallness of the market and the effective customization of products, these initial producers are almost invariably small. As the market expands, and both producers and consumers become better informed, there is an explosion of competition. A rash of new firms enters the industry to exploit the commercial potential offered by the new technology and the rate of product innovation begins to slow. Crucially, in these early days producers compete not so much with each other as against customer scepticism towards the new technology (embodied, as it is, in unrefined products). However, the appearance of a dominant design, says Utterback,[34] shifts the bases of competition:

. . . as product capabilities and features are crystallized through the emergence of a dominant design, competition between firms stabilizes. The number of competitors drops off quickly after this landmark event for the industry, and the bases of competition shift to refinements in product features, reliability and cost. From the crystallization, a set of efficient producers usually emerges.

(p. 87)

Following the emergence of a dominant design the product begins to take on many of the characteristics of a commodity. In the growing market, firms become focused upon producing higher volumes at lower costs, with scale economies assuming greater importance. This, in turn, tends to favour those firms with greater facility in process innovation and integration and with more highly developed engineering and technical expertise. The explosion of competition witnessed prior to dominant design is mirrored in an implosion of competition, post-dominant design and a move to stable oligopoly.

This 'shifting ecology of firms' is nicely illustrated by the evolution of the US automobile industry (see Figure 9.6). The early days of this industry were marked by considerable variation in the fundamentals of the product. Early pioneers experimented with steam and electric engines, as well as with the enduring, petrol-driven internal combustion engine. An astonishing variety of unique styles emerged from hundreds of workshops, many based on the open-body 'horseless carriage'. Concurrently, many new firms entered, often formed to exploit 'innovations' – new body designs, transmission systems, steering mechanisms, and so on. As the data in Figure 9.6 suggest, the number of manufacturers rose from 4 in 1895 to a peak of 274 by 1909. However, after this point, the number drops away rapidly, with a slight reversal of the trend in the early 1920s. By 1929 there were only 30 firms in the industry and by 1960 the figure had fallen to a low of 7. Importantly, that this 'shakeout' began after 1909 is probably not coincidental; nor is the second peak witnessed in the early 1920s. In the first instance, late 1908 saw the introduction of Ford's Model-T. Following the introduction of the Model-T, company policy was to keep up with demand by developing more specialized machine tools and innovations in the production process. Although the 'Tin Lizzie' was a technically advanced automobile, it was by no means technically revolutionary. Rather, it was Ford's emphasis on manufacturability and on process innovation that revolutionized the industry. The second wave of exits appears to coincide with the introduction, by Dodge, of the all-steel, closed-body automobile. As well as dramatically improving the strength and rigidity of the chassis, this innovation allowed manufacturers to shift from hand-forming of exterior body panels to the highly capitalized, but highly efficient, process of machine stamping.[34] Both cases ushered in eras of larger-scale production of more standardized products at lower cost, with the attendant economies of scale leading to fewer firms of larger size.

One of the more reassuring implications of dynamics theories of the sort presented by Utterback[34] is their ability to reconcile the apparently contradictory Schumpeter 'Mark I' and 'Mark II'. According to Freeman and Soete[2] there are essentially two types of Schumpeterian models of innovation: 'entrepreneurial innovation' and 'managed innovation'. In the former, new basic technologies emerge, drawn from new scientific developments, largely outside existing large firms. Risk-taking, fast-reacting entrepreneurs take advantage of the technological opportunities offered and through radical innovation develop and grow new industries and new product groups. During this stage of the industry cycle small, fast-growing firms play the major innovative role.

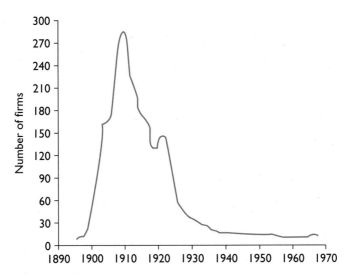

FIGURE 9.6

Population of US automobile manufacturers

SOURCE: Simon (1995).[35]

Over time the initial technology and markets mature, average firm size and industry concentration increases and inventive activity becomes increasingly undertaken in the large-scale, in-house R&D laboratories of large firms (which may have previously been the small entrepreneurial firms of the initial cycle stages). Little scope exists for major product innovation. Consumers become more informed and market requirements are increasingly well specified, resulting in minimal differentiation between competing products. As a result, price competition moves to the fore and the focus of development efforts rests primarily with process improvement aimed at cost reduction. Thus, small firms are involved in radical new product innovation and major improvements, while large firms are concerned with process innovation and minor product improvement.

A LESS DYNAMIC VIEW

If the models described above are taken to be universally applicable, then one must inevitably conclude that the role of small firms in innovation is likely to be transitory or confined, in the long run, to small specialist niches that are unattractive to large firms. However, this is not the case. Compelling though the models are, their applicability is largely restricted to mass-production industries where customer preferences are (or become) relatively uniform. In industries where customers value variety, a different pattern is likely to prevail. This is likely to apply to many service sectors and, within manufacturing, to such diverse industries as scientific instruments and textiles. Indeed, the success enjoyed by small Italian textile and leather manufacturers (in what has been termed the 'Third Italy'), during the 1970s and 1980s, provided much of the impetus for the development of the 'Flexible Specialization' thesis by Piore and Sabel,[36] as a counterpoint to the prevailing, large-firm-orientated 'Fordist' mass-production views that dominated (see also Chapter 2). The flexible specialization thesis sees mass production giving way to networks of specialist small firms, employing skilled workers to produce a variety of customized goods. According to this view, mass production progressively dominated the period 1900–70, but has been in crisis since. The breakdown of international regulatory mechanisms, more diverse markets and new manufacturing techniques, combined with flexible work practices, have served to lessen the impact and importance of scale economies. Relatedly, a common refrain in the management literature has been concerned with the value of concentrating on 'core competencies' as a means of accessing 'economies of specialization'.

Unfortunately, however, the debate is traditionally couched in bipolar terms. Flexible specialization is replacing Fordism; it is 'post-Fordist'. Presenting the theories in this 'either/or' way has made it easy for critics of flexible specialization to question its validity by simply pointing to the many industries and locations where Fordist practices continue. The 'Third Italy', then, is merely representative of a special case rather than a general trend. Though the debate is ongoing, and considerably more involved than this discussion permits, allowing for the co-existence of both mass production and flexible specialization seems a more reasonable position. In this way one may conceive of the two models as occupying extremes in some continuum of industrial organization. The point taken on the continuum, by any given firm or industry, is likely to be a function of a number of factors, which may include: the maturity of the technology, the uniformity of demand, the level of skilled labour required, the availability of finance, the culture of the industry or locale and so on. The issue, however, is that some industries continue to value product variety and producer flexibility, irrespective of their age and show no signs of shifting to models of mass production. In these industries smaller firms dominate and dominate innovation activity. This view is not 'less dynamic' in the sense that time or history does not matter, but in the sense that innovative advantage does not inevitably pass from small to large firms.

Empirical studies tend to confirm these sectoral variations in the relationship between innovation and firm size. Freeman and Soete,[2] for instance, note that smaller firms are apt to make a larger contribution to innovation activity in fields characterized by radical, but relatively inexpensive, innovation and where both development costs and entry barriers are low. Similarly, Acs and Audretsch[26; 27] found that small firms enjoy relative innovation advantages in industries where the total rate of innovation is high, R&D intensity is low and where there is a large component of skilled labour. In contrast, large firms dominate industries that are capital-intensive, concentrated and advertising intensive, and where development costs are generally high. For example:[2]

> In the chemical industry, where both research and development work are often very expensive, large firms predominate in both invention and innovation. In the mechanical engineering industry, inexpensive ingenuity can play a greater part and small firms or private inventors make a larger contribution.
>
> (p. 234)

SMALL-FIRM ADVANTAGES AND DISADVANTAGES

Consideration of the sectors in which small firms appear to hold a comparative innovation advantage might lead one to conclude that smaller firms do well in industries that place a premium on flexibility and resourcefulness, while they do less well in industries where resources and resource management are critical. This is also true of the dynamic theories. At the genesis of the industry, firms' structures are organic, there is limited task definition and few formal procedures. Such structures facilitate rapid communication both within the organization and with the marketplace and are necessary to accommodate the frequent major changes in products and, to a lesser extent and latterly, processes. However, as the innovation focus shifts from product to processes and from radical to incremental, informal control gives way to an emphasis on structure, goals and rules. The organizational becomes hierarchical and rigid and individuals' tasks are more clearly defined. In essence, we are witnessing a shift from an *organic* to a *mechanistic* organizational form. The former rewards entrepreneurship, while the latter rewards superintendence and administration.

Regardless of whether one is interested in the innovative advantages and disadvantages of small firms at a particular stage in a given industry's evolution or, more generally, *ex tempus* in a given sector of the economy, it is tempting to describe small firms as behaviourally advantaged, but materially constrained. This is a common and well-established view and Table 9.1 (again, adapted from Rothwell's work) gives more detail to the general statement. Whether in fulfilling the role of rapid product developer and diffuser, or in more mature markets, small firms are thought to enjoy unique advantages associated with: lack of bureaucracy; flat management structures; efficient, often informal, internal communications systems; resourcefulness and flexibility and adaptability through nearness to markets. By contrast, small firms face constraints associated with: lack of technically qualified labour; poor use of external information and expertise; difficulty in attracting/securing finance, and related inability to spread risk; unsuitability of original management beyond initial prescription and high cost of regulatory compliance. To reiterate, in the process of industrial innovation small firms appear to be behaviourally advantaged and resource constrained. The challenge, then, for both small-business managers and policymakers, is to find ways to preserve these behavioural advantages while simultaneously mitigating the resource constraints.

The resolution of this dilemma is not as simple as one might initially suppose. For instance, as stage models of firm growth indicate (see Chapter 10) increasing firm size is invariably accompanied by problems of control. That is, as the firm gets larger, it becomes more difficult for the entrepreneur to monitor effectively and supervise all facets of the firm's activities. Moreover, the measures employed to effect control, reduce waste or prevent unilateralism by subordinates, commonly reduce flexibility. Layers (or hierarchies) of management are introduced, ways of doing things become proceduralized and paper systems evolve. In essence, the organization becomes less an entrepreneurial firm and more a bureaucratic firm. There seems to be implicit trade-off between the alleviation of resource constraints and the preservation of behavioural advantages. This is simply a rephrasing of the 'innovator's dilemma'.[37] However, as noted earlier, one fashionable solution involves encouraging small firms to engage in innovation networks, thereby accessing the necessary resources for innovation through external linkages (with supplier, customers, and so on), while maintaining the flexibility and adaptability associated with smaller size.

TABLE 9.1 ADVANTAGES AND DISADVANTAGES OF SMALL FIRMS IN INNOVATION

Advantages	Disadvantages
Management: Lack of bureaucracy; greater risk acceptance; entrepreneurial management; rapid decision-making	Lack of formal management skills
Marketing: Nearness to markets ensures fast reaction to changing market requirements; may dominate niche markets	Little or no market power; poor distribution and servicing facilities; geographic market expansion may prove prohibitively costly
Technical manpower: Considerable scope for cross-functionality; technologists often 'plugged-in' to other departments	Often lack suitably qualified specialists (which may also constrain external networking); often unable to support formal R&D efforts
Communications: Efficient and informal internal communication facilitates rapid internal problem-solving	Lack of time and resources to forge external technological linkages
Finance: SMEs often considered more 'R&D efficient' (i.e. innovation can be relatively less costly); 'boot-strapping' possible	Difficulties accessing external finance; cost of capital relatively high; reliance upon short-term debt; inability to spread risk
Growth: Potential for growth through 'niche' or differentiation strategies	Difficulties accessing finance for growth; entrepreneurs often unable to manage growth
Government schemes: Government schemes established to facilitate small-firm innovation (e.g. SMART, innovation grants)	High transaction costs involved in accessing schemes; few resources available to manage collaborative schemes; lack of awareness
Regulation: Some regulations are applied less rigorously to small firms	In general, however, the relative unit cost of regulatory compliance is higher for small firms; patent system prohibitively complex and costly
Collaboration: Flexibility and rapid decision-making may make firms attractive partners	Firms suffer from power asymmetries in collaboration with larger partners; little, or no, supply chain influence
Organization: Suffer less from routinization and inertia	Suffer more from uncertainties and associated costs
Human resources: Flat management structures and local project ownership are likely	High staff turnover; little formal training

Source: Adapted from Rothwell (1989).[28]

INNOVATION NETWORKING AND 'OPEN INNOVATION'

There is a longstanding body of both conceptual and empirical literature on the promise of innovation networks for small firms that has had, in its turn, considerable influence on industrial policy.[38; 39; 40] Frequently, advocates of network approaches to innovation highlight an increasing division of labour among organizations as a first principle compelling collaboration or interaction. That is, increasing uncertainty, associated with changing technology and global competition, has encouraged many firms (and, indeed, many nations) to concentrate on fewer and fewer core competencies, relying upon trade, or co-operation, for others.[41] This effective disintegration of the vertical value chain has been taken as evidence of a move from hierarchical governance structures (based upon threat and coercion) to network governance structures (based upon reciprocity and trust).[42] In contrast to the pre-eminence of Fordist and Taylorist practices during the immediate post-war period, in many industries the efficient organization of production is increasingly associated with vertical disintegration and flexibility. In consequence, many of the valuable resources and activities required to deliver a given product or service reside outside of the individual firm.

The idea that valuable resources and activities are often external is likely to be particularly true for firms engaging in innovation. One cannot hope to employ all the smart people, hold all the patents, serve all the sophisticated customers, and so on. This is most clear if we concede that many of the most innovative ideas occur at the interfaces of different knowledge bases – through a process that is often termed 'creative abrasion'. Simply put, firms are increasingly relying upon external knowledge and expertise as a source of new technologies and as an alternative means to commercialize their own discoveries. This is the idea of *Open Innovation* recently popularized by Henry Chesbrough[43; 44] and depicted (with the 'old' *Closed Innovation* model as a contrast) in Figure 9.7 below.

While one might wonder about the extent to which it represents old wine in new bottles, there is little doubt that the concept of 'open innovation' has enjoyed growing popularity over the last few years. In short, open innovation holds that businesses must increasingly utilise both internal and external sources of innovation – rather than rely solely on internal research and development efforts. Moreover, firms must recognise that both internal and external paths to the market exist (in the latter case, for example, through technology licensing). This popularity is evident in a recent OECD (www.oecd.org/dataoecd/48/35/41721342.pdf) briefing, which notes that 'companies' innovation activities are increasingly international, and they are embracing "open innovation" – collaborating with external partners, whether suppliers, customers or universities, to keep ahead of the game and get new products or services to market before their competitors'. This, we are told, is 'a new logic of open innovation that embraces external ideas and knowledge in conjunction with internal R&D. This change offers novel ways to create value – along with new opportunities to claim portions of that value' (p. 41).[44]

While most of the literature regarding open innovation has been concerned with large firms, recent empirical evidence suggests that open strategies are increasingly widespread in small firms.[22] Given internal resource constraints to innovation in small firms,[38] the potential offered by 'openness' ought not to be too surprising. While one may conceive of large firms undertaking most innovation activities internally, small firms, with

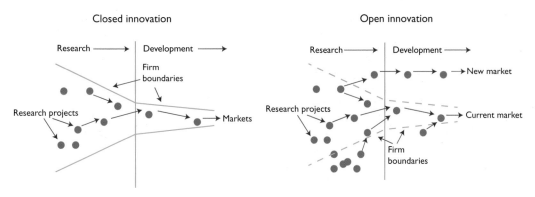

FIGURE 9.7

Models of open and closed innovation

SOURCE: Chesbrough, 2003.[44]

limited internal resources, are likely to look to others for access new ideas, to leverage additional resources, to find new markets, or to complete significant research projects.[46]

In this regard, the instrumental benefits of innovation networking are thought to revolve around the amelioration of internal resource constraints or competency gaps. More specifically, a review of the literature[47] suggests that the innovation benefits of networking include those listed in the accompanying box.

BENEFITS OF NETWORKING

- Cost and risk sharing
- Obtaining access to new technologies and markets
- Speeding products to markets
- Pooling complementary skills
- Safeguarding property rights when complete or contingent contracts are not possible
- Acting as a vehicle for obtaining access to external knowledge

By and large, empirical evidence tends to support the hypothesized link between openness and innovation. Figure 9.8, for instance, is taken from a study of 'Northern British' SMEs.[45] As the figure clearly suggests, there is an increasing propensity to co-operate, with all potential partners, as firms become more innovative. Indeed, while Figure 9.8 only relates to product innovation within manufacturing firms, broadly similar patterns were recorded for process innovation and within services. However, the danger is that one interprets these findings to indicate that innovation networks are inevitably good and that more networking activity is inevita-

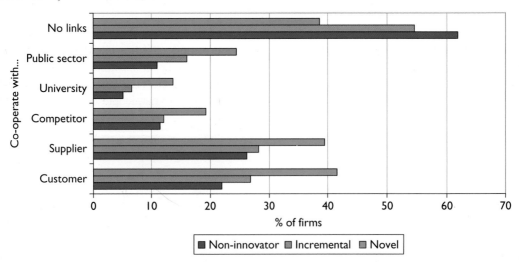

FIGURE 9.8

Product innovation and co-operation (manufacturing)

SOURCE: Freel and Harrison (2006).[45]

bly better. What is also clear from the data in Figure 9.8 is that a great many of even the most innovative firms were not involved in formal innovation networks. That is, networking is neither a necessary nor sufficient condition for innovation.

All of this suggests an important caveat: that the network view of innovation over-emphasizes an inter-organizational approach to processes that are ultimately intra-organizational. Crucially, the evidence points to the importance of extensive internal resource. As Angel[46] notes, 'it is likely that the impact of technological partnering on innovation and economic performance is mediated by a variety of other variables, including the internal resources of the firm involved' (p. 335). In short, 'firms must have resources to get resources' (p. 137)'.[47] While there are many theoretical and practical reasons for believing that networks may be an important mechanism for alleviating small-firm resource constraints and facilitating their innovation activities, such networks are unlikely to simply substitute for internal capability. Moreover, if the network model of innovation is to be seen as the panacea for small-firm resource constraints, much remains to be done to elaborate the conditions under which innovation networks generate economic benefits and the processes through which these are captured.

INNOVATION IN SERVICES

Early in the chapter we noted that the narrow technology view of innovation may serve to understate the innovativeness of small firms generally and small service-firms specifically. This echoes a common lament in studies of services innovation: that 'decades after services outdistanced manufacturing from an employment perspective, manufacturing has continued to dominate innovation studies' (p. 551).[48] The traditional view of service firms has been as innovation laggards. Services were thought to be incapable of innovation and, at best, to confine themselves to the adoption of technological innovations generated by manufacturing. Indeed, it has been common to characterize services as 'supplier dominated'.[49] Such firms tend to be small, have no R&D function, are recipients of embodied technologies originating in other sectors, serve price-sensitive customers and follow a technology trajectory underpinned by a logic of cost-cutting.

While this caricature may comfortably apply to some service industries (in particular, many personal services), its blanket application has profound implications for economies dominated by services.[a] As Gallouj[50] notes, such a position may 'preclude serious thought (particularly on the part of the public authorities) about ways of energising an area of activity of great importance for the future of firms, industries and nations' (p. 144). One of the most striking features of the service sector is its tremendous diversity. The highly heterogeneous nature of services should discourage bland generalizations about innovation in services. For instance, recent statistics have shown sharply increasing innovation expenditures within a number of service sectors, even where one employs traditional manufacturing derived measures. In particular, small, knowledge-intensive business services (KIBS) are increasingly recognized as occupying a dynamic and central position in 'new' knowledge-based economies, as creative innovators in their own right, rather than as mere adopters and users of new technologies. This recognition, in turn, has stimulated significant recent research effort.

While much of the early literature sought to assert a distinct services innovation process, it is increasingly thought that innovation processes may vary by degree rather than by kind (between different service sectors and between these sectors and manufacturing). For instance, though it is clear that interactive models of innovation are by no means unique to services,[48] a common conjecture sees services innovation as more reliant on 'soft' sources of knowledge and technology (such as co-operation with customers and suppliers), rather than 'hard' sources (such as R&D). In particular, emphasis is placed on the relationship with customers.[51] For example, Gallouj and Weinstein[52] note that 'one of the fundamental characteristics of service activities,

---

[a] In the developed economies services typically account for around 70 per cent of total employment and 70 per cent of gross value-added (*OECD Factbook* (2009)).

particularly 'knowledge-intensive' ones, is client participation (in various forms) in the production of the service' (p. 541).

In terms of internal resources; one of the most persistent stylized facts concerns the role of R&D. Notwithstanding the recent growth in R&D expenditure in a number of service sectors, the common view holds that, even within 'knowledge-intensive' sectors, service firms will perform less R&D and internal R&D will make a smaller marginal contribution to innovation than will be the case for manufacturing firms. In contrast, the importance of human resources – i.e. 'the labour embodiment of technological change' (p. 552)[48] – figures prominently in most academic accounts of services innovation. For Tether and Hipp,[53] this is one of the supposed 'peculiarities of services' (pp. 164–65) and holds, particularly, for KIBS. In this vein, Johnson et al.[54] note that 'in the service sector, knowledge itself is the product and human capital is the dominant form of capital . . . human capital formation and innovation are one and the same in [service] industries' (pp. 113–14).

Other commonly held views concern the appropriability of services innovations and the external financing of services innovation. In the former case, services firms are thought to be less able to protect their investments through standard appropriability mechanisms (such as patents), given the often disembodied nature of the new knowledge they create. In the latter, services frequently bemoan the unsympathetic attitudes of banks and venture capitalists, which may themselves reflect the limited asset base of many small service firms and the intangibility of investments. Unfortunately, many of these ideas lack substantiation. Research into services innovation, while gathering remarkable pace, is still relatively young. Here, it is sufficient to note the likely importance of services to the wider conception of innovation suggested by Schumpeter.

CONCLUSIONS

Innovation, or the presence of novelty, is often taken as a prerequisite for entrepreneurship. Moreover, the rhetoric of policymakers and small-firm academics frequently implies that small firms enjoy a comparative advantage with respect to certain types of industrial innovation. In this chapter we have argued that the innovative contributions of small firms vary across industry sectors and through the industry life-cycle, at least with respect to technical innovations. In new industries, where technology is still evolving, small firms have a more significant role to play than in mature mass-production industries, where the innovation focus has switched to cost-reducing process innovation and minor product enhancements. However, in these industries, small firms may benefit from innovations in structure, supply or markets, as producers of complementary products or in serving specialist niches. In addition, small firms may enjoy comparative advantage in industries that serve smaller, fragmented markets, where consumers value variety and where manufacturing flexibility carries a premium – irrespective of the *age* of the industry.

As innovators, small firms enjoy a number of advantages relative to their larger counterparts. These advantages are fundamentally behavioural and relate to the internal organization of activities and the manner in which small firms articulate with customers and markets. Flexibility, resourcefulness and speed are at the root of the small firm's innovation advantage. However, small firms also face a number of constraints. These are manifest in the high proportion of small firms failing to innovate. Studies of small firms regularly report in excess of 40 per cent of firms introducing no new products or processes in a given time period[55] – irrespective of whether these are new to the industry or new to the firm only. Such constraints, or barriers, to innovation seem largely to relate to resources: to skills, finance, information and so on. Consequently, increasing levels of small-firm innovation, as an objective of policy, is likely to involve measures aimed at improving access to resources, but that also go some way to preserving organizational flexibility. At the time of writing, innovation networks and the idea of 'open innovation' have quickly established themselves as popular policy responses, though there remain significant gaps in our knowledge of when and how openness and networking work.

As a final comment in this chapter, it is worth reiterating one important, but often overlooked, 'fact' about innovation. That is, there is substantial evidence that the majority of commercially significant innovations are technologically incremental, rather than radical.[56] Innovation is about borrowing more often than it is about invention. In other words:[19]

> [t]he first step in recognizing innovation as a ubiquitous phenomenon is to focus upon its gradual and cumulative aspects . . . Almost all innovations reflect already existing knowledge, combined in new ways.
>
> (p. 8)

Accordingly, we must be wary of the presumption that innovation is something only a few large, high- or new-technology-based firms do. The scope for small firms to add value through innovation is not limited to a narrow range of industries or classes of firms.

REVIEW QUESTIONS

1 Why does Schumpeter have two diametrically opposed views on the role of the entrepreneur in innovation (Schumpeter Mark I and Mark II)?

2 What are Schumpeter's forces of creative destruction?

3 To what extent is the Internet revolution an example of 'creative destruction'? (Hint: see also Chapter 1.)

4 How would you advise a local development agency wishing to encourage innovative entrepreneurship, particularly in relation to the creation of conducive environments?

5 What are the advantages of small firms over large firms in the entrepreneurship and innovation process?

6 Why has technological change encouraged innovative activity associated with entrepreneurial, small firms? (Hint: see also Chapter 2.)

7 Why are large firms suited to innovative activity in certain sectors? What are these sectors?

8 Is innovative activity linked to a firm's life-cycle? (Hint: see also Chapter 10.)

9 What are the external interactions that can exist for innovative entrepreneurs that will influence the process of innovation?

10 How does your answer relate to the question of networking by firms and innovative activity?

11 What are the principal ways that customers can be used to advantage by innovative entrepreneurs?

12 What role could support agencies take with innovative entrepreneurs?

SUGGESTED ASSIGNMENTS

These questions refer to the Aquamotive case study, which is available from the student online learning centre.

As a basis for discussion

1 With hindsight, was the strategy to use MBS to gain time and finance, as well as business experience, correct?

2 What are the difficulties faced by entrepreneurs in the innovation process as demonstrated by Aquamotive?

3 How can these be overcome?

4 What are the risks for a potential investor in Aquamotive?

As a role play

Students are allocated roles through a briefing sheet that asks them to adopt one of the following roles.

- Two students play the roles of Alex and Marion.

- One student plays the role of a business angel who has £100,000 to invest and is searching for an engineering opportunity.

- Students who take on the roles of Marion and Alex must sell their idea to the business angel, who then has to justify his/her decision as to whether or not to invest in Aquamotive.

Additional assignments

1 Identify a significant innovation introduced by a small firm or solo entrepreneur. What factors may have contributed to the success of this innovation? What barriers might the firm or entrepreneur have faced? (This is likely to be a web-based exercise.)

2 Identify a local small firm that has recently (in the last three years) introduced a new product and/or process. Interview the lead entrepreneur with respect to the motivation driving their innovation, the difficulties encountered and the success achieved.

3 Hold a class discussion around the theme of e-commerce generally and dotcom enterprises specifically. What opportunities are available to small firms? What factors are likely to determine the success of dotcoms?

REFERENCES

1 **OECD (**2010) *The OECD Innovation Strategy: Getting a Head Start on Tomorrow*, June, OECD, Paris.

2 **Freeman, C. and Soete, L.** (1997) *The Economics of Industrial Innovation*, 3rd edn, Pinter, London.

3 **Freel, M. S. and Robson, P. J. A.** (2004) 'Small firm innovation, growth and performance. Evidence from Scotland and Northern England', *International Small Business Journal*, vol. 22, no. 6, pp. 561–75.

4 **Coad, A. and Rao, R.** (2008) 'Innovation and firm growth in high-tech sectors: a quantile regression approach', *Research Policy*, vol. 37, pp. 633–48.

5 **Mansury, M.A. and Love, J.H.** (2008) 'Innovation, productivity, and growth in the US business services: a firm-level analysis', *Technovation*, vol. 28, no. 1, pp. 52–62.

6 **Rothwell, R.** (1983), 'Innovation and firm size: a case for dynamic complementarity; or is small really beautiful?', *Journal of General Management*, vol. 8, no. 3, pp. 5–25.

7 **Schumpeter, J.** (1934) *The Theory of Economic Development*, Harvard University Press, Cambridge, MA.

8 **NESTA** (2006) 'The Innovation Gap: Why policy needs to reflect the reality of innovation in the UK', available at http://www.nesta.org.uk/library/documents/Nesta%20Report%20TIG.pdf (accessed at 28 October 2011).

9 **Muller, E. and Doloreux, D.** (2009) 'What we should know about knowledge-intensive business services', *Technology in Society*, vol. 31, pp. 64–72.

10 **Cooper, R.G.** (1993) *Winning at New Products: Accelerating the Process From Idea to Launch*, 2nd edn, Perseus Books, Reading, MA.

11 **Schmookler, J.** (1966) *Invention and Economic Growth*, Harvard University Press, Cambridge, MA.

12 **Freel, M.S. and Harrison, R.T.** (2006) 'Innovation and cooperation in the small firm sector: Evidence from "Northern Britain"', *Regional Studies*, vol. 40, no. 4, pp. 289–305.

13 **Thornhill, S.** (2006) 'Knowledge, innovation and firm performance in high- and low-technology regimes', *Journal of Business Venturing*, vol. 21, no. 5, pp. 687–703.

14 **Freel, M.S.** (2007) 'Are small innovators credit rationed?', *Small Business Economics*, vol. 28, pp. 23–35.

15 **Rothwell, R.** (1994) 'Towards the fifth-generation innovation process', *International Marketing Review*, vol. 11, pp. 7–31.

16 **Balconi, M., Brusoni, S. and Orsenigo, L.** (2010) 'In defence of the linear model: An essay', *Research Policy*, vol. 39, pp. 1–13.

17 **Kline, S. and Rosenberg, N.** (1986) 'An overview of innovation', in R. Landau and N. Rosenberg (eds), *The Positive Sum Strategy: Harnessing Technology for Economic Growth*, National Academic Press, Washington, DC.

18 **Rothwell, R. and Zegveld, W.** (1985) *Reindustrialization and Technology*, Longman, Harlow.

19 **Lundvall, B.** (1995) *National Systems of Innovation: Towards a Theory of Innovation and Interactive Learning*, Pinter, London (first published 1992).

20 **Smith, K.** (2000) 'Innovation as a systemic phenomenon: rethinking the role of policy', *Enterprise and Innovation Management Studies*, vol. 1, pp. 73–102.

21 **Tether, B.** (2002) 'Who cooperates for innovation, and why? An empirical analysis', *Research Policy*, vol. 31, pp. 947–68.

22 **Van de Vrande, V., de Jong, J.P.J., Vanhaverbeke, W., de Rochemont, M.** (2009) 'Open innovation in SMEs: trends, motives and management challenges', *Technovation*, vol. 29, pp. 423–37.

23 **Schumpeter, J.** (1942) *Capitalism, Socialism and Democracy*, Harper & Row, New York.

24 **Galbraith, J.K.** (1956) *American Capitalism*, Houghton Mifflin, Cambridge, MA.

25 **Acs, Z. and Audretsch, D.** (1993) 'Innovation and firm size: the new learning', *International Journal of Technology Management*, vol. 8, no. 5/6, pp. 23–35.

26 **Acs, Z. and Audretsch, D.** (1987) 'Innovation, market structure and firm size', *The Review of Economics and Statistics*, vol. 69, no. 4, pp. 567–74.

27 **Acs, Z. and Audretsch, D.** (1988) 'Innovation in large and small firms: an empirical analysis', *The American Economic Review*, vol. 78, no. 4, pp. 678–690.

28 **Rothwell, R.** (1989) 'Small firms, innovation and industrial change', *Small Business Economics*, vol. 1, no. 1, pp. 51–64.

29 **Pavitt, K., Robson, M. and Townsend, J.** (1987) 'The size distribution of innovating firms in the UK: 1945–1983', *Journal of Industrial Economics*, vol. 35, pp. 297–316.

30 **Van Dijk, B., Den Hertog, R., Menkveld, B. and Thurik, R.** (1997) 'Some new evidence on the determinants of large and small firm innovation', *Small Business Economics*, vol. 9, pp. 335–43.

31 **Kaplinsky, R.** (1983) 'Firm size and technical change in a dynamic context', *The Journal of Industrial Economics*, vol. 32, no. 1, pp. 39–59.

32 **Rothwell, R. and Zegveld, W.** (1982) *Industrial Innovation and Public Policy*, Francis Pinter, London.

33 **Abernathy, W. and Utterback, J.** (1978) 'Patterns of industrial innovation', *Technology Review*, vol. 80, no. 7, pp. 41–7.

34 **Utterback, J.** (1996) *Mastering the Dynamics of Innovation*, HBS Press, Cambridge, MA.

35 **Simon, K.** (1995) 'Shakeouts: firm survival and technological change in new manufacturing industries', unpublished dissertation, Carnegie Mellon University, www.rpi.edu/~simonk/pdf/ksimonsphd.pdf (accessed at 28 October 2011).

36 **Piore, M. and Sabel, C.** (1984) *The Second Industrial Divide: Possibilities for Prosperity*, Basic Books, New York.

37 **Miller, D. and Friesen, P.** (1982) 'Innovation in conservative and entrepreneurial firms: two models of strategic momentum', *Strategic Management Journal*, vol. 3, pp. 1–25.

38 **Rothwell, R.** (1991) 'External networking and innovation in

small and medium-sized manufacturing firms', *Technovation*, vol. 11, pp. 93–112.

39　**Freel, M.** (2003) 'Sectoral patterns of small firm innovation, networking and proximity', *Research Policy*, vol. 32, pp. 751–70.

40　**Nieto, M. J. and Santamaria, L.** (2010) 'Technological collaboration: Bridging the innovation gap between small and large firms', *Journal of Small Business Management*, vol. 48, no. 1, pp. 44–69.

41　**Archibugi, D., Howells, J. and Michie, J.** (1999) 'Innovation systems and policy in a global economy', in D. Archibugi, J. Howells and J. Michie (eds), *Innovation Policy in a Global Economy*, Cambridge University Press, Cambridge, pp. 1–18.

42　**Nelson, R.** (2000) 'National innovation systems', in Z. Acs (ed.), *Regional Innovation, Knowledge and Global Change*, Pinter, London, pp. 11–26.

43　**Chesbrough, H., Vanhaverbeke, W. and West, J.** (2006) *Open Innovation: Researching a New Paradigm*, Oxford University Press, Oxford.

44　**Chesbrough H.** (2003). *Open Innovation*, Harvard University Press: Cambridge, MA.

45　**Freel, M. and Harrison, R.** (2006) 'Innovation and cooperation in the small firms sector', *Regional Studies*, vol. 40, pp. 289–305.

46　**Angel, D.** (2002) 'Inter-firm collaboration and technological development partnerships within US manufacturing industries', *Regional Studies*, vol. 36, pp. 333–44.

47　**Eisenhardt, K. and Schoonhoven C.** (1996) 'Resource-based view of strategic alliance formation: strategic and social effects in entrepreneurial firms', *Organization Science*, vol. 7, pp. 136–50.

48　**Drejer, I.** (2004) 'Identifying innovation in surveys of services: a Schumpeterian perspective', *Research Policy*, vol. 33, pp. 551–62.

49　**Pavitt, K.** (1984) 'Sectoral patterns of technical change: towards a taxonomy and a theory', *Research Policy*, vol. 13, pp. 343–73.

50　**Gallouj, F.** (2002) 'Innovation in services and the attendant old and new myths', *Journal of Socio-Economics*, vol. 31, pp. 137–54.

51　**Miles, I**. (2001) *Services Innovation: A Reconfiguration of Innovation Studies*, PREST Discussion Paper 01–05, University of Manchester, Manchester.

52　**Gallouj, F. and Weinstein, O.** (1997) 'Innovation in services', *Research Policy*, vol. 26, pp. 537–56.

53　**Tether, B. and Hipp, C**. (2002) 'Knowledge intensive, technical and other services: patterns of competitiveness and innovation compared', *Technology Analysis and Strategic Management*, vol. 14, pp. 163–82.

54　**Johnson, J., Baldwin, J. and Diverty, B.** (1996) 'The implications of innovation for human resource strategies', *Futures*, vol. 28, pp. 103–19.

55　**Cosh, A.D. and Hughes, A.** (eds) (2007), *British Enterprise: Thriving or Surviving? SME Growth, Innovation and Public Policy 2001–2004*, ESRC Centre for Business Research, University of Cambridge, Cambridge.

56　**Audretsch, D.** (1995) 'Innovation, growth and survival', *International Journal of Industrial Organisation*, vol. 13, pp. 441–57.

RECOMMENDED READING

Coad, A. and Rao, R. (2008) 'Innovation and firm growth in high-tech sectors: A quantile regression approach', *Research Policy*, vol. 37, pp. 633–48.

NESTA (2006) 'The Innovation Gap: why policy needs to reflect the reality of innovation in the UK', available at http://www.nesta.org.uk/library/documents/Nesta%20Report%20TIG.pdf (accessed at 28 October 2011).

Balconi, M., Brusoni, S. and Orsenigo, L. (2010) 'In defence of the linear model: An essay', *Research Policy*, vol. 39, 1–13.

Nieto, M. J. and Santamaria, L. (2010) 'Technological collaboration: Bridging the innovation gap between small and large firms', *Journal of Small Business Management*, vol. 48, no. 1, pp. 44–69.

Van de Vrande, V., de Jong, J.P.J., Vanhaverbeke, W. and de Rochemont, M. (2009) 'Open innovation in SMEs: trends, motives and management challenges', *Technovation*, vol. 29, pp. 423–37.

Muller, E. and Doloreux, D. (2009) 'What we should know about knowledge-intensive business services', *Technology in Society*, vol. 31, pp. 64–72.

10 ENTREPRENEURIAL AND GROWTH FIRMS

LEARNING OUTCOMES

At the end of this chapter you should be able to:

- Discuss the strengths and weaknesses of the main entrepreneurial growth theories.
- Describe the important factors that may affect the growth of small firms.
- Discuss the importance of an understanding of the process of growth to the development of small firms' policy.
- Describe and discuss the complexity of the growth of entrepreneurial firms.
- Discuss the current developments in growth theory in the light of empirical evidence and existing knowledge.

INTRODUCTION

There is a basic distinction between the person or entrepreneur that wishes to go into self-employment to pursue their own interests (and perhaps enters self-employment because there is no or little alternative) and the person or entrepreneur that enters small business ownership because they have a desire to develop their business, to achieve growth, expand employment and grow into a medium-sized or a large firm. The former type of small-business owner has very different managerial objectives from the latter. The objectives of the first will be concerned with survival and maintenance of lifestyle, whereas those of the second type will be concerned with growth and expansion, with the entrepreneur perhaps eventually owning several companies.

Many people enter into self-employment, as business owners, with little or no growth ambition. They are frequently sole traders, employ few or no people, and their major objectives are likely to be concerned with survival and maintaining sufficient income to ensure that the business provides them and their family with, in their turn, sufficient income. These small businesses, which are the overwhelming majority of small firms in developed economies, are sometimes called 'lifestyle' businesses. In other words, the owner-manager is only concerned with maintaining a lifestyle that he or she may have been accustomed to, or aspires to. A minority of small firms may be called 'entrepreneurial firms'; their owners will be concerned mainly with the strategic objective of achieving growth and will often go on to own more than one firm.

There has been much speculation about whether 'entrepreneurial firms' can be identified *ex ante*, that is, before they achieve growth, rather than *ex post*, i.e. after they have demonstrated growth. Of course, one may reasonably be able to identify the prior growth intentions of entrepreneurs. However, and crucially, intentions are not inevitably realized. This presents a problem for researchers and policymakers and for investors such as venture capitalists who will want to identify high-growth and high-performing firms. It is a classic adverse selection problem created by uncertainty and limited information. Despite the inherent difficulties in (pre-) identifying growth firms, this has not stopped governments from establishing policies targeted at supporting growth firms. This problem has also not stopped researchers from attempting to identify the characteristics and features of growth firms and their entrepreneurs. Specifically, attention has focused on identifying archetypical growth firms rather than identifying the constraints that may block the growth potential of many entrepreneurs and small firms. In this way, research and policy often appear to believe that the characteristics shown to associate with firm growth are independent of context or environment.

More fundamentally, and quite remarkably, there is no agreement on exactly what measure to use to distinguish a high-performing firm. Should performance be measured on the basis of employment created or by some other criterion, such as profits, turnover or financial assets? Certainly, the bulk of policy instruments take employment growth as the measure of superior performance. This may be reasonable given the focus of governments on providing jobs and income. However, few entrepreneurs are likely to identify increasing employment as a business objective. Rather, their concern is likely to be with sales, assets or profits. Unfortunately, for practical purposes, assets and profits have shortcomings which are difficult for the objective observer to resolve: asset values are highly sensitive to the capital intensity of industries and to changes over time; reported profits, in their turn, are notoriously unreliable measures of performance in small firms, given disincentives to their declaration. Accordingly, most studies (including those discussed in this chapter) adopt either sales growth or employment growth. These measures are relatively uncontroversial (methodologically) and data tend to be easily available, increasing the scope for cross-study comparability. However, research has shown the correlates of growth to be sensitive to the definition of growth and has suggested the use of multiple measures in studies (see Dobbs and Hamilton for a review).[1]

Perhaps in consequence of these difficulties (and narrow methodological choices) our understanding of small-business growth remains limited. This is not to say that we know nothing about growth. Rather, a remarkable body of research literature and case study work exists which has sought to extend our understanding and, no doubt, efforts will continue. In this chapter, we devote our attention to the most enduring approaches and to those avenues which appear to offer the greatest prospect for further breakthroughs. We also briefly touch upon failure, as the inverse of growth. However, we begin with a much quoted passage from the late Edith Penrose:[2]

> The differences in the administrative structures of the very small and the very large firms are so great that in many ways it is hard to see that the two species are of the same genus ... we cannot define a caterpillar and use the same definition for a butterfly.
>
> (p. 19)

Not all new firms are small firms, but most are. And it is, for instance, difficult to connect Steve Jobs and Steve Wozniak building the prototype Apple 1 computer in Job's parents' garage with today's US$43 billion Apple Inc. so beloved of design-conscious gadgeteers the world over. Clearly, there must be a process through which small firms become large. In addition to Apple, one need only think of Microsoft, Walmart, Dell and Ikea to be convinced of this and of the attractiveness of reconciling Penrose's caterpillars and butterflies. Accordingly, processes of growth, and growth firms themselves, have been and remain one of the most popular avenues for research into entrepreneurship and small firms. This focus is further heightened by consistent evidence that a few rapidly growing firms generate a disproportionately large share of net new jobs.[3] A common rule of thumb holds that: out of every 100 small firms 4 will be responsible for 50 per cent of the employment created over a 10-year period. Perhaps predictably, very few entrepreneurial caterpillars become corporate butterflies.

CHANCE MODELS OF GROWTH

Though mainstream economists have made contributions to our understanding of firm growth, these have largely been concerned with identifying the growth of 'average' firms, or growth distributions within populations. Stochastic models, for instance, have proven to be particularly popular. As a starting point, causal observation of real-world data on firm size suggests a highly skewed size distribution, with a few large firms and a larger tail of smaller firms. Such skewed distributions, of which the log-normal is perhaps the most familiar, may be generated by a stochastic process in which the variate (i.e. the size of firms) is subjected to cumulative random shocks over time. That is, with a sufficient number of observations, a mechanical chance model can be used to infer the size distribution of a *population* of firms that resembles actual empirical distributions. In other words, viewed in aggregate, firm size follows a 'random walk'. This 'fact' is the almost universal conclusion of econometric studies of both large- and small-firm growth.

The first, and most famous, exposition of this theory is Robert Gibrat's[4] 'Law of Proportionate Effect'. Leaving aside the associated mathematics, Gibrat suggested that:

- The causes of size change are numerous
- No single cause exerts a major influence on the phenomenon
- Any influence is independent of firm size

The final premise (that growth is independent of size), which gives the law its name, may be rephrased as 'the probability of a given proportionate change in size during a specified period is the same for all firms in a given industry – regardless of their size at the beginning of the period' (p. 1031).[5] It is this element of Gibrat's Law that has been subjected to the most rigorous testing, with generally negative conclusions. All in all, empirical results show a general tendency for growth rates to be negatively correlated with size, while their variance appears to decrease as size increases. In other words, taken in aggregate, small firms exhibit higher, but more erratic, growth rates. However, notwithstanding the falsifiability of Gibrat's proportionality hypothesis, it is the first two premises that, conceptually, present the most compelling logic. To illustrate, consider an older, but not untypical, study by Westhead and Birley;[6] having identified *88* variables hypothesized to influence firm growth, and subsequently conducted a large-scale postal survey, they found two (in the case of manufacturing) or three (in the case of services) factors exerted a statistically significant influence on growth rates. However, the authors acknowledged that these factors '"explain[ed]" a relatively small proportion of the variance [in sample firm growth]' (p. 28). Many factors may be thought to influence firm growth, but their influence is seldom significant or consistent.

Obviously, to suggest that all successful businesses or entrepreneurs were merely lucky is to considerably overstate the case. However, while acknowledging that eliminating all factors but chance from the equation is to put the case too strongly, it would be equally wrong to ignore the role of chance in determining the fortunes of a small entrepreneurial firm. Most small firm researchers will be able to offer anecdotal evidence, from their experiences with entrepreneurs and business owners, supporting the influence of chance – of 'lucky breaks' and grateful perplexion, as well as the predictable 'hard luck stories'. Such evidence, though lacking in scientific rigour, serves as an important caution to overly deterministic views. It is surely undeniable that, in the presence of uncertainty and bounded rationality, fortune will play a significant, if variable, role in determining which firms will succeed. As Nelson and Winter[7] note, 'luck is the principal factor that finally distinguishes winners from near-winners – although vast differentials of skills and competence may separate contenders from non-contenders' (p. 524).

Yet, in spite of a general belief in the influence of serendipity, it is clear that abstract stochastic models, of the type developed by econometricians, have little predictive or explanatory power at the level of the individual firm. Crucially, a better understanding of the growth processes of individual firms is central to the agenda of small firm academics and the business and public policy communities.

STAGE MODELS OF GROWTH

With respect to the development of firm-level models of growth, much of the early theoretical and empirical work, during the 1970s and 1980s, attempted to conceptualize the metamorphosis of Penrose's caterpillar in terms of stage, or life-cycle, models of firm growth. These models, normally incorporating five stages, envisage an inevitable and gradual movement along a known growth trajectory – the classic 'S-curve' (Figure 10.1).[8] At each stage the organization undergoes changes in management practices and style, organizational structure,

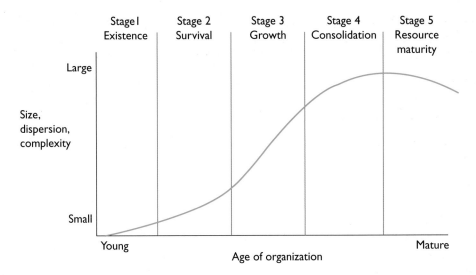

| Stage I | Stage 2 | Stage 3 | Stage 4 | Stage 5 |
| Existence | Survival | Growth | Consolidation | Resource maturity |

FIGURE 10.1

Life-cycle model of the entrepreneurial firm

degree of internal formality of systems and strategy, in such a way that the stage-5 firm (the butterfly) is truly distinct from the stage-1 firm (the caterpillar) from which it evolved.

In this section we briefly outline two of the more enduring and typical stage models of growth: those by Greiner[9] and Churchill and Lewis.[10] Taking them chronologically, the Greiner model posits a linear, continuous relationship between time and growth, postulating periods of incremental, trouble-free growth (evolution) punctuated by explicitly defined crises (revolution). Each period of evolution has a clear set of attributes that characterize it, and each stage, which ultimately degenerates into crisis, is a solution to the crisis of the previous stage (Table 10.1).

The crises outlined by Greiner form the bottom row of Table 10.1. In more detail these are as follows.

- Crisis of leadership – the shift from a phase-1 firm to a phase-2 firm is triggered by a crisis of leadership. More sophisticated knowledge and competencies are required to operate larger production runs and manage an expanding workforce. Capital must be secured to underpin further growth and financial controls must be put in place. The company must hire additional executive resource and restructure to meet these challenges.

- Crisis of autonomy – the control mechanisms implemented as a result of the first crisis become less appropriate as the physical size of the company increases. Line employees and line managers become frustrated with the bureaucracy attendant upon a centralised hierarchy. Line staff are more familiar with markets and machinery than executives and become[9] 'torn between following procedures and taking initiative' (p. 42). It has become necessary for the company to delegate to allow sufficient discretion in operating decision-making.

- Crisis of control – top executives begin to perceive a loss of control as a consequence of excessive discretion resting with middle and lower managers. There exists little co-ordination across divisions, plants or functions:[9] 'Freedom breeds a parochial attitude' (p. 43). Top management must seek to regain control, not through recentralization, but through the use of (undefined) 'special coordination techniques'.

- Crisis of red tape – the 'watchdog' approach adopted by senior management, in phase 4, and the proliferation of systems and programmes leads to a crisis of confidence and red tape. Line managers object to excessive direction and senior managers view line managers as unco-operative and disruptive. Both

TABLE 10.1 GREINER'S MODEL OF FIRM GROWTH

Attribute	Phase 1 Creativity	Phase 2 Direction	Phase 3 Delegation	Phase 4 Co-ordination	Phase 5 Collaboration
Management focus	Make and sell	Efficiency of operations	Expansion of market	Consolidation of organization	Problem-solving and innovation
Organization structure	Informal	Centralized and functional	Decentralized and geographical	Line staff and product groups	Matrix of teams
Top management style	Individualistic and entrepreneurial	Directive	Delegative	Watchdog	Participative
Control system	Market results	Standards and cost centres	Reports and profit centres	Plans and investment centres	Mutual goal-setting
Management reward emphasis	Ownership	Salary and merit increases	Individual bonus	Profit sharing and stock options	Team bonus
Crises	Crisis of leadership	Crisis of autonomy	Crisis of control	Crisis of red tape	Crisis of ?

groups are unhappy with the cumbersome paper system that has evolved to meet the challenges of the previous period. The company has become too large and complex to be managed through an extensive framework of formal procedures and controls. Movement to phase 5 requires a shift to 'interpersonal collaboration'.

- Crisis of ? – the crisis into which phase 5 degenerates remains undefined in Greiner's model. He can find no 'consistent' empirical evidence that points to the nature of this crisis and the subsequent phase 6. However, he hypothesizes that this crisis will revolve around the 'psychological saturation' of employees, which will occur as a logical result of the information age. Consequently, organizations will evolve with dual structures of 'habit' and 'reflection', allowing employees to move periodically between the two for periods of rest – or some alternative format whereby 'spent' staff can refuel their energies.

The revolutionary components of Greiner's paradigm are perhaps atypical of the broader set of stage models (although Scott and Bruce[11] imply a similar set of crisis triggers). By contrast, Churchill and Lewis,[10] although commenting upon Greiner, present a more general depiction of growth models where transition from stage to stage has no explicit trigger (Table 10.2). Further, Churchill and Lewis include a sixth stage by dividing the standard 'Success', or 'Growth', stage into growth firms and what may be described as 'comfort' or 'lifestyle' firms; comfort firms (stage 3-D) are those that, having achieved economic viability and chosen not to proactively seek further growth, can be assured of average or above-average profits in the long run, provided that managerial incompetence is avoided and the environment does not change to destroy their market niche.

In addition to those represented in Table 10.2, Churchill and Lewis include a further two factors in their paradigm that do not allow for easy tabulation: 'Organization' and 'Business and owner'. Addressing 'Organization', in the first instance, the authors[10] posit an internal organizational structure of progressively increasing horizontal

TABLE 10.2 THE CHURCHILL AND LEWIS MODEL OF FIRM GROWTH

	Stage 1 Existence	Stage 2 Survival	Stage 3-D Success – disengage	Stage 3-G Success – growth	Stage 4 Take-off	Stage 5 Maturity
Management style	Direct supervision	Supervised supervision	Functional	Functional	Divisional	Line and staff
Extent of formal style	Minimal to non-existent	Minimal	Basic	Developing	Maturing	Extensive
Major strategy	Existence	Survival	Maintaining profitable status quo	Get resources for growth	Growth	Return on investment

and vertical complexity, thus allowing for greater managerial sophistication and delegation. In the first instance 'the organization is a simple one – the owner does everything and directly supervises subordinates' (p. 33). Ultimately, however, as resources allow and complex operations require, 'the management is decentralized, adequately staffed, and experienced'; extended hierarchies have evolved with detailed reporting relationships.

With regard to the 'Business and owner' factor, this tracks the importance of the original owner-manager from an initially increasing central role to an eventual peripheral capacity when the organization has reached 'resource maturity' (Figure 10.2). In the early stages the owner *is* the business. He or she performs all the major tasks and is the principal supplier of energy, direction and capital. In contrast, by the resource maturity stage,[10] the 'owner and the business are quite separate both financially and operationally' (p. 40).

Following both Tables 10.1 and 10.2, along individual rows, from left to right, we see a logical progression in the extent and sophistication of the individual factors. The implication appears to be that firms move from an 'organic' to a 'mechanistic' form. While there are obvious differences in the nuances of these models, they are sufficiently alike to permit consolidation. Thus, generalizing, these models are explicitly intended to facilitate owner-managers and senior executives in recognizing the stage at which their organization stands and consequently identifying the skills required for further progression or, in the case of Greiner, the likely impending crises. Yet, while these models have the advantage of highlighting the notion that managerial skill requirements are not of a 'once-and-for-all-time' nature, there are fundamental difficulties associated with their rigidity. The standard critique is fivefold.[12; 13]

1   First, most firms experience little or no growth and, therefore, are unlikely ever to reach stages 3, 4 or 5. While Greiner allows for the conscious decision to remain in a particular stage, and Churchill and Lewis

FIGURE 10.2

Business and owner*

NOTE: *Smaller circle represents owner. Larger circle represents business. Adapted from Churchill and Lewis (1983).[10]

provide numerous 'break-off' paths for disengagement or failure, it nonetheless remains implicit that the norm for firms is to follow and complete the process.

2   Second, the models do not allow for a backward movement along the continuum or for the 'skipping' of stages. It is surely conceivable that many firms will reach 'take-off' only to find themselves plunged back into a struggle for survival due to unexpected changes in markets, technology or consumer preferences. In addition, the requirement for the firm to complete each individual stage, before moving forwards, seems excessively limiting. In the case of the Churchill and Lewis model, we can envisage some firms moving from 'existence' to 'growth' with such speed that 'survival' is either negligible or non-existent. We can also conceive of a start-up that is sufficiently large as to fulfil the criteria for Churchill and Lewis's stage 3-G.

3   Third, the models do not permit firms to exhibit characteristics from one or more stages, to become hybrids. As brief illustrations: from Greiner we can conjecture a situation whereby top-management style is participative (phase 5) while the organization structure is informal (phase 1) – e.g. many professional services firms; from Churchill and Lewis, a situation such that formal systems are either maturing (stage 4) or extensive (stage 5) and yet the major strategy is survival – a new franchisee may be one such example.

4   Fourth, the idea that firms are occasionally able to learn and adjust with greater effect in response to crises than in periods of relative stability seems entirely plausible. Yet, that crises occur in the non-random manner suggested, given the inherent uncertainty within which firms operate, is far less credible. It is conceivable that some firms will lurch from crisis to crisis and that these crises will not be of leadership, autonomy, control and red tape, but of market stagnation, market saturation, technology, finance or skills (i.e. a mixture of internal and external crises, rather than the purely internal crises Greiner conjectures). It is also conceivable that other firms will enjoy smooth growth over a relatively uninterrupted horizon.

5   Fifth, and following point 4, the models are generally thought to be too inward looking. In Greiner's model, the crises which occur (and their solutions) are exclusively internal. Similarly, Churchill and Lewis characterize the development of the firm solely in terms of internal motivations, processes and structures. Yet, there may be any number of external constraints or opportunities which condition small firm growth processes. For instance, changes in technology, regulations, interest rates or customer tastes may serve as sources of new growth opportunities or, conversely, undermine the viability of existing operations. We return to these external factors in the discussion of barriers to growth later in the chapter.

Stage models do place a welcome emphasis on the role of history in defining the future shape and success of an organization. Greiner explicitly notes the importance of 'historical actions . . . [as] . . . determinants of what happens to the company at a much later date' (pp. 45–46). Where difficulties arise is in the interpretation of this historicity, path dependency and crisis-stimulated growth. The frameworks suggested are overly rigid. The inevitability of each stage and each crisis is implausible. To assume that firms move from one stage to another along a narrow path, shaped only by periods of regularly recurring crises, ignores the variability and complexity of firm growth, the copious causes and the inconsistency of their influence.

PREDICTIVE MODELLING OF GROWTH

In his final criticism of stage models, Storey[12] notes that the 'models describe, rather than predict' (p. 122). Accordingly, it is to the body of literature concerned with predictive modelling of firm growth that we turn in this section.

FINANCIAL MODELS

The early work undertaken by Storey et al.[14] concentrated on the role of standard financial variables in predicting successful small firms. This method, adapted from use with large corporations, adopted an inverted approach to predicting small firm success – predicting failure and identifying success by implication. After initial testing of 'univariate ratio analysis' (consideration of individual financial ratios in progression rather than as a composite) proved inappropriate, Storey and colleagues shifted their focus towards methods of multivariate inquiry (principally 'multiple discriminant analysis'). In short, while univariate analysis suggested, predictably, that low profitability and high gearing ratios were positive correlates of small firm failure, the researchers' 'optimum' multivariate model utilized cash-flow and asset-structure variables as their primary predictors. On the basis of this final model, Storey et al.[14] claimed a 75 per cent success rate in distinguishing between failed firms and survivors.

Several criticisms can be levelled at this technique, as listed in the accompanying box.

CRITICISMS OF PREDICTIVE FINANCIAL MODELS

- The technique offers no historical insight. That is, there is little consistent evidence to suggest that the variables alter significantly as the companies approach failure, nor is there any indication of the underlying causes of failure.

- As a predictive model for rapid-growth firms, the technique would appear inadequate. Since its purpose is to identify firms that will fail, the model is unable to distinguish between the small proportion of growth firms and the bulk of survivors.

- The model takes little account of the human capital factors that assuredly play a considerable role in determining survival and growth.[15]

CHARACTERISTICS APPROACH

Subsequently, efforts to distinguish growth firms from their stable or declining contemporaries have tended to place a greater emphasis on non-financial characteristics of the owner-manager and the firm, with some attempt at generating integrated models of growth.[16] Of these integrated models, the one developed by David Storey has probably enjoyed the greatest longevity and had the broadest impact. In his review and synthesis of the extant research literature, Storey[12] postulated that small-firm growth was driven by three overlapping component sets: characteristics of the entrepreneur (identifiable pre-start); characteristics of the firm (identifiable at start); characteristics of the corporate strategy (identifiable post-start). From the empirical studies reviewed, Storey isolated those factors where 'consistent' evidence of influence was available (Table 10.3).

The entrepreneur

Motivation

The conjectured influence of motivation has a tidy, intuitive and appealing logic. It is suggested that individuals who are 'pulled' (to exploit an opportunity) into business ownership, and whose motivations are consequently positive, are more likely to develop growth firms than those who are 'pushed' (by unemployment, career dissatisfaction and so on) and whose motivations are correspondingly negative. One can see the analogy to the distinction between opportunity and necessity entrepreneurship discussed in Chapter 2. However, in common with other areas of entrepreneurship, motivation is likely to be a more complex process, often the result of the interplay of factors.[17] Moreover, motivation is unlikely to be stable over time;[13] nor does it necessarily translate into growth. In short, simplifying motivation into an artificial dichotomy ('pull' versus 'push') is likely to be misleading.

TABLE 10.3 STOREY'S CHARACTERISTICS APPROACH

The entrepreneur	The firm	Strategy
Motivation	Age	External equity
Education	Legal form	Market positioning
Managerial experience	Location	New product introduction
Teams	Size	Management recruitment
Age	Market/sector	
	Ownership	

Education

There are two contrasting hypotheses presented for this factor. First, it may be argued that education provides a foundation from which the entrepreneur can undertake the personal and professional development necessary for successful entrepreneurship and that education will endow the entrepreneur with greater confidence in dealing with bankers, customers and suppliers. This, again, seems entirely plausible. There is some evidence that a person's imagination, search and communication skills and computational abilities may be developed through education.[1] Conversely, however, it may also be argued that 'business ownership is not an intellectual activity'[2] (p. 129) and that the educated entrepreneur will quickly become wearied with the many tedious tasks that form the remit of most owner-managers. From the 18 studies that form Storey's review, evidence is found to support the former hypothesis in preference to the latter. More specifically, further research[18] has indicated that, while a first degree in a science or engineering subject may be most appropriate for high-technology entrepreneurs, it is likely that a trade qualification is more suited to success in many mainstream firms. It would appear that education, not to a level but of a type, influences the entrepreneur's ability in the given environment and, consequently, the firm's chances of growth. However, since little effort is made to explain the effect education has on firm processes we cannot explain why various types or levels of education *occasionally* influence growth. For instance, Barkham et al.,[19] in their four-region study of the determinants of growth, note that 'Education matters . . . but in an indirect way and the disadvantage of poorer education can be overcome by those who adopt similar strategies to graduates' (p. 140); the authors suggest that education per se does not influence growth, but instead education influences strategic choice, which, in turn, influences growth. This may suggest that the ability to learn, rather than prior formal education, is what matters.

Managerial experience

Management is fundamentally concerned with the management of people. In this vein, it is often suggested that, in all but the very smallest firms, the principal activity of the entrepreneur is the co-ordination of the work of other individuals. Hence prior managerial experience and, consequently, experience in the co-ordination role will allow the entrepreneur to attend to his or her remit more effectively and subsequently meet business objectives. There is also a parallel argument regarding the higher 'reservation wages' those with managerial experience are likely to have. Individuals with high reservation wages are unlikely to enter into self-employment without a corresponding high degree of confidence in a successful outcome. In either instance, prior managerial experience is thought to positively impact upon firm growth.

Teams

Storey[12] notes that 'Since the management of a business requires a range of skills . . . businesses owned by more than a single individual are more likely to grow than businesses owned by a single person' (p. 130). This is one of the stylized 'facts' in the small firms research and policy communities. However, from his research with high-technology firms (often viewed as the industrial sector representing the greatest growth potential) Oakey[20] noted that, 'rapid firm growth is strongly related to "single founder" businesses' (p. 16). It may be that, in this context, technology champions fare better – at least in the short run. On a different note, but perhaps as significantly, Vyakarnam et al.[21] argue that the core competency of successful entrepreneurs is the ability to build and manage effective teams – not the team itself. In this way, we may more appropriately conceive of the 'entrepreneurial team' as a dynamic and evolutionary phenomenon rather than the static entity implied by characteristics or predictive models of firm growth.

Age

In line with the evidence viewed by Storey,[12] Cressy[18] argues that the critical characteristics of growth firms are associated with human capital variables – most significantly founder(s) age and team size. Much as with Gibb and Richie's 'social dynamic' model, age may be used as a proxy for accumulated capital (both human and material), though Gibb and Richie imply a degree of trade-off between accumulated capital, on the one hand, and energy and tolerance of risk, on the other. Notwithstanding this, it is interesting to note that research frequently points to a strongly increasing self-employment rate up to the 35–44 age group, declining thereafter, before rising dramatically again to peak in the post-65 age range.

The firm

Legal status

In his review, Storey[12] finds overwhelming support for the contention that 'United Kingdom studies consistently point to more rapid growth being experienced by limited companies' (p. 140). Credibility with customers, suppliers and financial institutions is argued to be the principal benefit of incorporation. However, to the extent that incorporation limits downside risks, it may be associated with less persistence on the part of entrepreneurs. In this vein, recent evidence points to higher loan default rates on the part of limited liability companies.[22] However, from the perspective of predictive modelling the real issue is that legal form is not static. As Storey points out, 'we cannot reject the hypothesis that current legal status is a consequence rather than a cause of growth' (p. 141).

Age and size

The issues of firm size and age are often dealt with concurrently since it can be safely assumed that they are often related variables. While the relationship between size and age is by no means linear, we can plausibly suggest that in general '[t]he more a firm grows (the bigger it is) the more likely it is to survive another period (the older it is)'.[23] With regards to growth, accepted wisdom states that small firms grow faster than large firms and that younger firms grow faster than older firms. From the point of view of policy, logic would superficially seem to endorse the support of small, new firms as a means to achieving employment policy objectives. On a cautionary note it should be understood that most studies deal with changing *rates* of growth and not with absolute growth. An additional caveat would be to note that since in practice all failures are omitted from empirical samples, there is a tendency to overestimate small firm growth rates in relation to their larger counterparts. Indeed, recent research suggests that for the fastest growing firm (what are often termed 'Gazelles') it is age that matters not size, with the fastest growing firms typically much younger than their slow- and no-growth counterparts.[3] However, one must also recognize the liabilities of newness and smallness. As Storey notes 'the fundamental characteristic, other then size *per se*, which distinguishes small firms from large is their higher probability of ceasing to trade' (p. 78). Again, we return to this later in the chapter.

Location

Since the bulk of small firms operate in localized markets, location (as a proxy for the buoyancy of these local markets) will presumably influence firm performance. In this vein, Storey suggests that, on balance, the empirical evidence indicates a higher propensity to grow more rapidly for firms located in accessible rural areas than for firms located both in urban areas and in remote rural areas – although no attempt is made to rationalise this finding. By contrast, work by Westhead[24] found that 'the majority of firms suggested more than half their customers were located outside the county region of the businesses' main operating premises' (pp. 375–76) and that 'urban firms had recorded the largest absolute and standardised employment increases since business start-up' (p. 375). The literature is equivocal on the crude influence of location on growth. Even the studies reviewed by Storey fail to reach consensus. Regardless, this factor does little to enhance our understanding of cause and effect. Location itself does not directly influence growth; rather, a number of inconsistently related variables, such as physical and support infrastructure, resource munificence and availability of skilled labour, are the 'true' factors for which location acts as a fallible proxy variable. A more nuanced view of the environment is appropriate since, as we will discuss later, the environment (physical and otherwise) has an important contingent effect on growth.

Market/industry sector

With regard to markets or industry sector, high-technology small firms have often been viewed as a potential panacea for the structural unemployment attendant upon the decline of traditional industries over the last 30 years. This view is reflected in the plethora of policy initiatives directed at this sector of the economy. However, studies outside of the USA provide limited supporting evidence.[20] Indeed, research on Gazelles suggests that they exist in all industries, with no over-representation in high-technology industries.[3] Concerned by policy-makers' excessively optimistic view of high- and new-technology small firms, Tether[25] notes that 'expectations of small firms as "atomistic" innovators and employment creators have become over-inflated' (p. 109). While high-growth businesses are over-represented in young and growing industries, these are not exclusively in technology sectors, but are as likely to be in knowledge-intensive business services, health care or education.

Ownership

Recently, a number of academic studies have speculated on the extent to which a large component of small-firm growth is inorganic (i.e. growth through acquisition and through the development, by individual entrepreneurs, of other distinct businesses). In the former case, evidence suggests that growth through acquisition is rare in small and young firms.[26] However, the latter notion, often called 'portfolio entrepreneurship', has enjoyed a considerable recent popularity.[27; 28] Scott and Rosa[29] contend that the predilection of small-firm researchers for firm-level analysis fails to recognize the contribution of the individual entrepreneur to wealth and capital accumulation. While this might be true, the survey-based methodologies employed have a tendency to overstate the case. For example, such remote, and often general, studies are unable to distinguish between those who have started another trading business and those who have merely registered another company for legal reasons. In addition, regardless of the merits of identifying portfolio entrepreneurs and shifting the focus of research from firm-level to individual-level analysis, the substance of the research findings to date has not advanced our ability to 'explain' the process through which wealth and capital are accumulated; merely illuminated, indirectly, how it is distributed.

The strategy

External equity

It is generally accepted that the sources of finance accessed and the corresponding financial structures of small firms will influence their propensity to grow. The relative reliance of firms on short-term, often overdraft, debt finance[30] is clearly far from ideal. To this end, Storey suggests that firms that have sold equity, or indicated a willingness to do so, have outperformed those that have been unwilling to dilute ownership. This capital-for-equity exchange allows firms to circumvent constraints imposed by short-term debt funding.

Yet, we note two points that indicate the need for caution. First, as Storey himself points out, it may be the case that the only firms that attract external equity are those that have grown or exhibit obvious potential for growth. Consequently, there is no indication of the direction of causation. Second, irrespective of the inclination, or indeed disinclination, of small firms towards equity sharing, there undoubtedly exists some form of 'equity gap' (see Chapters 7 and 8).[31] In other words, many small firms, regardless of desire and strategic stance, are unable to obtain equity funding. It may be that this factor is, in part, not a true measure of strategy but is, instead, a measure of the beneficence of the external environment – an exogenous variable rather than an endogenous variable.

Market positioning

The temptation has always existed to characterize small-firm competition as perfect in the economic sense,[32] with the implication that there are no consumer loyalties and products are largely commodities. In this way, firms are 'price takers', have no incentive to expand output, are unable to erect entry barriers and are overly vulnerable to market uncertainties. Clearly, if a little superficially, we can identify in many industries or markets a large number of small firms competing and this is undoubtedly part of the attraction of this view.

The argument for market positioning, then, is that growth firms overcome this lack of market power and pricing discretion by inhabiting niches or Penrosean interstices. Competition becomes monopolistic and the firm is able to set prices above marginal cost – making above normal profits, which help to finance growth and increase relative market share (thus reducing uncertainty). The general idea that competing on cost/price considerations is less attractive than a differentiation strategy is captured in Michael Porter's popular generic strategies (Figure 10.3; see also Chapter 13). Simply put, being the cheapest is, on its own, unlikely to be a winning strategy – particularly for small firms. Lower price has implications for margins and the ability to finance future growth. In addition, price frequently acts as a signal of quality and too low a price may suggest,

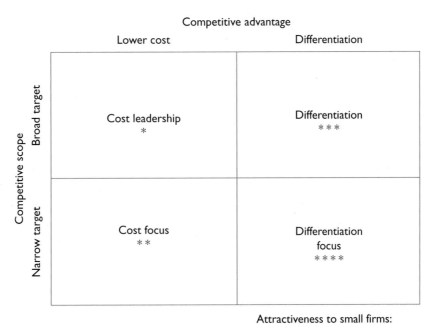

FIGURE 10.3

Porter's generic strategies

rightly or wrongly, poor quality to many customers. This is not to suggest that having lower costs (or prices) is a bad thing. Simply, that if this is the sole basis of a firm's competitive advantage it is less likely to provide the platform for growth.

However, although a niche strategy may initially be advantageous, it is unlikely to provide the basis for long-term sustainable growth. Barber et al.,[33] for instance, suggest that,

> [t]he challenge facing the growing firm can be stated in terms of a move from relatively narrow market niches in which it exploits a narrow range of distinctive assets into a situation in which it serves a larger number of market segments with a much broader skills and knowledge base.
>
> (pp. 15–16)

Another, and related, component of market position involves competitor characteristics. It may plausibly be argued that fast-growth firms, occupying market niches, see their primary competitors as other small firms occupying the same or adjacent niches.[32] Conversely, poorer-performing firms would be in direct competition with large firms where no niche exists. Accordingly, the large firms are able to take advantage of a relatively large market share (and associated market power) to the detriment of the small firm. While there is an internal logic to this argument the empirical evidence is, once again, inconclusive. For instance, Westhead and Birley[6] note that '[Growth] firms are associated with a strategic stance of competing with large employment sized firms rather than a decision to operate in markets saturated by fellow new and small firms' (p. 28).

New product introduction

New product introduction is, as a means of differentiating one firm's products from another's, related to the above discussion of product differentiation and market niches. Given the frequent inability to capture scale economies, it is unlikely that many small firms will be able to effectively compete on price. As such, competition on non-price factors such as innovation becomes crucial to business development.[34] New products frequently allow firms to address existing customers better and to attract new customers. Certainly, the empirical evidence that innovative firms outperform non-innovators is substantial.[35; 36; 37] However, injunctions to innovate must be conditioned by an understanding that an innovation strategy is typically a risky strategy. While successful innovation may confer a host of advantages on the firm, unsuccessful innovation may lead to business failure – most especially in small firms. Indeed, recent evidence suggests that the performance benefits of innovation may be heavily skewed towards a small number of 'superstar' fast-growth firms[37] and that aggregate observations on the relative performance of innovators and non-innovators may be misleading.

Management recruitment

Recalling the stage models discussed in the earlier part of this chapter it can be seen that, as the firm grows, the managerial function becomes progressively more complex. This is likely to hold true, though perhaps not in the inevitable and incremental manner suggested by the stage models. As the firm grows the manager can no longer maintain effective control over the minutiae of day-to-day operations and is required to delegate certain tasks to wage employees within the firm. The owner-manager's task becomes the identification or recruitment and motivation of suitable individuals who can 'manage' in his or her stead – sometimes characterized as a move from 'doing' to 'managing' to 'managing managers'. In a very general way, this is linked to Penrose's 'Theory of the growth of the growth'. Penrose[38] argued that the presence of sufficiently experienced executive resource was required for confident planning and subsequent growth. In this way, firms' growth is generated by successful managerial learning by doing. Accordingly, executive resource would ideally be internally experienced. In contrast, Storey suggests that growth firms are more likely to recruit managers *externally*. Regardless, as Storey notes, there has been insufficient research in this area. Intuitively, it is likely that management recruitment is both a consequence and a cause of growth and any subsequent growth will be significantly influenced not by the presence of, but by the efficacy of, new management.

At this point some general comment on the issue of firm strategy seems in order, not least because many similarly motivated texts devote considerably more space to the issue than we have allowed here. However, while there is undoubtedly a growing, if somewhat patchy, literature concerned with strategy in small firms, it is not clear to what extent this has improved our understanding of firm growth. Indeed, O'Farrell and Hitchens's[39] conclusion seems as pertinent now as it did more than 20 years ago:

> Numerous studies testify to a strategy–performance relationship, although the findings are significant more for establishing the importance of a strategy than for telling what strategies to follow under particular circumstances.
>
> (p. 1370)

Given the importance of context, attempts to be more specific often appear unreasonably prescriptive. The 'right' strategy is likely to be contingent upon a host of factors, both internal and external to the firm. On the other hand, simply making a value distinction between strategy and tactics, between long- and short-term planning, is not entirely helpful either. For the majority of small firms, the luxury of a three- or five-year planning horizon is one that they simply cannot afford amid the struggle for short-term survival.

However, to return to Storey's model: in addition to his triumvirate, Storey notes the importance of the 'wish to grow' in achieving growth (pp. 119–21). This conjecture is supported by Smallbone et al.,[40] who contend that 'One of the most important factors [in influencing growth] is the commitment of the leader of the company to achieving growth' (p. 59). While it can plausibly be argued that all small firms that grow do not do so willingly, occasionally being 'dragged' by a growing dominant customer, it would nonetheless seem prudent to include this factor in any predictive growth model.

The model described above clearly has a number of weaknesses – most of which are identified by Storey himself. Nonetheless, it represents the best available model, of its type. Moreover, the logic underlying the inclusion of individual variables is compelling and, in aggregate, they probably impact upon firms in much the way Storey envisages. Accordingly, it is emphatically not our intention to suggest that any of the factors discussed above do not influence firm growth – they undoubtedly do. Rather, there exists concern over the consistency of impact. And consistency is a prerequisite for prediction. Fundamentally, the influence of each variable is neither consistent nor, by consequence, predictable. Storey's model, and models of its ilk, neither describe, predict nor, more importantly, explain very well. To this end, we would echo Smallbone et al.[40] in suggesting that '[w]hile it may be possible to identify key success factors that affect the growth of SMEs, it is unlikely that a comprehensive model with predictive capability will emerge'.

It should be noted that Storey, in his turn, is chary of 'picking winners', most especially at start-up. Likening the process to a horse race, where the odds of backing a winner are unknown (though factors such as form or lineage may influence the outcome), Storey[41] suggested that, when 'gambling' with public money, it would be better to back horses after a significant number of hurdles had been cleared – that is, after the high number of failures, associated with the initial two- to three-year trading period, have occurred.

BARRIERS TO GROWTH

At the same time as the predictive modelling literature has grown, other commentators have argued that the focus of research and policy should be towards relieving barriers to growth for small firms, rather than identifying generic characteristics or sets of characteristics.[17] Although such an approach does not concern itself directly with growth theories, it has merits that recommend its inclusion in a review chapter of this type. The suggestion that 'artificial' barriers to growth exist and that firms may grow more readily were these barriers to be removed may be viewed from a different perspective. Implicitly, this approach suggests that a particular external state or internal structure is more appropriate for growth than that which prevails in the absence of suggested interventions.

As part of an ACARD (Advisory Council for Applied Research and Development)- and DTI (the former UK Department of Trade and Industry)-sponsored study designed to examine the barriers to growth faced by 'high flyers', Barber et al.,[33] summarizing the literature, suggest that these constraints consist of three types: management and motivation; resources and market opportunities; and structure.[a] Specifically, these would include, *inter alia*: lack of management training, relatively low qualifications, reluctance to delegate and the need for new management skills and techniques as the organization grows; access to finance, access to skilled labour and access to technology; market growth rates, size and frequency of purchases, degree of segmentation and opportunities for collaboration or merger. Many of the factors in this list are complements of, or related to, variables discussed in the previous sections. For example, lack of management training may equate with prior management experience, low qualifications with education, degree of segmentation with market positioning and so on. However, the variable that sits least comfortably, although arguably loosely related to the earlier discussion of external equity, is that of access to finance. In addition, this is the most commonly cited and vigorously debated 'barrier' to growth.

Although the issue of finance was discussed in greater detail in Chapters 7 and 8, the following represents a brief recounting with a view to the current context. The argument generally focuses upon either the 'equity gap', discussed earlier, or access to bank finance – since most firms rely principally upon the latter method of funding. With regard to banks, it is often argued that some form of market failure or 'finance gap' in the provision of debt to small firms exists. In short, small-firm demand for bank loans exceeds supply and the market fails to reach equilibrium at prevailing prices (interest rates set, by the Bank of England, below market equilibrium price). However, such an argument assumes homogeneous loan proposals, which is unlikely to be the case. Undoubtedly, some proposals will be of greater inherent worth than others. It is more likely that any difficulties relate to the relationship between small firms and their banks. Due to the nature of the banking relationship, in the presence of information asymmetries and moral hazard, adverse selection and credit rationing are liable to prevail, the risk-averse character of banks favouring potentially not selecting 'good' proposals in preference to potentially selecting 'bad' proposals.[42] As a 'remedy' it is suggested that, while perfect information is an unattainable ideal, there exists scope to improve information flows between small firms and their bankers.[43] There are further issues regarding the inconsistency of criteria used in, and the often subjective nature of, bank appraisal procedures.[44] Regardless of the plausibility of the above argument, and the laudability of the suggested response, there exists little empirical evidence that access to finance represents a significant barrier to growth.[18]

More generally, there is some suggestion that it is the impact of the external environment, and the pace and unpredictability with which it changes, that bears most heavily on the success (and failure) of small firms.[45] Because small firms frequently occupy narrow market niches and rely upon limited resources they are both more vulnerable to environmental change and less capable of predicting or adapting to it. In this way, government intervention to support small firms may be a legitimate means of ameliorating the disproportionate impact of, among other things, changes in regulations, interest rates, labour markets or tax laws.

However, there exists a counter-argument to the removal of such barriers. In this, it is suggested that entrepreneurs, or small-business owner-managers, trading in hostile environments are more likely to develop the characteristics of self-reliance and determination required to succeed.[46] Consequently, policy should avoid lowering

---

[a] The work of the ACARD- and DTI-funded study was built upon by a later ACOST (Advisory Council on Science and Technology) study. The findings of this second study served to support those of the first. In particular, it suggested that 'the ultimate barriers to growth relate to strategic management and lack of internal resources to make key business transitions' (p. v).

barriers or providing incentives that dull the development of these attributes. This is a generally untested hypothesis built upon principally anecdotal and *ad hoc* observations and it is doubtful whether such an extreme position would be of value in the generality of policy. While we might feel a policy of erecting or maintaining barriers is a step too far, Cressy's[18] suggestion that a stricter German model which, by making start-up more difficult (or less easy), aims at raising the threshold quality of new ventures, has some merit. By analogy, one might view business ownership as an obstacle race, littered with a series of walls that have to be scaled. Policy may take a variety of approaches to assisting the entrepreneur: (1) it may knock down the wall; (2) it may provide the entrepreneur with a ladder; or, (3) it may teach the entrepreneur how to scale walls. Too often expediency appears to favour 1 and 2, where 3 may develop more capable and independent entrepreneurs.

CONCLUSIONS

If this chapter were to provide a comprehensive review of all contributions to our understanding of small-firm growth it would require a dedicated text in itself. Instead, we have contented ourselves with presenting key strands, which have had considerable influence on public policy and mainstream academic debate: stage models and predictive models. Though frequently criticized, stage models are truly process orientated and grant due attention to the role of history in determining the actions and structures of firms. However, we concur with Storey: the models describe rather than predict or, more significantly, explain (unless through equally implausible, non-random, defined crises).

On the other hand, the characteristics or predictive modelling approach to small-firm growth has, itself, reached an impasse. The factors influencing growth are innumerable and are likely to defy classification in a simple, usable model. Attempting to isolate those where evidence of effect is 'consistent' appears fruitless. Perhaps more importantly, while many of the factors incorporated in such models *may* have considerable influence on the growth of small firms, any influence is likely to be contingent upon the given context.

More recently, emphasis has begun to shift from static analysis of, often categorical, proxy variables towards a more dynamic analysis of the processes of adaptation and learning.[47; 48; 49; 50] Simplistically, it may be suggested that, since growth necessitates change, those firms that have enjoyed sustainable growth are those that were most receptive to change and/or have managed change most effectively. This is in line with the view of growth as a process of adaptation and learning,[47] in which firms learn from their experiences of things going well and, perhaps more importantly, things going badly. Variations in how well firms learn and apply that learning may ultimately differentiate successful firms.[49] Within this context, learning is seen as a process of adaptation to changes in internal and external environments. This view owes much to Edith Penrose's[2] early work on competency- or resource-based theories of the firm. Penrose, for instance, noted that:

> the growing experience of management, its knowledge of the other resources of the firm and of the potential for using them in different ways, create incentives for further expansion as the firm searches for ways of using the services of its own resources more profitably.
>
> (p. xii)

Where limitations on growth exist, these relate to managerial competency and to the endowed resources (technology, skills, finance etc.) of the firm and its ability to meet challenges posed by a changing environment. Moreover, in the sense that learning is cumulative, so the development of the firm is likely to be history- or path-dependent:[51] 'Like the great men of whom Tolstoy wrote in *War and Peace*, "[e]very action of theirs, that seems to them an act of their own free will, is in bondage to the whole course of previous history"' (p. 333). In other words, past decisions (and past capabilities) are likely to constrain future options.

The aim of such research is to discover and delineate the underlying processes of adaptive learning and growth, irrespective of context. Or, indeed, to determine whether such processes exist. Unfortunately, no coherent, testable model has been developed to date. The development of a suitable process theory of (small) firm growth remains one of the major challenges in entrepreneurship and the wider social sciences, though interested students are directed to a paper by Elizabeth Garnsey,[50] which serves as an excellent starting point.

Finally, in this chapter, it is worth briefly commenting upon the converse of growth: viz. failure. As Storey (p. 3)[41] notes, 'ceasing to trade is endemic and central to the small firm sector'. This is well illustrated by Figure 10.4, which records monthly survival rates for the cohort of new VAT registrants in 1995. The limitations in using VAT data to measure survival are well known (see Storey[12]). However, the picture painted in Figure 10.4 is likely to be broadly accurate. To this end, almost 70 per cent of firms fail to make it to their tenth birthday. Of course, studying failure is as fraught as studying growth: samples are hard to construct, since failed entrepreneurs are less forthcoming than successful ones. And, issues of definition are even more contested than those concerning growth. Nonetheless, it seems remarkable, given the regularity with which it occurs, that failure features so infrequently in academic discussions and policy debates. Another familiar Tolstoy quote (this time from *Anna Karenina*), may help explain this neglect: 'All happy families resemble one another, each unhappy family is unhappy in its own way.' Social scientists often (rather unscientifically) draw the analogy that success has common antecedents, while failures are unique. Successful firms resemble one another, while those that falter do so idiosyncratically. This proposition is an artefact of reliance upon inadequate research methods. If the focus is upon 'emergence and dynamics' rather than comparative statics, one finds that success may be reached by a variety of paths. This observation leads one to wonder if, given the idiosyncratic nature of success, failures might have some common causes. As in other areas of the social sciences, the study of failed firms is neglected when one might reasonably hope to learn as much from failure as from success.

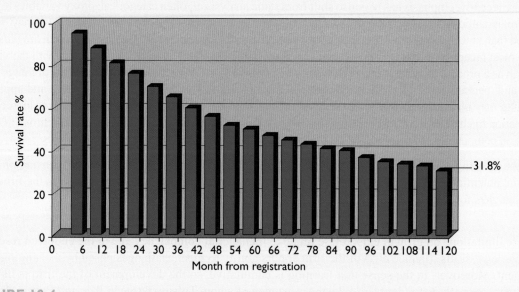

FIGURE 10.4

Survival rate of firms registering for UK VAT in 1995

REVIEW QUESTIONS

1 How small is the proportion of new firms that may achieve significant growth?
2 Why are policies to select 'growth firms' attractive to policymakers?
3 Is there any evidence to support Gibrat's Law that growth will be independent of firm size? Explain your answer.
4 Why do you think 'chance' plays a large part in successful (or unsuccessful) firm growth? Do any of the case studies discussed in this book support the role of chance in growth?
5 Compare Churchill and Lewis's and Greiner's models of firm growth. Why are they characterized as life-cycle models? How are they different?
6 What are the three broad categories of 'characteristics' in Storey's approach?
7 Can the characteristics approach explain firm growth?
8 Do any of the case studies in this book fit a life-cycle approach to entrepreneurial growth?
9 Why might finance be regarded as a barrier to entrepreneurial firm growth?
10 It was suggested that support agencies such as the Business Links might attempt to target their support at entrepreneurial growth firms. Why does evidence presented in this chapter suggest that this policy might be unproductive?
11 From the previous discussion in this chapter, and the illustration shown in Figure 10.3, why might the legal ownership of an entrepreneurial firm be a major barrier to growth?

SUGGESTED ASSIGNMENTS

The following assignment is based on the Nichol McKay case study provided in the students' online learning resources material. Further information on this case and teaching notes are also available in the lecturer's online resources.

Prepare a written report or plan for a classroom discussion to answer the following.

1 Consider the Nichol McKay case in light of Storey's tripartite model. How closely does Nichol McKay fit the criteria suggested in the model?

2 Where possible, can the direction/nature of cause and effect be determined?

3 At start-up would we have predicted Nichol McKay's subsequent growth and success?

REFERENCES

1 **Dobbs, M. and Hamilton, R.T.** (2007) 'Small business growth: recent evidence and new directions', *International Journal of Entrepreneurial Behaviour & Research*, vol. 13, no. 5, pp. 296–322.

2 **Penrose, E.** (1995/1959) *The Theory of the Growth of the Firm*, Blackwell, London.

3 **Henrekson, M. and Johansson, D.** (2010) 'Gazelles as job creators: a survey and interpretation of the evidence', *Small Business Economics*, vol. 35, pp. 227–44.

4   **Gibrat, R.** (1931) *Les Inégalités Economiques*, Sirey, Paris.

5   **Mansfield, E.** (1962) 'Entry, Gibrat's Law, innovation and the growth of firms', *American Economic Review*, vol. 52, pp. 1023–51.

6   **Westhead, P. and Birley, S.** (1995) 'Employment growth in new independent owner-managed firms in GB', *International Small Business Journal*, vol. 13, no. 3, pp. 11–34.

7   **Nelson, R. and Winter, S.** (1978) 'Forces generating and limiting concentration under Schumpeterian competition', *Bell Journal of Economics*, vol. 9, pp. 524–48.

8   **Phelps, R., Adams, R. and Bessant J.** (2007) 'Life cycles of growing organisations: a review with implications for knowledge and learning', *International Journal of Management Reviews*, vol. 9, no. 1, pp. 1–30.

9   **Greiner, L.** (1972) 'Evolution and revolution as organisations grow', *Harvard Business Review*, vol. 50, July–August, pp. 37–46.

10 **Churchill, N. and Lewis, V.** (1983) 'The five stages of small business growth', *Harvard Business Review*, vol. 61, May–June, pp. 30–50.

11 **Scott, M. and Bruce, R.** (1987) 'Five stages of growth in small business', *Long Range Planning*, vol. 20, no. 3, pp. 45–52.

12 **Storey, D.** (1994) *Understanding the Small Business Sector*, Routledge, London.

13 **McKelvie, A. and Wiklund, J.** (2010) 'Advancing firm growth research: a focus on growth mode instead of growth rate', *Entrepreneurship Theory and Practice*, March, pp. 261–88.

14 **Storey, D., Keasey, K., Watson, R. and Wynarczyk, P.** (1987) *The Performance of Small Firms: Profits, Jobs and Failures*, Croom Helm, London.

15 **Gallagher, C. and Robson, G.** (1996) 'The identification of high growth SMEs', paper presented to the 19th National Small Firms Policy and Research Conference, Birmingham.

16 **Davidsson, P., Achtenhagen, L. and Naldi, L.** (2005) 'Research on small firm growth: A review', paper presented at the 35th EISB Conference, Barcelona, Spain.

17 **Hessels, J., Van Gelderen, M. and Thurik, R.** (2008) 'Entrepreneurial aspirations, motivations, and their drivers', *Small Business Economics*, vol. 31, pp. 323–39.

18 **Cressy, R.** (1996) 'Are business start-ups debt rationed?', *The Economic Journal*, vol. 106, no. 438, pp. 1253–70.

19 **Barkham, R., Gudgin, G., Hanvey, E. and Hart, M.** (1996) *The Determinants of Small Firm Growth*, Jessica Kingsley, London.

20 **Oakey, R.** (1995) *High-technology Small Firms: Variable Barriers to Growth*, Paul Chapman, London.

21 **Vyakarnam, S., Jacobs, R. and Handelberg, J.** (1996) 'Building and managing relationships: the core competence of rapid growth business', paper presented to the 19th National Small Firms Policy and Research Conference, Birmingham (unpublished, amended version).

22 **Cowling, M.** (2003) 'Is the small firm loan guarantee scheme hazardous for banks or helpful to small businesses?', *Small Business Economics*, vol. 21, pp. 63–71.

23 **Jensen, J.B. and McGuckin, R.H.** (1997) 'Firm performance and evolution: empirical regularities in the US microdata', *Industrial and Corporate Change*, vol. 6, no. 1, pp. 25–47.

24 **Westhead, P.** (1995) 'New owner-managed businesses in rural and urban areas in Great Britain: a matched pairs comparison', *Regional Studies*, vol. 29, no. 4, pp. 367–80.

25 **Tether, B.** (2000) 'Small firms, innovation and employment creation in Britain and Europe: a question of expectations', *Technovation*, http://www.oecd.org/dataoecd/10/60/2090756.pdf (accessed at 28 October 2011) vol. 20, pp. 109–13.

26 **McKelvie, A., Wiklund, J. and Davidsson, P.** (2006) 'A resource-based view of organic and acquired growth', in J. Wiklund, D.Dimov, J.Katz and D.Shepherd (eds), *Advances in Entrepreneurship, Firm Emergence, and Growth*, Vol. 9, *Entrepreneurship: Frameworks and Empirical Investigations from Forthcoming Leaders in European Research*, Elsevier, Amsterdam, pp. 179–99.

27 **Scott, M. and Rosa, P.** (1996) 'Existing business as sources of new firms: a missing topic in business formation research', paper presented to the Babson Entrepreneurship Research Conference, Seattle, WA.

28 **Westhead, P. and Wright, M.** (1997) 'Novice, portfolio and serial founders: are they different?', paper presented to the Babson Entrepreneurship Research Conference, Boston, MA.

29 **Scott, M. and Rosa, P.** (1996) 'Has firm level analysis reached its limits? Time for a rethink', *International Small Business Journal*, vol. 14, no. 4, pp. 81–9.

30 **Deakins, D. and Hussain, G.** (1994) 'Financial information, the banker and small business: a comment', *British Accounting Review*, vol. 26, pp. 323–35.

31 **Murray, G.** (1994) 'The second "equity gap": exit problems for seed and early stage venture capitalists and their investee

companies', *International Small Business Journal*, vol. 12, no. 4, pp. 58–76.

32 **Storey, D. and Sykes, N.** (1996) 'Uncertainty, innovation and management', in P. Burns and J. Dewhurst (eds), *Small Business and Entrepreneurship*, Macmillan, London.

33 **Barber, J., Metcalfe, S. and Porteous, M.** (1989) 'Barriers to growth: the ACARD study', in J. Barber, S. Metcalfe and M. Porteous (eds), *Barriers to Growth in Small Firms*, Routledge, London.

34 **O'Gorman, C.** (2001) 'The sustainability of growth in small- and medium-sized enterprises', *International Journal of Entrepreneurial Behaviour & Research*, vol. 7, pp. 60–70.

35 **Freel, M.S.** (2000) 'Do small innovating firms outperform non-innovators?', *Small Business Economics*, vol. 4, pp. 195–210.

36 **Freel, M.S. and Robson, P.J.A.** (2004) 'Small firm innovation, growth and performance: evidence from Scotland and Northern England', *International Small Business Journal*, vol. 22, pp. 561–75.

37 **Coad, A. and Rao, R.** (2008) 'Innovation and firm growth in high-tech sectors: a quantile regression approach', *Research Policy*, vol. 37, pp. 633–648.

38 **Penrose, E.** (1971) 'Limits to the size and growth of firms', in *The Growth of Firms, Middle East Oil and Other Essays*, Frank Cass, London (first published in 1952 in *American Economic Review*, vol. 45, no. 2).

39 **O'Farrell, P. and Hitchens, D.** (1988) 'Alternative theories of small-firm growth: a critical review', *Environment and Planning A*, vol. 20, pp. 1365–83.

40 **Smallbone, D., Leigh, R. and North, D.** (1995) 'The characteristics and strategies of high growth SMEs', *International Journal of Entrepreneurial Behaviour & Research*, vol. 1, no. 3, pp. 44–62.

41 **Storey, D.** (1992) 'Should we abandon support to start-up businesses?', paper presented to the 15th National Small Firms Policy and Research Conference.

42 **Deakins, D. and Hussain, G.** (1991) *Risk Assessment by Bank Managers*, Birmingham Polytechnic Business School, Birmingham.

43 **Binks, M. and Ennew, C.** (1996) 'Financing small firms', in P. Burns and J. Dewhurst (eds), *Small Business and Entrepreneurship*, Macmillan, London.

44 **Deakins, D., Hussain, G. and Ram, M.** (1992) 'Overcoming the adverse selection problem', paper presented to the 15th National Small Firms Policy and Research Conference, Southampton.

45 **Hawawini, G., Subramanian, V. and Verdin, P.** (2003) 'Is performance driven by industry- or firm-specific factors? A new look at the evidence', *Strategic Management Journal*, vol. 24, pp. 1–16.

46 **Dewhurst, J.** (1996) 'The entrepreneur', in P. Burns and J. Dewhurst (eds), *Small Business and Entrepreneurship*, Macmillan, London.

47 **Wiklund, J.** (1998) *Small Firm Growth and Performance: Entrepreneurship and Beyond*, dissertation series no. 3, Jönköping International Business School.

48 **Costello, N.** (1996) 'Learning and routines in hightech SMEs: analysing rich case study material', *Journal of Economic Issues*, Jönköping, Sweden, vol. 30, no. 2, pp. 591–97.

49 **Freel, M.** (1998) 'Evolution, innovation and learning: evidence from case studies', *Entrepreneurship and Regional Development*, vol. 10, no. 2, pp. 137–49.

50 **Garnsey, E.** (1998) 'A theory of the early growth of firms', *Industrial and Corporate Change*, vol. 7, no. 3, pp. 523–556.

51 **David, P.** (1985) 'Clio and the economics of QWERTY', *AEA Papers and Proceedings*, vol. 75, no. 2, pp. 332–337.

RECOMMENDED READING

Dobbs, M. and Hamilton, R.T. (2007) 'Small business growth: recent evidence and new directions', *International Journal of Entrepreneurial Behaviour & Research*, vol. 13, no. 5, pp. 296–322.

Greiner, L. (1972) 'Evolution and revolution as organisations grow', *Harvard Business Review*, vol. 50, July–August, pp. 37–46.

Henrekson, M. and Johansson, D. (2010) 'Gazelles as job creators: a survey and interpretation of the evidence', *Small Business Economics*, vol. 35, pp. 227–24.

McKelvie, A. and Wiklund, J. (2010) 'Advancing firm growth research: a focus on growth mode instead of growth rate', *Entrepreneurship Theory and Practice*, March, pp. 261–88.

11 INTERNATIONAL ENTREPRENEURSHIP

LEARNING OUTCOMES

At the end of this chapter you should be able to:

- Describe how different cultures can affect entrepreneurial activity.

- Discuss the factors that affect the level of entrepreneurial activity in different nations.

- Describe the characteristics of the process of internationalization.

- Discuss competing theories on the process of internationalization.

- Discuss how all entrepreneurs are affected by the global economy.

- Discuss opportunities and threats posed by globalization.

- Describe examples of the nature of entrepreneurship in advanced, transition and emergent economies.

- Discuss the relevance of the concepts of necessity and opportunity entrepreneurship in the context of developing economies.

- Describe examples of innovative enterprise activity in the context of micro-finance in a developing economy.

INTRODUCTION

Chapter 10 examined some of the factors in the growth process of entrepreneurial firms. One factor likely to be involved in the growth process is the ability to export or to internationalize through an overseas operation. For high-growth firms, establishing overseas markets is an essential part of the growth process. The ability to internationalize operations will be an important part of that process. Some start-up entrepreneurs may be able to start in global markets; such firms are sometimes referred to as 'born globals'.[1] The case study of Skype could be considered to be a born global. Other firms may take longer to enter overseas markets and start from a domestic base. There are competing theories of this process of internationalization, which will be examined in this chapter. Trading overseas requires some understanding of different cultures, different economies and different ways of 'doing business'. In this chapter we examine some of the characteristics of different cultures (which affect entrepreneurial behaviour), risk-taking and economic production methods in other nations – factors that need to be taken into account by entrepreneurs who are seeking to expand in overseas markets. We begin by noting the importance of the global economy, a trend, it is argued, that cannot be ignored by any small-firm entrepreneurs, whether trading internationally or not.

GLOBAL MARKETS

As we have stated before, the majority of small-firm entrepreneurs do not wish to grow (and, by definition, do not wish to export or expand overseas). However, it is arguable that all entrepreneurs are affected by the globalization of the economy. A number of forces have led to increased globalization. All entrepreneurs have to trade in an economy that is affected by the trends or forces forming the global economy. Even if a firm's market is restricted to its local geographical area, it may face competitors that are based overseas and trading locally. Equally, the firm may be part of a supply chain whose end markets are global. For example, the West Midlands region of the UK is well known for the number of small firms based there that produce car components, supplying to local car manufacturers. All firms in the supply chain will be part of the global market and unable to ignore trends in that market. A small firm producing car components in Coventry is probably affected more by events in China than by those in its locality. While small firms are often embedded in local communities and dependent on the local infrastructure, they are also dependent on global supply chains and markets.[2]

Despite the widely reported stalling of the latest WTO trade talks at Doha, there continues to be a growth in bi-lateral and multi-lateral free trade areas and associated pressures to harmonise regulatory codes and regulations.

Nowadays we are all affected by economic events in other economies whether they are taking place in China, India or closer to home. This is due in part to increased 'superstructures' which bring increased connectivity to the 'global village', a feature predicted to become more important in the future (http://www.iftf.org).

Ability to respond to these events, to manage with the increasing pace of change, will affect the sustainability and viability of all small firms; part of that increasing pace of change is the globalization of the economy. A number of factors have contributed to the development of the global economy, factors that are increasing in importance. Some of these factors are listed in the accompanying box on future trends.

Many commentators say that we are in danger of being overwhelmed by the increasing pace of technological change. But exactly what do we mean by technological change? Let us consider a rather different view in a

FUTURE TRENDS IN THE GLOBAL ECONOMY

The development of superstructures of connectivity.

> We have built an extraordinary technological infrastructure to support our sociability. (Institute for the Future (2010) http://www.iftf.org)

By building networks into superstructures on a global scale SMEs can exploit opportunities to develop strategic partnerships. As the Skype case illustrates, in such circumstances location does not matter.

The *pace* of technological change. There is much hype about the *pace* of technological change. If we think about new products that have appeared in the twentieth century, the speed of diffusion appears to have increased. For example, motor cars took 50 years to be adopted by most people, colour TVs 10 years and mobile or cell phones 5 years. A dynamic view of the increasing speed of diffusion is shown in Figure 11.1.

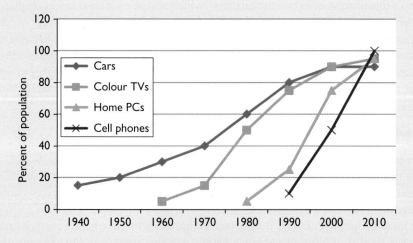

FIGURE 11.1

The increasing speed of diffusion

seminal article by Daniel Levinthal[3] called 'The slow pace of rapid technological change'. Levinthal argues that the image of technological change may well be rapid and discontinuous, but when we apply an evolutionary economics approach much technological change can be explained through the application of existing technology to a new domain of application: for example, wireless technology.

Thus, the important trend is that it is *pace of diffusion* that has increased, not the pace of technological change itself. In addition, increased discontinuities are producing more opportunities.

The implications for small firms and entrepreneurs are that they will increasingly need to:

- Build international networks
- Collaborate in R&D on a national and global basis
- Seek strategic partners
- Scan for opportunities as Schumpeterian discontinuities increase
- Be aware that new products will rapidly succeed or fail

These are factors contributing the development of the global economy and others are summarized in the following box.

FACTORS CONTRIBUTING TO THE DEVELOPMENT OF THE GLOBAL ECONOMY

- The development of e-business methods, as discussed in detail in material in the students' online learning centre.
- Increased superconnectivity.
- Increased pace of diffusion (but not the pace of technological change).
- Greater mobility of the labour force and labour skills.
- New technological developments that favour smaller firms (e.g. biotechnology/micro-technologies).
- Increased pace of change requiring flexible and speedy responses.
- Privatization and reduced barriers in emerging nations, with the development of economies in transition, the emergence of 'tiger economies' and the emergence of China as a major overseas market.
- Growth of global capital markets.
- Increasing number of bilateral and multilateral trade agreements between individual nations and groups of nations.
- Reduction of cultural barriers.

THE PROCESS OF INTERNATIONALIZATION

There are a large number of potential reasons why firms go global, which may be only partly explained by globalization. It is also evident from observation that some firms go global immediately or quickly (born globals), while for others the process of internationalization takes a longer period of time. The factors that might explain why firms go global include:

- Entrepreneurial growth reasons, such as those examined in Chapter 10 (associated with growth of the firm)
- More market-based factors associated with internationalization through participation in overseas markets; these factors may be associated with more effective use of ICT and e-business, as explained in more detail in the students' online learning centre.

Theoretical approaches to the process of internationalization have been developed that offer competing perspectives. These have included the traditional stage model, a network model and a more recent model that can explain born globals as international new ventures. Each of these is briefly examined.

THE TRADITIONAL STAGE MODEL OF INTERNATIONALIZATION

The first model, or stage model, is based on the hypothesis that a small-firm entrepreneur will expand overseas only as more knowledge is gained about operating in overseas markets. Uncertainty and lack of knowledge act as a constraint, which means that a staged approach is taken to internationalization. Often this staged approach is to export to the nearest overseas geographical market; thus for a UK-based entrepreneur this would mean an EU country such as France or Germany.

The model assumes that the process of internationalization is achieved through a series of stages and incremental decision-making by small-firm owners and entrepreneurs. It is a gradual process that starts with an established small-firm with an established domestic market.[4] Figure 11.2 illustrates the potential stages. Traditionally, the small-firm owner/entrepreneur enters overseas markets through agents, having established a

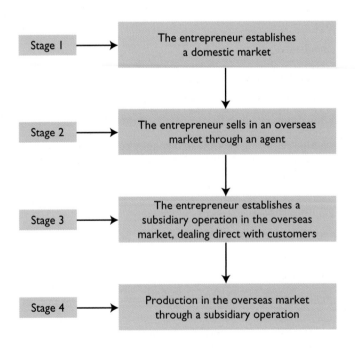

FIGURE 11.2

The process of internationalization: stage model

secure domestic base. Only when this stage is established, does the firm gain sufficient knowledge to open its own subsidiary as an overseas market is established, eliminating the need to operate through an agent and selling direct through its own employees working abroad. As knowledge of the market and practices increases, the final stage will involve overseas production.

It is worth noting that there is no connection between the stage models of internationalization and the (stage) models of growth discussed in Chapter 10, such as those of Churchill and Lewis and Greiner. The approaches have been developed totally separately.

THE NETWORK MODEL

The network model offers an alternative explanation to the internationalization process of small-firm entrepreneurs.[4] The principle on which the model is based is the importance of social capital for entrepreneurs. Entrepreneurs through their networks (e.g. other entrepreneurs) receive enquiries from overseas; this leads to exporting and, with the development of trust, the firm internationalizes. However, unlike the stage model, there are no distinct and discrete stages; rather, it is a smooth process. The network model suggests that business associations such as chambers of commerce or trade associations will be natural channels for the development of enquiries and orders that will lead to internationalization.

INTERNATIONAL NEW VENTURES MODEL

The international new ventures (INVs) model recognizes the importance of the development of globalisation, by identifying entrepreneurs that are in overseas markets from start-up. Such entrepreneurs are assumed to have global vision and seek to operate in international markets before domestic markets, and, in some cases, domestic sales only result from international sales. This was recognized in a study of software companies by Bell.[5] The characteristics of INVs have led to the term 'born global' to denote new entrepreneurial ventures that are established in global markets from inception. They are likely to be technology-based, with vested property interests in IPR that may be protected by the seeking of worldwide patents. An example of such a born global is provided by the Skype Parts I and II case.

The characteristics of such companies are associated with:[6]

- Entrepreneurs who have global markets in mind
- Entry strategies that seek to establish a strong market presence overseas
- The establishment of successor products early in their development

The characteristics of INVs or born globals attract the attention of policymakers since they represent the type of entrepreneurial activity that provides most benefit for local economies, and they are likely to be high-growth entrepreneurial firms.

Fletcher[7] comments: 'These firms were technology based firms in knowledge-intensive sectors, often operating in volatile markets. Rapid internationalisation is facilitated by the knowledge intensity of a firm's core resources and essential to its growth' (p. 3).

INTERNATIONALIZATION: IMPLICATIONS FOR ENTREPRENEURS

High growth entrepreneurial firms seeking to internationalize have to assess how to tackle globalization and the penetration of overseas markets. Operating abroad usually involves one of four approaches:

1 Production at home and *exporting* through partners or agents
2 Production at home and *licensing* another firm to produce abroad

3 Entering into a strategic joint venture agreement or partnership to exploit overseas markets

4 Owning and controlling an overseas operation through either a *de novo* operation or buying an existing operation

These alternative methods are illustrated in Figure 11.3. The strategy adopted will depend on the nature of the product or service, the requirements of the customer and the growth aspirations of the international entrepreneurial firm.

Figure 11.3 illustrates different strategic choices for the entrepreneurial growth firm. The strategy chosen will depend on a number of factors; these include cost, availability of finance, regulations in different countries, risk involved, availability of strategic partners and exchange-rate risks, but not least the entrepreneurial culture of different areas and nations.

DIFFERENT ENTREPRENEURIAL CULTURES

In Chapter 1 we discussed how the entrepreneur is increasingly seen as a key actor in the economy and an *agent* of economic change. To perform this function the entrepreneur becomes a *problem solver*, reconciling limited resources with the environment. The entrepreneur may be seen as having the same function in each economy, yet the environment and resources will vary. In different economies, different cultures will affect the degree to which the entrepreneur is able to be the key actor and hence influence economic change. Some economies are perceived to contain environments that are more conducive to entrepreneurship than others.

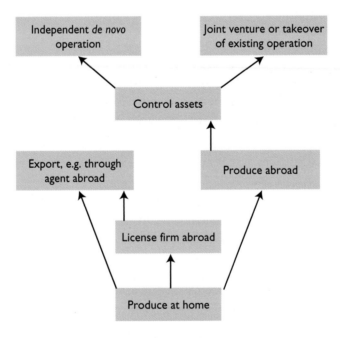

FIGURE 11.3

Strategies for internationalization

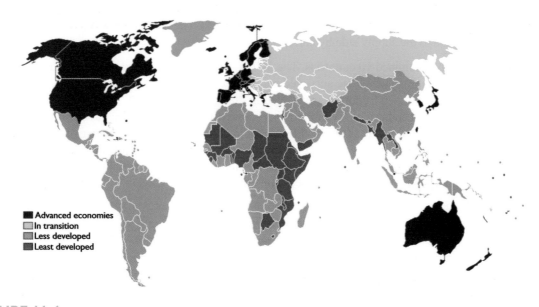

FIGURE 11.4

A world in transition

SOURCE: World Bank 2010.

Figure 11.4 illustrates that we live in a world in transition, although traditionally, following the IMF[8] we allocate rather pejorative terms to divide up our world into:

– Developed nations (or advanced economies)

– Developing and emerging nations (or economies in transition)

It is probably best to view all nations as in a state of transition and indeed some of the current developing economies are expected to outperform the developed economies. Indeed China's GDP surpassed that of the USA in 2010. However, after stating such caveats, in the following sections we examine some of the factors that determine whether the nature of the environment and culture in different economies is entrepreneurial.

ADVANCED ECONOMIES

Two contrasting attempts to assess the level of entrepreneurial culture and activity in different advanced nations are examined in this section. The first of these is the Global Entrepreneurship Monitor (GEM) approach;[9; 10] this is contrasted with the approach of Casson.[11]

The GEM approach proposes that a causal relationship exists between the level of entrepreneurial activity in an economy and the level of economic growth. It should be noted that this assumption of such a one-way causal relationship has been criticized, as has the methodology applied by the GEM studies. An assessment and critique of this methodology has been given in Chapter 2 and the reader should also refer to that chapter; we are interested here in claims made about differences in entrepreneurial activity as a result of the GEM studies.

Economies will differ in their level of entrepreneurial activity, which will directly affect the growth of a nation's gross domestic product (GDP). The GEM approach further proposes that factors affecting the level of entrepreneurial activity can be represented by means of a model. The GEM model consists of demand-side and supply-side factors that can be measured (represented in Figure 11.5). The demand side is represented by entrepreneurial opportunities and the supply side by entrepreneurial capacity.

The 1999 GEM report[9] examined 10 countries. The 2001 GEM report expanded the number of countries of 29, including developing nations, which are surveyed annually to arrive at the measurement of entrepreneurial activity.[12] After an expansion to 37 countries surveyed in 2002, the latest 2010 GEM report (at the time of writing) included 59 surveyed countries.[13] Comparisons across different cultures are obviously problematical. For example, GEM does not attempt to measure differences in culture. In addition, the use of a standard questionnaire survey across all 59 countries in 2010, when infrastructures are very different, is also, of course, problematical; nevertheless, the GEM reports have received much attention as a benchmarking approach to the level of entrepreneurial activity. This approach owes something to that of Casson,[11] but is contrasted with it below.

Casson has attempted to analyse and classify the 'entrepreneurial' cultures of advanced, or developed, economies.[11] He made a distinction between 'high-level' entrepreneurial behaviour, which he claimed is associated with the Schumpeterian concept of entrepreneurship, and 'low-level' entrepreneurial behaviour, which he claimed is associated with the Kirznerian concept of entrepreneurship (as discussed in Chapter 1, where an explanation is given of these contrasting entrepreneurship concepts). Casson compared, at the time, seven

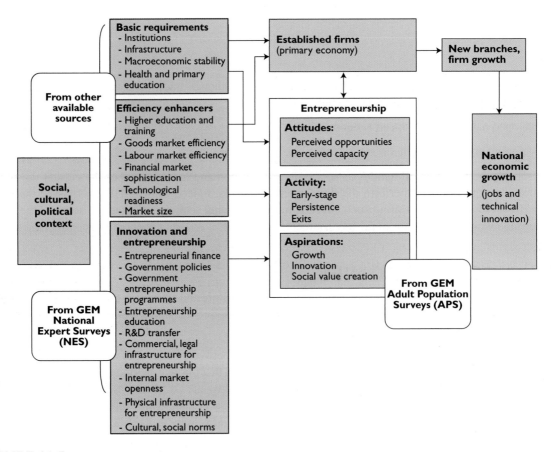

FIGURE 11.5

The GEM model of entrepreneurial activity

SOURCE: Global Entrepreneurship Monitor (2009).[14]

advanced industrial economies (the USA, Japan, the UK, France, Canada, Sweden and Italy) and used a scoring system for certain characteristics of cultural attitudes and environment that are discussed below. Using this (weighted) scoring system he found that Japan and the USA had the highest and most conducive entrepreneurial cultures, whereas (of the seven nations), the UK and Italy had the lowest ratings.[11]

Casson claimed that there were two groups of characteristics of national cultures that determined these ratings. First, technical aspects of a culture, which included attitudes to the importance of scientific measurement, to taking a systems view and hence to the degree of sophistication in decision-making. Second, moral characteristics of a culture, which included the extent of voluntarism, types of commitment and attitudes to achievement. These groups of characteristics determined the extent to which a culture was conducive to 'high-level' (Schumpeterian) entrepreneurship as opposed to 'low-level' (Kirznerian) entrepreneurship. For example, Japan scored well on the national characteristic of a scientific approach to problems and a systems view to planning, which meant a willingness to accept logistical planning and awareness of interdependency. It scored lower with voluntarism – the extent of willingness to allow freedom for transactions – an area where the USA scored highly. For example, this was explained by Casson[11] as:

> The philosophy of voluntarism . . . supports a political framework within which people are free to transact with whomever they like. Voluntarism opposes the concentration of coercive powers on institutions such as the state.
>
> (p. 92)

Casson's hierarchy of national entrepreneurial cultures was an attempt to provide objective measurements of subjective and intangible values of different national cultures. As such, the measurements could be subject to widely different interpretations. For example, Germany was a rather surprising omission from Casson's countries chosen for comparison and might score quite low on some of Casson's criteria, yet it would be accepted by many observers as a nation having, at the time, at least a medium level of entrepreneurial activity. Nonetheless, Casson's approach was an interesting attempt to analyse different levels of entrepreneurial culture in different economies. In identifying factors that affect attitudes to scientific endeavour, to moral codes, to commitments, the approach provided a useful framework for discussion of features of different national cultures and different levels of entrepreneurial activity.

It would be a mistake, however, to view certain economies as 'model' or prototypical entrepreneurial economies. Quite different cultures with different systems, attitudes and infrastructures can result in high-level, advanced entrepreneurship. For example, in the early 1990s, the Scottish Enterprise *Business Birth Rate Enquiry* investigated two advanced regional economies to examine factors that accounted for their relatively high levels of entrepreneurial behaviour.[15] The two contrasting regions, Massachusetts in the USA and Baden-Württemberg in Germany, had quite different attitudes, characteristics and environments. Massachusetts was characterized by little state intervention and a dependence on private-sector venture capital to provide the risk capital to finance new ventures. Baden-Württemberg, however, was characterized by (regional) state-funded assistance and a reliance on bank-loan finance to provide new venture capital. These two powerful economic regions demonstrated that, despite different characteristics in society and different infrastructures, both could produce advanced 'high-level' entrepreneurship.

THE IMPORTANCE OF DEVELOPED NETWORKS

The common feature of advanced entrepreneurial economies is the extent of networking. As shown by the Scottish Enterprise study, Baden-Württemberg contained advanced networks focused through local chambers of commerce.[15] Massachusetts also had important networks, through venture capitalists and through integration with the Massachusetts Institute of Technology (MIT), which provided an important spin-out route for technology-based high value start-ups. The importance of such support networks in Baden-Württemberg (B-W) has been highlighted by Kitching and Blackburn.[16] In a three-region study including B-W, Aarhus (Denmark) and London, they concluded that small engineering firms in London were disadvantaged by the lack of effective support networks. The level of networking and co-operative behaviour is not one of either the GEM or Casson's criteria; however, it is a recognized factor behind the success of areas such as the north-east of Italy, the 'Third Italy'.

Scottish Enterprise, following its enquiry, identified networking arrangements among new firms as a way to achieve growth and hence job creation:[17]

> Networks are important: many of the solutions will be found in the actions of individual entrepreneurs, backed by their networks of family and friends. An important focus of action for the strategy is to improve the effectiveness of these networks and to make potential entrepreneurs more aware of what they can do themselves to achieve success. Part of this involves improving the support given by the formal support networks in the private and public sectors.
>
> (p. 4)

Similarly, in a later version of strategy, Scottish Enterprise claimed:[18]

> To compete, companies will need to build strong partnerships through which information and ideas can flow quickly and to best mutual advantage. Spanning customers, suppliers, competitors and other supporting institutions such as the universities, colleges, research bodies and the utilities, these specialist networks or 'clusters' create more of the sparks that fuel innovation and generate synergies that power them to greater competitiveness.
>
> (p. 1)

The benefits that can accrue to new firms operating in partnerships/networks/clusters are the potential advantages of economies of scope. Services and inputs, such as advertising, training, access to loan finance at advantageous rates, consultancy advice, financial services – items that a single firm cannot easily afford or secure when operating independently – can be secured when operating as part of a larger group. It has also been demonstrated that external linkages with other firms encourage innovation (see Chapter 9). For example, Edquist et al. have illustrated, in the case of Gothia in Sweden, the importance of networking for product innovation in small manufacturing firms.[19]

While the organizational structure of firms operating in some kind of cohesive way may be given the title 'networking', firms producing in any economy take on some of the attributes of a networking structure. For example, by engaging in production and trade a firm deals with suppliers and customers, which necessitates a degree of co-operation and trust. These factors are regarded as essential attributes of the successful functioning of a network. There is also an element of risk and uncertainty within any business relationship. Trust arises in response to the threat of risk and uncertainty. When trust exists it minimizes the potential risk and opportunism. Thompson underlines the importance of trust:[20] 'Co-operation is more secure and robust when agents have a trust because of the reputation of themselves and other agents in the network for honesty and consistency' (p. 58).

Risk and opportunism can also be reduced via contracting but, as Macaulay[21] notes, while detailed clauses are often written into contracts, they are seldom used:

[C]ontract and contract law are often thought unnecessary because there are many non-legal sanctions. Two norms are widely accepted.
(1) Commitments are to be honoured in almost all situations;
(2) One ought to produce a good product and stand behind it.

(p. 63)

In other words, an environment can develop where implicit contracting ensures a degree of trust and co-operation. Other, more established, relationships can develop beyond that of a purely contractual kind. Sako[22] identifies two other kinds of trust: competence trust, being a belief that a trading partner will fulfil a particular task; and goodwill trust, which occurs in situations where initiatives are undertaken beyond the specific remit of a contract:[23] 'The role of goodwill trust extends beyond existing relations and includes the transfer of new ideas and new technology' (p. 218).

While we have identified trust and co-operation as two attributes of an advanced economy, they can be strengthened to ensure the efficient operation of the network. This can be the key to the development of advanced entrepreneurial regional economies such as the 'Third Italy'. For this to happen, contractual trust must be developed into goodwill trust. Economists using a game theoretical framework have demonstrated that, where firms attach sufficient weight to future interactions, punishment strategies can be employed to secure co-operation; when joining a formal organization, such as a network, defectors and uncooperative players can be excluded. The problem with over-reliance on punishment strategies is that they could lead to distrust, which would threaten co-operation: 'If you trust me why are you monitoring my behaviour?' Axelrod suggests that co-operation can evolve over a period of time as firms gradually learn rules and norms of behaviour leading to co-operation.[24] In other words, through continual interaction and the belief of further interaction, the temptation to cheat diminishes. The participating firms build up reputations for co-operation and these reputations have to be protected.

We have indicated that, where established networks exist, these can involve policing by member firms in an attempt to prevent opportunistic behaviour on behalf of other member firms. Where no existing meaningful networking arrangements exist, policy bodies could attempt to facilitate such developments. In local economies where this has proven to be more successful, such as the industrial districts of the Third Italy, this has occurred in conjunction with the key agents in the region, such as the small firm entrepreneurs themselves, the equivalent of the local chambers of commerce, the relevant financial institutions and the local authorities. In other words, the key players in the local economy have been involved in the design and implementation of the strategy, which is a major factor in that these key players take on ownership of the organisation.

Thus it has been argued that the level of co-operation, trust and networking is a key factor determining the level (high/medium/low) of entrepreneurship in different cultures. This networking may be characterized by different forms, but it seems to be a necessary condition for high levels of entrepreneurship.

ECONOMIES IN TRANSITION

With the collapse of communism in eastern Europe and the former USSR, attention has focused on whether such nations can successfully transform into entrepreneurial economies (whether high- or low-level). Although it is well known, particularly with the high profile enjoyed by the Russian entrepreneur Roman Abramovich, that such economies do produce and provide opportunities for successful entrepreneurial activity, such nations are regarded as emergent economies, as potential new areas for entrepreneurs seeking new markets. Therefore, if they can achieve the features of advanced economies, as discussed in the previous section, new opportunities for firms seeking growth become available. Although, as we have seen, we can view all nations as part of a world in transition (Figure 11.4), in practice it is often the former communist nation states that have been given the title of 'economies in transition'. As in western Europe, this term obscures a great diversity of development: different nations are at different stages in the transition process. This partly reflects the situation before the breakup of the old Soviet bloc, where some states had semi-market economies (such as Poland) and others were completely government controlled (such as the Baltic states). It also partly reflects the different features and characteristics of such nations.

These transition economies have certain identifiable features, as listed in the accompanying box.

FEATURES OF ECONOMIES IN TRANSITION

- High levels of uncertainty and lack of information, implying opportunities for the Kirznerian entrepreneur.
- A lack of formal financial infrastructure and sources of finance.
- Limited markets and spending power within internal economies.
- No formal regulation (e.g. for regulating new firms/companies).
- Varying degrees of former 'market economies' giving different attitudes and approaches to entrepreneurial activity.
- Different levels of assistance, dependent on access to EU and western development aid.

While there are obviously opportunities for entrepreneurship to flourish in such nations (Roman Abramovich being merely the most high-profile example), innovative or high-level entrepreneurship is difficult due to the lack of infrastructure that can provide the level of finance or risk capital required; the lack of networks, co-operative behaviour and trust (identified above as an important feature of advanced entrepreneurial regions); and the lack of infrastructure to support the small-firm entrepreneur. In some nations, a tradition of co-operative ownership has led to problems with the establishment of individual entrepreneurship.[25]

Given the newness of 'economies in transition', there is still a limited literature on the characteristics of their culture and the way this affects entrepreneurial behaviour in such nations. However, Roberts and Tholen give some insights into differences within these nations.[26] For example, their research showed considerable differences in Russia compared with other former Soviet bloc nations, with business development in Russia being more ad hoc and unplanned. Common characteristics across eastern European nations included:

- Unstable political regimes and hence the need for businesses to grow quickly
- A lack of tradition of business ownership and comparatively few family firms
- The absence of support services

Differences were likely to be:

- The source of new entrepreneurs (in Russia new entrepreneurs were former workers, whereas in other eastern European nations they were more likely to come from management levels)
- Higher growth ambitions in eastern Europe compared to Russia

- Fewer women entrepreneurs in Russia (in other nations women entrepreneurs accounted for around 30 per cent of new business ownership)

- Attitudes could vary to 'doing business' (entrepreneurs in Russia were likely to seek the 'big deal', whereas in other nations, such as Poland, a more realistic incremental development was adopted by entrepreneurs)

The transition economies of eastern Europe and Russia can be seen as containing a wide spectrum of different stages of progression to higher levels of entrepreneurship. Undoubtedly, much of it is low level, characterized by Casson[11] as Kirznerian, with some areas struggling to shake off attitudes that restrict creativity and innovative behaviour. In a comment that is probably representative of many such transition economies of eastern Europe, one native writer on Slovenia comments perceptively that,[27]

> Traditionally, Slovenians have not been classified as exhibiting entrepreneurial traits. The collectivist culture, dependency upon the state, historical subordination by external powers and strong egalitarian values relative to the even distribution of social and material gains have combined with a conservative formal education system that rewarded obedience and diligence, and suppressed innovation and creativity.
>
> (p. 108)

A paper on entrepreneurship in Bulgaria[28] commented that the environment for entrepreneurial activity was 'hostile' and that entrepreneurial responses included the characteristics of 'short term orientation, informal networking, opportunism and surplus extraction' (p. 163).

The accession of some central and eastern European countries to the EU on 1 May 2004 illustrated that some transition economies had developed sufficient features to be acceptable new members of the EU; these included Poland, Hungary, the Czech Republic, Slovakia, the Baltic states (such as Latvia, Estonia and Lithuania) and Slovenia (other states acceding were Cyprus and Malta). Yet others, notably Turkey and the Balkan states (such as Croatia, Montenegro and Bosnia-Hercegovina), have yet to satisfy conditions for EU entry, although some preparatory negotiations have been taking place with some states such as Croatia and Turkey.[29]

Western European nations have been involved in assisting the development of infrastructures in transition economies in eastern Europe. However, as one writer comments,[30]

> It may well be that in the longer term, borrowing ideas which lead to a change in values and attitudes towards enterprise and small business and which change norms of behaviour, is a critical task in ensuring that a culture sympathetic to small business is created.
>
> (p. 26)

There can be considerable barriers to entrepreneurial and new-firm development in the 'transition economies'. For example, adjustments have to be made by employees used to working for non-profit organizations to new cultures and working practices in small, privately owned firms. During periods of transition, recruitment of sufficiently motivated staff has been an issue.[31]

Smallbone et al., in a review paper, have summarized the key barriers to small and medium-sized firm development in countries in different stages of transition.[32] Those countries still at an early stage included Ukraine and Belarus, and are characterized by a number of barriers to the development of higher levels of entrepreneurial activity. The main barriers are identified in the box entitled 'Economies in transition 1: early-stage barriers'.

ECONOMIES IN TRANSITION 1: EARLY-STAGE BARRIERS

- High levels of bureaucratic regulation.
- Inadequate legal frameworks.
- Inadequate financial institutions.
- High inflation.
- Slow acceptance of private enterprise by government.
- The existence of relatively high levels of corruption.

By contrast, those countries at a later stage of transition, such as Poland, are characterized by the features given in the box entitled 'Economies in transition 2: later-stage features'.

ECONOMIES IN TRANSITION 2: LATER-STAGE FEATURES

- Essential legislative framework in place.
- Financial infrastructure adjusting to needs of private sector.
- Limited supply of investment finance.
- Developing business support infrastructure, but still not comprehensive.
- Increasing competition from other indigenous entrepreneurs and small firms.

Lynn has also indicated that opportunities for entrepreneurial small-firm diversification vary across different economies in transition, providing greater entrepreneurial risk in those at earlier stages of transition.[33]

To explain different levels of entrepreneurial activity, there is a need to recognize the institutional environment within which entrepreneurship operates. In transition economies the level of entrepreneurial activity reflects the interplay between the individual and the state; market reforms will produce a more conducive environment over time. For example, Smallbone and Welter contrast the level of entrepreneurship between two former socialist states, Belarus and Estonia, to illustrate the different influences of the institutional environment and the progress of market reform.[34] They argue that the need to introduce market and institutional reform in countries seeking accession to the EU, such as Estonia, has been the impetus to the creation of conditions that allow entrepreneurship to develop. By contrast, in a country such as Belarus, there are still institutional and legal obstacles that provide barriers to entrepreneurial activity developing on any significant scale. However, entrepreneurial activity may still develop despite the nature of such an environment. For example, Smallbone and Welter comment:

> Evidence from empirical surveys in former Soviet republics, such as Russia, Belarus and Ukraine, suggest that many enterprises have set up, survive and sometimes even grow *despite* government, because of the entrepreneurship of individuals [their emphasis].
>
> (p. 5)

The following 'Entrepreneurship in Action' box illustrates some of the difficulties in entrepreneurship in one of the former Socialist economies.

ENTREPRENEURSHIP IN ACTION

Former socialist nation – Belarus
Reproduced from Smallbone and Welter[34] with permission of the authors

As is evident from our empirical evidence, entrepreneurs in Belarussian conditions often cope with an inadequate institutional framework through 'evasion' strategies, which allow private entrepreneurship to survive, despite the hostility of the external environment. 'Typical' evasion strategies include combining legal and informal production; setting up a 'fictitious' enterprise; and cash payments to employees, which are undeclared to the tax authorities. A further example is diversification into unrelated activities. This can be both seen as a necessary coping strategy in an environment where banks typically do not serve new and small firms, but also as an attractive development path for successful entrepreneurs, who are keen to avoid being publicly noticed as being too successful because of the unwarranted attention this can attract from officials and representatives of the KGB.

Unrelated diversification as a coping strategy made necessary by a hostile environment can be illustrated with reference to a small firm which started its operations in 1991 in Minsk. Although seeking to focus on its core business (embroidery), the firm has engaged in simple, but unrelated, trading activity in order to generate cash for investment in the core business initially and to attempt to deal with a cash-flow crisis several years later. Embroidery was viewed as the core-business activity from the outset, although only by initially trading in detergents was the enterprise able to accumulate capital that was subsequently invested (in 1993–94) in developing hand-made embroidery products. This included the development of a design capability for products and patterns. However, following political changes in Belarus in the period 1995–97, the number of foreign tourists declined dramatically and the demand for embroidered goods largely dried up. An attempt was made to enter foreign markets directly at this time, although this was thwarted by a lack of partners who understood the structure of foreign markets, as well as by difficulties resulting from foreign exchange controls. In 1998, the firm became involved in wholesale trade for certain types of forage and vitamin additives in order to ensure the survival of the embroidery production line.

Source: Smallbone, D. and Welter, F. (2007) 'Entrepreneurship and Government Policy in Post Socialist Economies', paper presented to the 30th ISBE National Conference, Glasgow, November.

As illustrated above, transition economies are at very different individual stages of development, characterized by different levels of entrepreneurship. They face unique problems in transforming their society and cultures from former state dependency to ones where individual risk-taking is accepted and supported.

The diversity of development, however, is such that to treat such economies collectively is probably mistaken. Each nation, and indeed each region, will evolve its own entrepreneurial characteristics and activity. It would also be mistaken to prescribe solutions from the West. Exporting support frameworks and practices may not be appropriate in different environments, even though lessons may be learned from practice elsewhere.[35] Lessons from emergent nations suggest that unique developments and infrastructures are required to overcome some of the barriers to entrepreneurial development. Some of these lessons are examined in the next section.

How important small-firm entrepreneurs are in such transition economies has been the subject of some disagreement by writers. For example, one writer at least has claimed that small firms are still unimportant in such economies.[36] Others have claimed, in the case of Poland, that small-firm entrepreneurs have become the engine of the Polish economy.[37] Such diametrically opposed opinions will take some time to reconcile as the transition economies continue to evolve and further evidence of the different levels of entrepreneurial activity emerges.

EMERGING ECONOMIES

In contrast to some transition economies, emerging economies contain examples of nations for which the entrepreneur and the small firm have always played a role in their economic development. In India the small-firm sector has been a prominent part of the economy for the past 50 years.[38] Other emerging nations, of course, provide examples where entrepreneurial behaviour has been far longer in developing. For example, Kenya is still considered to have low levels of entrepreneurial activity.[39] Recent GEM reports put the emergent economies of Brazil, Mexico and Korea in their high band of entrepreneurial activity, India in their middle band, whereas some of the advanced industrial economies are in their low band.[12] The analysis given by the GEM reports also makes a distinction between 'opportunity' and 'necessity' entrepreneurship, claiming that opportunity entrepreneurship is characteristic of advanced nations and necessity entrepreneurship of emergent nations.[10] However, other writers have suggested that the distinction between opportunity and necessity entrepreneurship is too simplistic to be used to describe different entrepreneurial activities across different nations.[40]

NECESSITY ENTREPRENEURSHIP AND EMERGING ECONOMIES

It is outside the scope of this text to comment to any meaningful extent on the diversity and characteristics of entrepreneurship in developing economies. However, in this section, we do consider the validity that the main forms of entrepreneurial activity will be associated with 'necessity entrepreneurship' as defined in the annual GEM reports (http://www.gemconsortium.org). As defined in their 2001 *Executive Report*,[12] necessity entrepreneurship is described as where the participant has 'no better choices for work' (p. 8) and that 'such actions presented the best options available for employment, but not necessarily the preferred option'. Rosa et al., in a study of entrepreneurs in Uganda and Sri Lanka,[41] found that opportunistic entrepreneurship flourished once resources were acquired and they said that 'The results question recent attempts to classify countries on the basis of distinctive forms of entrepreneurship based on necessity and opportunity'. Other studies have demonstrated that entrepreneurs in developing nations are innovative and characterized by diversity. For example, Irwin, on the work of support agencies in contrasting African nations, refers to 'Africa's entrepreneurial heterogeneity'.[42]

In addition, far from being limited to models of entrepreneurship, based on incentives of necessity, developing countries have demonstrated and fostered innovative models of entrepreneurship, especially in rural environments and rural entrepreneurship. In some cases these have served to form the basis for models adopted by western countries. The best example, that of micro-finance and the founding of the Grameen Bank, is illustrated in the 'Entrepreneurship in Action' box below.

ENTREPRENEURSHIP IN ACTION

Muhammad Yunus and the Grameen Bank

Muhammad Yunus was awarded the Nobel Peace Prize for 2006 for his work in establishing the micro-credit system and as founder of the Grameen Bank. He established a system of micro-credit in rural Bangladesh, realizing that rural women, lacking collateral, could not raise funding through normal banking credit lines. Muhammad Yunus realized that western forms of credit provision were inappropriate for the vast majority of rural women in a developing nation such as Bangladesh. Particularly he wanted to provide a way that rural women, often in situations of desperate poverty, could achieve independence and in 1983 he established a system of micro-credit based on mutual trust. He introduced very small amounts of credit – micro-credit loans – which were necessary to enable a transformation of the income of rural women through self-employment. The micro-credit is used to start their own profit-making enterprises in agriculture, craft and services. It has been the means by which many very poor women have been able to transform their lives through self-employment and enterprise. Now recognized by many writers, the Grameen Bank has become a very successful model of social entrepreneurship.[43] Muhammad Yunus himself is recognized as one of the world's leading social entrepreneurs.[44] Not only has the micro-credit system transformed lives in Bangladesh, it has become recognized as the starting point and basic model for the introduction of micro-finance schemes in some deprived areas of the UK, the Community Development Finance Institutions (CDFIs) which have been discussed in more detail in Chapter 7. The mutual trust that underpins the micro-credit system provides a powerful incentive for borrowers to repay and has also been the model for mutual credit schemes in the UK.

The principle that has enabled the remarkable success of the Grameen Bank is based on the assumption that if individual borrowers are given access to credit they will be able to engage in opportunities for enterprise. According to the Grameen Bank, women in Bangladesh, once given the opportunity, have proved to be astute entrepreneurs and as a result 'they have raised their status, lessened their dependency on their husbands and improved their homes and the nutritional standards of their children' (http://www.grameen.org).

The Grameen Bank has now expanded as an organization and has over 7 million borrowers, 97 per cent of whom are women. The Grameen Bank itself operates in over 80,000 villages in Bangladesh (http://www.grameen.org). The experience of the Grameen Bank demonstrates how enterprise and innovation can flourish in developing countries once some initial resources are provided.

ENTREPRENEURSHIP IN DEVELOPING NATIONS AND DISASTER RECOVERY

We can identify the increased importance of entrepreneurship in disaster recovery programmes. Many of the developing nations are located in areas of the world that suffer from natural disasters such as earthquakes, volcanic eruptions and others such as the devastating tsunami that hit many nations on 26 December 2004. In such circumstances, the self-sufficient economy of such areas is devastated through the loss of agricultural land on which the economy is based. Despite such devastation, communities have successfully rebuilt once initial resources were provided to enable self-employment and small scale enterprises to flourish. For example, Nugroho and Susilawati describe one such scheme in Central Java,[45] a region devastated by a major earthquake in May 2006; they demonstrate that enterprise development has successfully begun to rebuild communities.

There are obviously vast differences that exist in cultures and concomitant entrepreneurial levels of activity in different emergent nations. We have not attempted to discuss such diversity here. However, we have noted examples of successful entrepreneurial behaviour, how certain groups have overcome barriers to entrepreneurial development and the factors associated with such success. Such examples may have wider applications and lessons for advanced and transition economies.

In India a high need for co-operation to overcome substantial limitations on resources has been observed and seems to be characteristic of entrepreneurial behaviour.[46] High levels of trust and co-operative behaviour have provided the basis for micro-credit unions,[47] examples of micro-business finance, which have provided the basis for models of investment trusts and alternative sources of micro-finance in cities in advanced nations.[48] They have also been the forerunners of micro-credit schemes established by policymakers in transition economies.[48] Such attributes of entrepreneurial behaviour were discussed in an earlier section; India provides examples of flourishing networks and clusters.[49]

Other emergent nations often have complex factors that may have arisen from their history and inheritance as former colonial states, which affect cultural attitudes to entrepreneurship. For example, South Africa, according to one writer,[51] 'with its many cultures and dynamic and transforming socio-political environment, represents a particularly problematic case study' (p. 27). The legacy of apartheid in South Africa has caused some black entrepreneurs to respond entrepreneurially to adversity, whereas enterprise in other members of the black population has been stifled.[51]

The diversity of emergent economies is such that it is difficult to draw coherent patterns on factors that affect the level of entrepreneurship. For example, factors that may be important and conducive to entrepreneurial behaviour in one culture, such as co-operative behaviour and networks in India, may be restrictive in others. For instance, a study of small-firm entrepreneurs in Turkey found that networks were dependent on traditional values, sectarian affiliations and the family environment.[52] The researcher claimed that such networks enforced their own inertia, preventing innovation in small firms in Turkey.

This complexity of factors reveals the infinite variety of entrepreneurial behaviour in emergent nations, variety to which we can only give the briefest of indications. In many cases we are only just beginning to learn about and appreciate this diversity. What is apparent is that we can't apply 'western' solutions to such diversity.

The following 'Entrepreneurship in Action' case illustrates how one entrepreneur, Ho Kwon Ping, from a developing nation, has overcome adversity to build a very successful business in the tourist sector.

ENTREPRENEURSHIP IN ACTION

Triumph Over Adversity: Ho Kwon Ping and Banyan Tree

Ho Kwon Ping is the founder of Banyan Tree, a worldwide chain of luxury resorts now based in Singapore in South-East Asia.

His story is one of remarkable resilience and triumph against adversity. When in the USA and attending Stanford University, he protested against the Vietnam war. Later, while working as a journalist, Mr Ho ended up in jail in Singapore as a result of controversial articles he'd written for the *Far East Economic Review*. He describes his two months in prison as a 'sobering experience'; yet now he has been able to draw upon that experience to have a worldwide chain of luxury, boutique hotels.

Ho Kown Ping commented to the BBC:

> You realise in solitary confinement who you are and who you are not. I realised I was not a Nelson Mandela. I was not ever going to be. The causes for which I might have been imprisoned were not the causes that ... I really could identify with.

Nevertheless, Mr Ho feels that he and many of his generation have not completely lost touch with the spirit of those times.

> Many of those people who were young, idealistic and got into jail or got kicked out of universities, and are successful people today, haven't forgotten their ideals. They've just found different ways to express them.

Ho Kwon Ping says his experience changed his life. While in jail, he was prompted to propose to his wife. 'All the time when I was inside prison, I could see my parents ... but I couldn't see the woman who is now my wife.'

What did she make of his proposal? 'That's my idea of romance ... I think it was romantic. She probably doesn't think so'.

After his release Mr Ho continued to work as a journalist, settling on one of Hong Kong's offshore islands with his wife. They lived in a small fishing village. But despite the fact that they were 'pretty impoverished', he says it was an 'idyllic' period of time. Indeed his company is named after Banyan Tree Bay where they lived for three years.

> 'We wanted to choose a name that evoked, at least to us, the values which we think Banyan Tree stood for and that was ... romance and intimacy,' he explains. He points out that this is not limited to 'hot blooded young couples'.
>
> 'It can be the romance of travel, the romance of being in a beautiful fishing village ... and that is essentially the essence of Banyan Tree ... captured, I think, in the origins of the name itself.'

Ho Kwon Ping's foray into the business world came several years later when he decided to join the family business after his father suffered a stroke. He says he quickly decided that it needed a completely new direction.

> The primary thing that we were doing, which I felt was not viable and which today remains to me in many ways the curse of Asian businesses, was contract manufacturing ... just a technical term for being a sub-contractor.
>
> Adversity is not a bad thing. That's how Banyan Tree was born – because we had no beach front. You never owned the market, you never owned the brand ... the margins are squeezed all the time. I decided we had to have a brand and we had to be global in nature ... With that intent, I needed to find some business other than what we were doing,

The opportunity came when a hotel they built in Phuket in Thailand was proving difficult to let because of its lack of a beach front.

Ho Kwon Ping was inspired to build villas rather than rooms, each with its own swimming pool. Since then the formula has been the basis of its success.

CURRENT FACTS ON BANYAN TREE

- Turnover (2009) : Singapore $313.3 million
- HQ location: Singapore

- Number of employees: 15,000 worldwide
- Year founded: 1994
- Ownership: listed on Singapore stock exchange

DISCUSSION QUESTIONS

1 How have the critical events in the previous experience of Ho Kwon Ping affected his current approach to business and being an international entrepreneur?

2 What factors have contributed to the worldwide success of the model chosen for Banyan Tree luxury hotels?

3 How does the case illustrate the importance of global trends and globalisation for entrepreneurial activity?

Source: http://www.bbc.co.uk/news/11910973

ENTREPRENEURSHIP IN CHINA: A SPECIAL CASE

Really an economy in transition rather than an emergent economy, China has seen a number of phases of SME development as the Chinese State Government has relaxed regulatory controls and introduced regulatory reforms to encourage SMEs' development and individual entrepreneurial activity. Within the last 30 years there are three phases that have been recognized:[53] from 1978 to 1992 when there was a period of encouragement for self-employment and the development of township and village enterprises (TVEs). These were collective-based enterprises such as rural co-operatives, which have become an important distinctive feature of entrepreneurial activity in China.[54] A second phase from 1992 to 2002 saw a reduction in state ownership to allow opportunities for small firms development and individual entrepreneurial activity and a third period of promotional policies for SMEs and encouragement of innovation post 2002.

There are a number of distinctive features of Chinese entrepreneurial activity which are worth highlighting, which are discussed in more detail below.

THE ROLE OF SOCIAL CAPITAL AND CHINESE ENTREPRENEURSHIP

In Chapter 1, we discussed the role of social capital in the process of entrepreneurship. It may have negative (constraining) as well as positive (enabling) roles, but it involves the development of personal networks that allow the entrepreneur to acquire resources or access markets. In China the acquisition of social capital through a network of personal contacts has a much more important and key role in entrepreneurial development. Chinese culture places great importance on personal networked relationships; not only are they more important than in western societies, they also carry more significance in the form of cultural legitimacy, a feature in Chinese society known as *guanxi* (gwanshee), and these personalized networks carry social capital that has conditioned the nature of Chinese entrepreneurial activity.[55] It is only through the development of personal networks that an individual entrepreneur can 'do business' and in the absence of regulation and laws it permits business owners to acquire resources and develop their businesses. The significance of *guanxi* is further enhanced by limited formal sources of finance that exist in emerging nations. For example, the banks have a much more limited role in financing entrepreneurial business development with Chinese entrepreneurs dependent upon personal resources and personal contacts for acquiring financial capital.[56]

Township and village enterprises

Township and village enterprises (TVEs) are a further distinctive feature of Chinese entrepreneurial activity.[54] They are an important feature of the large rural areas of China and have developed following government encouragement, introducing greater opportunities for rural co-operatives, but also for manufacturing through industrial collectives in the townships. Chen et al. have commented that: 'TVEs in particular can be seen as important contributors to the re-emergence of contemporary Chinese entrepreneurship'[54] (p. 249). This is a form of quasi-state entrepreneurial activity that has been described as 'local state entrepreneurship' or mini-state enterprises. In this context, there is no real equivalent of this model in western economies, although they also exist in other east Asian countries such as Indonesia. In the Chinese model, local government officials were given decentralized powers which allowed the development of localised entrepreneurship. However, the owners of the enterprises are independent, although they often pay a fee, in return for the concession, to the local government body. For this reason they are sometimes referred to as 'red hat' enterprises.[56]

Regional disparities

As with any nation, China has large regional disparities in entrepreneurial activity.[57] However, not only are they much more marked than other nations, they also characterized by large differences in the main forms of entrepreneurial activity. Provinces where individual entrepreneurial activity is the greatest are those centred on the large urban centres such as Shanghai. Thus, it is more appropriate to identify regional variation in the characteristics of entrepreneurship in China, rather than attempt to refer to any model of Chinese entrepreneurship.

CONCLUSIONS

In this chapter we have argued that individual entrepreneurs cannot isolate themselves from the globalization of the economy. Every business trades in a global economy, which effectively means adopting strategies that enable the entrepreneur to optimize opportunities. These strategies will depend on resources available, key staff, type of product and the nature of technology. It may mean adopting joint venture strategies; it may mean adopting quality benchmarking techniques as part of a network of firms in a supply chain; it may mean forming networks to share resources, information and gain externalities. Entrepreneurs must think globally, even if they operate only in local markets.

Entrepreneurs who do 'internationalize' by operating in more than one country, must be aware of different entrepreneurial cultures in different nations. We have examined how, in advanced economies, different regions can have very different cultures yet still be successful. We have suggested that advanced networks may hold one key to successful entrepreneurial development in advanced economies. In transition economies the legacy of communism and state control has affected entrepreneurial development in different ways in different nations. Some have been more successful at overcoming this legacy; in others, lack of a recent history of business ownership has been more of a hindrance. Similarly, in emergent nations entrepreneurs have reacted in different ways to historical legacies, whether this is apartheid in South Africa or colonialism in the Indian subcontinent.

Casson[11] has suggested that it is possible to identify characteristics in the cultures of different nations that will determine whether they have high or low levels of entrepreneurship. The GEM project has also attempted to identify factors affecting high- or low-level entrepreneurial activity. However, we have also seen that the infinite variety of international entrepreneurship defies classification and it can be claimed that inconsistent factors affect the level and success of entrepreneurial activity (such as networks). All entrepreneurs need to be aware of the global economy, but all entrepreneurs who wish to operate internationally must be aware of the infinite variety of cultures that still exists in the world economy.

REVIEW QUESTIONS

1　What are the main forces of increased globalization?
2　Why should no entrepreneur ignore these forces of globalization?
3　What methods and approaches might enable a firm to become international in operation? Why might international entrepreneurial strategies vary?
4　Distinguish between high-level and low-level entrepreneurial activity. Give examples of countries that demonstrate such different levels of entrepreneurial activity.
5　What are the main components of an economy that might affect the level of entrepreneurial activity according to the Global Entrepreneurship Monitor (GEM) approach?
6　Give examples of nations that may be considered to be 'economies of transition' for the level of entrepreneurial activity.
7　Why are there likely to be large differences in the levels of entrepreneurial activity in such nations?
8　What features are likely to mark out the more advanced economies that are in this category?
9　Why should levels of networking, trust and co-operative behaviour affect the level of entrepreneurial activity in different economies whether advanced, transition or emergent?
10　Give examples of nations that may be considered to be 'emergent economies' for the level of entrepreneurial activity.
11　Why are there likely to be large differences in the levels of entrepreneurial activity in such nations?
12　Using factors discussed in this chapter, why might they encourage high levels of entrepreneurial activity in such nations?

SUGGESTED ASSIGNMENTS

1 Students are required to work in a small group with an identified small-firm entrepreneur in their locality. They are required to assess how the firm could be affected by global trends and globalisation. A group report should cover the following points:

- Introduction with case material on the firm

- Analysis of strengths and weaknesses

- Analysis of opportunities and threats within the global economy

- Research with potential markets (the Department for Business, Innovation and Skills in the UK provides publications on overseas markets)

- Conclusions

2 Students are divided into small groups and each group is given a country to research, classified as a transition economy. Their tasks are to:

- Research information on the country, from sources such as the Department of Business, Innovation and Skills' exporting publications.

- If relevant, provide information from the GEM report on the level of entrepreneurial activity.

- Present findings for full class discussion with students discussing differences between transition economies.

3 You are a consultant to a local firm wishing to obtain advice on exporting to eastern Europe. Write a report detailing national and local assistance, indicating differences in the nature of local and national support provided in your region or local area.

REFERENCES

1 **Chell, E.** (2001) *Entrepreneurship: Globalisation, Innovation and Development*, Thomson, London.

2 **Curran, J. and Blackburn, R.** (1993) *Local Economic Networks: The Death of the Local Economy*, Routledge, London.

3 **Levinthal, D**. (1998) 'The slow pace of technological change', *Industrial and Corporate Change*, vol. 7, no. 2, pp. 217–47.

4 **Ghauri, P.** (2000) 'Internationalisation of the firm', in T. Monir (ed.), *International Business,* *Theories, Policies and Practices*, Prentice Hall, London.

5 **Bell, J.** (1995) 'The internationalisation of small computer software firms: a further challenge to stage theories', *European Journal of Marketing*, vol. 29, no. 8, pp. 60–75.

6 **Jolly, V.K., Alahuta, M. and Jeannet, J.P.** (1992) 'Challenging the incumbents: how high technology start-ups compete globally', *Journal of Strategic Change*, vol. 1, no. 1, pp. 71–82.

7 **Fletcher, M.** (2006) 'Learning processes of internationalising SMEs', paper presented at the 29th ISBE National Conference, Cardiff, November.

8 **International Monetary Fund** (2010) *World Economic Outlook October 2010 Recovery, Risk and Rebalancing*, IMF, Washington, DC.

9 **Global Entrepreneurship Monitor** (GEM) (1999) *Executive Report*, GEM Project, Babson College/London Business School, Boston, MA.

10 **Global Entrepreneurship Monitor** (GEM) (2007) *Executive Report*, GEM Research

Consortium, Babson College/London Business School, Boston, MA.

11 **Casson, M.** (1990) *Enterprise and Competitiveness*, Clarendon Press, Oxford.

12 **Global Entrepreneurship Monitor** (GEM) (2001) *Executive Report,* Babson College/London Business School, Boston, MA.

13 **Global Entrepreneurship Monitor** (GEM) (2011) *2010 Global Report*, GEM Project, Babson College/Universidad del Desarrollo, Boston, MA.

14 **Global Entrepreneurship Monitor** (GEM) (2009) *Executive Report,* Babson College/London Business School, Boston, MA.

15 **Scottish Enterprise** (1993) *The Business Birth Rate Enquiry*, Scottish Enterprise, Glasgow.

16 **Kitching, J. and Blackburn, R.** (1999) 'Management training and networking in SMEs in three European regions: implications for business support', *Government and Policy*, vol. 17, no. 5, pp. 621–36.

17 **Scottish Enterprise** (1993) *The Business Birth Rate Strategy*, Scottish Enterprise, Glasgow.

18 **Scottish Enterprise** (1998) *The Clusters Approach*, Scottish Enterprise, Glasgow.

19 **Edquist, C., Eriksson, M.-L. and Sjögren, H.** (2000) 'Collaboration in product innovation in the East Gothia regional system of innovation', *Enterprise and Innovation Management Studies*, vol. 1, no. 1, pp. 37–56.

20 **Thompson, G.** (1993) 'Network coordination', in R. Maidment and G. Thompson (eds), *Managing the United Kingdom*, Sage, London.

21 **Macaulay, S.** (1963) 'Non-contractual relations in business: a preliminary study', *American Sociological Review*, vol. 45, pp. 55–69.

22 **Sako, M.** (1992) *Prices, Quality and Trust: Inter-firm Relations in Britain and Japan*, Cambridge University Press, Cambridge.

23 **Burchell, B. and Wilkinson, F.** (1997) 'Trust, business relationships and the contract environment', *Cambridge Journal of Economics*, vol. 21, no. 2, pp. 217–37.

24 **Axelrod, R.** (1981) 'The emergence of cooperation among egoists', *American Review of Political Science*, vol. 75, pp. 306–18.

25 **Carlisle, B. and Gotlieb, A.** (1995) 'Problems, training and consultancy needs in SMEs in Russia – an exploratory study', paper presented to the 18th ISBA National Small Firms Policy and Research Conference, Paisley, November.

26 **Roberts, K. and Tholen, J.** (1997) 'Young entrepreneurs in the new market economies', paper presented to a Conference on Enterprise in the Transition Economies, Wolverhampton, September.

27 **Glas, M.** (1998) 'Entrepreneurship in Slovenia', in A. Morrison (ed.), *Entrepreneurship: An International Perspective*, Butterworth-Heinemann, Woburn, MA, pp. 108–24.

28 **Manolova, T.S. and Yan, A.** (2002) 'Institutional constraints and entrepreneurial responses in a transforming economy: the case of Bulgaria', *International Small Business Journal*, vol. 20, no. 2, pp. 163–84.

29 **Samardzija, V. and Cuculic, J.** (2003) 'Regulatory impact assessment: importance for the process of Croatia's integration into the European Union', paper presented at the 4th International Conference on the Enterprise in Transition, University of Split, Hvar, Croatia.

30 **Batstone, S.** (1998) 'SME policy in Slovakia: the role of bi-lateral and multi-lateral aid', paper presented to a Conference on Enterprise in the Transition Economies, Wolverhampton, September.

31 **A&O Research** (1999) *Report on Entrepreneurial Activity in Görlitz: Regional Partnerships as a Means of Safeguarding Employment*, A&O Research, Berlin.

32 **Smallbone, D., Welter, F., Voytovichc, A. and Egorovd, I.** (2010) 'Government and entrepreneurship in transition economies: the case of small firms in business services in Ukraine', *The Service Industries Journal*, vol. 30, no. 5, pp 655–70.

33 **Lynn, M.** (1998) 'Patterns of micro-enterprise diversification in transitional Eurasian economies', *International Small Business Journal*, vol. 16, no. 2, pp. 34–49.

34 **Smallbone, D. and Welter, F.** (2007) 'Entrepreneurship and government policy in post socialist economies', paper presented to the 30th ISBE National Conference, Glasgow, November.

35 **Danson, M., Helinska-Hughes, E. and Whittam, G.** (2001) 'SMEs and regeneration: a comparison between Scotland and Poland', paper presented to the Regional Studies Association Conference, Gdansk, Poland.

36 **Scase, R.** (1998) 'The role of small businesses in the economic transformation in Eastern Europe', *International Small Business Journal*, vol. 16, no. 1, pp. 13–21.

37 **Erutku, C. and Vallée, L.** (1997) 'Business start-ups in today's Poland: who and how?', *Entrepreneurship and Regional Development*, vol. 9, no. 2, pp. 113–26.

38 **Das, K.** (1998) 'Collective dynamism and firm strategy: a study of an Indian industrial cluster', *Entrepreneurship and Regional*

Development, vol. 10, no. 1, pp. 33–50.

39 **Dondo, A. and Ngumo, M.** (1998) 'Entrepreneurship in Kenya', in A. Morrison (ed.), *Entrepreneurship: An International Perspective*, Butterworth-Heinemann, Woburn, MA, pp. 27–41.

40 **Smallbone, D. and Welter, F.** (2003) 'Entrepreneurship in transition economies: necessity or opportunity driven', paper presented at the Babson Entrepreneurship Research Conference, Babson College, Boston, MA.

41 **Rosa, P., Kodithuwakku, S. and Balunywa, W.** (2006) 'Reassessing necessity entrepreneurship in developing countries', paper presented at the 29th ISBE National Conference, Cardiff, November.

42 **Irwin, D.** (2007) 'Learning from business support in Africa', paper presented to the 30th ISBE National Conference, Glasgow, November.

43 **Mair, J. and Schoen, O.** (2007) 'Successful social entrepreneurial business models in the context of developing economies: an explorative study', *International Journal of Emerging Markets*, vol. 2, no. 1, pp. 54–68.

44 **Cozzi J.** (2007) 'The greatest entrepreneurs of all time', *Business Week*, 27 June.

45 **Nugroho, A. and Susilawati, H.** (2007) 'Building a sustainable livelihood of the earthquake victims in Indonesia', paper presented to the 30th ISBE National Conference, Glasgow, November.

46 **Schmitz, H.** (1990) 'Small firms and flexible specialisation in developing countries', *Labour and Society*, vol. 15, pp. 257–85.

47 **Kashyap, S.P.** (1988) 'Growth of small-scale enterprises in India: its nature and content', *World Development*, vol. 16, pp. 667–81.

48 **Nicholson, B.** (1998) 'Aston Reinvestment Trust', paper presented to the ESRC Seminar Series, The Finance of Small Firms, University of Middlesex, January.

49 **Cicic, M. and Sunje, A.** (2003) 'Micro-credit programmes in Bosnia-Herzegovina', paper presented at the 4th International Conference on the Enterprise in Transition, University of Split, Hvar, Croatia.

50 **Das, K.** (1996) 'Flexibility together: surviving and growing in a garment cluster, Ahmedabad, India', *Journal of Entrepreneurship*, vol. 5, pp. 153–77.

51 **Allie, F. and Human, L.** (1998) 'Entrepreneurship in South Africa', in A. Morrison (ed.), *Entrepreneurship: An International Perspective*, Butterworth-Heinemann, Woburn, MA, pp. 27–41.

52 **Özcan, G.B.** (1995) 'Small business networks and local ties in Turkey', *Entrepreneurship and Regional Development*, vol. 7, no. 3, pp. 265–82.

53 **Chen, J.** (2006) 'Development of Chinese small and medium-sized enterprises', *Journal of Small Enterprise and Development*, vol. 13, no. 2, pp. 140–47.

54 **Chen, G., Li, J. and Matlay, H.** (2006) 'Who are the Chinese private entrepreneurs?', *Journal of Small Enterprise and Development*, vol. 13, no. 2, pp. 148–60.

55 **Carlisle, E. and Flynn, D.** (2005) 'Small business survival in China: guanxi, legitimacy and social capital', *Journal of Development Entrepreneurship*, vol. 10, no. 1, pp. 79–96.

56 **Xiao, L.** (2007) 'Financing high-tech SMEs in China', unpublished PhD dissertation, Middlesex University, London.

57 **Yang, K. and Xu, Y.** (2006) 'Regional differences in the development of Chinese SMEs', *Journal of Small Enterprise and Development*, vol. 13, no. 2, pp. 174–84.

RECOMMENDED READING

Global Entrepreneurship Monitor (GEM) (2011) *2010, Global Report,* GEM Project, Babson College/ Universidad del Desarrollo, Boston, MA.

International Monetary Fund (2010) *World Economic Outlook October 2010 Recovery, Risk and Rebalancing*, IMF, Washington, DC.

World Bank (2010) *Doing Business 2011: Making a Difference for Entrepreneurs*, International Bank for Reconstruction and Development, Washington, DC.

PART FOUR
MAKING IT HAPPEN

In this section we continue the theme of strategic decision-making, but focus on the challenges of the exploitation of entrepreneurial opportunities, of generating ideas, recognising opportunities and the important issues in the start-up and planning process that need to be considered. This part draws upon concepts and material from all the previous chapters in order to bring together the different elements that are required to achieve the action of entrepreneurship: creating and starting a business.

In Chapter 12 we examine the strategic issues in business start-up and break down the start-up process into different phases. Having looked previously, in Part 3, at strategies to acquire resources, we examine the requirements to put plans into action. We look at what is required to create the action of entrepreneurship, drawing on material from previous sections. Chapter 12 examines issues in different phases of the start-up process, pitfalls that exist and how decisions can be made. Concepts introduced in this chapter are placed in the context of 'Entrepreneurship in Action' case examples.

In Chapter 13 we examine the planning process in detail as the preparation for business start-up. As in Chapter 12 this is broken down into separate steps, outlining how the business planning process could be undertaken, what issues to consider and outlining the requirements of business planning and financial forecasting. Examples are provided of pro-formas, requirements for sections of business plans and sources of detailed guidance and information.

E-WAITER

by Arnis Sauka and Aivars Timofejevs, Stockholm School of Economics, Riga (Latvia)

Rickie Moore, Em Lyon Business School, France

INTRODUCTION

Maarika Ansip looked at the latest version of the business plan and wondered if she would ever get it right. After writing the first version, she had shown it to the entrepreneurial team that she was leading. Worryingly, they had questioned the viability of the business model and had highlighted numerous areas where the plan could be improved. She had rewritten the main body of the report, but had had no time yet to adjust the financial figures. These were a mess and she would have to redo them completely before going back to the team. But as she reread the business plan she realized that there were still many other faults to the plan itself. She would have to improve the whole document yet again. However, she only had twenty-four hours before she was scheduled to meet with the other members of the entrepreneurial team. What she urgently needed was someone who was an expert in writing business plans to help her.

MAARIKA AND THE BUSINESS IDEA

Maarika was a 25-year-old IT graduate of the Institute of Technology Tartu and throughout her years in school and in college she had never taken a single class in business or management. After completing her undergraduate degree she took employment with the ITH Group and worked as an IT specialist on client projects. While working on one such project, Maarika spotted the opportunity that is E-Waiter and discussed it with her boss.

E-Waiter is a user-friendly IT-based technical solution for restaurants, bars, pubs and other public places, to be used as a digital menu and interactive tool to order food and drinks from the restaurant and bar. There would be one device for each dining table and a computer data server is required to operate the device. The devices will be built and designed especially for restaurants to fit with their particular needs (for example, to fit with the decor or atmosphere). There will be choice of colours for the frame, and the restaurant can choose where it would like the device to be installed. For example, the device can be placed on the wall by the table, or built into the table of the restaurant, so that it can be removed when it is not being used. The device can also be offered in a hand-held portable format for tables that are located in the middle of a restaurant and where there is no possibility of attaching it to a wall.

After numerous discussions about the idea, Maarika's boss suggested that a spin-off business was the best way to pursue the opportunity. The concept was very different from ITH's core activities, and spinning it off would avoid unnecessary competition for resources and time with current products and services. He also suggested that because the expertise required to advance the business was quite diverse, it would be beneficial if they had partners. He proposed and approached two other companies with whom he had existing relationships. However, he was very clear that Maarika should be the lead entrepreneur of the project as it was her idea. Therefore, the entrepreneurial team would consist of Maarika and the CEOs from three companies:

- One Baltics – a company working in the tourism and hospitality fields
- Microdators – a company that produces 'Mazzy' touch screen monitors and computing hardware solutions
- ITH Group – a company that develops software solutions, web pages, web applications and accountancy systems

The business would be supported by experts from different fields such as design, finance and marketing, while a couple of local professors would act as consultants to the project. It had already been broadly agreed that each company would contribute €50,000 share capital to the business. But to carry through on the plan, they would need additional funding of €150,000 if the business was to have a good chance of being successful. Therefore the initial focus of the entrepreneurial team was to prepare a business plan that would convince investors that the concept was a good investment. However, because Maarika had no prior business management experience, she had no idea how to write a business plan or how to put together financial projections. She decided it was time to phone a friend who worked with an enterprise support agency for advice. She wanted him to read the current draft of the business plan (see Online Learning Centre) and then to tell her what changes she should make, what additional information was required, and to help her rework the financial projections so that they made sense. She also wanted him to advise her on how much equity she should offer to potential investors, what the expected return on investment might be, and what exit strategy she should offer them. She needed his advice urgently if she was to present a high-quality business plan to potential investors and to the other members of the entrepreneurial team 24 hours from now.

12 ISSUES IN BUSINESS START-UP

LEARNING OUTCOMES

At the end of this chapter you should be able to:

- Discuss the importance of different factors that affect the business creation process.
- Discuss the importance of factors that inhibit or block creativity and ideas formulation.
- Describe the importance of developing, modifying and refining ideas over time.
- Discuss the importance of processing information in opportunity recognition.
- Describe the opportunity recognition process in the context of examples from entrepreneurship in action case studies.
- Discuss the different paradigms involved with the start-up process in different types of new ventures.
- Describe successful post-entry development marketing strategies in competitive sectors.
- Discuss whether special issues apply to business start-up in rural areas.

INTRODUCTION

In this chapter, we focus on the process of new entry entrepreneurship by exploring in greater detail some of the issues in business start-up. It is worth bearing in mind that this start-up and development process can occur over a considerable period of time. Initial business ideas take time to formulate, research, raise funding for and find partners/investors and may be considerably refined before the launch of the business. Every business start-up is a unique event; the circumstances that contribute to success are intangible and may be different for each individual entrepreneur. Thus we need to be careful about recommending 'paths to success'; what may work for one entrepreneur may not work for another. However, we suggest later that intervention and support still have a role in the start-up process. The business start-up process can be broken down into a number of stages, as listed in the accompanying box.

STAGES IN THE START-UP PROCESS

- Formation of the idea.
- Opportunity recognition.
- Pre-start planning and preparation, including pilot testing.
- New entry into entrepreneurship.
- Launch and subsequent development.

Each of these stages is a process in its own right, as we will examine in more detail in this chapter, and each stage will have a number of factors that will impinge on its process. These may either encourage further development or have a negative influence, perhaps causing the individual nascent entrepreneur to terminate the process. These factors will include the nature of the local environment, culture, access to finance, local support networks, role models and enterprise support and encouragement. A representation and suggested paradigm of this process is illustrated in Figure 12.1. For the sake of simplicity the representation abstracts from reality. In practice a host of factors may affect each stage – for example, the psychology of the individual entrepreneur, mental processes and personal characteristics such as tenacity and perseverance in overcoming obstacles and barriers. These factors could affect each of the processes associated with each stage. Some of these factors will be brought out in the 'Entrepreneurship in Action' case studies that are included in this chapter (and in other

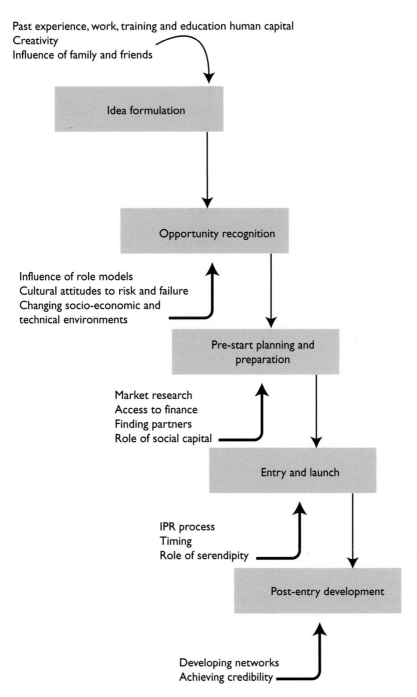

FIGURE 12.1

Business creation and start-up process: a suggested paradigm cases in other chapters of this book), but for this part of the chapter we discuss some of the more 'external' factors that can impinge upon the different processes and stages. Again, we do not attempt to capture all of these, but some of the most important are represented in Figure 12.1 and discussed below. It is also worth noting that:

- The nature of the process outlined in Figure 12.1 could apply to entrepreneurial teams rather than entrepreneurial individuals seeking to start a new business
- The nature of the process will be affected by feedback at different stages – for example, the nature of the business idea and the start-up approach will be modified over time as a result of feedback from different stages in the process

IDEA FORMULATION

The formation of business ideas will be affected by a nascent entrepreneur's past experience, training, education and skill development. This accumulation of knowledge, skills and experience is termed 'human capital', a concept used particularly in the context of labour markets by economists following the pioneering work of Gary Becker.[1] Formulation of business ideas may be influenced by work experience, by individual training and recognition that a particular product or process 'could be done better'. Recognizing that a process or product could be done in a superior way has been the spur behind many new businesses. For example, in the case study of Aquamotive (available from the students' online learning centre resources), the entrepreneurs in question developed an innovative new product after identifying a problem and realizing that they could provide a better solution. The majority of new business ventures are known to be in sectors or industries where the new business owners have had previous experience. For example, Cressy[2] has argued that human capital is an important determining factor in new business creation. The importance of human capital tends to be reinforced by external financial institutions, since research has shown that bank managers rate previous experience as an important factor in lending to new-venture entrepreneurs.[3]

For younger entrepreneurs, who will have limited human capital, it can be argued that education can have an important role in providing a conducive environment for idea formulation. It has been suggested that younger entrepreneurs (up to the age of 30) are underrepresented in entrepreneurship because of limited personal capital and limited access to finance.[4] The limited experience (or human capital) that potential entrepreneurs in this age range can draw upon will limit the scope of opportunities for developing ideas. Youth, however, can also be an advantage. Young entrepreneurs may be more willing to test different ideas and bring a different perspective to trading opportunities. For example, research undertaken by the author with ethnic minority entrepreneurs in Scotland has suggested that, in some cases, young second-generation entrepreneurs are more willing to take on the risks and strategies associated with innovation and business growth than first-generation entrepreneurs, partly because of the greater ambition of second-generation entrepreneurs when succeeding their first-generation parents.[5] Idea formulation here will be affected by educational experience and early training. It is arguable that education should provide scenarios that encourage creativity, lateral thinking and problem-solving. However, there can be a conflict in providing sufficient scope within a curriculum for the development of such transferable and 'core' skills. There are indications that greater importance is being placed on 'enterprise' abilities including problem-solving, group work and ideas generation, although previous schemes in the UK, such as the Enterprise Insight initiative,[6] which was designed to highlight the success of young entrepreneurs, have had rather limited appeal and success. Similarly, in Scotland, a comprehensive strategy, Determined to Succeed,[7] was introduced, aimed at introducing enterprise-related skills at all levels of primary and secondary education, but the success can be determined by the extent of local enthusiasm of teachers across schools and colleges, as much as by the content of such programmes, and initiatives can be rather variable in impact.[8] Other examples of attempts to widen the curriculum, such as Young Enterprise,[9] can also be variable in impact and unfortunately be 'add-ons' rather than developments that are embedded in the curriculum.

Education systems are important in the development of creativity and idea formulation. For example, Timmons[10] comments, 'The notion that creativity can be learned or enhanced holds important implications

ENTERPRISE EDUCATION INITIATIVES: SOME EXAMPLES

- *Young Enterprise*: a programme encouraging young people to form a trading company: http://www.youngenterprise.org.uk

- *Determined to Succeed*: a Scottish programme aimed at introducing enterprise in the curriculum to all primary and secondary school children: http://www.scotland.gov.uk/publications/2007/03/07101713/13

- *National Council for Graduate Entrepreneurship*: a programme to support graduate entrepreneurs in higher education institutes (HEIs): http://www.ncge.org.uk

- *Enterprise Centres UK*: a national network of enterprise educators: http://www.enterprise.ac.uk

- For a review see: Entrepreneurship Education and Training in Europe report: http://ec.europa.eu/enterprise/policies/sme/documents/education-training-entrepreneurship/

for entrepreneurs who need to be creative in their thinking' (p. 43). Thus, education is an important conditioning experience. Creative thinking can be enhanced or constrained by the education system and this will affect the way we view opportunities, not just in our formative years but later in life as well.

CREATIVITY

Figure 12.1 indicates that creativity will affect idea formulation. The process of creative thinking is now recognized as an important element in management. It has spawned a literature in its own right,[11] so we can only recognize and comment on its importance here. Such literature suggests that obtaining the right environment and the right team of individuals is important for creative thinking and hence idea formulation.[12] According to Clegg, creativity is the ability to connect previously unrelated things or ideas.[13] A creative individual will think laterally rather than vertically (defining a problem in one way), perceive many possible divergent options rather than focus on a unique convergence, use imagination rather than apply logic. The alternative to creative thinking is analytical and logical reasoning: these different ways of thinking are appropriate in different circumstances; however, creative thinking is a necessary, but not sufficient, condition for idea formulation. Providing sufficient conditions implies providing the appropriate circumstances and environment for creativity. There are known techniques that can be employed to improve creative thinking and hence idea formulation, such as 'brainstorming' techniques, but equally important can be the removal of barriers.

BARRIERS TO CREATIVE THINKING

- Vertical thinking: defining a problem in only one way.
- Stereotyping situations and compartmentalism.
- Compressing information.
- Complacency and non-inquisitiveness.

Reacting and conforming to 'norms' often limits creative options. To encourage individuals to think creatively, it may be necessary to change the environment or employ different techniques. John Kao's 'idea factory' is one example of an attempt to provide an environment as an incubator of new business ideas and to nurture creativity, being designed to provide an environment that is safe, casual and liberating.[14]

Finally, it should be realized that idea formulation can take considerable time. The sudden breakthrough is comparatively rare. Ideas take time to refine; they benefit from discussion with others, from research, from information-gathering and from feedback. Thus, being creative is only part of the process. Additional skills must be developed that can take basic ideas, then modify and refine them – perhaps involving considerable research – before ideas become viable business start-up ventures.

As John Kao[15] has illustrated in his popular text *Innovation Nation*, there is no accepted definition of creativity or innovation. He comments (excerpt p. 2):

> Is innovation about being creative or is creativity about being innovative? I believe we are in what might be called a pre-Copernican period with regard to innovation. It's as if we don't yet know which heavenly bodies revolve around which others. We don't even know where all the planets are located, nor do we have a viable theory of planetary motion. We rely on metaphors and images to express an as yet imprecise and unsystematic understanding.

Creativity is essential to innovation. In Kao's terms it is 'innovating innovation'.

OPPORTUNITY RECOGNITION

Converting an idea into a business opportunity is the key element of the process of business creation. Moving from the idea stage to the exploitation of the opportunity requires many elements to be in place. The economic environment has to be conducive, the culture must be appropriate for risk-taking and the nascent entrepreneur must have the self-confidence to take an idea suggested by opportunities through to fulfilment. Opportunities are generated by change. Change may be political, economic, social, demographic or technical. For example, economic change may be characterized by a period of economic growth and expanding demand, which may create opportunities for new business ideas that take advantage of increased affluence, leisure time and spending power of the population. The growth in the leisure industry has spawned many new developments and opened niche markets in areas such as sports, holidays and travel. At the time of writing, greater concerns with the environment are providing new opportunities in 'green entrepreneurship', 'clean tech' or in eco-tourism. The increased pace of technological change has created opportunities for new business ventures in new technologies, in new developments in information technology such as the Internet and in new applications in biotechnology. Social and demographic change may provide opportunities through changing attitudes or through creation of new markets in ageing population structures. Even during recessionary times there will still be opportunities that entrepreneurs are able to exploit. For example, it is likely that the demand for second-hand cars will have increased in the post global financial crisis (GFC) period post 2008, as people delay spending on expensive items such as a new car.

These factors are the engines of change, but harnessing such change to create new business ventures requires entrepreneurs to formulate ideas and fit them to the opportunity. It is this combination that is important. The idea has to be right for the opportunity. For example, in the Aquamotive case, the entrepreneurs recognized an opportunity to develop a new fish-farming application service, but the market required considerable development. The market was not ready or receptive to the new technology. Thus the correct timing of the idea with the opportunity, created by forces of change, can be critical.

These environmental change processes provide the nascent entrepreneur with imperfect information on opportunities, information which will require research and refinement. Pech and Cameron have illustrated the role of 'informational cues' from opportunity seeking and investigation for the entrepreneur in the opportunity recognition process.[16] They propose an entrepreneurial decision-making model based upon information processing associated with opportunity recognition. In the process of identifying opportunities entrepreneurs will act upon information received about market opportunities. The information will then be processed by individual entrepreneurs. How that information is processed may lead one person to act, but others not to. Entrepreneurs analyse information, then seek to acquire resources to act upon information. They comment that: 'entrepreneurs seek and diagnose opportunities and then access required resources needed to exploit that opportunity' (p. 73).

Figure 12.2 illustrates their proposed model. It indicates the role of some of the environmental factors discussed above and elements of this process, including processing and refinement by the entrepreneur of informational cues and the role of 'filters' in the process.

Perceptions of opportunity, that is, of the same informational cues, differ between individuals. One of the 'filters' may be the extent of self-confidence of an individual in their own abilities and skills to take advantage of an opportunity, known as self-efficacy (see also Chapter 1). Kreuger and Dickson claim that greater self-efficacy leads to a greater propensity to take decisions associated with risky opportunities.[17] In an experimental study

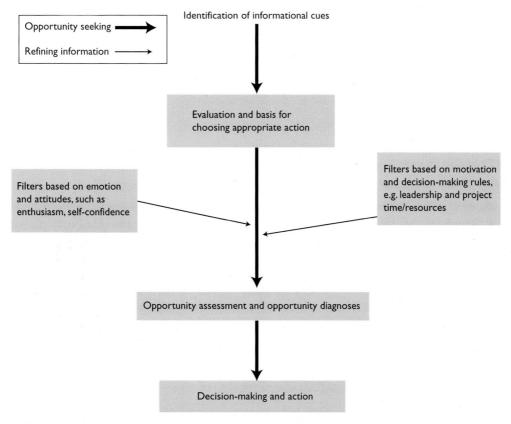

FIGURE 12.2

Model of opportunity recognition and entrepreneurial decision-making process following Pech and Cameron with permission of the authors

they claim that 'subjects who are led to believe they are very competent at decision-making see more opportunities in a risky choice and take more risks' (p. 385).

The opportunity recognition process has also been described by Rae.[18] For Rae, entrepreneurship and entrepreneurial activity are based on identifying and creating opportunity, then using resources to plan and realize the opportunity. He terms the process 'opportunity-centred entrepreneurship', which he considers to be based upon four interconnected themes: acting on opportunity; personal enterprise; creating and exploring opportunity; and planning to realize opportunity. However, such a process may have barriers or hazards at any stage. The processing and gathering of information can be imperfect, refinement may be inappropriate. Hseih et al. demonstrate that there are barriers to this process of information assimilation with opportunity recognition.[19] They identify two barriers:

* Knowledge appropriation hazard – extraction of value without payment poses a hazard to the entrepreneur's efforts to promote knowledge transfer or exchange
* Strategic knowledge accumulation hazard – actors act independently rather than collectively yet they need collective action to solve complex problems

They indicate that 'the entrepreneur's critical task is to efficiently govern the process of discovering opportunities' (p. 1255).

As indicated earlier, it is also the case that the process of opportunity recognition will change over time, and opportunities vary over time. For example, Schwartz et al. indicate that the process varies over time and varies between sectors.[20] From their longitudinal study they find differences between manufacturing and non-manufacturing sectors and differences in each sector over time.

The role of opportunity recognition in business start-up has received increased attention and recognition, particularly following the work of Shane and Venkataranam.[21] They argued for a framework based upon the existence, discovery and exploitation of entrepreneurial opportunities. The roots of such research lie in Austrian economics and the recognition of how opportunities arise from uncertainties and asymmetric information held by individuals. Shane's (2000) influential paper proposes that opportunity discovery is a function of the distribution of information in society and that entrepreneurs discover opportunities related to the information they already possess. Shane's key finding was that the source of entrepreneurship lies in differences in information about opportunities.[22]

Cultural attitudes to risk and failure can also impinge at this stage. For example, it has been suggested that, in the UK, we have lower tolerance levels of failure than other nations, such as the USA, and different attitudes to risk-taking.[23] Cultural factors are obviously intangible and difficult to gauge, but they help to determine whether the entrepreneur who has a business idea – that is, has recognized an opportunity – will be encouraged or discouraged from attempting to exploit that opportunity. If failure is heavily punished, as we have suggested it is in the UK, then fear of failure may act as a significant constraint on this process.[24] We suggest that the existence (or otherwise) of role models will also affect such a process. Role models remove one of the stumbling blocks in the process of new business creation – they help to identify with success and encourage the next step of developing the business idea and identifying the right opportunity. Such role models should not be too successful though; potential nascent entrepreneurs need to be able to identify with them, where they came from and how they were successful and more publications that help to identify entrepreneurs from many different ethnic and cultural backgrounds are needed as source material.[25]

Taking this further, an alternative approach to opportunity recognition has been identified by Fletcher who has argued that opportunity formation is relationally and communally instituted.[26] That is, that the opportunity recognition process needs to be understood within the context of the social environment within which entrepreneurs operate. Fletcher argues that the development of the entrepreneurial opportunity discovery literature has failed to take account of the social and economic contexts in which the process of entrepreneurial opportunity discovery is framed. Put another way we need to take account of the reality of how social relations are constructed in order to understand the opportunity discovery process.

The following 'Entrepreneurship in Action' on Lord Karan Bilimoria and Cobra Beer illustrates how ethnicity and culture can influence how an opportunity is recognized and exploited.

ENTREPRENEURSHIP IN ACTION

Lord Karan Bilimoria and Cobra Beer
Case contributed by Dr Spinder Dhaliwal, University of Surrey

Karan Bilimoria was born in India and came to London to study. He stayed at the Indian YMCA on Fitzroy Square in London which was surrounded by Indian restaurants and it was here that Karan first discovered European lager. He was not impressed: 'I found them gassy, very fizzy, very bland, very harsh and very bloating.' Lager was the curry lover's choice of beer but it did not seem suitable to the young Karan. An idea had formed in his mind.

Karan soon enrolled to study law at Cambridge University and threw himself head first into student life, picking up some useful entrepreneurial skills along the way. 'It was at Cambridge that I realised that I could sell. I had to do door canvassing to get myself elected to the Union.' His sales patter paid off and he was elected vice president of the Student Union.

Karan finished his degree and was £20,000 in debt but was set to be an entrepreneur. A&K International was formed in 1986 by Karan Bilimoria and Arjun Reddy, his long-term friend, and this is where the Cobra story really begins.

Karan and Arjun went to India and researched products that they could market and they also made a list of all their contacts in India. When they returned to England they established who their contacts were and how they could pursue their goals. Then, through luck as much as good judgement, Karan and Arjun decided to import seafood from a company called Pals. After closer examination of the brochure they found they were less interested in Pals seafood and more in Pals beer, which was a division of the Mysore Brewery. The Mysore brewery was a former Coca-Cola bottling plant and had grown to become the biggest privately owned brewer in India.

Karan was increasingly frustrated with trying to communicate with their contacts in India – so much so that he jumped on a plane and went to India to talk face to face. He was shrewd enough to recognise who the key players were. He made a convincing pitch with evident self-belief, passion and confidence to a sceptical audience. He made the deal of his life and secured the brewing contract. He used his network of family contacts to get in touch with big-bottle manufacturers. The snag was the size of the bottles, in the UK the regular size is 330ml, but in India it is 650 ml.

They were to encounter several problems. There was a lot of red tape to deal with before they could get samples out of India and into the UK. They managed to get it freighted. However, many of the bottles were broken by the time they landed in the UK, thus rendering the exercise useless.

Another major stumbling block was dealing with the excise authorities in India, which insisted that bottles be labelled with the state where the beer was to be sold. Cobra was brewed in the state of Karnataka, but for export, so Karan was obliged to write '*not for sale in Karnataka, for export only*' on each bottle. Of course he did not want to write all that as it took up valuable space on the label and would be meaningless to UK customers. He eventually managed to convince the authorities of this.

The next challenge was to sell his lager. He turned his sights to the Indian restaurant trade. The restaurants had paved the way for his business. They had opened doors and made the British aware of Indian food and lagers. Cobra's initial base was the niche market of Indian restaurants. Indian restaurants were expanding rapidly in the UK and becoming a familiar sight in every high street. 'I had a battered old 2CV as a company car and we used to park it down the road from the restaurants we were delivering to,' says Karan.

Apart from being new in the Indian restaurant marketplace, which already had established beers in place, Cobra also faced a problem with its large bottles. Indian restaurant customers were more used to the smaller bottles. Ever quick to turn a negative into a positive, Karan pointed out to his potential clients just how authentic this method was of drinking the beer, and the benefits of the sharing aspects of one bottle and two glasses. It worked, and the cases began to shift. It was, he recalls, a real struggle but after five years his revenue hit the £1 million mark.

During the first five years, he recalls feeling 'very demoralised, but I never once thought of giving up'. Arjun decided otherwise, leaving the company in 1995 to return to India and pursue other avenues once everything was in place and Karan became sole owner. Now Cobra Beer is one of the fastest growing beer brands in the UK.

Source: Dhaliwal, S. (2008) *Making a Fortune – Learning from the Asian Phenomenon*, Capstone, West Sussex.

DISCUSSION QUESTIONS

1 How did Karan Bilimoria discover the opportunity for Cobra Beer?

2 What challenges did he face and how did he overcome them?

3 What have been the success factors behind the growth of Cobra Beer in the UK?

4 What are the cultural and business problems with dealing with other countries?

SERIAL AND PORTFOLIO ENTREPRENEURS

The phenomenon of the serial entrepreneur – an entrepreneur who repeatedly starts new businesses through the development of new ideas and exploitation of opportunity – has been identified by several writers.[25; 27] The recognition of opportunity does not have to come from new entrepreneurs; existing entrepreneurs will be in a position to recognize new opportunities, buy other businesses and use previous success to develop new ideas. New opportunities will arise just from being in business. These may be exploited by setting up additional businesses (portfolio entrepreneurs); or perhaps through selling an existing business, perhaps to a large-firm competitor, and using the harvested capital resulting from the business sale to launch another (new) business, a process that may be repeated several times by the same entrepreneur (i.e. serial entrepreneurship). Richard Branson and Stelios Haji-Ioannou (see the 'Entrepreneurship in Action' box) are classic examples of the former. Examples of the latter, which are more common, but less well known, include Sir Clive Sinclair (ZX computers) and Tom Hunter (Sports Division).

ENTREPRENEURSHIP IN ACTION

Stelios Haji-Ioannou and the 'easy Group'

The son of a Greek-Cypriot shipping tycoon, Stelios Haji-Ioannou is well known as the entrepreneur responsible for starting easyJet, yet he has also started other ventures, including easyCar, easyInternetcafe and easyCinema. These qualify him as a portfolio entrepreneur or, as he describes himself, a 'serial entrepreneur'. He founded easyJet in 1995 with a £5 million loan from his father. The company achieved spectacular growth in nine years by exploiting a successful model from the USA of a low-cost airline, South-West Airlines. By 2001 easyJet was carrying 8.25 million passengers on 40 routes. Far from being affected by the events of 9/11 and the post Global Financial Crisis recession, easyJet has continued to expand, thrive and increase profits, while the major airlines have, of course, struggled to survive, with famous names such as Sabena going bankrupt. Adopting an aggressive price-cutting strategy with Internet bookings and ticket distribution, easyJet seeks to fill seats at the lowest cost. As a result, in 2007 easyJet was continuing to expand and was handling more passengers than ever. Although the 'no frills' business model will not work in all countries as it needs latent demand to succeed, the airline illustrates how a successful and high-profile entrepreneur has achieved success by copying a business model from elsewhere.

In April 2002, however, after floating easyJet on the London Stock Exchange, Stelios Haji-Ioannou found himself up against City institutional shareholders concerned about corporate governance practices and was forced to resign as chairman of the company. He was quoted as saying his skills lay in 'starting new ventures, taking risks and being a serial entrepreneur' and has turned his attention to launching yet more new ventures, such as easyHotel and easyCruise.

DISCUSSION QUESTIONS

1 How does this 'Entrepreneurship in Action' case illustrate how some serial entrepreneurs may be (more) suited to starting early-stage development of ventures rather than their subsequent development?

2 By importing and adopting the South-West Airlines business model, would you consider that Stelios Haji-Ioannou has been an innovative entrepreneur?

PRE-START PLANNING AND PREPARATION

A further combination of factors will be important to the eventual success of new business creation. Among the most important are research, obtaining information (to determine entry strategy), raising sufficient finance and the role and influence of social capital. For obvious reasons, little research has been done on new business ventures that subsequently fail, but it is commonly asserted that one of the main reasons for the reported high failure rates of such new ventures is undercapitalization.[28] Researching the market and the competition is dealt with in more detail in Chapter 13, but, in addition, search activity will be required in raising finance. Previous research into the causes of small-firm failure rates, however, has been with third parties. A study by Benson,[29] with directors of small companies that had failed, suggests that the reasons for failure are more complex, with undercapitalization only one of a number of factors that were more reflective of real-world complexity, including the importance and quality of professional advice.

The length and time of the search activity will depend on the opportunity and the characteristics of the new venture. If formal venture capital is required, raising such finance may take some time, because of due diligence procedures (12 months), as well as research and preparation, although for certain businesses, such as Internet start-ups, such time periods may be compressed into a matter of weeks or even days. Research undertaken by the author with entrepreneurs using non-executive directors, produced a number of cases where the entrepreneurs had spent some time researching opportunities in preparation for a management buy-in (MBI).[30] In these cases, the entrepreneurs had researched a large number of potential candidate companies (up to 100) as a target for an MBI. If informal, or business angel, finance is sought, this will still involve a search and matching process by the entrepreneur before a suitable investor may be found.[31] Even raising bank finance can involve a search procedure and time to find sufficient bank finance and the best terms and conditions.[32]

Preparation means finding the right management team with complementary skills. Evidence on entrepreneurial team start-ups suggests that they can have advantages over individual entrepreneurs because of the match of skills brought together within the team.[33] However, the evidence is far from conclusive. For example, Oakey has suggested previously that, with technology-based small firms, the best performers were those with a single founder.[34] Team starts have been the focus of policy 'best practice',[35] but it must be remembered that it is important to get the right 'mix' of skills in the proposed entrepreneurial team. Our research with entrepreneurs that had appointed non-executive directors demonstrated that the matching process was crucial to the success of the relationship and affected the growth and performance of the firm.[30] Chapter 13 discusses in more detail the process of business planning, focusing on designing, writing and implementing business plans. Therefore, we do not go into the planning process in detail in this chapter but, as indicated in Chapter 13, the importance of pre-start preparation through market research, competitor analysis and careful planning of entry strategy cannot be underestimated for determining the success of the business start-up process.

THE ROLE OF SOCIAL CAPITAL

It is arguable that the role of social capital (the resources, trust, support and advice available from extended family and social networks) is of key importance in start-up and entrepreneurial development. Its role is complementary to that of sources of financial capital, yet it has received relatively limited attention in research with start-up and nascent entrepreneurs, although this is beginning to change. For example, Daviddson and Honig[36] have commented that, 'From an entrepreneurial perspective, social capital provides networks that facilitate the discovery of opportunities, as well as the identification, collection and allocation of scarce resources' (p. 309). They conclude in their study that sources of social capital are important for predicting start-up entrepreneurial activity.[36] The author's research with ethnic minority entrepreneurs in Scotland has highlighted the complementary role of social capital.[5] Social capital replaces the role of institutional sources of advice in the same way that informal finance can replace and substitute for the role of institutional sources of formal finance. The complementary nature of its role was revealed through the involvement of family, relatives and the general local community as sources of advice. In addition, it was found that ethnic minority entrepreneurs might also rely on access to business advice through a network of business contacts via their own community.

ENTRY AND LAUNCH

As suggested before, the timing of entry is important. While advantages exist for first movers, moving too early can result in insufficient customers to make heavy investment worthwhile. The issue of timing becomes crucial if the protection of intellectual property rights (IPR) is involved. The entrepreneur with a new product or process needs to decide whether and when to patent. The process of patenting is expensive and time-consuming, but obtaining patents may be a necessary prerequisite for formal or informal venture capital. Developing the entry strategy is an important part of the launch of the new business; attention will need to be paid to marketing, a factor that is sometimes neglected by the technology-based entrepreneur.[34] The important relationship between marketing and entrepreneurship has been noted by a number of writers,[37] but the concept of the development of the idea and formulation of strategies has been explored by relatively few. The issue of developing entry and early-stage strategy has been illustrated with a number of cases in this book and, later in this chapter, we also suggest an alternative paradigm for technology-based small firms.

The role of serendipity is often an underplayed factor in the business creation process. To the casual observer, the entrepreneurial and marketing strategies developed in the case study firms may appear to contain a strong element of chance, yet precursor developments can be highly important as preparation for exploitation of the business opportunity. With cases involving technology-based small firms, non-technology-based development beforehand was an important preparation for the development of entrepreneurial and marketing strategies concerned with the technology-based ventures. This arose partly because of the well-known difficulty in funding technology development and raising finance for a technology entrepreneur (see Chapter 7). Alternative business development became a way of funding the 'real' growth start-up business. The role of serendipity has scarcely been acknowledged, let alone researched, in entrepreneurial development and strategies,[38] yet our evidence demonstrates that chance is only one element; the entrepreneur must be prepared to exploit opportunities, recognize and take advantage of them. The role of the non-technology phase of development lies in learning to deal with customers, with suppliers and bank managers and in gaining general business experience.

POST-ENTRY DEVELOPMENT

Early-stage development is a crucial phase for the novice entrepreneur. The entrepreneur is naïve and must learn quickly to understand customers, suppliers, cash flow and how to deal with other stakeholders in the new business, which may include the bank manager or other financiers. For businesses in a team start, it is only the post-entry stage that leads to the testing of relationships between individuals, confirmation of their role and the value that each of them can bring. One of the most important issues that a new business faces is credibility. Being new, especially if markets are competitive, means that customers have to take quality on trust, that suppliers will be unwilling to give trade credit and that banks will be unwilling to extend significant credit facilities. One strategy that can overcome this lack of credibility is to include an experienced entrepreneur as a part-time director in early-stage development. From our research with small companies that employed non-executive directors, we isolated a subsample of start-up companies only; in this subsample the most important reason for employing a non-executive director was to achieve credibility.[39] Alternatively, the use of an experienced entrepreneur as a mentor may also lead to introductions to key customers, to achieving credibility with suppliers and to bringing invaluable experience that overcomes the relative naivety of the start-up entrepreneur.

In addition to achieving credibility, the establishment of early-stage networks can be important in the development of new ventures. Part of the reason for bringing in experienced entrepreneurs will be to access their extensive network of contacts. Where this is not possible, new entrepreneurs need to establish their own network of contacts that may help them to break into new markets during the crucial early-stage development of the new business. There is now an extensive literature and evidence on the importance of networks, especially in a competitive sector.[40]

There are a number of factors in the post-entry development stage that new start-up entrepreneurs may not prepare for, or may underestimate in importance. Through naivety, inadequate approaches may be taken to cash flow, dealing with late payers, payment of VAT, cost and stock control, putting in place employment contracts for staff – to name just a few examples of common areas that may be neglected by early-stage entrepreneurs. The Ace Cleaning case study, available in the online resources for this chapter, provides one example of how an entrepreneur has dealt with such issues in early-stage development.

MARKETING: A NEGLECTED FUNCTION IN POST-ENTRY DEVELOPMENT?

Early-stage entrepreneurs may suffer from a form of myopia through too much focus on the product or service, rather than attention to entry and subsequent marketing strategy. This may be particularly true with technology-based entrepreneurs and we discuss their situation as a special case below. However, any entrepreneur may take a mere reactive approach to customers, rather than a proactive marketing strategy.

In marketing terms, products or services may be seen to have an efficiency dimension. Customers will buy products and services because they do what they are meant to do and often entrepreneurs will focus on ensuring that their product or service is as good or better than their competitors', or that it provides something that is different. However, this is not the only explanation for purchase. Customers may also buy products due to 'reputation effects' or 'symbolic effects'.

During early-stage development new entrepreneurs may have to compete with established firms that have established reputations and find ways of attracting and retaining customers. This may mean that the early-stage entrepreneur has to find novel ways of delivering the service or product. Two examples are given from material in the text.

1   Adopting a complementary marketing strategy, as was the case with Cobra (see the separate 'Entrepreneurship in Action' box). Although Cobra focused on ensuring that its product was of high quality, it also adopted a complementary marketing strategy to reach a market through 'Indian' restaurants.

2   In the case of Ace Cleaning (given in the online resources) the entrepreneur purchases an existing contracts list to 'buy out' a previous owner. In a competitive industry, such a move saves an initial expensive marketing campaign to attract customers and, instead, the focus can be on retaining customers rather than winning new customers. Although such a strategy may appear expensive, in reality this was less expensive than establishing a new company and trying to win new customers.

TECHNOLOGY-BASED ENTREPRENEURS: A SPECIAL CASE?

It is generally accepted that start-up for a technology-based entrepreneur may not involve a product on the market during the post-entry and early-development stage. For example, such entrepreneurs can decide to start trading while still undertaking R&D or still developing a prototype, perhaps funded by grant aid to overcome negative cash flow. A standard paradigm for such a start-up is shown in Figure 12.3, where the technology-based entrepreneur comes from one of two sources: a public-sector research institution or the R&D department of a larger private-sector firm. For such entrepreneurs, obtaining patents (to secure markets and funding) may be more important than achieving credibility. Also, because the market may still have to be developed, such entrepreneurs are generally seen to face special marketing problems.[41]

TECHNOLOGY-BASED ENTREPRENEURS: AN ALTERNATIVE PARADIGM

Figure 12.4 presents an alternative paradigm for early-stage development of such technology-based entrepreneurs. Drawn from case-study evidence, it suggests that technology development can occur after an initial non-technical start-up. The non-technical start-up provides an important preparation for the entrepreneur through the learning experience, providing the basis for the development of more advanced strategies

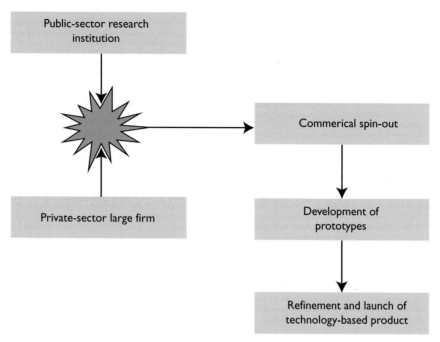

FIGURE 12.3

Technology-based entrepreneur start-up

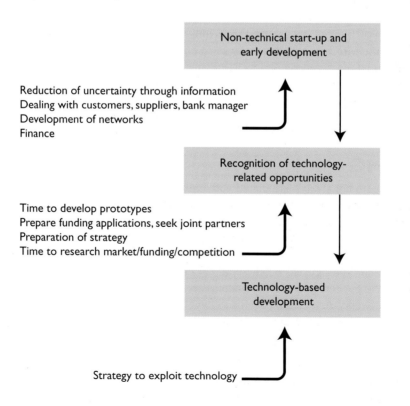

FIGURE 12.4

An alternative representation of start-up and early-stage development for the technology-based entrepreneurs and small firms concerned with marketing, finance and risk-management for the technology-based development. The importance of this preparation should not be underestimated. It provides the novice entrepreneur with a valuable window of development when potential mistakes can be overcome, lessons can be learned, and contacts and networking can be developed. The entrepreneur, during this period, learns to recognize the importance of marketing strategies, while moving away from ad hoc developments. The traditional view normally sees the technology-based entrepreneur as a technical expert, in a high-technology environment, and lacking commercial expertise. We suggest that an alternative paradigm can be presented; that a precursor non-technical period of development can be valuable and necessary in the preparation of entrepreneurial strategies appropriate for the technology-related development.

MANAGEMENT BUY-OUTS AND MANAGEMENT BUY-INS

Both management buy-outs (MBOs) and management buy-ins (MBIs) have not been regarded traditionally as examples of entrepreneurship and business creation. Management buy-outs involve the buy-out of the equity of a company by the existing management team, often funded by a venture capital institution. Although this can lead to changes in management style and strategy, it can be argued that little new is created. Management buy-ins involve an outside entrepreneur or management team buying into the equity of an existing company, again often funded by a venture capital institution. As stated before, our research with small companies that employed non-executive directors, revealed MBIs where a single outside entrepreneur was often involved in the processes of new business creation, thus entailing considerable pre-MBI planning, research and search activity.

Management buy-outs, by their nature, do not lead to new business creation per se and have been regarded as very different from new-start business creation. This may well be the case where an existing management team is given an opportunity to 'buy out' the equity of previous owners, a situation that does not lead to new business creation. However, some MBOs can be much closer to entrepreneurship, where either a team or an individual can virtually transform an old company and its associated way of doing business. In addition, where an MBO is undertaken by an individual, rather than, say, the previous management team, this can be virtually equivalent to new business creation. The Ace Cleaning case study (see the students' online learning centre resource material) is an example of this type of transformation and 'new' business creation.

FRANCHISING

Another entry route, again not always associated with entrepreneurship, is to take on, or take over, a franchise. Franchising still involves new business creation and, therefore, all the aspects of the process that have been identified in this chapter. The difference, of course, is that the franchisor, rather than the franchisee, undertakes much of this process, including idea formulation, opportunity recognition, pre-start planning and market research. The interested reader might like to note that franchising can cover a range of self-employment activities; for a discussion and typology see Brodie et al.[42] Franchising has become a growth industry in its own right, with claims that 50 per cent of franchise systems are less than five years old,[43] although the rapid growth of the 1990s and early twenty-first century seems to have levelled off pre and post GFC.[44] Although the large franchises are well known and are present on almost every high street, the vast majority of franchises are much smaller with 43 per cent having fewer than 10 outlets.[45]

Buying a franchise, rather than undertaking *de novo* entrepreneurship, can have advantages as well as disadvantages for the individual. The main advantages and disadvantages are illustrated in Table 12.1.

Despite the considerable disadvantages, shown in Table 12.1, arising from the loss of control in a franchise, their popularity, as noted above, has mirrored the importance and growth of small firms in the economy, as

TABLE 12.1 THE MAIN ADVANTAGES AND DISADVANTAGES OF BUYING A FRANCHISE AS A MEANS OF BUSINESS START-UP

Advantages	Disadvantages
The franchise is usually based on a proven and tried and tested recipe for business success	Proven track records have their price – successful franchise systems require very large investments by the franchisee
The franchisee can benefit from economies of scale, e.g. in marketing, advertising and buying supplies	Although you can sell on to someone taking over your role as franchisee, this may be less than could be achieved with *de novo* entrepreneurship
Market research may be undertaken by the franchisor	Trading is limited by geographical area and location, hence growth of the business will be finite and limited
Training is provided by the franchisor	Problems may exist in the relationship with the franchisor, leading to financial and legal or contractual disputes
The franchisor may act as a business mentor providing early-stage advice	Innovation may be limited because the franchise operates to a strict formula for production and sales and marketing
Stationery and other business systems may be provided as part of the franchise package	Specialised 'franchise lawyers' may have to be hired when a dispute occurs
Benefits from the strong brand name	
Franchise systems are often favoured by banks due to an established track record	

discussed in earlier chapters. The appeal of the reduced risk, while still retaining elements of entrepreneurship, has obviously been a powerful motivating factor for many people and the popularity of franchising seems likely to continue in the second decade of the twenty-first century.

THE ENVIRONMENT AND BUSINESS CREATION

Chapter 4 examined diversity in entrepreneurship and the role of ethnic minority entrepreneurs who have created new ventures in inner-city environments; by operating in ethnic enclaves, such entrepreneurs have achieved remarkable success in a difficult environment. Similarly, it is arguable that rural environments provide environmental problems associated with limited access and limited (or peripheral) markets, and should be treated as a special case.

BUSINESS CREATION IN A RURAL CONTEXT

It is arguable that business creation in a rural environment is distinctive from that in an urban environment, although precisely what is defined as 'rural' as opposed to 'urban' has been the subject of some academic discussion.[46] It is arguable that business creation can be more difficult in rural environments.[47] For example, the more scattered population may mean that business opportunities are more limited and the nature of the infrastructure may mean that resources, such as skilled labour, are scarcer. In addition, demographic features of rural areas are different from urban areas. In the UK, as in most European countries, rural areas suffer from emigration of younger people, increasing the scarcity of resources such as a trained and skilled labour force. However, rural areas may offer attractions to entrepreneurs seeking to establish businesses in such areas due to a perceived (higher) quality of life in a rural environment.

Therefore, business creation will be affected by the nature of individual entrepreneurs that may be attracted to the rural environment.[48] There are further distinctive features of business creation in a rural environment – for example, networks are more difficult to establish.[49] This affects the nature of entrepreneurial development; greater emphasis for entrepreneurial growth may be placed on global rather than local networks. Entrepreneurs in urban areas may have the luxury of achieving early growth through local markets; for entrepreneurs in rural environments, local markets are rarely sufficient to sustain substantial growth, but this may force rural entrepreneurs at an early stage to develop distinctive and resourceful growth strategies.[50]

It is also claimed that creativity and innovation are more limited and develop at a slower pace in rural environments.[51] This is because of the more limited pace of technological and infrastructure developments, but it has also been claimed that there is a lower speed of technological take-up by rural entrepreneurs.[52] For example, a lack of competition and local monopolies may result in producing more inertia and technological lock-in than may occur in urban environments.[53] A further implication of lower creativity and innovation is that it is reasonable to hypothesize that entrepreneurial learning may be more restricted.[54] An example of the nature of technological change and rural environments is provided in the accompanying box.

TECHNOLOGY AND RURAL ENVIRONMENTS: BROADBAND

The UK's Coalition Government has recently announced a commitment to a roll-out of 'super-fast' broadband across the country.[55] The increased focus on the need for fast communication has highlighted some of the features of rural environments. As the availability, capacity and speed of broadband has increased, this has led to a widening 'gap' of provision in rural areas.[56] However, the recent discussion paper has a commitment to 'introduce broadband in remote areas at the same time as the more populated areas'.[55] Until recently, fast broadband has been available only in the main urban areas or in areas of 'significant settlement'. A widely held perception has been that this would hold back business development in rural areas; indeed it was expected to cause further migration of new businesses to urban areas.[57]

However, the story so far has been either that business owners were sufficiently adjusted to rural environments not to need the enhanced capability of broadband, or that there have been sufficient incentives to increase demand. For example, the Highlands and Islands region of Scotland has been enjoying high start-up figures for new business creation with increasing numbers of people seeking alternative lifestyles.[52] This phenomenon is also noticeable in other rural areas of the UK, partly affecting the approach of British Telecom and other infrastructure providers in their decision to roll out 'super-fast' broadband to a greater number of rural areas.

LIFESTYLE OR GROWTH BUSINESSES

From the discussion so far we can see that environments are dissimilar, each possesses distinct advantages and disadvantages, and the entrepreneur has to engage with his or her environment in order to survive and prosper. This environmental dissimilarity is another reason why there is a wide variation in the kinds of new ventures. Since environments vary, different kinds of entrepreneur exist and many influences may interact to cause a particular individual to form a particular business at a particular time and place. Two specific factors have been highlighted as determining the level of new business creation.[58] First, the perception of environmental munificence – that is, the extent to which the entrepreneur perceives the availability of critical resources. Second, resource acquisition self-efficacy, where the small-business owner's ability to mobilize and gather the required resources from his or her environment becomes vital.

The rural environment is perceived as being disadvantaged, but it also offers the ideal circumstances in which to study business creation. First, rural areas, by most definitions, are less concentrated in terms of business activity than urban areas and this means it is easier to trace out patterns of activities. Second, rural areas are viewed as being lean in terms of those resources associated with business start-up. As discussed earlier, they may be perceived as being distanced from main markets and main centres of business activity, have a lower and more dispersed population, a weaker infrastructure, more limited local markets, higher cost of both obtaining and having raw materials due to the remoteness of location and, as indicated earlier, suffer from shortages of skills within the local labour market. Therefore, rural areas are perceived to be scarce in terms of environmental munificence and the critical resources associated with the entrepreneurial process. Consequently, examining the process within the context of rurality is interesting, since it enables us to see how entrepreneurs overcome what could be viewed as being potential difficulties and hindrances to growth and development. The associated discussion, in the students' online learning centre resources, uses the rural context to investigate what entrepreneurs do and develops this into a working definition and description of entrepreneurial actions, together with additional case examples.

The level of growth in business creation in rural areas reported earlier has been attributed, at least in part, to the attraction of the quality of life that the countryside was perceived to provide, drawing people to rural areas.[47] These were often lifestyle businesses. It has also been suggested that the flexibility associated with rurality, the need to be more innovative and competitive, has meant that the more dynamic expansionist firms have tended to be concentrated in smaller towns and rural areas.[50] Further discussion of the impact of rural environments is given in the students' online learning centre resources, which also includes two case studies of business creation in a rural environment. Despite the problems of peripherality and limited local markets, these examples demonstrate that entrepreneurship associated with business creation in rural areas can be successful, with growth rather than lifestyle businesses. This supports some evidence that rural firms are more profitable and enjoy greater business growth (in certain size ranges) than their urban counterparts, possibly because rural environments have compensating factors such as a high-quality and loyal labour force.[51] Thus, although the environment may be a limiting factor, in practice, if sufficient pre-start preparation, planning and research is undertaken, an opportunity for business creation can still be exploited successfully.

The nature of rural entrepreneurship means that there are distinctive policy implications.[48] Governments cannot assume that policies to encourage entrepreneurship will have similar impacts in urban as in rural areas; for example, a number of writers have suggested that there is a premium associated with support programmes in rural areas.[49] In the final section of this chapter, we consider in greater detail whether enterprise support can influence the nature of business creation.

THE ROLE OF ENTERPRISE SUPPORT AND BUSINESS START-UP

INTRODUCTION

In the UK, it is arguable that the role of enterprise support has evolved in an ad hoc manner, but for reference purposes a simplified version of the framework of support agencies that will be referred to in this chapter is shown, for England, in Figure 12.5; for Scotland, which has different support agencies, the equivalent structure

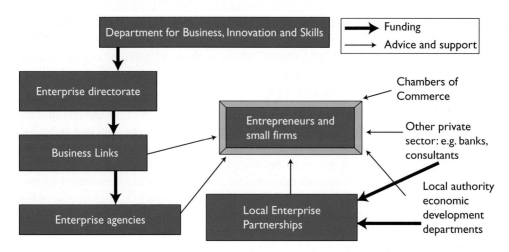

FIGURE 12.5

Enterprise support system for England following the White Paper on Local Growth, October 2010

is shown in Figure 12.6. Wales and Northern Ireland also have different structures: in Wales administered by the Welsh Assembly, which absorbed the former Welsh Development Agency; and in Northern Ireland a separate agency, Enterprise Northern Ireland. These illustrations do not attempt to show all the agencies involved in providing start-up advice and support to entrepreneurs and small firms, but show the relative funding links between different agencies. The general relationship that might exist between the entrepreneur and the enterprise support agency, via a business adviser or mentor, is shown in Figure 12.7.

THE NEW LOCAL ENTERPRISE PARTNERSHIPS

The Coalition Government's White Paper on Local Growth published in November 2010 announced the first 24 Local Enterprise Partnerships or LEPs across England.[59] At the time, large areas of England were still left without an LEP. The intention is to empower local communities to achieve local economic development and 'local growth'. It is too early to see whether LEPs will be more effective than the former Regional Development Agencies, but in principle, they should be more responsive to local needs and local environments. Obviously one way to achieve local economic development is from business start-ups and to 'stimulate enterprise by providing support for projects and programmes with significant potential for economic growth' (p. 32).[59]

This evolution of enterprise support has meant varying importance placed upon supporting start-ups. However, the publication in 2004 of the former Small Business Service's (now the Enterprise Directorate) Action Plan[60] emphasized a government policy commitment to 'making the UK the best place in the world to start and grow a business' (p. 4). However, it is not possible to support all new start-up entrepreneurs and one of the principles of enterprise support that has enjoyed varying importance is the concept of selectivity.

SELECTIVITY

It is too expensive to provide business advice to all new business owners on a one-to-one basis. Business advisers have to meet their clients frequently and may have intensive periods of counselling sessions; in many areas this has led to segmentation of support. For example, in Scotland local support agencies will provide a basic level of advice to most start-ups, but have specialist high-growth programmes for selected perceived high-growth start-ups. It should be noted, following our discussion of rural environments, that segmentation is difficult to achieve in rural areas, due to the smaller pool of start-up business owners.

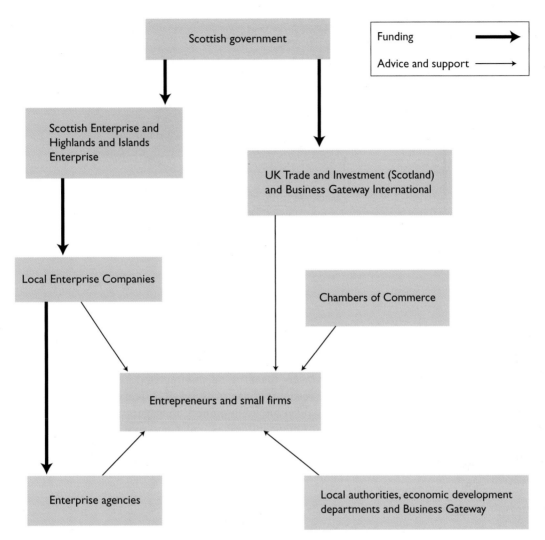

FIGURE 12.6

Support agencies for Scotland

CONTINUITY

It is arguable that some businesses will need continuity of pre-start, start-up, aftercare and business development adviser support. In the same way that start-up support has varied across areas and, historically, practice has varied, not only has the extent and length of aftercare varied but so has the continuity of support. In principle, early stage clients may be passed on to general business development adviser support, but in practice there has been a sharp division in support, with different agencies focusing on different types of support and, in some cases, overlapping areas of responsibility.[61] Many early stage business clients, perhaps at a critical stage in their development, however, will not have access to further support. Segmentation, driven by public and EU funding, has meant that only higher growth potential clients have received intensive and proactive aftercare support in a limited number of areas in the UK.

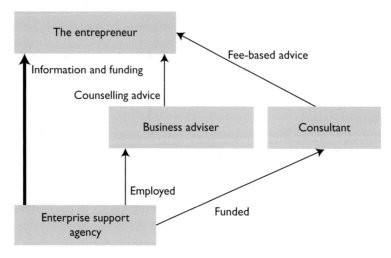

FIGURE 12.7

Enterprise support: the entrepreneur–adviser relationship

INTEGRATED MODEL: THE BUSINESS LINK MODEL

Business Links (introduced in the early 1990s) were meant to be an integrated model of business support: a one-stop shop. This has some attractions since resources, information and delivery can all be provided in the one location. Advisers can easily speak to each other and with trainers, managers and specialist advisers. The Business Links were also meant to combine different initiatives under one roof, such as the former DTI's Information Society Initiative to provide, for example, an IT centre for training, advice and consultation. However, as reviewed by a number of writers, the provision of such an integrated one-stop shop has been highly variable.[62; 63]

SPECIAL NEEDS GROUPS

The provision of volume adviser support, where limited start-up advice is given, can ignore the needs of special groups where there is a case for more targeted and more specialized support. For example, in Birmingham, specialized agencies such as Black Business in Birmingham (3bs) aim to cater for the needs of ethnic minorities in business. In Glasgow, the Wellpark Enterprise Centre has been promoted as an example of specialized support for women from socially excluded groups, by a Bank of England report.[64] Other cities have similar targeted support agencies. The advantage of providing specialized, targeted support for special needs groups is that it can integrate business development with economic inclusion and establish business forums that maintain links with such business groups.

It is arguable that technology-based start-ups should receive specialized start-up support and longer aftercare provision, given their special requirements for funding and, in some cases, R&D. The current focus on exploiting commercialisation is important for the UK's economy, and some Business Links and Local Enterprise Companies (LECs) have integrated support linked to higher education institutions. For example, in the east of Scotland, Dundee Technopole combined with BioDundee has established a partnership linking world-class expertise at the University of Dundee in biosciences to an incubator and Medipark, and a successful bioscience cluster.

The complexity of the support picture across the UK, however, is illustrated by the confusing range of specialist support agencies that may provide advice to technology-based start-up firms, women in business, ethnic minority firms and other categories of firm, which may qualify for a range of support, funding and specialized advice.

PROVIDING START-UP SUPPORT: A REVIEW OF EVIDENCE

Storey[65] has compared the provision of start-up support to 'a lottery in which the odds of winning are not good' (p. 16). The basis for this view has been that the blanket coverage of start-up support programmes, such as the former Enterprise Allowance Scheme (EAS), has not resulted in a noticeable impact on the quality of firm starts and may have encouraged low-quality firm start-ups, even though Storey considered the EAS to be one of the 'better schemes'. The vast majority of new firm starts are known to be poor job creators. [65] Thus, it has been argued that the opportunity cost of such start-up enterprise support is high, since the careful targeting of public funds, in the form of enterprise support, at the small number of high-performing growth firms that are new starters, should result in a more cost-effective way of supporting new-venture development.

However, research by the author and colleagues with local area programmes has found evidence that mentoring and business adviser support had beneficial effects on the subsequent business development and the development of entrepreneurial learning with start-up owners involved in business creation.[66] More recent research by the author, with a local area targeted support programme with new-start ethnic minority entrepreneurs, also found that adviser support had beneficial effects, in particular enabling new-start ethnic minority entrepreneurs to link into a wider network of mainstream funding and further training.[67]

One of the problems with evaluations of such assistance is that the benefits of support are difficult to measure and quantify objectively. Without going into details, benefits tend to be subjective, related to the quality of advice, in areas such as managing change, problem-solving or accessing finance. Thus, support that attempts to improve the quality of new-business creation may be difficult to evaluate.

Initiatives to improve the quantity of new business creation are a different matter and have proved to be much more problematical. For example, an evaluation of a period of seven years of a Business Birth Rate Strategy in Scotland concluded that the strategy had made little impact on business creation or the nation's business birth rate.[68] A study by Mole et al.[69] comparing three English counties – Cleveland, Buckinghamshire and Shropshire – concluded that 'policies to boost new firm founding rates would lead to more firms in low-income elasticity demand sectors, such as hairdressing and motor vehicle repair', the implication of the authors being that support that is designed to increase the rate of business creation would merely lead to more firms in competitive sectors; the disadvantage being that such business creation is likely to have both displacement (where established firms close down) and deadweight (zero impacts on the beneficiaries of public funding) effects.

We suggest that there is a need to make a distinction between support that addresses the quality of new business creation, where interventions with good-quality advice can make a critical difference, and support that seeks to address the rate or quantity of new business creation, where there is little evidence that such support makes a perceivable or measurable impact. In addition, there is emerging evidence that targeted in-depth support programmes, rather than broader and less targeted programmes, such as those geared to women entrepreneurs, ethnic minority entrepreneurs and young people, who may face additional barriers, are beneficial in contributing to the diversity of business creation, to increasing the quality and quantity, and therefore to local economic development, and have recently been considered to have more impact.[70]

CONCLUSIONS

This chapter has considered the process of business creation, often regarded as the distinguishing feature of entrepreneurship, especially in the process of opportunity recognition. We have seen that just one stage in this process, that of opportunity recognition, is itself a complex process affected by informational and environmental factors that impinge on decision-making by the entrepreneur. We have seen that the entrepreneur is required not just to generate ideas, but more importantly to process imperfect information correctly in order to recognize the correct opportunity and the correct timing for exploiting perceived opportunities. Although chance may be involved, pre-start preparation and planning is also critical. For example, case evidence, drawn from research undertaken for this text, has demonstrated that precursor preparation before launching technology-based products was an important factor, allowing development of networks, learning and appropriate marketing strategies by the entrepreneurs concerned. This evidence was drawn from cases used in this text, including Alternative Publishing and Aquamotive (see the students' online learning centre resources).

Although each new business start-up is a unique creative event, we have noted that start-up is diverse and complex: it may involve serial and portfolio entrepreneurs; it may involve new franchise systems and franchisees; it may involve MBIs and MBOs and it may be different in nature in rural and urban environments. It is arguable that intervention in the start-up and business-creation process may not be valuable or productive. However, we have also argued that in-depth, targeted support can be beneficial and that it is possible to improve the quality, if not the quantity, of new business creation.

REVIEW QUESTIONS

1   Why is the environment important for creativity?
2   List barriers to creativity in your organization/university.
3   How can group dynamics affect creativity?
4   Give an example of an enterprise education initiative. Why might an emphasis on creativity be an important part of such an initiative?
5   What are the start-up stages before market entry and launch?
6   Why should creativity be encouraged in young people with potential business ideas?
7   Discuss, either individually or in a group, whether the traditional education system encourages creativity.
8   Why does change affect the formation of business ideas? Can this explain the explosion of dotcom business ideas with the growth of Internet use and trading?
9   What are the research and search procedures necessary in the pre-start and planning stage?
10 Suggest ways in which new-start entrepreneurs can overcome the credibility problem.
11 What is the difference between an MBO and an MBI? Would you consider MBOs and MBIs as valid new entrepreneurial activity?
12 Why can timing be crucial to the business entry decision?
13 Describe why a rural or urban environment can affect the business-creation process.
14 How might mentors/business advisers help new start-up entrepreneurs?
15 What start-up assistance is provided in your locality for new start-up entrepreneurs?

SUGGESTED ASSIGNMENTS

The following assignments are based on the case of Ace Cleaning Ltd, which can be found in the students' online learning resource centre.

1 Students discuss the case of Ace Cleaning Ltd in a small group. They are required to identify the options available to Mary Anderson, and recommend and present a course of action.

2 Students are required to consider the Ace Cleaning case as consultants, discuss how Mary should change her management style and practices, and make recommendations as consultants to Ace Cleaning Ltd.

3 Compare the Ace Cleaning case to the Alternative Publishing case (see students' online learning centre resources for Chapter 4). What are the similarities and differences between the two cases? How does the business-creation process differ in each case?

Additional questions

4 Argue the case for and against intervention in the start-up process by public-sector enterprise support agencies.

5 Why might the use of previous entrepreneurs as mentors to new-start entrepreneurs be beneficial in terms of impact and development of such new-start businesses?

REFERENCES

1 **Becker, G.S.** (1962) 'Investment in human capital', *Journal of Political Economy*, vol. 70, pp. 9–49.

2 **Cressy, R.** (1996) *Small Business Failure: Failure to Fund or Failure to Learn?*, Centre for SMEs, University of Warwick, Coventry.

3 **Deakins, D. and Hussain, G.** (1994) 'Risk assessment with asymmetric information', *International Journal of Bank Marketing*, vol. 12, no. 1, pp. 24–31.

4 **Scottish Enterprise** (1993) *Scotland's Business Birth Rate: A National Enquiry*, Scottish Enterprise, Glasgow.

5 **Deakins, D., Ishaq, M., Whittam, G. and Wyper, J.** (2004) Unpublished Interim Progress Report for the Scottish Executive, Scottish Executive, Edinburgh.

6 **Enterprise Insight** (2001) *Enterprise Insight*, DTI, London.

7 **Scottish Executive** (2003) *Determined to Succeed – Enterprise in Education: Scottish Executive Response*, Scottish Executive, Edinburgh.

8 **Deakins, D., Glancey, K., Menter, I. and Wyper, J.** (2004) *Columba 1400 HTLA: Developing Enterprise Culture*, Scottish Executive, Edinburgh.

9 **Gavron, R., Cowling, M., Holtham, G. and Westall, A.** (1998) *The Entrepreneurial Society*, IPPR, London.

10 **Timmons, J.A.** (1994) *New Venture Creation: Entrepreneurship for the 21st Century*, 4th edn, Irwin, Chicago, IL.

11 **Goodman, M.** (1995) *Creative Management*, Prentice-Hall, London.

12 **Proctor, T.** (1998) *Creative Problem Solving for Managers*, Routledge, London.

13 **Clegg, B.** (1999) *Creativity and Innovation for Managers*, Butterworth-Heinemann, Oxford.

14 **Kao, J.J.** (1997) *Jamming: The Art and Discipline of Business Creativity*, HarperCollins, London.

15 **Kao, J.J.** (2007) *Innovation Nation*, Free Press, Simon and Schuster, New York

16 **Pech, R.J. and Cameron, A.** (2006) 'An entrepreneurial decision process model describing

opportunity recognition', *European Journal of Innovation Management*, vol. 9, no. 1, pp. 61–78.

17 **Kreuger, Jr, N. and Dickson, P.R.** (1994) 'How believing in ourselves increases risk taking: perceived self-efficacy and opportunity recognition', *Decision Sciences*, vol. 25, no. 3, pp. 385–400.

18 **Rae, D.** (2007) *Entrepreneurship: From Opportunity to Action*, Palgrave Macmillan, Basingstoke.

19 **Hseih, C., Nickerson, J.A. and Zenger, T.R.** (2007) 'Opportunity discovery, problem solving and a theory of the entrepreneurial firm', *Journal of Management Studies*, vol. 44, no. 7, pp. 1255–277.

20 **Schwartz, R.G., Teach, R.D. and Birch, N.J.** (2005) 'A longitudinal study of entrepreneurial firms, opportunity recognition and product development management strategies', *International Journal of Entrepreneurial Behaviour and Research*, vol. 11, no. 4, pp. 315–29.

21 **Shane, S. and Venkataranam, S.** (2000) 'The promise of entrepreneurship as a field of research', *Academy of Management Review*, vol. 25, no. 1, pp. 217–26.

22 **Shane, S.** (2000) 'Prior knowledge and the discovery of entrepreneurial opportunities', *Organisation Science*, vol. 11, no. 4, pp. 448–69.

23 **Birley, S. and Macmillan, I.** (eds) (1995) *International Entrepreneurship*, Routledge, London.

24 **Reynolds, P. and White, S.** (1997) *The Entrepreneurial Process: Economic Growth, Men, Women and Minorities*, Quorum, Westport, CT.

25 **Wanogho, E.** (1997) *Black Women Taking Charge*, E.W. International, London.

26 **Fletcher, D.** (2006) 'Entrepreneurial processes and the social construction of opportunity', *Entrepreneurship and Regional Development*, vol. 18, no. 5, pp. 421–40.

27 **Carter, S.** (1999) 'The economic potential of portfolio entrepreneurship: enterprise and employment contributions of multiple business ownership', *Journal of Small Business and Enterprise Development*, vol. 5, no. 4, pp. 297–306.

28 **Cressy, R.** (1996) *Small Business Failure: Failure to Fund or Failure to Learn?*, Centre for SMEs, University of Warwick, Coventry.

29 **Benson, A.** (2004) 'Reasons for cessation of trading of incorporated SMEs in manufacturing and engineering in the Humber sub-region 1998–2000', unpublished DBA thesis, University of Hull, Humberside.

30 **Deakins, D., Mileham, P. and O'Neill, E.** (1998) 'The role and influence of non-executive directors in growing small firms', paper presented to Babson Entrepreneurship Research Conference, Ghent, Belgium.

31 **Mason, C.M. and Harrison, R.T.** (1995) 'Informal venture capital and the financing of small and medium sized enterprises', *Small Enterprise Research*, vol. 3, no. 1, pp. 33–56.

32 **Deakins, D. and Hussain, G.** (1991) *Risk Assessment by Bank Managers*, Small Business Research Centre, University of Central England, Birmingham.

33 **Vyakarnaram, S., Jacobs, R. and Handleberg, J.** (1997) 'The formation and development of entrepreneurial teams in rapid growth businesses', paper presented to Babson Entrepreneurship Research Conference, Babson College, Boston, MA.

34 **Oakey, R.P.** (1995) *High Technology New Firms: Variable Barriers to Growth*, Paul Chapman Publishing, London.

35 Former **Department of Trade and Industry** (1996) *Small Firms in Britain Report 1996*, now Department for Business, Innovation and Skills, London.

36 **Daviddson, P. and Honig, B.** (2003) 'The role of social and human capital among nascent entrepreneurs', *Journal of Business Venturing*, vol. 18, no. 3, pp. 301–31.

37 For example, **Carson, D., Cromie, S., McGowan, P. and Hill, J.** (1995) *Marketing and Entrepreneurship in SMEs: An Innovative Approach*, Prentice-Hall, London.

38 **Martello, W.E.** (1994) 'Developing creative business insights: serendipity and its potential', *Entrepreneurship and Regional Development*, vol. 6, no. 2, pp. 239–58.

39 **Deakins, D., Mileham, P. and O'Neill, E.** (1998) *The Role and Influence of Non-executive Directors in Growing Small Firms*, ACCA research report, ACCA, London.

40 **Shaw, E.** (1997) 'The real networks of small firms', in D. Deakins, P. Jennings and C. Mason (eds), *Small Firms: Entrepreneurship in the Nineties*, Paul Chapman Publishing, London, pp. 7–17.

41 **Jones-Evans, D.** (1997) 'Technology entrepreneurship, experience and the management of small technology-based firms – exploratory evidence from the UK', *Entrepreneurship and Regional Development*, vol. 9, no. 1, pp. 65–90.

42 **Brodie, S., Stanworth, J. and Wotruba, T.R.** (2002) 'Direct sales franchises in the UK', *International Small Business Journal*, vol. 20, no. 1, pp. 53–76.

43 **Tikoo, S.** (1996) 'Assessing the franchise option', *Business Horizons*, vol. 9, no. 3, p. 78.

44 **Watson, A. and Kirby, D.A.** (2004) 'Public perceptions of franchising in Britain: releasing the potential', *Journal of Small Business and Enterprise Development*, vol. 11, no. 1, pp. 75–83.

45 **Dickie, S.** (1993) *Franchising in America: The Development of a Business Method*, University of North Carolina Press, North Carolina.

46 **Anderson, A.R.** (1997) 'Entrepreneurial marketing patterns in a rural environment', paper presented at the Special Interest Group Symposium on the Marketing and Entrepreneurship Interface, Dublin, January.

47 **McKain, R.** (2003) 'Social constructions of environmental quality and opportunities for enterprise in rural Scotland', unpublished PhD thesis, University of Highlands and Islands, Perth College, Perth.

48 **Vaessen, P. and Keeble, D.** (1995) 'Growth-oriented SMEs in unfavourable regional environments', *Regional Studies*, vol. 29, no. 4, pp. 489–505.

49 **Smallbone, D., North, D., Baldock, R. and Ekanem, I.** (2002) 'Encouraging and supporting enterprise in rural areas', research report for the DTI's Small Business Service, London.

50 **Deakins, D., Galloway, L. and Mochrie, R.** (2004) 'Rural business use of ICT: a study of the relative impact of collective activity in rural Scotland', *Journal of Strategic Change*, vol. 13, no. 2, pp. 139–50.

51 **Galloway, L., Mochrie, R. and Deakins, D.** (2004) 'ICT-enabled collectivity as a positive rural business strategy, *International Journal of Entrepreneurial Behaviour and Research*, vol. 10, no. 4, pp. 247–59.

52 **Highlands and Islands Enterprise** (2004) *HIE Annual Report*, HIE, Inverness.

53 **Cooper, A.C. and Dunkelberg, W.C.** (1981) 'A new look at business entry: experiences of 1805 entrepreneurs', in K.H. Vesper (ed.), *Frontiers of Entrepreneurship Research*, Babson College, Boston, MA.

54 **Curran, J. and Storey, D.** (1993) 'The location of small and medium enterprises: are there urban–rural differences?', in J. Curran and D. Storey (eds), *Small Firms in Urban and Rural Locations*, Routledge, London.

55 **Department for Business, Innovation and Skills** (2010) 'Broadband deployment and sharing other utilities' infrastructure: a discussion paper', BIS, London.

56 **Talbot, H.** (2008) 'The perpetual broadband gap', paper presented to the 6th Rural Entrepreneurship Conference, Dumfries.

57 **Galloway, L., Sanders, J. and Deakins, D.** (2011) 'Rural small firms' use of the Internet: from global to local', *Journal of Rural Studies*, vol. 27, no. 3, pp. 254–62.

58 **Anderson, A.R.** (1995) 'The Arcadian enterprise: an enquiry into the nature and conditions of rural small business', unpublished PhD thesis, University of Stirling.

59 **HMSO** White Paper (2010) *Local Growth: Realising Every Place's Potential*, Department for Business, Innovation and Skills, London.

60 **Small Business Service** (2004) *A Government Action Plan for Small Businesses: The Evidence Base*, SBS, DTI, London.

61 **Ram, M.** (1996) 'Supporting ethnic minority enterprise: views from the providers', paper presented to the 19th ISBA National Small Firms Policy and Research Conference, Birmingham, November.

62 **Bennett, R., Robson, P. and Bratton, W.** (2000) 'Government advice networks for SMEs: an assessment of the influence of local context on Business Link use, impact and satisfaction', working paper no. 182, Centre for Business Research, University of Cambridge, Cambridge.

63 **Mole, K.** (1999) 'Heuristics of personal business advisers', unpublished PhD thesis, University of Wolverhampton.

64 **Bank of England** (2000) *Finance for Small Businesses in Deprived Communities*, Bank of England, London.

65 **Storey, D.J.** (1993) 'Should we abandon support to start-up businesses?', in F. Chittenden and M. Robertson (eds), *Small Firms: Recession and Recovery*, Paul Chapman Publishing, London, pp. 1–26.

66 **Deakins, D., Sullivan, R. and Whittam, G.** (2002) 'Developing support for entrepreneurial learning: evidence from start-up support programmes', *International Journal of Entrepreneurship and Innovation Management*, vol. 2, nos. 4/5, pp. 323–38.

67 **Paisley Enterprise Research Centre** (2002; 2004) *Interim Evaluations of the Ethnic Minority Business Support Programme*, Glasgow City Council, Glasgow.

68 **Scottish Enterprise** (2001) *Review of the Business Birth Rate Strategy*, Fraser of Allander, Scottish Enterprise, Glasgow.

69 **Mole, K., Greene, F. and Storey, D.** (2002) 'Entrepreneurship in three English counties', paper presented at the 25th ISBA National Small Firms Policy and Research Conference, Brighton, November.

70 **Mole, K.F., Hart, M., Roper, S. and Saal, D.S.** (2011) 'Broader or deeper? Exploring the most effective intervention profile for public small business support', *Environment and Planning A* vol. 43, pp. 87–105.

RECOMMENDED READING

Daviddson, P. and Honig, B.
(2003) 'The role of social and
human capital among nascent
entrepreneurs', *Journal of
Business Venturing*, vol. 18,
no. 3, pp. 301–31.

**Mole, K.F., Hart, M., Roper, S.
and Saal, D.S.** (2011) 'Broader
or deeper? Exploring the most
effective intervention profile for
public small business support',
Environment and Planning A,
vol. 43, pp. 87–105.

Shane, S. (2000) 'Prior
knowledge and the discovery of
entrepreneurial opportunities',
Organisation Science, vol. 11,
no. 4, pp. 448–69.

13 PREPARATION FOR BUSINESS START-UP: RESEARCH, DESIGN AND IMPLEMENTATION OF BUSINESS PLANS

LEARNING OUTCOMES

At the end of this chapter you should be able to:

- Describe different sources of information.
- Discuss the potential of online databases for information gathering.
- Discuss the importance of primary and secondary sources of information for entrepreneurs.
- Describe the importance of qualitative research for the business plan.
- Construct the main sections of a business plan.
- Describe the importance of strategic planning for the successful development of a business.
- Discuss the importance of careful research for the accuracy of forecasts in the business plan.
- Construct a cash-flow forecast from some income and expense assumptions.
- Discuss the advantages and limitations of business plans for the adequate monitoring of business performance.
- Discuss the wide variety and flexibility of business plans.

INTRODUCTION

In this chapter, we examine the steps required for researching, developing and designing business plans in relation to the business start-up process. References to sources of advice and support are also included.

Designing and writing the business plan should be seen as the outcome of a careful research process and subsequent planning procedure as illustrated in Figure 13.1. We will discuss some of the stages of this research process in more detail; however, the business plan should be regarded as part of that procedure, but not as the end of that process.

The business plan is part of the ongoing process of strategic planning for the entrepreneur and small business, whether produced for a start-up business or for an existing business. The business plan can have several purposes (see box).

PURPOSES OF A BUSINESS PLAN

- It may be produced to raise funding from banks or venture capitalists, or it may be required to obtain funding from an agency such as a Business Link or a Local Enterprise Company.
- It may serve as a strategic planning document for entrepreneurs, a plan to guide the business and as a basis for taking strategic decisions.
- It may serve as a subsequent monitoring document for a business.

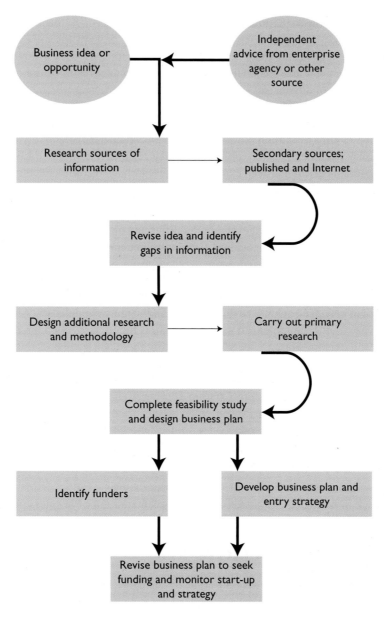

Business start-up: the strategic planning process

Nowadays there are many guides produced by banks, enterprise agencies and accountants, as well as books published on this ongoing planning process.[1] These are often also available online (see useful Internet sites given at the end of this chapter) with a business plan template and format already provided. This chapter does not attempt to replicate these guides, which are often excellent summaries of the essential first steps in starting in business for new entrepreneurs. These guides are often a framework for organizing ideas and formulating a draft business plan. Many agencies and bankers would say that most new business start-ups are now required to produce a business plan. This is a major advance on what might have existed in the past, when a person with a business idea could talk it over with their bank manager, produce some rough 'back-of-the-envelope' calculations and walk out of the bank with a start-up overdraft. The majority of start-ups and even expansions of existing businesses are still planned on the basis of some cash-flow forecasts with a few introductory pages of explanation. Although there have been major improvements, partly as a result of the development of agency and other professional sources of advice and support, there remains tremendous variety in the standard of business plans that are produced, with many that are severely limited in scope. There is an often-quoted statement that a business plan is 'out of date as soon as it is produced'; yet, if a business plan is to be effective, this should not be the case. This chapter aims to explain how a business plan can be used effectively as an ongoing monitoring and strategic planning document, which, although it may need revision, should be effective for several years. After all, if considerable effort has been expended on research, as recommended in this chapter, then this should have some pay-off in the future planning and monitoring of the business.

One problem when designing and writing a business plan is that different funding bodies can have different requirements. We have seen in Chapter 7 that even among different bank managers there can be different expectations in terms of what was expected and required from entrepreneurs when producing a business plan.[2] In addition, venture capitalists will require a much more detailed business plan and perhaps more market analysis than a bank manager will, for the obvious reason that the venture capitalist will not be able to take security to safeguard his or her investment. Mason and Stark have found that there are significant differences in what is expected in a business plan between bankers, business angels and venture capitalists.[3] An enterprise or development agency will also vary in its requirements if a business plan is required to secure grant-aided funding. Thus, the advice to potential and existing entrepreneurs before writing the business plan is to seek to determine what format is preferred by the potential funder in terms of presentation and content. In the case of banks, this is usually obtainable from their own start-up guides and suggested templates which are provided online. This will avoid unnecessary rewrites or changes to the presentation. It is best to have a full business plan that you are satisfied with and that will serve you as the entrepreneur when taking strategic decisions for the business. However, remember that the business plan should be produced for yourself, not for the potential funder; it can be modified, shortened, summarized or extended for different potential funders (or users) and you should be prepared to make these changes. Some additional suggestions on the presentation of business plans are given later in this chapter.

Following the process illustrated in Figure 13.1, we discuss sources of information and research methods before moving on to look in more detail at the design and implementation of business plans.

SOURCES OF INFORMATION

A business is often at its most vulnerable when launching because it will not have the same knowledge or information as its competitors. It will face issues of credibility, yet it will need to establish a network of contacts with suppliers and buyers, its credit rating will inevitably be low and it may not be aware of what credit it can take advantage of, or what are the best sources of advice. There may also be shortages of skilled labour and other resources and it will still have its reputation to establish. These problems can at least be reduced if a new business takes advantage of the wide range of sources of information that are now available.

SECONDARY DATA SOURCES

Sources of information are conveniently classified as either primary or secondary information sources. All secondary information sources include officially published data, provided by the government or its agencies or by other institutions, such as banks, the Confederation of British Industry (CBI), trades unions, local authorities and Chambers of Commerce. In addition, institutions have online web pages that may provide access to sources of information. For example, national data provided by the Office for National Statistics (ONS) is available from its website at http://www.statistics.gov.uk.

It is likely that, in the future, printed sources of statistical data will become redundant as online access methods are developed further. However, at present it can still be necessary to make reference to published sources. The main sources of published data are illustrated in Table 13.1, with some comments provided on the relevance and value of each source. Each of these sources will have a website where breakdowns, reports and additional data sources may be available.

TABLE 13.1 SECONDARY DATA: PUBLISHED SOURCES OF INFORMATION

Source	Type of data	Comment
Annual Abstract of Statistics	Summary tables on population, national income and the labour force	Useful summary reference
2011 Census	Demographic and socio-economic data	Data analysis and trends often published separately
Labour Force Survey	Labour market data including earnings and employment	Valuable and up-to-date source of data on the UK labour market. Summary data published monthly, full data published quarterly
Monthly Digest of Statistics	Components of national income	
Economic Trends	Data on economic indicators	Useful indicator of major economic trends
Regional Trends	Regional economic indicators	
Population Trends	Demographic indicators	Useful predictor of future market trends
Financial Statistics	Data on financial indicators	Gives indications of credit activity
Bank of England Quarterly Bulletin	Gives detailed money supply and lending data	Summarizes current economic conditions with forecasts
New Earnings Survey	Income and hours worked of the labour force	Useful source on wage rates
Business Monitors	Data on specific industries	Useful indicator of trends in industry
Census of Production	National output data	
Labour Market Trends	Data on earnings and employment rates	Useful source of data with occasional articles
MINTEL	Market intelligence reports	Valuable source of intelligence and market data if available (fee-based)
Trade and industry journals	Qualitative data	Occasional articles can be useful
Patent office	Information on existing patents	Provides a search facility
Euro-information centres	Various information on EU funding	Selected localities

Online and PC-based databases

The development of online and PC-based databases has meant that it is possible to gain direct access to some databases, giving an advantage in terms of convenience in access and downloading data. These can be powerful packages, providing additional graphical illustrations and analysis. Libraries have databases that store basic statistical data as a database on a CD. These may be databases of literature, journal articles or statistical and financial information. The development of these databases has made information searches far easier, and there is nowadays an increasing amount of information and basic data that is available online. Some examples are given in Table 13.2.

The Internet

Increasingly, an alternative approach to gathering information on competitors may exist through the Internet. All large firms have their own web page, and with the search engines that now exist, information on potential competitors can be obtained and downloaded. For suggestions of search engines in this area see the discussion of use of the Internet for business in the students' online learning support centre. Obviously, the importance of the Internet will still increase in the future as an increasing range of secondary sources of information becomes available through this medium. At present, however, printed versions of secondary sources are still in demand, because of the time taken to search the Internet and the variation in quality of web pages. For example, until a web address is accessed, at present the researcher is unlikely to know the extent and quality of information that is made available. Table 13.3 gives some useful web addresses that can be valuable sources of secondary data and information.

PRIMARY DATA SOURCES

Although there is a vast range of secondary sources of information, it will be appreciated that they often do not provide the right combination of data or perhaps the data are incomplete. There are many situations when this is going to be a problem, particularly with the requirements of entrepreneurs for specific information regarding products and potential demand. As an entrepreneurial student, you may be preparing for entrepreneurship. As a potential entrepreneur, who is considering launching a new product, the only way to obtain information concerning potential demand might be to carry out your own market research using survey techniques and questionnaires. For these reasons, we will concentrate on some of these survey techniques.

TABLE 13.2 EXAMPLES OF ONLINE AND PC-BASED DATABASES

Source	Type of data	Comment
EXSTAT	Micro-level data on companies	Brief summaries of trading records
FAME	Financial data on all companies	Powerful package including graphical illustration and financial ratios
DATASTREAM	Financial data	Financial analysis
KOMPASS	European database	Details on companies throughout Europe
Patent office	Existing patents	Fee-based service
Local industrial directories (usually produced by local authorities)	Information on local companies	Quality of information and source varies

TABLE 13.3 SOURCES OF INFORMATION ON THE WEB

Web address	Type of information	Comment
http://www.statistics.gov.uk	Range of national data	The Office for National Statistics website. Variable quality of information. Summary articles
http://www.bis.gov.uk/policies/enterprise-and-business-support	The Enterprise Directorate: a range of information on support with links to sources of advice	Comprehensive research reports, but on selective topics
http://www.bis.gov.uk/search?keywords = small+business+survey&type = all	Small Business Survey, a national UK survey of issues facing SMEs	Comprehensive coverage of a range of issues. Data is always a year out of date due to time to analyse and publish results so may not reflect current economic conditions. Specialist reports on themes
http://www.britishchambers.org.uk	Detail of reports and information on Chambers of Commerce	Useful source for occasional reports
http://www.scotent.co.uk	Information on support agencies in Scotland	Links to Local Enterprise Companies
http://www.cabinet-office.gov.uk	Up-to-date information on areas of government priority	Occasional reports available; employment reports, social inclusion reports
http://www.hmrc.gov.uk/index.htm	HM Revenue and Customs website and information	Information on VAT registration and threshold levels for businesses. General tax advice for start-up businesses
www.hm-treasury.gov.uk	Occasional reports. Tax information	Useful for updates on the budget and taxation changes

There are a number of ways that primary information can be obtained, the most obvious being through the use of questionnaires using an alternative variety of methods, including postal or telephone surveys, focus groups and face-to-face interviews. However, data may also be obtained by observation, by interview over a longer period of time (longitudinal research) to establish whether, say, there are changes in social attitudes, or by records of respondents (e.g. purchases of families recorded by the Family Household Expenditure Survey). A brief overview of some of the methods that can be used to obtain primary data is given below.

SURVEY METHODS

In a feasibility study and/or a subsequent business plan, you may wish to organize a survey of potential customers using a survey method. There is a danger that these surveys will be done superficially, often containing questions that reveal only the most basic information. You will need to aim for high-quality information and that can only be achieved if your questionnaire and survey are well designed. Since the information obtained from any survey is going to form the basis of conclusions and recommendations in the final business plan, the quality of this final business plan is going to depend crucially on the research techniques used and the design of your questionnaire. Giving careful consideration to the design of questions and survey method will improve the quality of analysis that can subsequently be carried out in either a feasibility study (market assessment) or a business plan.

Survey methods include questionnaire-based surveys, which are normally postal, and telephone or interview-based surveys that may be more open-ended. Their main advantages and disadvantages are summarized in Table 13.4.

TABLE 13.4 ADVANTAGES AND DISADVANTAGES OF THE MAIN SURVEY METHODS

Method	Advantages	Disadvantages
Postal survey questionnaires	Sample size can be large if response is adequate Relatively quick Inexpensive Can provide useful basic data May be the only option for some data Responses can be completely confidential Structured questionnaires make for easy analysis	Low response rates unless incentives are used Difficult to control for respondent bias Responses may be unreliable Sample is self-selecting and may be biased Only limited information can be obtained Responses may be incomplete Questionnaire needs careful construction
Telephone survey questionnaires	Saves time over postal survey Response rates are often much higher than postal survey Control over respondent and responses Sample less likely to be biased	Questions may be more limited Respondent has little time to consider question Data may not be available easily
Web-based surveys, see http://www.monkeysurvey.com	Saves postal cost and time by using web software. Guidance on construction and convenient	Similar low response rates to postal surveys. Requires e-mail contact address
Face-to-face interviews	Provides qualitative, in-depth information Complete control for researcher Flexible, allowing additional issues to be pursued Most reliable method in terms of validity of responses	Relatively expensive and time-consuming May be difficult to analyse Subject to personal bias of researcher
Focus groups	Group-based interviews to give synergy and encourage greater response Can save time and expense Well-tried method in market research	Requires a trained facilitator to get best results and requires careful preparation and appropriate environment Group needs to be carefully balanced Difficult to record outcomes in a coherent manner

Any survey method will depend for accurate and coherent subsequent analysis on the research design, which includes questionnaire design. It may be acceptable to combine these different survey methods (for example, short interviews of a reasonable sample may be combined with more in-depth material with a small number of respondents). In-depth interviews are designed to obtain qualitative information whereas larger surveys are designed to obtain quantitative information.

RESEARCH DESIGN

The research design and survey method used will depend on the aims and objectives of the research. For example, a full feasibility study undertaken in advance of a business plan will aim to provide both quantitative data and analysis and more in-depth qualitative information so that a combination of methods will be appropriate. Research design involves the selection of the appropriate survey method(s), the sample and the design of appropriate questions. The design involves matching the survey method or combination of methods to the aims of the study and research. Good research design and some thought given to the survey method used will pay dividends later in analysis and the production of the final business plan. This is shown in diagrammatic form in Figure 13.2.

Sampling method

Some attention should be paid to how you are going to choose your sample. The sampling frame may be provided, such as the provision of a membership list of an association; you may then decide to survey the whole

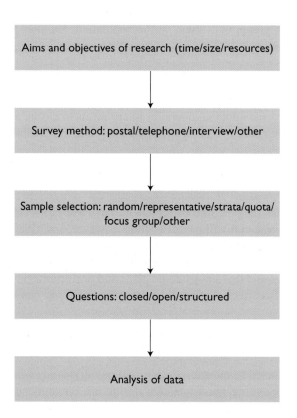

FIGURE 13.2

Research design

membership, the population, or choose a sample. How this sample is chosen will affect the interpretation that can be placed on the final results. The sample will be drawn from some sampling frame, such as a membership list or perhaps the electoral roll in a local area. Samples may be of the following types.

Purely random

To select a true random sample, each member of the population must have the same chance of being selected. One way to choose a random sample is to generate random numbers using a computer program. You then use these numbers to select respondents from your sampling frame.

Representative sample

A representative sample contains a microcosm of the features of the population in their appropriate proportions. Thus if you are surveying firms, you may wish to have representations of different firm sizes in true proportions to their numbers in the population of all firms. That is, say, 97 per cent of your sample should employ fewer than 20 employees. The extent to which your sample can be representative will depend on having information about the population. Samples can only be representative if features of the full population are known, such as the proportion that earn less than '£X' per week, or the proportion that are male/female, married/ not married, and so on.

Stratified sample

A stratified sample attempts to break down the population in a coherent manner, using one or two criteria. One example might be the industrial sector of businesses that are respondents. The sample is not representative in having true proportions but you use the criteria of, say, the industrial sector as a way of ensuring some representation is included from each group, or 'strata', of the population. Samples may be chosen randomly from each strata if the sampling frame permits this.

Quota sample

Quota sampling is a commonly used technique in market research where a characteristic of the population (often age/gender) is used to provide quota numbers for interviewers to ensure a minimum number of respondents is identified in each category. In contrast to stratified sampling, this method is often used where no sampling frame is available.

The importance of research

Given limited resources and time, the potential entrepreneur may have little scientific basis for the selection of the sample. A small amount of research will pay dividends, however, and give a more logical approach to the business plan. A short discussion of methods used to research data in a section in the business plan (or feasibility study) will indicate that some thought has gone into the research behind the plan and that assumptions are well founded, have a good basis, and that the strategic plans and projections have a solid basis. This can make a tremendous difference and also affects the confidence with which you can present a business plan to any potential funders.

Question design

As noted before, some care devoted to question design will pay dividends when analysing the results of any research. Some simple rules regarding good question design are recommended and these are listed in the accompanying box.

QUESTION DESIGN: SOME SIMPLE RULES

Questions should:

- Be unambiguous

- Be relatively short

- Not be biased or leading in some way

- Be designed to achieve the objectives of the research

- Be structured (semi-structured or open-ended, but open-ended are generally best avoided with postal, phone or web-based questionnaires).

NEW DEVELOPMENTS

As with project planning there are now relatively sophisticated software packages available that offer a full business-planning and start-up package. They have inbuilt flexibility and could be a good investment for potential high-growth new start businesses. These packages provide the essential sections and help you to produce financial forecasts. Of course, software cannot replace the basic planning process, which requires adequate research. A business plan, however well produced and presented, will be only as good as the quality of data and information input to the software that is being used. Reliable data are still required that will be processed by the software into a business plan that will serve the business as a valuable planning tool for a number of years.

In addition to software packages, there are templates and guidelines that can be downloaded direct from websites with step-by-step guides on information that include: standard section headings, research information, market analysis sections and pro-formas for financial statements. A good example is the free online downloadable business plan template format provided by Business Link available at: http://www.businesslink.gov.uk/bdotg/action/detail?itemId=1087369151&type=RESOURCES. This provides an easy-to-follow guide with step-by-step instructions and a downloadable template for producing a business plan. Alternatively the main commercial banks have free downloadable templates which can be accessed direct from their websites; see 'Internet Resources' for a list of useful websites at the end of this chapter.

DESIGNING THE BUSINESS PLAN

The templates indicated above all take a similar approach in that there are a number of standard sections that would normally be included in any business plan. These should include sections on the business, the people, the market, aims and objectives, competitive analysis, marketing strategy and strengths, weaknesses, opportunities and threats (SWOT) analysis. However, the sections required for the business plan will vary depending on the nature and sector of the business. A manufacturing business requires a different business plan from a service-sector based business. An exporting firm requires a different business plan from a components supplier that relies on large UK customers. A small start-up concern requires a different business plan from a medium-sized firm that is planning an expansion into different products. Although software packages can be flexible, they aim to provide a standard package that can be used by any business. A business plan has to be flexible and it is impossible to be prescriptive since every business plan will be different and will be produced for different requirements. Having said that, there are certain sections and guidelines that can be discussed and we attempt this below. We look at what might be expected from any business plan; you may not wish to include all of the sections – not everyone will have the time or resources to produce a full and detailed business plan. However, some thought given to the following suggestions will help to plan for the possible different scenarios, competition and future changes that may be faced. Putting in effort at the research and design stage will improve the process of decision-making, which is one of the main purposes of any business plan.

The following sections are recommended when designing the content of the business plan. As emphasized above, these sections are not prescriptive and can be modified to suit the purposes of individual entrepreneurs and business plans. They do not attempt to replace a business-plan template and pro-formas that can be obtained from the sources identified earlier.

EXECUTIVE SUMMARY

If your plan is carefully researched, constructed and written, then an executive summary will be very useful to the users of the business plan, who may be potential funders or partner entrepreneurs in the business. Although the executive summary should be the first section of the plan, it is likely to be the last to be written and can be the most difficult because you have to summarize the main contents of the business plan succinctly yet provide enough information for a potential investor to make a decision to give the plan serious attention. It can be useful to build the executive summary around the competitive strategy.

INTRODUCTION

A short introduction should give some background to the business, the key people, and an introduction to the nature of the business and the industrial sector. This section can be used to give the main aims and objectives of the business. In this section you will need to explain the purpose of the business plan. Is it to map out an expansion plan for the business? Or is it to provide a strategy for the launch of a new business? The aims and objectives could be placed in a separate section. You can also use this section to explain the rationale for the business and the business plan. It is important to communicate quickly and in a short space the key purpose and activities of the business in a succinct manner. A common fault is to provide too much background detail without specifying the main purpose, products, services and activities of the business.

In the introduction you can provide additional information such as the nature of incorporation if a start-up, whether the company is registered, whether you have registered for VAT, in which case a VAT number should be quoted, starting employment levels, resources and whether there is a need for recruitment of staff and personnel.

MARKET ANALYSIS AND RESEARCH

In this section you can report the findings of market research that might have been undertaken, if primary research has been completed, along the lines suggested in this chapter. You should avoid the temptation to give too much information although, as suggested before, illustrations of the main findings can be quite useful for presentation purposes and for potential readers of the plan. However, those readers will not want to wade through a large amount of information and data. If the questionnaire that has been used as the basis for the research has been well designed, then it should be possible to present the information and analysis in the form of summary tables with brief comments on the significance and importance of market analysis and summaries of the potential total market and market share. It is important to identify a proposed market share rather than (just) the overall size of the target market.

Some of the software packages that were mentioned above will give a market opportunity analysis. Additional analysis provided by such software can be a useful way of impressing any potential funder.

This section should be used to explain the assumptions behind income generation in the cash-flow statements. Are the income levels based on the market research findings, or perhaps on other factors, such as seasonality or state of economic levels of activity, or capacity levels if a manufacturing concern? Other factors should also be included, such as the basis of payment; income may be generated on the basis of commission, fees or sales.

If sales of products and services are involved, then some form of normal credit period will be assumed. Standard practice is, of course, 30-day credit periods between the sale taking place and income shown in the cash flow. If the business is subject to strong seasonal factors, such as high sales in the Christmas period, then this should be shown in the income statement of the cash flow, with allowance made for any credit period.

You may wish to consider outlining a brief marketing and distribution plan. This can be contained within the business plan, or if distribution is a major part of the firm's operations, then it is recommended that a separate document is produced. The marketing plan effectively sets out how sales are to be achieved. It may include all aspects of the 'marketing mix' (see box).

THE MARKETING MIX

- Pricing policy.
- Promotion (advertising and other forms of sales promotion).
- Production (the outlets and marketing strategy should reflect the production capabilities of the business).
- Place (the location of the business and outlets used).

It is important to have these aspects of the business integrated, so that distribution channels and outlets do not overburden the production process and capabilities and the outlets are appropriate to cope with production capacities. An example is used to illustrate such concepts below (see box).

EXAMPLE: MATCHING MARKETING WITH PRODUCTION

A small firm had produced a new form of hanging basket bracket that was produced to a new design and to a high quality. Yet the marketing strategy adopted bore no relation to production capabilities. The bracket was marketed through a major chain gardening store and as soon as one large order was placed, the firm could not cope with the production quantities required by a major multiple retailer.

This problem of matching production to outlets and distribution channels cannot always be resolved, but planning for different outcomes in the business plan can help to resolve this problem if it does arise and a separate marketing plan can be a valuable planning tool for any business.

Access to retail outlets can be a critical problem for some businesses. However, a marketing strategy can still be developed that takes into account barriers to entry, potential outlets and distribution and any secured retail outlets if appropriate.

PRODUCTION STRATEGY

If the business is concerned with manufacturing and production, a separate section should be devoted to the planning of production. If the business is concerned merely with expanding using existing production facilities, through perhaps obtaining new market outlets, then a separate production plan will not be necessary. However, it may be necessary to plan for additional production facilities, new machinery and increased capacity. Additional resources and capabilities will be required for new production levels. Additional skilled staff may be required and recruitment policies should be explained.

For a new start-up business that requires production facilities, the business plan will obviously need to describe how these are to be obtained and how staff are to be recruited.

The assumptions described in this section will form the basis behind the projections in the expenses of the cash-flow statements. There may be some research necessary in order to predict these forecasts accurately. As far as possible, quotations for ordering the supplies and equipment required can be used as a basis for some of the forecasts.

Timing

An important element of any manufacturing business is timing production to co-ordinate with sales orders and matching supply of materials with production capabilities and sales orders. This is the importance of integrating market predictions and sales back through the production process and ensuring that the supply of materials and components is of the quality required to ensure that customers are satisfied with the product. It must be stressed that orders can be lost if insufficient attention is paid to quality in the production process and quality obtaining from suppliers. This can be a particular problem for a new (producing) firm, which can be vulnerable if certain specifications have been laid down to suppliers with no guarantee that these are going to be met. If possible, although this may use up some resources, it is worth trying to get some prototypes made to check quality. Of course, this will be a particular problem where new technology or new production techniques are being employed, which is one of the reasons why financing technology-based firms gives rise to different and special issues from other types of start-up.

Timing is important because resources and finance will be required before products are made, before sales are made and certainly well before income is received. This should be reflected in the cash-flow statements. Any manufacturing and producing firm is certain to have a negative balance in the first part of the cash flow. It is better to plan properly for this, so that financial resources can either be set aside, if internal resources are available, or funding requirements can be made clear in the business plan.

Action plans

To aid the planning process it is worth providing an action plan. The purpose of this is to map actions against time and the production process. This will allow the planning of different requirements into the production and marketing stages as they are required over time.

An action plan can be produced for any type of business and modified to produce a Gantt chart, which maps out the sequential timing of decisions against production/sales levels and can serve as an action plan for the business.

SWOT ANALYSIS

A section on SWOT analysis involves the identification of strengths, weaknesses, opportunities and threats for the business. There can be some dispute over how a SWOT analysis can be presented and explained. To some extent, a SWOT analysis should consist of a series of short bullet points so that the reader can see easily and in summary the main strengths and weaknesses of the business and the opportunity. However, the statements that comprise the bullet points should not be so short that they become perfunctory statements, leaving the reader wishing for further explanation or elaboration. Again, a balance has to be struck between the need to keep the statements short (and preferably punchy) and the need to provide an adequate statement that the reader or user of the business plan can understand and comprehend.

A long list of strengths and weaknesses is not necessary; the list should be relatively short, perhaps half a dozen bullet points under each heading. It is also better to be honest. A long list of strengths followed by short list of weaknesses is more likely to raise suspicions from potential funders than it is to impress them.

The SWOT analysis should 'fit' the business plan. If many strengths are shown but other aspects of the business plan are perhaps weak (such as limited analysis of market projections), then the SWOT analysis will look out of place in the context of the rest of the business plan.

There are few guidelines that can be given for the SWOT analysis. The entrepreneur(s) is (are) the best person (people) to write the SWOT analysis but, bearing in mind the points raised above, it is worth taking time to identify strengths. These may reflect the skills of the entrepreneur and business team, they may include extensive experience in the industry, a reputation for quality, a sound knowledge of working practices and employment conditions in the industry, existing contacts with potential customers, and knowledge of new techniques/technologies that can be applied to existing production processes.

A SWOT analysis will always remain subject to personal preferences and views. The reader of the business plan should be aware of this and will make some allowances for this. A different individual could interpret strengths and weaknesses in different ways. Unless a business plan is put together by an independent consultant, a SWOT analysis will remain a personal statement by the entrepreneur(s) of their view of the strengths and weaknesses of the business and the opportunities provided by the business creation or development.

COMPETITION

The competition and a section dealing with competitive analysis will follow from the identification of threats in the SWOT analysis. The extent of knowledge of competitors will probably vary, but it should be possible to identify the major competitors and what their relative strengths are. It is also useful to identify what strategies they have used to establish their market position. For example, have they used market-niche strategies, or perhaps more aggressive market penetration strategies? Or have they established their position by reputation and word of mouth?

In Chapter 2, we discussed the increased importance of small firms across European economies and some of the reasons for this increased importance. Often the reason for the start-up of a new firm by an entrepreneur is that they have recognized a market niche in an industry that is not being catered for by existing (large) firms. A small firm/entrepreneur will have the flexibility to respond to new market opportunities and market niches. While it is likely that the competition may consist of well-established firms, these may not have the flexibility to respond quickly to new market opportunities and challenges.

The analysis of competition should match the market analysis that is presented in the business plan as discussed earlier. If the business plan is predicting a relatively large market share, this will not fit with a competitor analysis which suggests that the major competitors are strong, well established and that the market is difficult to penetrate. This analysis should also fit the marketing strategy. A market-niche strategy will probably aim for high quality services or products and likely outlets should have been identified that are willing to take the business's products, or potential customers should have been identified if a service is being marketed.

Some thought should be given to potential competition. As opportunities develop, it could be that the business will face competition, either from additional entrepreneurs who start up, or as a result of retaliation on the part of the existing competition. If the business plan is to be a valuable document over a three- or five-year planning period, then some thought must be given to future competition and the likely sources of that competition.

It is possible to provide contingency plans. However, given that the number of different possible scenarios is infinite, it will not be possible to provide a contingency plan to cope with all possible eventualities, possible reactions and strategies of the competition. However, it is feasible to recognize that the outcomes that are predicted in the business plan can change and that the business plan should be used to monitor operations and then adjustments can be made to predictions and/or strategy as circumstances change. It is desirable to conduct a limited amount of sensitivity analysis, which will demonstrate to potential funders that some thought has been given to different outcomes and the reaction of existing and potential competitors.

BUSINESS MODEL AND COMPETITIVE STRATEGY

In some ways this is the most important section of the business plan, since it should identify an appropriate business model for the value proposition of the business (e.g. low cost/low price; high quality/high price; web-based/non web-based/hybrid) and map out the complementary strategy for the survival, development and growth of the business. Building on the business-entry model adopted, a strategy should be identified that will enable the business to meet the aims and objectives that will have been set out in the early part or sections of the business plan. The development of competitive strategy will be the natural outcome of the process of researching the market opportunity, the nature of the product or service, the SWOT analysis and the competitive analysis. Porter has provided a well-known taxonomy of generic market strategies, which are outlined below.[4] It is likely that your strategy will fall into one of these three categories. Porter shows that competitive strategies are a response to the environment in which the business operates; in other words, they are generic to the environment and the nature of competition faced by the business. Porter's three generic strategies are described below.

Cost leadership

Under this strategy, the emphasis is on maintaining a competitive edge through a cost advantage over competitors. It may, but does not necessarily, involve undercutting competitors on price and maintaining a competitive edge on price. Undercutting through price does contain disadvantage: it may lead to some form of price war and, even if competitors are at a cost disadvantage, they may be better placed to sustain losses that might be incurred through any price-cutting war to gain customers. The advantage of cost leadership for entrepreneurs will lie in the generation of additional income that may result from cost reduction and that may be reinvested to provide new production techniques or new products.

Differentiation

This strategy may follow from a need to diversify production or services. It should not be confused with the third (focus) strategy. It is a strategy that is more likely to apply to existing and well-established producers where, perhaps, products have entered a maturity stage of their life-cycle and there is a need to diversify production to maintain growth in the firm.

Focus

This third strategy is the one that is most likely to be adopted by new-firm entrepreneurs. It recognizes that many market opportunities result from specialization. Small firms have the advantage that they can be flexible as well as specialized. The development of a focus strategy involves the identification of a market niche that has not been exploited by existing producers. The firm should quickly be able to gain a reputation for satisfying this market niche. Identifying the correct time to launch and exploit the market opportunity can be crucial. Thus, there are market 'windows of opportunity' that appear at different times. Launching too early or too late can result in missing this opportunity.

Although Porter's categories have been very influential, they may be seen as a bit limiting. Kay has produced a useful alternative analysis of competitive strategy that focuses on the importance of value added that a firm can bring to the industry.[5] The extent to which a firm will produce value added to its costs of production will determine its success. For example, in an analysis of the retail food industry Kay shows that the strategies adopted by Tesco have been very successful at adding value to its operations. Since Kay's analysis, Tesco has proceeded to be the dominant retailer, despite increased competition, by focusing on quality and value added.

These analyses stress the importance of getting the strategy right for the type of market that you are in. There is no right or wrong strategy, but it must match the business model adopted, be appropriate for the business, the operation, the market and the business development plan.

CRITICAL SUCCESS FACTORS

The identification of critical success factors is a useful section that should be included in the final business plan. It can serve as a useful summary and checklist of factors that have been identified in other sections of the business plan and is best placed towards the end of the business plan. Like the SWOT analysis, it will tend to be a personal reflection on the most important factors that are going to be critical to the success of the business. Thus, again, it is impossible to be at all prescriptive about this section, but you may like to think about the following issues.

- What factors does the success of the business hinge upon? Are they factors concerned with gaining orders or are they concerned with securing quality from suppliers?
- How important are the key personnel to the success of the business? If a key member of staff leaves, how will this affect the performance of the business? Can they be replaced?
- How important is the recruitment strategy of the business? Does the success of the business depend on obtaining appropriate skilled staff?
- Does the success of the strategy adopted depend on how competitors react?

It is worth considering each section of the business plan and identifying just one or two key factors from each section that will be critical to the performance of the business and to its success. For an entrepreneur, this will help to identify key and critical success factors and, at later stages, to monitor performance. Having identified such factors, the entrepreneur can adopt strategies that can ensure success or lead to alternative arrangements. For example, if dependence on a single supplier is identified as a critical factor, the entrepreneur may wish to investigate alternative arrangements for ensuring supply.

THE MANAGEMENT TEAM

Although a business plan may be developed by a single start-up nascent entrepreneur, it is likely that a management team will be required and involved from the beginning. For some funders, especially venture capitalists, the management team, who they are, what their qualifications and experience are, will be very important and forms the basis on which they might seek to add value to the existing management business team. Therefore, it is important to include a section that outlines the key skills, how they complement each other and the roles that each member will take in the business. It should indicate who is responsible for the main functional areas of any business: finance, sales/marketing, production and employment/recruitment.

FINANCIAL FORECASTS

The extent of financial forecasting undertaken can vary considerably across different business plans, but it will be essential to include a cash-flow statement, indicating assumptions and a profit and loss forecast. These are dealt with in more detail in the following sections.

CASH-FLOW STATEMENT

The cash-flow statement contains the projected income from sales and other sources and all the expenses concerned with the launch and operation of the business. It is best prepared on a computer spreadsheet package, although business planning software, as mentioned before, will have its own spreadsheet and financial analysis built in.

The importance of the cash-flow statement is that it shows the timing of income and expenses and should show all these figures for 12 monthly periods of up to three or perhaps five years, depending on the potential users of the business plan. It shows the liquidity of the business at any one time and reflects the need or otherwise to raise funds and credit. If the business plan is being prepared for a bank manager then it is unlikely that cash-flow forecasts will be required beyond three years. If, on the other hand, it is being prepared for a venture capitalist then it is more likely that five years' cash-flow forecasts will be required.

A pro forma cash-flow statement is shown as an example in Figure 13.3, but the detail of the cash flow will obviously depend on the individual business. The notes given in the pro forma are referred to below.

1   Income will consist of sales, fees and commission. It may include income from grants or loans. The timing of the receipt of this income should be as accurate as possible. A small adjustment to the timing of the income can affect the extent of any negative or positive net cash flow.

2   Total income just calculates the total for each month. On a spreadsheet this is easily calculated by inserting the appropriate formula to sum cells and then copying across different cells.

3   Expenses can either be summarized under different headings or shown individually, but they should identify all expenses from the operations of the business. These will include equipment, materials, computing equipment, staffing, leasing of vehicles, insurance and promotional expenses. Again, timing is important and should be as accurate as possible since a small adjustment will affect the extent of the positive or negative cash flow.

4   Staffing should include National Insurance (NI) contributions, although NI payments can be shown separately.

5   It is important to consider and include items such as insurance. If the business is a producer it will need products' liability, public liability and employers' liability insurance. If insurance is a relatively small part of sales, perhaps only 2 per cent, it can be paid in just one annual premium.

6   If the business is registered for VAT, then it will be entitled to a VAT rebate on VAT payments. These can be claimed every three months. Registering for VAT becomes mandatory over a threshold (taxable; i.e. eligible for VAT) turnover of currently £73,000, at the time of writing, but voluntary registration is advisable at levels below this to claim VAT rebates. This VAT threshold usually changes once a year and is announced in the UK Chancellor's annual budget. The actual rate of VAT that is levied can change occasionally, as announced in 2010. The standard rate of VAT increased from 17.5 per cent to 20 per cent on 4 January 2011.

   To calculate VAT liability three months in arrears it is assumed that VAT liability is incurred on sales and commission, but VAT is paid on materials and fixtures and fittings bought. Thus for the first three months, January to March income is £14,250 giving a VAT liability of £2,850. However, during the first three months VAT eligible expenses total £22,850, VAT paid is £4,570. This gives VAT rebate of £1,720. After March, VAT liabilities on sales and income exceed VAT paid on VAT eligible expenses, hence a net VAT liability is incurred for this hypothetical company example with two net VAT payments calculated as £1,125 over the April to June period and £1,385 over the July to September period.

7   Total expenses merely add up the expenses in each column and this is easily done on a spreadsheet.

8   Subtracting the total expenses from the total income shows the net cash flow for each month. A general point to consider is that you will want to take advantage of any credit. This will be reflected in the liquidity of the business as shown in the net cash flow.

9   The opening balance for the first month is normally shown as zero, although it is possible to have reserves (from previous operations) shown in the opening balance.

Hypothetical company, year 1

	JAN	FEB	MAR	APR	MAY	JUN	JUL	AUG	SEPT	OCT	NOV	DEC	TOTALS (11)
INCOME (1)													
SALES		3500	4000	5000	5500	5000	6000	3000	6500	6500	7000	10000	62000
FEES	2025	2025	2700	2025	2700	2700		1350	3375	2700	3375	2025	27000
GRANT													0
ENTERPRISE AGENCY	7000												7000
													0
TOTAL INCOME (2)	9025	5525	6700	7025	8200	7700	6000	4350	9875	9200	10375	12025	96000
EXPENSES (3)													
MATERIALS	3500	3000	3000	3500	3000	3000	3500	3000	5000	4000	4000	3000	41500
EQUIPMENT													
MACHINERY	5000	5000	5000	5000									20000
COMPUTERS		3600											3600
PRINTER		1000											1000
VIDEO			750										750
TABLES			600										600
CHAIRS		600											600
BOOKCASES			300										300
													0
WAGES (4)													
PRODUCTION	2893.75	2315	2893.75	2315	2315	2315	2893.75	2315	2893.75	2315	2315	2315	30095
OFFICE	607.5	607.5	810	607.5	810	810		405	1012.5	810	1012.5	607.5	8100
HEAT AND LIGHT			1000			1000			800			1200	4000

(continued)

													TOTAL
RATES					1000						1000		2000
INSURANCE (5)					1500						1500		3000
TELEPHONE			200		200					150		250	800
CONSUMABLES													0
PRODUCTION		200	200	200	200	200	200	200	200	200	200	200	2200
OFFICE STATIONERY	300		100	100	100	100	100	100	100	100	100	100	1300
VAT (REBATE) (6)					−1720					1125		1385	790
TOTAL EXPENSES (7)	12501.25	16422.5	14853.75	14222.5	6425	5905	6393.75	6020	11281.25	9925	7627.5	9057.5	120635
NET CASH-FLOW (8)	−3476.25	−10897.5	−8153.75	−7197.5	1775	1795	−393.75	−1670	−1406.25	−725	2747.5	2967.5	−24635
OPENING BALANCE (9)	0	−3476.25	−14373.8	−22527.5	−29725	−27950	−26155	−26548.8	−28218.8	−29625	−30350	−27602.5	
CLOSING BALANCE (10)	−3476.25	−14373.8	−22527.5	−29725	−27950	−26155	−26548.8	−28218.8	−29625	−30350	−27602.5	−24635 (12)	

FIGURE 13.3

Pro-forma cash-flow statement for a hypothetical company

10 The closing balance adds the opening balance to the net cash flow. The closing balance is automatically carried forward to become the opening balance in the next month (period).

11 The totals are added horizontally. They need not be shown, but they are a useful check on calculations and can show the total income and expenses for the year.

12 The last closing balance for the year will become the opening balance for the next year and should be carried forward as in previous months.

If drawings are made by the entrepreneur, perhaps as a sole trader, then these are best shown as part of the expenses concerned with the operation of the business. These are likely to be regular withdrawals and they should be shown monthly rather than a total figure at the end of the year.

It is important to note that the cash-flow statement is not the same as profit and loss. As stated before, the net cash flow reflects the liquidity of the business. The cash-flow statement can show additional income, say borrowings, that are not part of the profit and loss account.

FORECAST PROFIT AND LOSS ACCOUNT

It is essential to forecast an end-of-year profit and loss account. This shows the trading position of the business and gives the level of profit (loss) that is expected. This involves adding up all the trading income, subtracting cost of goods sold, to get the trading profit and loss. General expenses for the year can be totalled, including depreciation subtracted from the trading profit to get the net profit. Note that it can be perfectly acceptable to show loss-making in the start-up period of the business, indeed it would normally be expected as goods and supplies have to be bought, premises rented, staff paid and other overheads paid before income can be earned on goods sold.

Further examples of cash-flow statements and forecast profit and loss accounts are available in the students' online learning centre.

FORECAST BALANCE SHEET

A forecast balance sheet is sometimes required, particularly by bank managers, and this can be relatively easily calculated from the projections for the end of year.

The balance sheet is a statement of assets and liabilities at any particular time period. As a planning tool it is not very useful since it provides only a snapshot at any one time, but it may be required by bank managers.[6]

A number of financial ratios can be calculated and included in terms of profitability and liquidity. It is not necessary to go into detail on the calculation and usefulness of these, but standard business-planning software will calculate these automatically.

SENSITIVITY ANALYSIS

The purpose of the sensitivity analysis is to provide a test of the susceptibility of the business to changes, or a test of the robustness of the business proposition to cope with unforeseen changes. We can assume that most of the expense forecasts will be accurate. Despite careful research, income forecasts will still contain some uncertainty and the purpose of sensitivity analysis is to examine the consequences of changing some of the income forecasts on the net cash flow.

There is little point in developing any sensitivity analysis beyond the first year of operation, but it is worth formulating for the first year with what may be called an optimistic and a pessimistic scenario.

The optimistic scenario might *increase* sales and other income by 10 per cent. Expenses will need to be adjusted to allow for this – for example, through increased cost of materials, and perhaps through increased salary costs. The pessimistic scenario might *decrease* sales and other income by 10 per cent with appropriate adjustments of expenses.

A further purpose of sensitivity analysis is to examine the effects of changes in timing on the net cash flow and funding requirements. For example, a delay in securing orders can be as important as a fall in income and will increase the funding requirements for the business plan. Therefore, a full sensitivity analysis would examine changes in timing of income flows as well as changes in their level.

Note that examples are not provided in the text of additional financial statements, such as the forecast profit and loss account and forecast income statement, but can be found in the students' **online learning centre**.

SOURCES OF ADVICE AND SUPPORT

There are a number of free sources of start-up advice and support; these have benefited from a higher profile recently, with the UK government's stated desire[7] to make the UK 'the best place in the world to start and grow a new business' (p. 4). As a key part of this aim, the UK government is seeking to build an 'enterprise culture' in which access to enterprise start-up advice is promoted and easily available. Although the nature and meaning of an 'enterprise culture' has been questioned previously by a number of studies,[8; 9] it appears that greater emphasis is again being placed on individuals having the ability to choose entrepreneurial and business start-up career choices as well as other employment and careers.[7] An important part of this policy is aimed at young people, where greater emphasis is being placed on the development of enterprise skills with young people at all levels of the education system.[10] In the UK, the Enterprise Education Trust is an umbrella organization that integrates a number of initiatives focused on young people, enterprise and the education system.[11]

These recent developments have meant that sources of advice have become more important and closer links have been established between educational institutions and agencies.[12] Links may be established with a number of sources of advice and support and some of these are listed with comments in Table 13.5. Research has indicated that satisfaction levels with public-sector agencies have recently improved,[13] but in the past the publicly funded support system has been criticized for being confusing and duplicative of resources.[14] The ad hoc development of the support agency movement over time has meant that provision of support, spatially and vertically, is the result of chance and accidents of geography, and the economic mix of the environment that happened to exist at the time that different agencies were formed. Despite the considerable framework of support that now exists (established in the 1990s), the delivery of small business advice can still vary considerably from agency to agency. There can be large asymmetries in the size, staffing and operation of individual agencies. However, the Enterprise Directorate of the Department for Business, Innovation and Skills (BIS), has provided greater consistency in the deliverers of support advice, the Business Link Operators. In Scotland, a comprehensive overhaul of the support network has led to a consistent service delivered by the Business Gateways, now brought within the responsibility of the local authorities, and in Wales the Welsh Assembly government provides support through its own funded agencies.

Overall there is certainly much consistency and accessibility to a range of sources of advice and support, some of which are listed in Table 13.5. When added to the list of sources of information and secondary data and a number of independent websites, the prospective entrepreneur now has a large range of sources of advice and support to turn to. It is important to consult as many sources as possible, to talk through ideas and development plans; the more this is done, the better and more reliable will be the final business plan.

TABLE 13.5 SOURCES OF ADVICE AND SUPPORT

Agency/organization	Type of information	Comment
Business Link Operators (BLOs)	Range of start-up and business management development advice and training	Funded by contract from Enterprise Directorate of BIS, some have closed and merged
Business Gateway	Range of start-up and business management development advice and training	Operate within funding arrangements for local authorities in Scotland
Chambers of Commerce	Fee-based membership	Can be valuable source through contacts and intelligence held for members Often provide specialist advice such as exporting Gives access to network of Chambers and the British Association of Chambers
Specialist Enterprise Agencies	Specialized advice and training	May operate in specialized locations on special schemes funded by BLOs
PYBT (PSYBT in Scotland)	Advice to young people under 26	Detailed aftercare support, can provide grants and loans and are, therefore, a source of funding for young entrepreneurs
Federation of Small Businesses (FSB)	Fee-based membership, a source of advice especially on legal and taxation issues	Largest association of small businesses in the UK
Other small business and entrepreneurial associations	Examples: Forum of Private Businesses (FPB) Entrepreneurial Exchange	Of variable value and all fee-based membership usually on a sliding scale Websites can be valuable source of free information
Confederation of British Industry	May provide specialist technical advice	Fee-based membership
Patent Office	Specialist advice and searches (fee based)	Can be a valuable source of advice for those seeking to patent
Professional bodies	Lawyers, accountants	Some may have special low rates for start-up businesses Expensive but often the most valuable source
Banks	May provide 'free information'	Useful for start-up guides and business plan template documents Often work locally with publicly funded support agencies such as BLOs and Business Gateway

CONCLUSIONS

The research, design and implementation of the business plan is part of the ongoing planning process within any firm. If the start-up entrepreneur adopts planning policies that are based on sound research and careful consideration of strategy, this will have benefits throughout the life of the business. We have already indicated that there are high birth rates of new small firms and entrepreneurs but, at the same time, these are accompanied by high death rates. One of the reasons for these high death rates has been insufficient thought and time given to proper and adequate planning of the strategy of the new business.

We started this chapter by commenting that, nowadays, business plans are much more common and much more detailed than they used to be. One of the reasons for the growth in the use of business plans has been the spread of the agency movement and the requirement of banks (sometimes working in co-operation with agencies) for business plans if any funding is required. However, another reason is that it has become accepted that a carefully constructed business plan is important to the survival and successful performance of any business.

Business plans are very flexible. They can be used for both large and small firms, for start-ups or for expansion, for private- or public-sector organizations; they can be a few pages or a substantial document running to 10,000 words or more supported by appendices. Despite the recent evolution of national standards, prompted by bodies such as support agencies, business plans are still very variable in quality, so it can be difficult to determine whether a business plan is of good quality. We are still left with that overused phrase, mentioned before, that a good business plan should 'stack up'. We have indicated that what this really means is that the different sections should produce a strategy document that is convincing, be interconnected, that it should be underpinned by careful research, by knowledge of the market opportunity and that the assumptions and research should underpin the financial forecasts.

REVIEW QUESTIONS

1 What are the different purposes for which we might need to develop a business plan?
2 What is the difference between primary and secondary sources of data?
3 You have been asked to advise a start-up entrepreneur on the most important sources of secondary data information. What advice will you give?
4 An entrepreneur wishes to research a new service. What advice could you give on different survey methods that might be used to identify customer needs?
5 Why is research design important for the collection of primary data?
6 In conducting surveys what would be wrong with just stopping people in the street to ask them questions?

7   What are the advantages of postal surveys (over other survey methods)?

8   What are the disadvantages of interview-based surveys?

9   What different competitive strategies could be adopted by a start-up entrepreneur?

10 What is the difference between a cash-flow forecast and a forecast profit and loss account?

11 How does a business plan differ from a feasibility study?

12 Assuming that the business plan has been completed, you have raised funding and you have started the business, what should you now do with the business plan:

   (a) Throw it away?

   (b) File it in case the funder needs to see it?

   (c) Continue to use it?

   Explain your answer.

SUGGESTED ASSIGNMENTS

1 Feasibility study

Students are divided into groups to research and produce a feasibility study for an existing firm/entrepreneur. The feasibility study may involve a new market opportunity or a change of strategy, perhaps involving diversification from existing markets. Students work as consultants to the client entrepreneur and are required to:

(a) Negotiate and agree terms of reference with the entrepreneur

(b) Use appropriate research methods, including market research with an appropriate questionnaire

(c) Identify and analyse existing and potential competition

(d) Identify the additional costs/resources that will be required to exploit the opportunity

(e) Examine the local labour market as appropriate if additional staff are required

(f) Produce a feasibility study as a written report with sections that include introduction, terms of reference, research methods, findings, conclusions and recommendations

(g) Present the findings to the entrepreneur and obtain feedback

2 Business plan

Students are required to complete a business plan through the development of research work carried out for the feasibility study. The business plan should follow the guidelines given in this chapter and include the following sections:

- Executive summary

- Introduction and background

- Management team
- Market analysis and assumptions for cash flow
- SWOT analysis
- Competition analysis
- Competitive strategy
- Required resources with budget
- Cash-flow forecast
- Profit and loss forecast, if required by client
- Notes to the accounts
- Conclusions
- Appendices, if required.

The business plan will be produced by the students working in small groups and working as consultants for a client entrepreneur/firm. The completed written business plan will need to be of high quality. Students should complete a final presentation to the entrepreneur/client.

REFERENCES

1 For example, **Barrow, C., Barrow, P. and Brown, R**. (2000) *The Business Plan Workbook*, 4th edn, Kogan Page, London, or any of the commercial banks' own guides.

2 **Deakins, D. and Hussain, G**. (1994) 'Financial information, the banker and small business: a comment', *The British Accounting Review*, vol. 26, pp. 323–35.

3 **Mason, C. and Stark, M**. (2004) 'What do investors look for in a business plan? A comparison of the investment criteria of bankers, venture capitalists and business angels', *International Small Business Journal*, vol. 22, no. 3, pp. 227–48.

4 **Porter, M**. (1980) *Competitive Strategy: Techniques for Analysing Industries and Competitors*, Collier Macmillan, London.

5 **Kay, J**. (1993) *Foundations of Corporate Success: How Business Strategies Add Value*, Oxford University Press, Oxford.

6 **Fletcher, M**. (1994) *Bank Managers' Lending Decisions to Small Firms*, Department of Entrepreneurship, University of Stirling, Stirling.

7 **Small Business Service** (2004) *A Government Action Plan for Small Business*, BIS London.

8 **Curran, J**. (2000) 'What is small business policy in the UK for? Evaluating and assessing small business support policies', *International Small Business Journal*, vol. 18, no. 3, pp. 36–50.

9 **Gray, C**. (1998) *Enterprise and Culture*, Routledge, London.

10 **Davies, H**. (2002) *A Review of Enterprise and the Economy in Education*, DfES, London.

11 **Enterprise Education Trust**, London, http://www.enterprise-education.org.uk/home.php (accessed September 2011).

12 **Deakins, D., Glancey, K., Menter, I. and Wyper, J**. (2004) *Columba 1400: Creating Enterprise Culture*, final research report for Scottish Executive and the Hunter Foundation, Scottish Executive, Glasgow.

13 **Bennett, R. and Robson, P**. (2003) 'External advice and business link', in A. Cosh and M. Hughes (eds), *Enterprise Challenged: Policy and Performance in the British SME Sector, 1999–2002*, CCBR, University of Cambridge.

14 **Deakins, D**. (1993) 'What role for support agencies? A case study of UK enterprise agencies', *Local Economy*, vol. 8, no. 1, pp. 57–65.

RECOMMENDED READING

Barrow, C., Burke, G., Molian, D. and Brown, R. (2011) *Enterprise Development: The Challenges of Starting,* *Growing and Selling Businesses*, Cengage, Andover.

Williams, S. (2011) *The Financial Times Guide to Business Start Up*, Financial Times Guides, London

Index